THE BALTIC STATES:
YEARS OF DEPENDENCE
1940–1980

THE
BALTIC
STATES

YEARS OF DEPENDENCE
1940–1980

by
ROMUALD J. MISIUNAS
and
REIN TAAGEPERA

UNIVERSITY OF CALIFORNIA PRESS
Berkeley   Los Angeles

University of California Press
Berkeley and Los Angeles, California

© 1983 by
Romuald J. Misiunas and Rein Taagepera

Printed in Great Britain

Library of Congress Cataloging in Publication Data

Misiunas, Romuald J.
  The Baltic States, years of dependence, 1940–1980.
  "Sequel to Georg von Rauch's The Baltic States: the years of
independence, 1917–1940 (1974)" — Pref.
  Bibliography: p.
  Includes index.
  1. Baltic States — History. I. Taagepera, Rein.
II. Rauch, Georg von. Geschichte der baltischen
Staaten. English. III. Title.
DK511.B3M57 1983   947'.40842   82–4727
ISBN 0–520–04625–0   AACR2

To Audra and Mare

CONTENTS

PLATES

(between pages 112 and 113)

I. Stalin, German Foreign Minister Ribbentrop and others at the signing of the Non-Aggression Treaty between Germany and the USSR, Moscow, 23–24 August 1939.

II. Two facets of Soviet-Estonian relations: the visit of the Soviet Marshal A.I. Egorov to Tallinn in 1939, and a Soviet armored car outside the Tallinn Central Prison on 21 June 1940.

III. Soviet-organized mass demonstration in Tallinn, 21 June 1940; a group of Lithuanian partisans, 1947.

IV. Bronze statue by the Estonian sculptor O. Männi, exemplifying the Stalinist historical canon; Lithuanian CP First Secretary A. Sniečkus at the dedication of a war memorial, 1972.

V. Independence Monument in Riga, a pre-war landmark which has survived.

VI. Two examples of monumental modernist architecture in the Baltic republics: the Academy of Sciences of the Latvian SSR and the Vilnius Opera House.

VII. Post-war housing developments: at Jelgava, Latvia, and Lazdynai, a suburb of Vilnius.

VIII. A new eight-pump gas-station which was front-page news in Estonia in 1972; an overturned tractor whose driver was drunk.

IX. Evidence of industrialization: docking facilities at Ventspils, Latvia; an oil-shale site on Estonia's north coast.

X. The Estonian Song Festival; athletes from the Baltic republics at the Moscow Spartakiad in 1956 demonstrating their national identity.

XI. Restored medieval buildings in Lithuania.

XII. The Church of Mary Queen of Peace, Klaipėda, Lithuania, built 1956–62, before and after conversion into the ''People's Philharmonic''; the Lutheran church at Vidsmuiža, Latvia, now a grocery shop.

XIII. The Hill of Crosses near Šiauliai, Lithuania.

ix

PREFACE

The present work has been undertaken at the request of the British publisher, Christopher Hurst, as a sequel to Georg von Rauch's *The Baltic States: The Years of Independence, 1917–1940* (1974). It seeks to fill a gap in scholarly literature. Apart from a seventy-page appendix by Evald Uustalu, "Events After 1940," to the second edition of August Rei, *The Drama of the Baltic Peoples* (1970), there does not seem to be any overview of the area in Soviet times. Most of the histories of the individual countries in English do not cover the period after World War II. Significant overviews of the Soviet period — in Estonia: Tönu Parming and Elmar Järvesoo (eds.), *A Case Study of a Soviet Republic: The Estonian SSR* (1978), and in Lithuania: V. Stanley Vardys (ed.), *Lithuania Under the Soviets, 1940–1965* (1965) — are multi-author efforts which cover these republics by specific topics rather than by chronological survey.

Like von Rauch, we approached the Baltic countries as an entity. Treating each republic separately would have simplified our task considerably, but it would have yielded a less useful survey and doubtless a somewhat repetitious one. Even more than in the interwar period, the Baltic peoples have come to identify themselves as a unit. And others have come to view them as a particularly distinct entity within the USSR. Such perceptions argue for a unitary approach.

A common approach stresses the similarities in the histories of the three countries. To a large extent, such similarities in their recent experience are present: common occupation by the Soviets, collectivization, deportations, Sovietization of culture, and search for Western ties. On the other hand, there are also significant differences in their postwar development. The Estonian purge of 1950 and that in Latvia in 1959 proved unique for both republics. And in many ways, Lithuania has tended to exhibit a markedly different pattern of postwar Sovietization: a later industrialization, a native Communist Party leadership and membership, and the existence of the Catholic Church as a strong focal point for national resistance. Although our approach is one of synthesis, which by its very nature tends to downplay distinctions, we hope that such major differences have received sufficient attention here.

The problem of postwar periodization emerged as a major one. Both Soviet and émigré treatments tend to avoid subdivisions of these years, considering them as one happy or unhappy period, as the case may be. But it is evident that thirty-five years cannot be so uneventful as to become practically indivisible in historiography. Some Soviet works, operating on the Marxist principle that historical periods should be based on the economic organization of the society they treat, use 1950 as one such divide. Collectivization was then nearly complete and guerrilla resistance was waning. Consistency in application of this principle of historical division would imply a need for subsequent divisions in 1958 and 1965, when the *sovnarkhozy* (regional economic councils) were established and abolished. But such division is evidently not forthcoming, as it could detract from the aura of infallibility of the party which the regime has so assiduously nurtured.

Western periodization of Soviet history is also not readily adaptable to the Baltic scene. It tends to be based on changes in all-Union leadership: the Stalin, Khrushchev, and Brezhnev years, which are not always consonant with developments on the republic scene.

We chose our own subdivisions. The postwar Stalinist years are continued to the end of 1953 and, in some aspects, even to 1955. Even though an appreciable change in mood can be said to have appeared in 1953, it took some time for concrete changes of the Thaw to filter down significantly to the republic level. The replacement of Khrushchev by Brezhnev in 1964 does not seem to have had any immediately notable impact on the Baltic republics. Therefore, we somewhat arbitrarily chose the year 1968 as a dividing line. The invasion of Czechoslovakia admittedly also had no immediately tangible repercussion on the Baltic scene. However, we chose to view it as a sort of psychological watershed in moods and expectations for improvement, particularly on the cultural scene – a focal point in the national lives of the three republics. Such change in mood or perception is admittedly hard to measure, define, or delineate. By its nature, it remains subjective. Nevertheless, we are of the opinion that change can definitely be said to have occurred in the aftermath of the events in Czechoslovakia, altering the guarded optimism which appeared pervasive up to that time. Its concrete manifestations took some time to surface, yet surface they did. The resignation and the dissent of the 1970s are both markedly different in quality from the hidden hopes of the preceding decade.

We realize that our subdivisions are arbitrary and debatable. Moreover, they might not always best suit developments in each of the three republics. However, they should be viewed as an attempt to integrate developments in each republic into a Baltic unit as well

as into the history of the USSR as a whole, of which such developments perforce form a part.

One obvious difficulty is our inability to use Latvian-language
literature in any detailed way. We have found secondary literature
in other languages sufficient to allow us to proceed with the overview. Nevertheless, our inability to operate with original Latvian
material, and our lesser familiarity with the distinctness of the
Latvian scene, may have introduced some imbalance in terms of
examples and illustrations. We hope this will not overly detract
from the validity of the survey as a whole.

The paucity of primary sources hinders the writing of Baltic
history in the West. Within the Baltic republics themselves,
primary sources are more readily available, but synthesis is
frequently restricted by a whole host of impediments typical of
Soviet academic life: restricted access to archives, self-censorship,
and formal censorship. Yet many valuable Soviet secondary
sources are produced. Taken in conjunction with corroborating
evidence available outside the USSR, a fairly accurate overall
picture can be constructed.

The present volume cannot pretend to be a definitive picture of
the Baltic states since 1940. The time perspective for the last decade
is too short to make valid generalizations. Key primary sources
have frequently been unavailable. Many times, even when they are
available, they are buried among considerable chaff in secondary
Soviet works. It has not always proved feasible to sift through this
bulk. This is particularly true for the Stalin years. But even when
perspective is sufficient and documentation adequate, there
remains a marked absence of detailed analytical studies on many
very important questions which would bring together all extant
primary and secondary sources and the findings of which could be
generalized in a survey work such as this.

This work can be said to be, in many sections, a condensation of
as-yet nonexistent specific studies. We earnestly hope that in-depth
research might be catalyzed by the numerous tenuously documented statements necessitated by the overview nature of the work
which were included in preference to total silence on the topics in
question. Perhaps a second edition, a decade from now, will be
able to utilize such studies to rectify some of these instances of
incompleteness, imbalance, and possible error in the present text.

All data tables are located in Appendix B. Footnote citations at
the end of a paragraph usually apply to the entire paragraph, or to
that part which follows a previous note.

We are grateful to all who have read and commented on the
manuscript. Many extremely useful suggestions have come from
these individuals and have shaped the final appearance of the

work. We are particularly indebted to Karl Aun, Nicholas Balabkins, Juris Dreifelds, Andrievs Ezergailis, Uldis Ģērmanis, Walter Hanchett, Gundar King, Benedict Mačiuika, Hain Rebas, Aleksandras Shtromas, Evald Uustalu, and Tomas Venclova. Valuable comments have also been received from Yaroslav Bilinsky, David Crowe, Neil Dale, Elmar Järvesoo, Ivar Ivask, Aušra Jurašas, Atis Lejiņš, Imre Lipping, Dietrich Loeber, Jānis Penikis, Jaan Pennar, Arnold Purre, Thomas Remeikis, Vello Salo, Rimvydas Šilbajoris, Adolfs Sprudzs, Dagmar Vallens, V. Stanley Vardys, George Viksnins, and Pranas Zundė. Important source materials have been given or loaned to us by Edgar Anderson, Jaan Puhvel, Toivo Raun, and Andris Trapans. Stephanie Komkov, Herwig Kraus, Hilja Kukk, and Stephen Rogers helped with the indexing. We should further like to thank Rolfs Ekmanis, Jurgis Anysas, Bronius Kviklys, Reino Sepp, Vitolis Vengris, the Lithuanian Information Center, the Estonian Archives in the U.S., the Relief Centre for Estonian Prisoners of Conscience in the USSR, and Vitauts Simanis, who lent us some of their photographs for the illustrations. We also thank Lorraine Thompson and various individuals at the UCI Social Sciences Word Processing Center — Kathy Alberti, Donna Dill, Cheryl Larsson, Jayne Putman, Marjorie Robinson, Dave Westhoff, Lillian White, and Helen Wildman — who have so valiantly struggled with the Baltic spellings. Needless to say, any short-comings remain our responsibility.

ROMUALD J. MISIUNAS
REIN TAAGEPERA

FINLAND

GULF OF FINLAND

Paldiski • Tallinn

Kohtla-Järve

Narva

•Kautla

HIIUMAA

ESTONIA

Lake
Peipsi

BALTIC

Pärnu · Pärnu · Viljandi

Tartu

SAAREMAA

Kilingi-Nõmme

Emajõgi

RUSSIA
(RSFSR)

SEA

GULF
OF
RIGA

LIVONIA

Petseri

Pskov

Haanja
Ruusmäe

•Ventspils

Valmiera

KURZEME
(COURLAND)

Cēsis

LATVIA

ABRENE

Augspils

Rīga

Jūrmala · Ogre

Madona

Liepāja

Dobele

Jelgava

Plaviņas

LATGALE

Daugava

Rēzekne

Mažeikiai

Žagarė

Akmenė

Venta

Šiauliai

Daugavpils

Minija

Klaipēda

Panevėžys

Zarasai

Lake
Drukštai

LITHUANIA

Nevėžis

Jurbarkas

Nemunas

Kėdainiai

Jonava

BELORUSSIA

Sovetsk
(Tilsit)

Šešupė

Kaunas

Žiežmariai

KALININGRAD
OBLAST (RSFSR)

Elektrėnai

Vilnius

Trakai

EAST
PRUSSIA

Skardupiai

Pirčiupis

Varėna

•Suwałki

Minsk

POLAND

0   100 KM

- - - - - 1938 borders
············· June 1940 border of
                    Lithuania
— — — Post–1945 borders

Lithuania's gains in
1939 and 1940

Estonia's and Latvia's
losses in 1945

xvi

CHAPTER I

INTRODUCTION: HISTORICAL BACKGROUND

BEFORE THE MODERN AGE

The three Baltic republics form a distinct and unique cultural unit — a Western enclave within the multi-national Soviet state. They are the only areas of the USSR to have experienced an independent modern national life and modernization not patterned on the Soviet model. Although bound by geographic proximity and a modern history of inclusion in the same empire, the Estonians, Latvians, and Lithuanians are ethnically and culturally diverse peoples. The Estonians speak a Finno-Ugrian language, related to Finnish, which is radically different from those of their two neighbors to the south. Latvian and Lithuanian are the only living varieties of the Indo-European Baltic family of languages. Estonia and Latvia developed within the north European Protestant world, while Lithuanian culture was shaped by the central and eastern European Catholic milieu. The histories of the three peoples during the present century, their emergence as independent nation-states after World War I, their mutual experiences during the interwar period, and their fate during World War II and its aftermath have served, however, to affirm a common identity which in some ways has superseded the cultural differentiation of the past.

The homeland of the Baltic peoples, the eastern littoral of the Baltic Sea, was medieval Europe's last pagan backwater. Although it straddled the commercially important waterway between the Varangians and the Greeks, its distance from the two European centers of civilization of the time, the Latin West and the Orthodox East, limited cultural contact between its indigenous inhabitants and the world of Christendom.

The first serious outside incursions into the area date from the beginning of the present millennium. While the occasional campaigns for booty and tribute by several princes of the East Slav Kiev realm failed to introduce lasting political dominance, the expansion of the Latin West was accompanied by settlement and the

1

imposition of suzerainty. The thrust began toward the end of the twelfth century and first touched the westernmost Baltic people, the Prussians. Within a few decades their lands were subjugated by the military monastic Order of the Teutonic Knights, which had transferred their crusades to this region after suffering reverses in the Near East. A few centuries later the Prussians became extinct, leaving only their name (until 1945) to the lands they had once inhabited. At around the same time the maritime Danish monarchy entrenched itself in northern Estonia, and German merchants colonized the region of the Daugava (Dvina) River. In 1201, a bishopric was established at the core of their operations, Riga. Another German military order, the Brothers of the Sword, pursued the conquest of the hinterland. As was the case with the Prussians, native resistance based on a rudimentary political organization proved sporadic and disunited. Within a century, the conquest of what would subsequently become Latvia and Estonia was completed. Their peoples were absorbed into the social and cultural structures of the world of Western Christendom of the High Middle Ages before they could develop a native political system. The invaders colonized, baptized, and gradually enserfed the indigenous population, reducing their identity to an ethnic character, politically dormant until the age of modern nationalism. After the Danes sold their holdings in Estonia to the Teutonic Order, in 1346, the area became a loose confederation of the domains of the Order, ecclesiastical estates ruled by princes of the Holy Roman Empire, and a few independent Hansa towns.

During their initial drive of the thirteenth century, the Latin Christians were unable to overwhelm the less accessible Lithuanians. A native chief, Mindaugas (Mindovg), successfully forged the Baltic tribes in the area of present-day Lithuania and parts of Belorussia into a lasting political entity. He inflicted a crushing defeat on the Brothers of the Sword which led, in 1237, to their amalgamation into the Teutonic Order. Seeking peace with the Germanic invaders, he attempted to integrate his newly established realm into the West European political system. He converted to Latin Christianity and was crowned King on authority of Pope Innocent IV. But internal strife thwarted his efforts. The Lithuanian state survived his violent end in 1263 at the hands of political opponents. Its society, however, returned to the pagan customs of their ancestors.

During the fourteenth century, a series of particularly able Lithuanian rulers, Gediminas (Gedimyn), Algirdas (Olgerd), and Kęstutis (Kenstut), managed not only to contain the assaults of the Teutonic Order but also to expand eastward in the wake of the recession of Tatar power. Considerable East Slav territory was absorbed into Lithuania, making it a major power in East Europe. The extensive state, whose rulers and ethnic core maintained their pagan religion, became a cultural battleground between Latin influences and the Orthodox traditions of the incorporated East Slav population. A resolution of this conflict came in 1386. Great Prince Jogaila (Jagiełło), pressed by continuing incursions of the Order, sought Polish support. As a condition of his marriage to the heiress of Poland, Jadwyga, and his accession to the Polish throne, he agreed to the baptism of his pagan Lithuanian subjects into the Latin rite. The rule of Jogaila's cousin Vytautas (Vitovt), as Viceroy according to theoretical West European designation but as an independent Great Prince in practice, saw the apogee of Lithuanian power. The realm stretched from the Baltic to the Black Sea, from the outskirts of Moscow to Poland. In 1410 the combined armies of Poland and Lithuania inflicted a crushing blow on the Teutonic Order at Grünwald (Tannenberg). It was never able to recover, and thereafter ceased to be the threat to Lithuania that it had been for two centuries.

The nearly two hundred years of personal union with Poland, never clearly defined in the political sense, lasted until 1569 and had two long-term cultural effects on the ethnic core of the Lithuanian state: the Christianization of the Lithuanians according to the Latin Rite and the Polonization of the Lithuanian nobility. The older and culturally richer Polish society proved irresistible to the Lithuanian nobles. While a sense of distinct political identity was preserved for a long time, the Lithuanian nobility became culturally indistinguishable from its Polish counterpart. The effect on the peasantry was similar to that in Estonia and Latvia — enforced Christianization and enserfment to a nobility which could not speak their language.

As a result of the Reformation, the Teutonic Order and the ecclesiastical domains in the Estonian and Latvian lands became politically anachronistic. Their secularization coincided in time with the colonization of the New World, which attracted adventurous Europeans, and led to a manpower problem in the successors to the Order. Unable to defend themselves adequately, they began to seek foreign protection. The major political realignments were triggered by a Russian push toward the Baltic launched by Ivan IV. In reaction, the rulers of northern Estonia preferred to submit to Sweden in 1561. The nobility of Livonia (southern Estonia and eastern Latvia) sought Lithuanian protection in 1560. Their lands were incorporated into the Lithuanian state; the western part of Latvia became the Duchy of Courland, a personal fief of the Lithuanian and Polish sovereign. Not long thereafter, also in a reaction to the Muscovite push, Lithuania regularized its personal political union with Poland into a formal constitutional arrangement. While duality of sovereignty was retained, a new Commonwealth structure with a joint sovereign and legislature was established at the Union of Lublin (1569).

The Commonwealth successfully resisted the Russian drive. However, it was not able to contain the Swedes. In 1629, Livonia was divided. Its northwestern half, including the city of Riga, came under Swedish overlordship; its eastern portion, Latgale, remained under Lithuanian rule. The status of the Duchy of Courland did not change. Except for Latgale, whose association with Lithuania for two centuries rendered it distinct from the rest of Latvia, the cultural boundary between Lithuania and the north acquired a long-standing character as one between Catholic and Lutheran worlds, between Polish and German social and administrative practices.

Although Sweden itself had never experienced enserfment, the system of peasant bondage continued in its Baltic provinces. As a result, the sympathies of the government were not always automatically on the side of the Baltic barons. However, Sweden depended on the barons for military service and on uninterrupted grain imports from the region, and could not afford wholly to alienate the local seigneurs. On the whole, conditions among the peasants worsened during the course of the seventeenth century. However, in view of even worse times later, Estonians and Latvians have come to regard the Swedish period in their history rather warmly.

The next major change in the political configuration of the region came with the renewed and successful Russian push to the Baltic Sea during the Great Northern War. The Treaty of Nystad (1721) confirmed Russian possession of Livonia and Estland (northern Estonia). The imposition of Russian rule allowed the local nobility to reassert some of their former prerogatives which had been whittled down during Swedish times. Among its provisions, the peace settlement guaranteed all former noble rights, among them self-government and unlimited rule over the peasants, which had fallen into disuse. It is doubtful whether any other area in Europe at the time produced quite the extent of legal argumentation designed to redefine and in so doing expand nobles' rights over their peasants. As a practical consequence, a closed corporation of 324 families established a monopoly of landholding in the area. The Baltic German barons proved loyal subjects of the Russian Empire. New opportunities for advancement in the administrative, diplomatic, and military service developed, allowing them to expand their influence in St. Petersburg far beyond what their relatively small numbers warranted. For the Latvian and

Estonian peasants, however, the late eighteenth century marked the nadir of their rights and living conditions.

In addition to the annexation of Livonia and Estland, the Russian Empire established *de facto* control over the Duchy of Courland, which had become virtually an independent state during the preceding century. Likewise, Russia managed to exercise preponderant influence over the decadent Polish-Lithuanian Commonwealth. Internal attempts at reform in this state triggered foreign intervention and its extinction as a political unit. During the course of the three partitions of the Commonwealth (1772, 1793, and 1795), the Lithuanian state fell under Russian rule virtually in its entirety.

THE ROAD TO THE MODERN NATION-STATES

In all three Baltic countries, the appearance and growth of national consciousness during the nineteenth century accompanied the social struggle of the peasantry against a culturally alien entrenched nobility. Matters were complicated by the desire of the Russian government to turn the region into a culturally integral part of the Russian state. The policy of Russification pursued by the Tsarist government, particularly during the latter part of the century, was aimed primarily at the old local elites and thus unwittingly facilitated the emergence of the indigenous peasant nations.

The Baltic provinces of Estland, Livonia, and Courland were the first regions of the Russian Empire in which serfdom was abolished. The first attempt to limit this institution was made by Alexander I in 1804, but the Baltic barons managed to minimize any practical results from his measure. By 1819, however, personal emancipation had been effected. The trend of the previous five centuries was reversed. Although the peasants were legally free, they had not been endowed with land. Changes in the agrarian economy coupled with a series of measures during the 1840s to 1860s enabled many peasants to acquire as personal holdings much of the land which they had formerly been forced to lease from the barons. At the same time, the abolition of compulsory guild membership among urban craftsmen permitted Estonian and Latvian peasants to settle in the hitherto primarily German cities.

Proselytizing for the Russian Orthodox Church, which proved quite successful in some districts among the peasantry, established a counterweight to the German-dominated Lutheran Church. The competition between the two churches led to an expansion of publications in Latvian and Estonian.

The railway age saw a considerable expansion of the cities. Riga,

Liepāja (Libau), and Tallinn (Reval) grew significantly with an increase in their importance as ports and industrial centers. A Latvian and Estonian middle class as well as a proletariat made their appearance. Tallinn, already more than 50% Estonian in 1871, was about two-thirds Estonian by 1897. The Latvian share in the population of Riga nearly doubled during the same period, from 23% to 42%. This expansion of urbanization was accompanied by the introduction of education in the native languages. By the end of the century, the Baltic provinces were unique within the Russian Empire for having virtually eliminated illiteracy.

The growth of national consciousness fostered by such socio-economic tendencies was furthered by the Russification policy pursued by the Imperial government during the reign of Alexander III. Its targets were the provincial administration, the courts, and the educational system, which were the bastions of the privileged German elements. This pressure helped the fledgeling political activity by the rising Estonian and Latvian elements, although forced imposition of Russian as the language of instruction in Latvian and Estonian schools resulted in an educational setback for the native languages. By the turn of the century, there were successes on the municipal level. In 1904, Estonians gained a majority in the municipal council of Tallinn. Between 1897 and 1906, Latvian majorities were elected to the municipal councils of four large towns.

A somewhat different socio-economic development occurred in Lithuania. In one portion of the country — the area southwest of the Nemunas River, which had belonged to Napoleon's Grand Duchy of Warsaw — the peasants were freed during the first decade of the nineteenth century. Emancipation, with the right to limited landholding, came to the rest of the country in 1861, along with the general abolition of serfdom throughout the Russian Empire. A social struggle with the Polonized nobility ensued.

The policy of Russification began earlier in Lithuania than in the other two Baltic countries. It became a marked feature of cultural life after the 1831 uprising which accompanied a revolt in Poland. Initially it was aimed at the Polonized nobility; after the 1863 revolt, however, its measures also hindered the Lithuanian national renaissance. The Lithuanian peasantry had shown itself to be more revolutionary than its counterpart in Poland. In 1865, the publication of Latin alphabet books in the Lithuanian language was prohibited, a measure not repealed until 1904. Policies of settling Russians in rural areas and of proselytizing for the Russian Orthodox Church were undertaken. The rights of the Roman Catholic Church were curtailed; in 1894, Roman Catholics were excluded from administrative positions in local government organs. A struggle for religious equality turned into one facet of the Lithuanian nationalist movement, in contrast to its Latvian and Estonian counterparts. The close identification of Catholicism with nationalism has persisted in Lithuania to the present day.

Cultural persecution by the Russian authorities led to the use of the compact ethnic Lithuanian population living across the border within the more liberal structure of Prussia as a *point d' appui*. The first journal in the Lithuanian language was published here. Books printed in Tilsit and elsewhere in that region were smuggled across the Russian frontier. These helped to nourish a system of *ad hoc*, almost secret, "schools of the hearth" through which the level of rural literacy was raised and national values were fostered during a half-century of intense Russification.

Unlike Estonia and Latvia, Lithuania remained an almost entirely agrarian country. Its few urban centers were not populated by the ethnic Lithuanian majority. As a result, by the turn of the century there was virtually no Lithuanian middle class or proletariat. Rural overpopulation at a time of rising anti-Russian sentiment fostered emigration — mostly to the United States and Canada. It is estimated that on the eve of World War I, one out of every three Lithuanians lived in North America.

The disorders which swept the Russian Empire in 1905 affected the entire Baltic area, though to different degrees. In Latvia and Estonia, the protests were heavily socio-political. Urban unrest was particularly severe in Riga and Tallinn. Freedom of the press and of assembly as well as a universal franchise were the principal goals of the strikers and demonstrators. Nationwide assemblies (1,000 Latvian delegates in Riga, 800 Estonian delegates in Tartu) convened in November and called for national autonomy. The situation in the countryside was even more turbulent. German nobles and clergymen were particular targets for the jacqueries; nearly 200 manor houses were burned and about 100 noblemen killed. The brutal suppression of the uprising included several thousand executions and the imprisonment and exile to Siberia of thousands of others.

The revolution in Lithuania was considerably less dramatic and remained largely confined to rural areas. It appeared aimed more at perceived cultural enemies. Its targets were mostly Russian schoolteachers and members of the Orthodox clergy; excesses were relatively few. The events in Lithuania were highlighted by the massive National Congress of 2,000 delegates which met in Vilnius (Vilna) in December 1905. The resolutions of the Congress sought autonomy, a centralized administration for the ethnic Lithuanian region of the Russian Empire, and the use of the Lithuanian language in administration. The reaction in Lithuania was likewise relatively mild. The Stolypin reform, which sought to create a rural class of prosperous farmers throughout the Empire as a social bulwark of the system, even benefited many Lithuanian peasants.

In spite of setbacks, the general political and cultural relaxation which set in after 1906 allowed for a steady intensification of the national consciousness of the Baltic peoples. Although the events of 1905 had forced many leaders into exile and emigration, Estonians and Latvians acquired representation through delegates to the Imperial Duma. The Lithuanians also acquired a group of experienced national politicians through this new Russian legislature. The elimination of restrictions on the press in the national languages equally affected all three, but was an especially pronounced cultural development in Lithuania.

THE YEARS OF INDEPENDENCE: 1918–1940

Modern Baltic history has been shaped by the conflict among great powers in the region. The simultaneous collapse of the Russian and German empires during World War I allowed the three Baltic peoples to seize a rare opportunity of creating their own nation-states. Before the end of the war, on 16 and 24 February respectively, Lithuania and Estonia declared their independence. An analogous Latvian declaration appeared on 18 November, shortly after the end of hostilities in the West. The circumstances under which each of the three countries established its independence varied considerably.

The Estonian movement for separate statehood emerged from the dissolution of the Russian Empire. Estonia was the only national region to which the Provisional Government of 1917, after a massive demonstration of Estonians in Petrograd, granted autonomy. The organ of autonomous self-government unilaterally declared complete independence one day before advancing German troops occupied Tallinn. The collapse of Germany in November of 1918 allowed for a reassertion of this proclamation. An invasion by the Red Army in December seriously threatened Estonia's independence, although a Soviet naval attack on Tallinn was foiled by a British naval squadron. While an appreciable minority of the population favored the Bolsheviks, the wide majority rallied to the cause of national statehood. By March 1919, Estonian territory had been cleared of foreign forces, although hostilities continued at the frontiers.

Circumstances in Latvia were far more complex. As the most industrialized part of the Russian Empire, Latvia had developed a strong working-class movement which had been affected by the revolution. Moreover, the Tsarist government had formed Latvian rifle regiments in the summer of 1915 after the German armies reached the Daugava (Dvina) River. These soldiers, along with the rest of the old Russian army, were affected by the revolutionary mood of 1917 and split their loyalties between a crystallizing national movement and the Bolsheviks. Such a division of sympathies immensely complicated the incursion of the Red Army into Latvia after the German collapse. Matters were further complicated by German attempts in 1919 to preserve a foothold in the Baltic lands. Utilizing the desperate Latvian nationalist need to stem the Red tide, a commander of the German *Freikorps*, General Rüdiger von der Goltz, tried to set up a puppet Latvian regime. The defeat of his army by Estonian-Latvian forces, British diplomatic and naval pressures, and the subsequent defeat of another German attempt to utilize a White Russian adventurer, Colonel Pavel Bermondt-Avalov, as a cover for their operations allowed the Latvians to concentrate on clearing their country of the Red Army. By 1920, this had been achieved.

The Lithuanian declaration of independence came while the entire country was still under German occupation. The Lithuanian National Council (*Taryba*), a group of nationalist leaders whom the Germans had originally sought to use as a cover for their expansionist aims, issued the resolution unilaterally. However, it could not be implemented because of German refusal to recognize any arrangement which would not permanently tie Lithuania to Germany. The German collapse in 1918 made possible the organization of an administration and an army. In early 1919, an invading Red force was repulsed. Later that year, the German forces of Bermondt-Avalov were also pushed back into Latvia.

The establishment of Lithuanian independence was also complicated by pressures from the newly arisen Polish state for a restoration of the political union of historic times. Although they were resisted, these demands delayed Lithuania's recognition by the Western powers. Matters were exacerbated by the conflicting territorial claims of the two states. The capital of the historic Lithuanian state, Vilnius, was occupied by the Poles after conclusion of an armistice leaving the city in Lithuanian hands. As a result, Polish-Lithuanian relations remained strained throughout the interwar period, and diplomatic relations between the two countries were not established until 1938.

In 1920, the three Baltic countries concluded peace treaties with the Soviet state (Estonia on 2 February; Lithuania, 12 July; and Latvia, 1 August). Russian claims to sovereignty over their territories were renounced in perpetuity. Nation-building could now proceed unhindered, although Lithuania's continuing problems with unsettled frontiers delayed this process somewhat in that country.

The achievement of independence brought similar problems to all three countries. They needed to reform their social, economic, and political structures to conform with their new status as nation-states. In societies which were still predominantly agararian, the question of land ownership was a pivotal one, from the social as well as the economic point of view. Economies which had suffered during the years of war needed adaptation to new international circumstances. And new constitutional structures had to be devised for an independent state life.

Land reform proved most drastic in Estonia and Latvia. There the holdings of the large landed estates were redistributed to peasants, particularly to volunteers in the war for independence, thus ending the economic and political power of the Baltic barons. Their legal corporations, which had dominated social life in the area, had already been dispersed in 1917. Land reform in Lithuania, where the local nobility had been considerably more repressed in Tsarist times, was less sweeping. Although the large estates disappeared, their former owners were left with somewhat larger portions of their former holdings.

Loss of the former Russian markets led to some hardship for the Estonian and Latvian industries. Realignment came slowly, but it was successfully achieved. Estonia developed a new oil-shale industry. Timber and related enterprises were built up as export industries. In 1930, manufacturing engaged 17.4% of Estonia's labor force and 13.5% of Latvia's , but only 6% of that of Lithuania, which remained unindustrialized to any degree.

The principal economic effort in all three countries was to create an export economy based on agricultural produce and specializing in meat, poultry, and dairy products. Government-sponsored cooperatives appeared in all three countries to handle the collection, processing, and marketing of farm produce. England and Germany became the two principal export markets. These moves were intended to benefit the new independent farming class which had been created through land redistribution and which emerged as the principal component in the socio-economic structures of the three states.

In accordance with prevailing Western political currents of the time, all three countries adopted liberal democratic constitutions. Their legislatures clearly predominated over their executives. Single-chamber parliaments emerged in all three. In Estonia, the Prime Minister was simultaneously Chief of State. Under such circumstances, a vote of no-confidence in Parliament left the country without even a titular head. Such assembly structures are perhaps the most difficult of all to operate, and none of the three societies possessed a proper social, economic, or political culture or tradition necessary to support their functioning. The radical parliamentary constitutions and electoral rules hampered the creation of stable governments. The pressures of radical interests and ideologies soon led, as it did throuhgout the rest of eastern Europe, to the emergence of some sort of authoritarian systems.

The earliest change came in Lithuania. A precarious political stability had been possible as long as the Christian Democrats and their allies managed to win majorities among the predominantly Catholic electorate. In 1926, however, a series of scandals led to their defeat. Later that year, the small Nationalist Party, supported by the passivity of the opposition Christian Democrats, was installed by the army, overthrowing a coalition government of Populists, Socialists, and minorities which had been in power barely half a year. An authoritarian presidential regime, similar to that of Piłsudski in Poland, emerged under the leadership of Antanas Smetona.

The process of democratic disintegration was somewhat more drawn out in Estonia and Latvia. Fragmentation into numerous small political parties made the formation of stable coalitions a difficult task. In Estonia, governments between 1919 and 1933 lasted eight months on the average. Political instability was aggravated by the social effects of the Great Depression. Pressures for political reform mounted, particularly from the right-wing League of Freedom Fighters, an association of veterans of the war for independence. In October 1933, their proposal for constitutional reform won by 72.7% of the votes in a referendum. The following March, the Acting President, Konstantin Päts, made use of the new authoritarian constitution to declare a state of emergency, deactivate Parliament, and disband the League of Freedom Fighters. He ruled by presidential decree until 1938.

A similar change occurred in Latvia a few months later. In a situation of extreme polarization between right- and left-wing forces, Prime Minister Kārlis Ulmanis declared a state of emergency, formed a government of national unity, dissolved all political parties, and governed without the legislature.

There were noticeable differences in the styles of the new regimes in the three countries. Authoritarianism proved somewhat milder in Estonia and Lithuania than in Latvia. The moderate Estonian leader considered his system as a transition to a more stable democratic system. A referendum on a new Constituent Assembly implicitly legalized his caretaker regime in 1936. Another new constitution provided for a Parliament which convened in 1938. Electoral rules were designed to favor Päts and his Patriotic

League. However, elections to the lower house were basically fair. Despite their fragmentation, opposition groups won 17 of the 80 seats. In Lithuania, the more dictatorially inclined rightist Prime Minister Augustinas Voldemaras, who had been installed along with Antanas Smetona during the coup of 1926, was dismissed in 1929. Thereafter Smetona, casting himself as the "nation's leader," tried to fashion his regime on the fascist Italian model. Although his Nationalist Party, the only political group allowed to function openly, was expanded into a mass organization, many politicians from the previously important political parties continued their activity unofficially. The worsening international climate during the late 1930s led Smetona to allow a *de facto* emergence of "coalition" governments of national unity, even though the parties represented in them could not legally function as such. Authoritarianism in Latvia proved more straightforward. Ulmanis did not bother to legalize his regime by a referendum or to organize his supporters into an official party. Adopting a policy of "a strong and Latvian Latvia," he combined the offices of President and Prime Minister. In search for a base of support, he pursued a policy of enlarging the state sector of the economy, primarily at the expense of the German minority.

No significant opposition to the suppression of the parliamentary governments arose. Many former politicians proved quite willing to cooperate with the new regimes, whose introduction was rationalized by a need to prevent foreign influence or takeovers by extreme local rightist or leftist elements. The continued support of the professional officer corps assured their stability. While the liberal-minded intelligentsia could not be won over, and chafed under the relatively mild restraints on political expression, the rural population and the business establishment welcomed the prosperity accompanying stability — which was largely due, however, to the passing of the world Depression. From the mid-1930s, foreign trade showed a steady increase in all three countries. While political dissatisfaction was not absent, potentially serious internal dissension did not arise. In Estonia, the general amnesty of 1938 left only a few dozen "political" prisoners, nearly all of them espionage cases. Even the Lithuanian regime proved able to weather two grave blows to its prestige in foreign relations. In 1938, following a frontier incident, Poland presented an ultimatum to recognize Polish possession of Vilnius. In March 1939, Hitler reannexed Klaipėda (Memel), which had been part of the pre-1918 German state.

The political authoritarianism was too mild to affect culture significantly. Indeed, the regimes supported the development of the national cultural life which had begun with the achievement of independence. The twenty-two year period of independence was one of significant cultural advance for the Baltic peoples. Literary, artistic, and musical life flourished. The increase in numbers of schools was phenomenal. Each of the three countries maintained a national university, where higher education in the native language became available for the first time. In Estonia, the German-Russian University of Iurev (Dorpat) became the University of Tartu. The Polytechnic Institute of Riga was expanded to become a full university. In Lithuania, as Vilnius was controlled by Poland, a new university was established at Kaunas in 1922.

The three Baltic countries attempted to pursue a path of neutrality in foreign policy as the war clouds gathered during the late 1930s. Even regional cooperation among the smaller states between Germany and the USSR proved minimal. Unreconcilable dif-ferences between Lithuania and Poland hampered cooperation in this quarter, and Finland was not interested in any southern alliance. An Estonian-Latvian defensive alliance of 1923 was supplemented in 1934 by a Baltic Entente including Lithuania. However, the level of practical cooperation remained minimal. This may have been due partly to differences in opinion as to where the principal danger lay. Lithuania and Latvia inclined toward a predominant fear of Germany; while Estonia, which was further away from Germany and which had experienced an abortive Communist coup in 1924, was more concerned with the threat from the USSR.

All three countries eventually signed non-aggression or neutrality agreements with the Soviet Union (Lithuania in 1926, Latvia and Estonia in 1932), and with Germany (Latvia and Estonia in June 1939, and Lithuania in the context of the Act of March 1939 ceding Klaipėda). Neutrality laws patterned on the Swedish law of 1938 were adopted by Latvia and Estonia in December 1938, and by Lithuania a month later.

If the foreign policies of the Baltic states can be said to have been inclined toward any of the great powers, it was toward Britain, which while far away supposedly could, as it had in 1919, exercise its naval power in the area. However, by 1939 Britain appeared increasingly weak. It also seemed to be moving in the direction of willingness to accept some sort of Soviet predominance in the Baltic states as a safeguard against German influence. The extent to which Britain was ready to tolerate Soviet control is unclear; one of the reasons for the failure of the Anglo-French military mission to the USSR in the summer of 1939 was its inability to grant the Soviets a free hand in the area.

The Baltic leaders strove to minimize and to balance both German and Soviet influences. Their attempts to maintain neutrality came to be criticized as pro-German by both Great Britain and the Soviet Union, who wanted the Baltic states to participate in collective defense against Germany. The sole area of direct German interest, Klaipėda, was wrested from Lithuania by force in March 1939, and German economic pressure on Lithuania increased; but German attempts to promote a military alliance with Lithuania directed against Poland, with Vilnius as a prize, were resisted by the Kaunas government. Baltic independence, however, was less dependent on efforts of the local governments than on arrangements among the great powers.

CHAPTER II

THE WAR YEARS: 1940–1945

THE COMING OF THE SOVIETS

The End of Baltic Independence

The fate of Baltic independence was sealed with the conclusion of the Molotov-Ribbentrop Pact on 23 August 1939 between Nazi Germany and the Soviet Union. Its secret "additional protocol" assigned Estonia and Latvia to the Soviet sphere of influence, while Lithuania was left to Germany. A subsequent modification concluded after the collapse of Poland placed most of Lithuania in the Soviet sphere as well. By late September, with the Baltic states completely cut off from Britain and France, Stalin could begin the process of annexation. He started with Estonia, which (in contrast to Latvia and Lithuania) had not mobilized even partially during the Polish campaign. About 160,000 Soviet troops were brought to the Estonian border.[1]

The first step on the road to the loss of independence was the least painful. With Soviet warplanes flying low over Tallinn, and Germany taking a stance of pro-Soviet neutrality,[2] Estonia was forced to accept, on 28 September, a Pact of Defense and Mutual Assistance with the USSR. Latvia's turn came on 5 October, and Lithuania's on 10 October. The pacts provided for sizable Soviet garrisons as well as naval bases on Baltic territory. The 30,000 Soviet troops in Latvia and 25,000 in Estonia surpassed in size the national armies (20,000 and 16,000, respectively); Lithuania haggled its share down to 20,000 Soviet troops. The Baltic

---

[1] For texts of Nazi-Soviet agreements, see Raymond Sontag and James Beddie (eds.), *Nazi-Soviet Relations, 1939–1941* (Washington, 1948), [henceforth cited as *Nazi-Soviet Relations*], pp. 76–78; or *Documents on German Foreign Policy, 1918–1945*, ser. D, vol. VIII (U.S. Department of State, 1954), p. 166; also Bronis Kaslas (ed.), *The USSR-German Aggression Against Lithuania* (New York, 1973), pp. 109–112 and 129–130. For Baltic mobilizations and Soviet troops, see Seppo Myllyniemi, *Die baltische Krise, 1938–1941* (Stuttgart, 1979), pp. 54–55 and 59.

[2] German representatives not only refused any support, but also said they would not allow sea transport of arms to Estonia from the West. See *Eesti NSV ajalugu*, III (Tallinn, 1971), p. 365.

governments could not verify the actual numbers brought to the Soviet bases. The treaties guaranteed Baltic independence and reiterated Soviet non-interference in Baltic internal affairs. Lithuania, which during September had resisted German promptings to become a satellite and to retake its claimed capital city Vilnius from Polish control, now received that city together with some surrounding territory as a "gift" from the USSR, which had occupied the area on 17 September.[3]

During the first few months following the pacts, Soviet military and naval presence was kept at an unobtrusively low profile. Stalin, having to face unexpectedly stiff resistance to his attempt to impose a similar arrangement on Finland, was also no doubt waiting to see which way the Germans' war with the West would go.

It is not clear how much the Baltic governments knew about the secret protocols in the Molotov-Ribbentrop Pact. Rumors were circulating already in August. The published documents seem to indicate that the Latvian and Lithuanian governments had been at least partially apprised of the clauses by the Soviets in early October.[4] The lack of German protest over the military arrangements in the Pacts of Mutual Assistance provided sufficient indication of German cognizance of and acquiescence in the matter. Repatriation of about 65,000 Germans from Latvia and Estonia in late 1939 was also ominous. What most likely remained unclear was the degree to which the USSR would effectively seek to impose its dominance. If the Baltic governments were aware of the gravity of the situation, their attempts to reassure their populations provided little indication of it. For instance, on 20 October the Lithuanian paper *Lietuvos aidas*, considered a mouthpiece for government opinion, reasoned:

> The present war shakes the foundations of our old order. The new peace radically changes, with a certainty, its exterior physionomy. Many new principles will be found and applied, not only in international relations, but also in the internal organization of many free and independent peoples. The new principles will equally affect our country.[5]

The policy of all three governments was to maintain good relations with the USSR and to avoid incidents with the garrisons until

---

[3] Kaslas 1973, pp. 148–158; see also Myllyniemi 1979, pp. 59–69. For Latvian and Estonian figures, see Arnolds Spekke, *History of Latvia* (Stockholm, 1957), p. 380, and Evald Uustalu, "Events After 1940," in the Appendix to August Rei, *The Drama of the Baltic Peoples*, 2nd ed. (Stockholm, 1970), p. 239.

[4] *Nazi-Soviet Relations*, pp. 114–117.

[5] Cited in Henry de Chambon, *La tragédie des nations baltiques* (Paris, 1946), p. 34.

the international political climate improved. As Baltic independence had originally been made possible in part by a German-
Russian conflict, not much could be done as long as Germany
supported the Soviet presence in the three states. The Finnish
Winter War confirmed that the Western powers could not be
counted upon. Perhaps the leading circles in Riga and Kaunas
shared Estonian President Päts' conviction of the inevitability of a
German-Soviet clash by late 1940.[6] Such reasoning affirmed the
prudence of docility vis-à-vis the USSR. It also dictated efforts at a
slow strengthening of the German stake in the area as a counter-
balance. Increased trade arrangements with the Reich reflected
such a policy. The war had interrupted Baltic trade with the West
and new outlets were badly needed. Between December 1939 and
April 1940, all three states had concluded trade treaties according
to which Germany was supposed to buy about 70% of all Baltic
exports. The Soviets voiced no objections; their own trade with
Germany was brisk.[7]

The winter of 1939-40 also saw the first meaningful and inten-
sive, albeit belated, collaboration among the three states, even
though the formal framework for such communality, the Baltic
Entente, dated from 1934. However, in view of the general attempt
on the part of all three governments to placate the Soviets, no
concrete preparations were undertaken. In May 1940 some instructions on contingency situations were issued to the diplomatic
services of Latvia and Lithuania. On 17 May 1940, plenipotentiary
power was issued to the Latvian Minister in Great Britain, Kārlis
Zariņš. He was authorized, were contact with the home country
broken, to exercise full authority over Latvia's resources and
representatives abroad and to liquidate all diplomatic missions
save that in the United States if he so saw fit.[8] The Lithuanian
Envoy in Rome, former Foreign Minister Stasys Lozoraitis, was
designated on 30 May head of the service in the event that the home
government should cease to exist or be unable to carry out its
duties. A portion of the Latvian and Estonian gold reserve was sent
to the United States and Great Britain, and some Estonian archives
were shipped to the Legation in Stockholm.[9]

[6] Heinrich Laretei, *Saatuse mängukanniks* (Lund, 1970), p. 241; Myllyniemi 1979,
p. 102.
[7] Actual figures were lower; e.g., Germany accounted for 53% of Estonia's exports
in May 1940, and 42% from January to May. The USSR actually urged Latvia to
export more to Germany. See Myllyniemi 1979, pp. 108-110.
[8] *Third Interim Report of the Select Committee on Communist Agression*, 83rd
Congress, 2nd Session (Washington, 1954) [henceforth cited as *Third Interim
Report*], p. 433.
[9] Hain Rebas, "Tallinn-Stockholm-Tallinn, 1940: Estonian Diplomatic Records
on a Mysterious Round Trip," JBS, VIII/3 (Fall 1977), pp. 205-213.

The Soviets obviously realized that in the case of any military conflict they could not depend on the Baltic states as allies — any hope for genuine alliance had been wrecked by the methods through which Soviet bases had been forced upon the Baltic states. A decision to occupy them fully may have been made in early February 1940, at a Moscow meeting attended by Soviet envoys in the Baltics, since Baltic Communist underground activity increased sharply in March.[10]

The Battle of France gave Stalin a unique opportunity for total occupation of the Baltic states; both German and Western forces were tied up far from eastern Europe. Lithuania was singled out for the first blow. On 25 May, a Soviet note to the Kaunas government accused Lithuanian authorities of kidnapping two Soviet garrison soldiers. The Lithuanians proposed an extraordinary investigatory commission including a representative of the Red Army garrisons, as well as an order for an energetic search for the two, but there was no Soviet reaction. On 30 May, Moscow published a communiqué on allegedly provocative activities of the Lithuanian authorities. The Lithuanian Minister of Foreign Affairs, Juozas Urbšys, went to Moscow in an attempt to settle the incident through direct negotiations. Molotov agreed to discuss the matter, but only with the Prime Minister, Antanas Merkys, who also flew to Moscow on 7 June. In two meetings with Merkys, Molotov castigated the Lithuanian Minister of the Interior as well as the Director of its Security Department for their allegedly hostile anti-Soviet attitudes. The Prime Minister himself was reproached for transforming the Baltic Entente into a military alliance directed against the USSR. Subsequent efforts by the Lithuanian government included a personal message from the President of the Republic to the Chairman of the Presidium of the Supreme Soviet giving explicit assurances of having at all times honored the Pact of Mutual Defense with the USSR.

After Merkys' empty-handed return to Kaunas, Molotov, at midnight on 14 June, handed the Foreign Minister (who had stayed in Moscow) the Soviet proposal for settling the issue. It came in the form of an ultimatum: (1) the arrest and trial of the two officials against whom Molotov had levelled charges; (2) the formation of a government "capable of assuring proper fulfillment" of the pact with the USSR; and (3) the entry into Lithuania of additional units of the Red Army, to be stationed in important centers "in numbers sufficient to assure proper enforcement" of the pacts. The numbers were not specified. As the country was to be occupied, this was irrelevant.

---

[10] Myllyniemi 1979, pp. 114–117.

The emergency Lithuanian cabinet session that followed decided to comply with the Soviet demands. President Smetona found himself in a minority in urging at least symbolic military resistance, to be followed by a collective withdrawal of the government from the country.[11] In accordance with Soviet wishes, Prime Minister Merkys resigned and Smetona asked the erstwhile Commander-in-Chief of the Army, General Stasys Raštikis, who had left that post not long before over political differences with Smetona, to form a new government. A few hours later, the Foreign Minister, still in Moscow, informed the government that Raštikis was also unacceptable to the Kremlin and that the Soviet Deputy Commissar for Foreign Affairs, Vladimir Dekanozov, would be sent to Lithuania as special emissary. He would supervise the formation of a new cabinet. Smetona, accompanied by a few high officials, left his country. The Red Army streamed into Lithuania. On the same day (15 June 1940), the Germans entered Paris.

The following day, Molotov sent similar notes to Latvia and Estonia accusing their governments of breaking their pacts with the USSR and of plotting to turn the Baltic Entente into an anti-Soviet alliance. His proof consisted in pointing to the December 1939 and March 1940 meetings of the Foreign Ministers of the three countries, which had hardly been secret, and publication of the *Baltic Review*, a journal appearing since February 1939 with articles in English, French, and German. Molotov's notes demanded the formation of governments capable of carrying out the pacts with the USSR and the introduction of unlimited additional Soviet military and naval units. Each ultimatum carried a six- to eight-hour time limit.

Latvia and Estonia also yielded to the Soviet demands, and on 17 June Soviet forces marched into both countries. The futility of any resistance had been increased by the Lithuanian surrender. Latvian combat preparations were called off when the Soviets threatened to bomb the cities, and when it became clear that Germany would not agree to sell any arms; President Päts of Estonia also seems to have tried through his unofficial contacts with the German Legation in Tallinn to persuade Germany to intercede.[12] Two special emissaries, Andrei Vyshinskii for Latvia and Andrei Zhdanov for Estonia, accompanied the Red Army to supervise the formation of new pro-Soviet governments. By 18 June, the occupation of the Baltic states was complete.

---

[11] Stasys Raštikis, *Kovose dėl Lietuvos* (Los Angeles, 1957), II, pp. 23–25.

[12] Jānis Jūrmalnieks, "Die Einverleibung Lettlands in die Sowjetunion," AB, XVII (1977), p. 152; Georg von Rauch, *The Baltic States: The Years of Independence, 1917–1940* (London; Berkeley and Los Angeles, 1974), p. 221.

At no time in May–June did the USSR accuse the Baltic governments of collusion with Germany. Indeed, a 28 May 1940 article in *Pravda* on "political feelings in Estonia" had chided the Estonians for their liking England and disliking Germany. Germany did not protest the Soviet occupation of the Baltic states. On 18 June, the German Ambassador in Moscow reported Molotov's comment on the necessity to put "an end to all intrigues by which England and France had tried to sow discord and mistrust between Germany and the Soviet Union in the Baltic states."[13]

The Formation of People's Governments

The first step toward a "constitutional" metamorphosis of the Baltic states into constituent republics of the USSR was the formation of transitional "People's Governments." Cabinet lists were presented by the Soviet emissaries, who refused to sanction even minor changes.[14] The Communist Parties in all three states were minuscule (see details in next section). During the first days of Soviet occupation, they were still officially illegal. Their leaders were not widely known. So, for the sake of appearance, the new governments were coalitions of broadly left-wing "popular" forces including several prominent opposition figures to the previous regimes. Only a few Communists received ministerial portfolios, albeit ones of key significance. In theory, the cabinets were installed according to constitutions still in force.

From the legal point of view, this task of forming a cabinet "normally" was most problematic in Lithuania. The President had left. Antanas Merkys was Acting President by virtue of a position , Prime Minister, which he had already resigned. His ability to fulfill the functions of the presidential office, including the appointment of a new cabinet, could be questioned. Dekanozov overcame this obstacle with an announcement, blatantly untrue, that the Lithuanian government considered Smetona's departure as his resignation.[15] The new Lithuanian cabinet was headed by Justas Paleckis, a journalist whose political sympathies could be best described as moderate left-wing populist. He also replaced Merkys as Acting President, an act of dubious constitutional validity. The Prime Minister's functions were taken over by his deputy who was simultaneously Minister of Foreign Affairs, the writer and literary scholar Vincas Krėvė-Mickevičius, the most eminent and widely

---

[13] *Nazi-Soviet Relations*, p. 154.
[14] Boris Meissner, *Die Sowjetunion, die Baltischen Staaten und das Völkerrecht* (Köln, 1956), pp. 71–81. The only exception seems to be the inclusion of Kruus in Estonia, on insistence by Vares; cf. Myllyniemi 1979, p. 131.
[15] Juozas Brazaitis, "Pirmoji sovietinė okupacija (1940–1941)," *Lietuvių enciklopedija* (Boston, 1968), XV, p. 360.

known personage in the new administration and the only one with genuine popularity throughout the land. His participation gave credence to the official line that the new government was only a replacement for the overthrown "fascist" regime. The retention of the Minister of Finance of the previous cabinet, Ernestas Galvanauskas, also served this purpose. Although the new Minister of Internal Affairs, Mečys Gedvilas, was a Communist, he was publicly known only as a left-wing activist. Somewhat later, three other Communists, Mykolas Junčas-Kučinskas, Karolis Didžiulis, and Stasys Pupeikis were added to the cabinet, though not in prominent positions.

From the constitutional point of view, the tasks in Riga and Tallinn were somewhat simpler. Vyshinskii and Zhdanov presented Presidents Ulmanis and Päts, respectively, with Soviet-proposed cabinet lists. The initial refusal of both incumbents to sanction such governments led to the organization of "popular" demonstrations by the "masses" — a mélange of Communist sympathizers, some of the recently released prisoners, civilian Soviet workers at Soviet bases, and Soviet military and naval personnel specially lent out and accompanied by armored cars for the occasions. In Riga, where on 18 June the cruiser *Marat* had brought a shipload of Soviet demonstrators, 25,000 people in all may have been involved in demonstrations. Their activity led to some bloody street disturbances. In Tallinn, there was a brief skirmish, with some shots fired between Estonian soldiers and civilians invading their barracks with armed Soviet support. Demonstrators and bystanders amounted to 2,000 to 7,000 people.[16] The futility of noncompliance became evident to both Presidents. In Latvia, an "announcement of the Secretariat of the President of the Republic," to the effect that a new cabinet had been formed, was published in the official government gazette on 20 June but without the signature of Ulmanis or of any other official.[17] Initially, the new government, led by Liberal Professor Augusts Kirhenšteins, a bacteriologist, also included, in addition to two Communists (Vilis Lācis and Vikentijs Latkovskis), Social Democrats, Populists, and various left-wing cultural figures.

[16] Alfred Bilmanis, *A History of Latvia* (Princeton, 1951), p. 394; August Rei, "Traagiliste sündmuste tunnistajana," in *Eesti riik ja rahvas teises maailmasõjas* (Stockholm, 1954-1962; 10 vol.) [henceforth cited as *Eesti riik*], III, pp. 17-25; A. Kurgvel, "Sõjavägede staabis 21 juunil," *ibid.*, pp. 32-37; Myllyniemi 1979, pp. 128-131. A demonstration attendance of 30,000 to 40,000 people in Tallinn is claimed in *Eesti NSV ajalugu*, III, p. 489, but a picture on p. 487 shows a half-empty square with only a few thousand people.
[17] *Latvju enciklopēdija* (Stockholm, 1950-1951), I, pp. 804-805; *Valdības vēstnesis*, 20 June 1940.

Only in Estonia were the constitutional formalities observed, as Päts, under coercion, approved the Soviet-proposed cabinet. Johannes Vares, a physician and poet, was the new Prime Minister; Professor Hans Kruus, a well-known historian from the University of Tartu, was appointed Deputy Prime Minister. The cabinet represented a coalition of three former social revolutionary intellectuals (Vares, Kruus, and Johannes Semper), four leftist members of the Estonian Parliament, and several non-party specialists. The Soviet-imposed cabinet of Estonia initially included no known Communists.

Presidents Ulmanis and Päts formally headed their respective countries until both were forced to resign in mid-July. But in a political sense, neither was of any significance once the new cabinets had been installed. After their resignations, both were deported to the USSR, Kārlis Ulmanis to Voroshilovsk on 22 July, Konstantin Päts to Ufa on 30 July; the locations became known only years later. Antanas Merkys, the former Lithuanian Acting President, was deported on 16 July.[18] Several other high officials of the previous Baltic governments were also taken to the USSR around this time. Lithuanian Foreign Minister Juozas Urbšys, who was in Moscow on 15 June, was simply not allowed to return home.

The formal incorporation of the Baltic states into the USSR had not yet taken place, and from the official Soviet point of view they were still independent states. The arrest and deportation of leading statesmen of one state by another state was perhaps an unprecedented event in the history of modern international relations.

People's Assemblies and Formal Incorporation

The earliest statements of the new cabinets denied any intention of setting up Soviet regimes, not to mention incorporation into the USSR.[19] The declared purpose of the invasion and of political changes was merely to remove the "fascist" politicians from office. Vyshinskii, in an address from the balcony of the Soviet Legation in Riga, rebuked overzealous pro-Soviet demonstrators demanding the incorporation of Latvia into the USSR. He even finished his speech in Latvian: "Long live free Latvia! Long live the unbreakable friendship between Latvia and the Soviet Union!" Lithuanian Minister of the Interior Gedvilas, one of the Communists in the new cabinet, declared on 21 June:

The essential fundamentals of our country have not been changed.

---

[18] Rauch, p. 226.
[19] See *Third Interim Report*, pp. 220, 301, and 338, as well as speech of J. Paleckis, 18 June 1940, in V. Kancevičius (ed.), *Lithuania in 1939–1940: The Historic Turn to Socialism* (Vilnius, 1976), pp. 160–162.

No one threatens rightful private property or wealth. The Red
Army came to our country not to change our way of life, but only
to protect us from the dangers of war and to help us maintain our
independence.[20]

On the other hand, it should also be stressed that Communist Party
appeals did not eschew allusions to the incorporation which was to
come. Slogans like "Long live Soviet Lithuania — the Thirteenth
Soviet Socialist Republic" began to appear in party leaflets.[21]

Nevertheless, the initial uncertainty among the populations of
the Baltic states over Soviet intentions following the events of
mid-June soon gave way to realization that establishment of the
"coalition cabinets" was not the end of the process. Real power lay
not with these governments but rather with the three Soviet
emissaries operating from the Soviet Legations.

Significant alterations in the political and social structures of the
three countries were begun soon after the occupation. In late June
and early July, the Communist Parties, which had been visibly
active (although still illegal) since the first days of the arrival of the
Red Army, emerged as the countries' only legal political parties.
Their position was somewhat anomalous. As all three countries
were predominantly agrarian, none had developed a Communist
movement of any significance. Moreover, most of the more
prominent Baltic Communists who had remained in the USSR
during the interwar period had perished during the purges of
1936-38. The Lithuanian party of some 1,500 members was
numerically the largest of the three. A significant portion of its
membership consisted of individuals from minority groups. The
Latvian party had about 1,000 members at the time of its
legalization. The supreme irony was that its traditions were still
those of 1905 and 1917-18. Soviet "liberation" galvanized the
remnants of such traditional political action: the distribution of
leaflets, hoisting of red flags, and the agitation of crowds. The
Muscovite functionaries who were running the show, however, had
emerged from the USSR of the thirties and tended to view such
"old-fashioned" spontaneous ebullience disapprovingly. According to the official party history, the Estonian party numbered only
133 members.[22]

[20] *Third Interim Report*, pp. 338–339; cited from *Lietuvos žinios*, 22 June 1940.
[21] *Istoriia Litovskoi SSR* (Vilnius, 1978), p. 422. Mentions of the currency of such
slogans in June 1940 seem to have been avoided in earlier Soviet sources.
[22] It is difficult to find exact figures for party memberships in June 1940. More
recent Lithuanian sources place the number at around 2,000; viz., K. Surblys,
Lietuvos KP veikla ugdant socialistinę darbininkų klasę, 1940–1975 (Vilnius,
1976), p. 12. Another source, *Lietuvos Komunistų Partija skaičiais, 1918–1975:*

All non-Communist-controlled public activity was proscribed; political, social, ideological, and religious groups which could not be subsumed into the circle of Communist fronts were disbanded. In late June, the process touched groups which were evidently political. By the end of the following month, even the Boy Scouts had ceased to exist. Changes in the administrative apparatus of all three countries began immediately after the occupation. There were massive layoffs of leading officers, district chairmen, police commanders, and school principals. In Lithuania, 11 of the 12 mayors of principal cities, 19 of the 23 mayors of towns, and 175 of 261 county heads were replaced by 18 July.[23] At the end of the month, the police force was replaced by a militia specially recruited from among workers in factories hiring more than fifty persons. The newly renamed "People's Armies," although still technically distinct from the Red Army, were rapidly Sovietized in preparation for their absorption into the Red Army. Already in late June, massive layoffs of senior officers began. Early during the following month, Institutes for Political Instruction were established in the three armies. Their soldiers were "allowed to participate" in politics during their off-duty time. In effect, they were marshalled as participants in the ever-increasing "spontaneous" demonstrations. By mid-July, the auxiliary Home Guard militias which had been conceived as a voluntary ready reserve were disbanded.

The course of Sovietization gave overwhelming and unmistakable evidence of a rapidly approaching loss even of formal

---

statistikos duomenų rinkinys (Vilnius, 1976), p. 10, claims 2,000 upon legalization on 25 June 1940; on p. 42, however, the figure of 1,690 is given for 15 June 1940. It also provides the puzzling explanation that, in late 1940, party cards could not be issued to 1,011 individuals for a variety of reasons. Of these, more than 500 had belonged to the underground before the occupation; therefore actual membership must have reached some 2,200. The prominent party historian R. Sharmaitis [Šarmaitis], "Kommunisticheskoi Partii Litvy — 50 let," Kommunist (Litvy), 1968, p. 69, also claims 2,000 upon legalization. However, at the bottom of the same page, he gives the figure of 1,470 for party membership from 1934 up to 1940, which would indicate that the underground party increased by a third during the first half of 1940, which is rather hard to believe. An earlier source, A. Butkutė-Ramelienė, Lietuvos KP kova už tarybų valdžios įtvirtinimą respublikoje (Vilnius, 1958), p. 166, estimates 1,500 for mid-June 1940 and adds that 673 were admitted soon after legalization. The Latvian figure is taken from Ocherki istorii Kommunisticheskoi Partii Latvii, II (Riga, 1966), p. 444. Myllyniemi 1979, p. 84, tabulates 1,150 LaCP members in 1934, only 400 in 1939, and 1,000 in June 1940, with the latter figure possibly applying to late June when the Soviet army was already in. The Estonian figure of 133 is from Aleksander Panksejev, in Töid EKP ajaloo alalt, II (Tallinn, 1966), p. 156. On 1 September 1940 only 124 pre-July ECP members received the new membership cards, according to Johannes Jakobson et al., Ülevaade Eestimaa Kommunistliku Partei ajaloost, III (Tallinn, 1972), [henceforth cited as Ülevaade EKP], p. 13.

23 A. Rakūnas, Klasių kova Lietuvoje, 1940–1950 m. (Vilnius, 1976), p. 22.

independence. It most alarmed those Baltic leaders who had felt that collaboration with the USSR was the only sensible way of riding out the crisis. Lithuanian Foreign Minister Vincas Krėvė-Mickevičius acted on such considerations in seeking an interview with the Kremlin leadership. Molotov saw no need for talks and refused his initial request. But Mickevičius' persistence changed Molotov's mind, and an interview was granted on 30 June. At first, according to his memoirs, the Lithuanian official presented a picture of the actual state of affairs in Lithuania and the impotence of the People's Government in running the country in the face of activity by Soviet officials. He requested a new convention to regulate Soviet-Lithuanian affairs more precisely. Molotov was quite blunt about the Soviet intention to occupy the whole region permanently, and defended the move as a historical necessity for the development of the Russian state which had been understood by the tsars. But historical imperative was not the sole criterion conditioning the Kremlin's actions. Molotov continued:

> You must take a good look at reality and understand that in the future small nations will have to disappear. Your Lithuania along with the other Baltic nations, including Finland, will have to join the glorious family of the Soviet Union. Therefore you should begin now to initiate your people into the Soviet system, which in the future shall reign everywhere, throughout all Europe; out into practice earlier in some places, as in the Baltic nations, later in others.[24]

Mickevičius tried to raise objections on practical grounds. He argued that Sovietization would merely introduce chaos into the Lithuanian economy, a situation obviously detrimental to Soviet interests. But such observations were useless. Not wanting to officiate over the burial of his country, a thoroughly disillusioned Krėvė-Mickevičius submitted his resignation upon his return to Lithuania. It was rejected, though he was given a leave of absence ostensibly for reasons of health. Lithuanian Minister of Finance Ernestas Galvanauskas also resigned and fled abroad.

In order of prevent *de facto* Sovietization from outpacing the formal constitutional structures by too wide margins, elections for "People's Assemblies" to be held on 14 July (and continuing to 15 July in Latvia and Estonia) were announced early that month. Changes in the electoral laws by decrees which accompanied the announcements contravened the constitutions then still formally in force. In Latvia the period for presentation of candidates was radically shortened from 40 days to 4–6 days after promulgation of

---

[24] *Third Interim Report*, p. 458.

the decree; in Estonia 35 days were reduced to 3 days. Candidates were to be "nominated" by cultural, educational, labor, and other legally functioning organizations — and for practical purposes, by that time only organizations dominated by the Communist Parties were legal. The obvious intention was the staging of a Soviet-style election with the unanimous victory of a single slate of candidates. The approved slates of the "Working People's Leagues" were heavily non-Communist in composition. As parliaments under the Soviet system were a formality anyway, such a ratio made no difference. In Lithuania, at least two candidates appeared on the slate without the knowledge of the individuals involved;[25] it is unlikely that they were an exception. At that stage, any talk of incorporation into the USSR was vehemently denied by the new rulers.

Efforts to organize alternate electoral slates in all three countries provide a swan song of attempts to maintain some autonomy within the new system. In Estonia, where only $3\frac{1}{2}$ days had been allotted for nominations, opposition groups nonetheless managed to present 78 candidates in 66 of the 80 electoral districts. The cabinet, acting on instructions from Zhdanov and without any legal basis, required all candidates to submit a platform within a few hours. Most of the alternate candidates managed to comply. They were removed by a combination of threats and violence as well as invalidations by district electoral commissions. As orders were received at the last minute, some alternate candidates did manage to obtain certification in several districts; this had to be summarily nullified. In Latvia, an abortive attempt was made to include on the ballot a Democratic bloc representing a coalition of all significant, by then banned, Latvian political parties with the exception of Social Democrats. The organizers were arrested soon after. It has been claimed that the formally dissolved Populist Party proposed a distinct slate in Lithuania; we are unable to verify this assertion.[26]

The goal of the occupation authorities was that the greatest number of individuals should vote and thus legitimize the new

[25] Liudas Dovydėnas, "Mano kelias į Liaudies Seimą," *Lietuvių archyvas: Bolševizmo metai* (Kaunas, 1942), III, p. 51; Dovydėnas, *Mes valdysim pasaulį* (Woodhaven, N.Y., 1970), I, pp 193ff.; A. Garmus, "Lietuvos įjungimas į SSSR — Maskvos diktatas," *Lietuvių archyvas*, ed. J. Prunskis (Brooklyn, N.Y., 1952), p. 8.
[26] At the Estonian government meeting of 9 July, Prime Minister Vares apparently showed a note from Zhdanov ordering elimination of alternate candidates; see Myllyniemi 1979, p. 133. On Latvian arrests, see Spekke, p. 386. Lithuanian Populist list: Leonas Sabaliūnas, *Lithuania in Crisis, 1939–1940* (Bloomington, Ind., 1972), p. 285, note 44.

system. Along with Latvian and Lithuanian newspapers, Estonia's main daily *Rahva Hääl* openly threatened non-voters on 14 July: "It would be extremely unwise to shirk elections. . . . Only people's enemies stay home on election day." As results had according to Soviet practice most likely been decided in advance, care in the electoral procedure itself did not warrant scrupulous attention. In Lithuania, no lists of eligible voters were drawn up; in effect, anyone could vote, and several times if he so desired. In all three countries, a stamp in the internal passports identified, for future purposes, those who had voted. However, even with this practical threat, the turnout was so low as to induce the Lithuanian cabinet to extend balloting by one day, 15 July.

The ballot carried only the Soviet-assigned candidate's name. The only way to register opposition was to strike it out. Use of an isolated booth was discouraged or prevented; in many places, open ballots had to be handed to an official who dropped it in the box. The vote count was often cynical. In one Estonian case, doubtless typical throughout the three countries, election officials computed the number of votes needed to show 99.6% participation, counted out the necessary number of used and unused ballots for that result, and submitted the appropriate return to the district committee. In Narva, Red Army troops guarded the ballot boxes overnight; in Tartu, they were even present in the polling room.[27] The elections in one sovereign state were physically conducted by the armed forces of another.

Officially, the results were to the Kremlin's satisfaction: in Lithuania, 95.5% of the electorate allegedly voted and gave 99.2% of its vote to the League; in Latvia, the figures were 94.7 and 97.6%; in Estonia, 81.6 and 92.9%. Privately, several leading members of the Lithuanian administration were quoted as having claimed a real total turnout not exceeding 32%.[28] Archives left behind by the Soviets during their retreat in 1941 indicate that Estonia's Central Electoral Committee forged 35,119 votes.[29] This apparently was in addition to the numerous tamperings at lower levels.

Once the elections had been staged, open reference to Sovietization and to incorporation into the USSR, which until then had been

[27] For Tartu: eyewitness report by Ants Oras, *Baltic Eclipse* (London, 1948), p. 73. For Narva: eyewitness report by A. Soom, "Seadusevastased valimised," *Eesti riik*, III, p. 42. For ballot-box stuffing: eyewitness report by E. Kuik, "Valimisvõltsimine Viljandimaal," *Ibid*, p. 48.

[28] Sabaliūnas, pp. 206–207. Acting President Paleckis of Lithuania is supposed to have expressed privately his opinion that the actual voter turnout in Lithuania stood at 15–16%: Brazaitis, "Pirmoji sovietinė," p. 362.

[29] Evald Uustalu, *The History of the Estonian People* (London, 1952), p. 242.

uncalled for by the scenarios, became commonplace. Indeed, exhortations along such lines now provided the topics for "discussion" of the principal tasks facing the elected assemblies. Before the elections, there had been virtual silence on the questions which those bodies would have to tackle. "Popular voices" consisting of organized street demonstrations began increasingly to express the "demand of the people" for the introduction of the Stalin Constitution in all three countries as well as their incorporation into the USSR.

All three People's Assemblies convened on 21 July 1940. In Estonia, Soviet troops were present in the assembly hall at least part of the time.[30] Within the first hour, the Estonian Assembly had proclaimed by acclamation the establishment of a Soviet socialist form of government. The following day, it formulated an application for membership in the USSR. In Latvia and Lithuania, both acts took place on the first day. The rest of the initial sessions were devoted to remaining essentials, such as nationalization of most urban and rural property, together with all industrial concerns and banks. As there was no real debate and as everything passed unanimously, the assemblies completed their assigned tasks within a few days. Before adjourning, they "elected" delegates to go to Moscow in order to present their countries' applications for membership in the fraternal Soviet brotherhood of nations.

The Supreme Soviet met on 1 August. After a lengthy exposition on Soviet foreign policy by Molotov, the recent tangible benefits of that policy were presented to the Soviet legislators. The Baltic delegations applied, on behalf of their governments and peoples, for membership in the USSR. The Supreme Soviet apparently "deliberated" the merits of their cases. It decided to grant the Lithuanian request on 3 August, the Latvian request two days later, and held out on the Estonian request until 6 August.

Thus in the space of less than two months, the Kremlin completed its formal takeover of the Baltic states. The Soviet military establishment in the region, which had been considerably augmented since June 1940, kept increasing now that the area had become a forward position. Russia's World War I loss of a broad littoral along the Baltic had been undone.

Lithuania, which had been "awarded" Vilnius in November 1939, now gained additional districts in the east. However, the sum total of Lithuanian territorial acquisitions, consisting of previously Polish-controlled territory, represented only about one-third of the

---

[30] *Eesti riik*, III, p. 59, has an unambiguous photo; pp. 21, 41, and 65 have photos of Soviet troops and armored cars participating in the 21 June demonstrations in Tallinn.

total area which the Soviet state had recognized as Lithuanian in 1920, but which had not been part of the interwar republic. The incorporation of Lithuania also included the southwest region of that state which had, according to the September 1939 secret "supplementary protocol" to the German-Soviet Boundary and Friendship Treaty, remained in the German sphere of influence. Not willing for the moment to raise the issue, Berlin agreed to a Soviet payment of 7,500,000 gold dollars for these "rights."[31]

Most of the Baltic diplomats stationed abroad ignored the instructions and threats of the new regimes to return home. Of the foreign powers, only Germany and Sweden recognized the annexation. While some governments subsequently extended *de facto* recognition, others (e.g., the United States) did not and continue to this day to accept the official continued functioning of the Baltic legations in their capitals.

THE FIRST YEAR OF SOVIET OCCUPATION

In comparison to what had preceded, the formal aspects of Sovietization after Moscow's acceptance of the Baltic "petitions" were anticlimactic. The People's Assemblies unanimously adopted new Soviet constitutions giving themselves as well as other offices and organs of state power proper Soviet nomenclature. No new elections to these bodies were held until 1947. In January 1941, however, all three republics elected their representatives to the USSR Supreme Soviet. The results more closely resembled the Soviet averages of popular approval in the upper-nineties percentiles than had the July 1940 elections.

According to Soviet practice, the First Secretaries of the republics' Communist Parties became the ranking loci of power in theory as well as in practice: Karl Säre, in Estonia; Jānis Kalnbērziņš, Latvia; and Antanas Sniečkus, Lithuania, all local Communists. While the state structure of the USSR is formally federal, the party organization in whose hands the monopoly of political power rests is centralized. The republic Council of Ministers (until 1946, Council of People's Commissars) does not govern, but is rather a channel for the implementation of decisions by a strictly disciplined body controlled by Moscow. Likewise, the Supreme Soviets of the republics serve merely to legitimize legislation frequently devised outside the republic. The transitional Prime Ministers were kicked upstairs to become Chairmen of the Presidium of the Supreme Soviet, i.e., the formal heads of state.

[31] *Nazi-Soviet Relations*, pp. 176, 186–188, 237, 267–268.

(For a systematic list of Baltic leaders and administrators, see Appendix A.) In November, the legal codes of the republics were changed; or rather, the code of the Russian Soviet Federated Socialist Republic (RSFSR) was adopted by each of them.

The Communist Parties which had emerged during the first weeks of occupation as the sole political organizations continued to grow rapidly (see Table 6 in Appendix B). The Estonian party mushroomed from 133 members in mid-June to 1,344 in early September; by 1 June 1941 it had grown to 3,732. By 1 January 1941 the Lithuanian party counted 2,504 members and 634 candidate members; six months later, the number of Communists in the republic stood at 4,625. The rapid increase was due in large part to the influx of officials from the other parts of the USSR whose party memberships were automatically transferred to the new Baltic republics once their parties had been integrated into the all-Union party in October 1940. In Estonia, 37% of the membership (1,009 people) were imports. However, the great need for party members in the situation of reorganization and expansion began to attract careerists of all stripes. Not everyone was accepted. Of the 133 pre-July Estonian CP members, only 124 had received CP membership cards by September 1.[32]

Changes in the civil service varied. Those institutions least concerned with the exercise of political power and most likely to be staffed by hard-to-replace experts tended to keep their former personnel. In Lithuania, for instance, as late as April 1941, 81.7% of the staff of the Ministry of Finance and 60% of the Ministry of Agriculture's had been appointed before the occupation.[33]

The Sovietization of Economic Life

Although formal rearrangements in the economic structures of the Baltic states had to wait until convocation of the People's Assemblies, dislocations affecting everyday life began with the arrival of the additional large numbers of Soviet military and political personnel. In Lithuania, the 15 June ultimatum led to lines at food stores, which were virtually empty by the following day. Chronic shortages can thus be said to have come with the Red Army. Later, hoarding and speculation began to have their effect as well. Demand was intensified by large-scale purchases by newly arrived Soviet personnel. A drop in production followed even the initial steps of Sovietization. The disruption of distribution also affected availability of goods, as did large-scale requisitions for other parts of the USSR. Shipment to the Baltic states of quantities

---

32 *Ülevaade EKP*, pp. 13–19; Rakūnas, p. 47.
33 Rakūnas, p. 41.

of some foodstuffs, such as watermelons, in boxcars allegedly decorated with slogans such as "for the starving *Pribaltika*," had no marked effect on the shortage situation which developed.

Expropriation of industry began in early July, even several weeks before promulgation of the appropriate decrees by the People's Assemblies. The first step consisted of the appointment of commissars, usually individuals without any experience in industrial management but with the "proper" social backgrounds, to positions of complete supervisory control. In early 1941, only 4% of enterprise managers in Latvian light industry had a college education, and 64% had only attended primary schools.[34] The effect on practical operations is not hard to imagine.

Formal expropriation came in late July. All factories employing more than 20 workers, and mechanized enterprises with 10 or more workers, were affected. In Latvia and Lithuania, but not in Estonia, all concerns exceeding a specified annual turnover (150,000 *litas* and 100,000 *lats*) were also expropriated. Although in theory small firms were excluded, they were, for all practical purposes, expropriated if they possessed machinery needed by some trust or organization. Repair shops for agricultural machinery provide the most frequent examples of this; they tended to be converted into machine-tractor stations (MTS). By early 1941, the state takeover of industry had been virtually completed. In May of that year, over 1,000 enterprises in Lithuania had been nationalized.

Expropriation of commercial enterprises began in the fall of 1940. At first, only larger units exceeding a specified annual turn-over were affected. In Lithuania, 1,597 stores, restaurants, and warehouses along with 43 hotels and 2,555 buildings were taken over. By June 1941, only 10% of the private shops in the country remained in private hands.[35]

The Russian *ruble* appeared as legal tender, circulating alongside the local currencies, from the first days of Sovietization. However, the rates of exchange were extremely unfavorable. The Estonian *kroon* (then valued at approximately 18 to one British pound) was pegged at 1.25 rubles; its earlier value had been between 10 and 15 rubles. The Latvian *lat*, which had officially been worth 10 rubles, was made equal in value. The Lithuanian *litas* was set at 0.9 rubles, whereas its earlier value had been 3 to 5 rubles. Such rates of exchange provided windfall profits for Soviet military and political *apparatchiks* (party officials) with high ruble incomes and little to

---

[34] Gundar J. King, *Economic Policies in Occupied Latvia* (Tacoma, Wash., 1965), p. 60.
[35] Details on Lithuanian expropriations are provided in Rakūnas, pp. 54ff.

spend them on in the rest of the USSR. The Baltic currencies were eventually abolished in late 1940.

The situation in banking paralleled that in industry and in commerce. Bank panics broke out with the Soviet ultimatums. In Lithuania, withdrawals soon had to be limited to 250 litas per week unless the account-holder could show a concrete business need for a larger withdrawal. The number of litas notes in circulation increased by 9% in June and by 13% by the end of the first month of Soviet occupation.[36] In spite of the phenomenal growth in business sales, deposits into bank accounts virtually ceased. Upon state takeover of banks in late July, all accounts were effectively frozen for several months. Upon their reopening, only 1,000 rubles (about equivalent to U.S. $500 in 1980) could be withdrawn from any account. The rest had been confiscated.

In July and August, salary increases were announced for individuals at the low end of the economic scale. These were, however, usually accompanied by "Stakhanovite" campaigns requiring considerable unpaid overtime. Prices also rose, resulting in an overall decrease in the purchasing power of money at a time when the availability of goods had become spotty. The semi-official rationalizations for the disappearance of goods as having been caused by a growth in the purchasing power of the population tended to be met with scorn. By November, further increases had tripled the money wages of Latvian industrial workers (compared to 1939) and nearly doubled most other wages. However, by May 1941 food prices tripled and textile and shoe prices had increased sixfold. In Estonia, the relative purchasing power of median wages dropped 15% for food and 65% for textiles between early 1940 and early 1941.[37]

Expropriation also affected housing. The aim was not merely the sequestration of property, but also the ruin of its owners. Real estate was classified as business. Houses exceeding 220 square meters in the cities and 170 sq. m in the rural areas were affected. In Kaunas, housing had been in chronically short supply during the period of independence. In 1937 rents had been stabilized, though at a high level. On 5 July 1940 they were lowered 15–25% in Kaunas and 10% in other cities. However, the demand had skyrocketed with the advent of Soviet bureaucrats and officials. The housing shortage was aggravated by the construction slowdown which accompanied the overall drop in production. The 1941 plan called

---

[36] Albert Tarulis, "Lietuvos ūkio katastrofos pradžia, 1940. VI.15 — 1940.VIII.25," *Lietuvių archyvas*, II, p. 133.

[37] For Latvia: King, p. 58; for Estonia: calculations based on price lists given by H. Nurk, "Eesti majandus punasel aastal," *Eesti riik*, III, pp. 124–125.

for only 1,148 new apartments in Kaunas, while 3,376 had been completed in 1939.[38] In order to make room for the new ruling class, the so-called parasite elements and their families — former real estate owners, merchants, clergymen, pensioners, and unemployed — were forced to relocate in the far suburbs. This situation was paralleled in Riga and Tallinn, which had not been as squeezed for housing during the independence period. The introduction of Soviet cadres resulted in the eviction of many urban residents, creating a housing shortage almost overnight.

All those who either left after the arrival of the Soviets or who had been abroad at the time and refused to return had their property confiscated. Individual craftsmen were pushed into cooperative artels through threats and high taxes. All existing consumer and producer cooperatives as well as credit unions were made state property. Only nonvoluntary cooperatives seemed to be acceptable.

The working class lost not only purchasing power but also its autonomous institutions. Trade unions which had organized many successful strikes during independence now became management tools to strengthen labor discipline. Unexcused absence, or even being late to work by 20 minutes, could mean six months of work at wages reduced by one-fourth. The Stalinist labor laws made the workers pay for damage or loss caused by carelessness (as determined by the management), sometimes at a punitive rate of five times the actual cost. Leaving employment without the manager's permission was punishable by two to four months in prison. The same applied to those refusing transfer to another plant. In December 1940, the workers at "Red Krull" in Tallinn went on a three-day strike against high prices, shortages, overtime, and abolition of workers' councils. They were broken through attrition tactics, and only won a two-day Christmas holiday which was abolished elsewhere.[39]

The Sovietization of Agriculture

All three Baltic states were predominantly agricultural countries. The expropriation of industrial, commercial, and banking institutions affected only a small portion of the population directly. As the likelihood of a backlash over these acts was minimal, the regime could proceed with impunity. Such was not the case with agricultural holdings, which did involve the majority of the population. Land reforms had been enacted in all three states during the first

[38] Brazaitis, "Pirmoji Sovietinė," p. 364.
[39] Uustalu 1952, p. 246; Aleksander Kaelas, *The Worker in the Soviet Paradise* (London, 1947), pp. 42–43.

years of independence. There were really no latifundia to provide convenient objects for negative Soviet propaganda. The regime certainiy possessed sufficient power to enforce collectivization, which was its ultimate goal in agricultural planning. It realized, perhaps as a practical result of experience gained during collectivization of the USSR in the early thirties, the dislocations and interruption in production which would result. The People's Assembly of Lithuania specifically expressed its condemnation of any collectivization attempts:

> Any attempts to infringe upon the personal property of peasants or to impose on them collective farms against their will shall be severely punished as harmful to the interests of the people and the state.[40]

Apparently collectivization rumors were widespread.

Although collectivization was not on the immediate program for the Soviet Baltic countryside in 1940, it is hard not to discern from concrete measures enacted that it was a long-term goal. According to the land legislation of the new Soviet Baltic governments, those portions exceeding 30 hectares (75 acres) were taken away from their former owners. In Lithuania, this affected only some 28,000 owners (10% of all owners), who as a group lost 604,000 ha. out of their total holdings of 1,440,000 ha. In Latvia about 15%, and in Estonia about 20% of farms were affected by the measure. About 3,700 Estonian farms were seized in their entirety. The untouched land remained in "perpetual tenure"; it could not be bought, sold, or given away. Significant portions of the sequestered land were slated for parcelling out to small landholders or to landless peasants. In Lithuania, 607,600 ha. were made available, and by November some 75,000 landless peasants or small landholders had received 394,000 ha. In Latvia, 52,000 landless peasants received land, and 23,000 small farms were increased in size. The plots granted by the Soviet regime were small; the maximums of 10 ha. in Latvia and Lithuania, and 12 ha. in Estonia, were too small to support a family. The grants were evidently meant to be temporary and were intended more to splinter the farmers as a class than to provide social justice in the countryside. Such a rationale was virtually admitted by Antanas Sniečkus, First Secretary of the Lithuanian Communist Party.[41]

---

[40] Kancevičius, p. 218.
[41] *Tarybų Lietuvos valstietija: istorijos apybraiža* (Vilnius, 1979), pp. 39–40; M. Gregorauskas, *Tarybų Lietuvos žemės ūkis, 1940–1960* (Vilnius, 1960), p. 82; taken from A. Sniečkus, *Ataskaitinis pranešimas V-me LKP(b) suvažiavime apie LKP(b) darbą* (Kaunas, 1941), pp. 24–27.

Other practical measures in agriculture undertaken during the first year of the Soviet regime also seem to confirm collectivization as an eventual goal. Production levels had dropped in the summer of 1940 as a result of the loss of work incentive coupled with rumors of all kinds. Public appeals by the new governments did not succeed in solving the problem. In early 1941, requisition norms appeared. In Lithuania, a 30-ha. farm with 20 ha. of plowed land worked by hired farmhands was assessed: 15 metric tons of grain, 11 tons of potatoes, 4,680 liters of milk, 390 kilograms of meat, and 13 kilograms of wool. Depending on farm size, 30–50% of total production went to the state; local authorities had the right to increase these figures by up to 30% if they saw fit. The farms were to receive 2,500 rubles for their produce, the market value of which was about 15,500 rubles. A further indication of planned collectivization was the appearance by early 1941 of about 50 MTS in Latvia, 42 in Lithuania, and 25 in Estonia. At the same time, the press began to devote attention to the subject.

A few *kolkhozes* (collective farms) were actually founded during this period, starting as early as 25 September 1940 in Estonia's eastern border land. Lithuania's first, named after Lenin, appeared in January 1941 in the Akmenė district. It was a small enterprise worked by 16 families consisting of 250 ha. (625 acres) of land, 20 horses, and 60 head of cattle. One week before the German attack, a kolkhoz named after Stalin cropped up near Augspils in northeast Latvia. Altogether, 9 kolkhozes were created in eastern Estonia and 12 in Lithuania.[42]

The Sovietization of Society and Culture

Changes in economic life were paralleled by those in education and culture. All private schools were taken over; the organizational systems of education and scholarship were somewhat altered. Latvia's 12-year and Lithuania's 13-year primary and secondary school systems were reduced to an 11-year system, similar to the Soviet Union's. Estonia already had an 11-year system.

The curricula saw more drastic revisions. Many writers in the native literary traditions had to be deleted from syllabi. Others, though not nearly as many, had to be introduced. Most had to

[42] Gregorauskas, p. 101; *Ülevaade EKP*, p. 77; *Lietuvos TSR istorija*, IV (Vilnius, 1975), pp. 44–45; Alfreds Ceichners, *Was Europa bedrohte: die Bolschewisierung Lettlands, 1940–1941*(Riga, 1943), pp. 400–402. Lithuania received 4 kolkhozes with territory transferred from Belorussia in 1940; the total number has been stated as 20 in a recent source, *Tarybų Lietuvos valstietija*, p. 49. The existence of Latvian and Estonian kolkhozes has been downplayed in Soviet historiography, possibly because most of them were located in territory transferred to the Russian republic in 1945.

undergo selective presentation. In Lithuania, for instance, the liberal turn-of-the-century poet Vincas Kudirka, who authored the national anthem, could not be totally excluded, though some of his work was demonstrably excised from plans of study. As it would have been a major and practically insurmountable effort to prepare new textbooks for the fall 1940 school year, the Lithuanian People's Commissar for Education issued a circular on 30 September instructing teachers to tear out unsuitable pages from old textbooks. In Estonia, bookstores were instructed to do so.

Press control appeared early. On 7 August (two days after formal annexation) all publishing houses and printing shops in Latvia were taken over by the Soviet state. They were consolidated into a single State Publishing House run by three expatriate Communists returning from Russia. As in the rest of the USSR, the function of newspapers became primarily the dissemination of official views rather than the reporting and discussion of events from a variety of viewpoints. Their total circulation of pre-Soviet times was not matched; the diversity reflected in the larger circulations was not needed. Only the major newspapers were allowed to continue, although their names and tone of coverage were altered. Pre-war Lithuania had had 7 daily newspapers, 27 weeklies, 15 biweekly reviews, and 27 monthly magazines, with a combined total circulation of around a million copies. During the Soviet regime, the total number of all titles in these categories shrank to 27, with a total circulation of 300,000.

An official *List of Banned Books and Brochures* was issued in Latvia in November 1940. Additional lists in February and March 1941 brought the total number of proscribed titles to 4,000: books on history, politics, philosophy, sociology, and any fiction by "nationalist authors." The pattern was similar in Estonia and Lithuania. All such books were to be removed from all bookstores and libraries. In many places throughout the three countries, the proscribed books were burned. Most writers, including many a leftist, were classified as "reactionary," and their work was banned. Among major writers, Latvia's Vilis Veldre, who had sung about chains, equality, and fraternity, committed suicide; Aleksandrs Grīns was shot; Atis Ķeniņš and Līgotnu Jēkabs were deported, and Jēkabs soon perished.[43]

At least in the short run, the organization of culture along Soviet patterns was a more difficult task than the reshaping of education. Creative artists lend themselves least to bureaucratic

---

[43] Rolfs Ekmanis, *Latvian Literature Under the Soviets, 1940–1975* (Belmont, Mass., 1978), pp. 45–49. Banned book lists: *Aizliegto grāmatu un brošūru saraksts*, nos. 1, 2, and 3 (Riga, 1940, 1941).

regimentation. Nevertheless, the foundations were laid in this domain as well, with the establishment of Baltic branches of the all-Union societies of writers, composers, etc. This transformation presented some difficulties to the cultural bureaucrats. In Latvia, which had some 200 active members of the writing profession, only 9 joined the Writers' Union at the time of its foundation. Most of the previously existing cultural organizations were disbanded, and Stalinist oddities began to be featured frequently and prominently at the operas and theatres.

For a variety of reasons, including personal ones, some prominent cultural figures did initially welcome the new order, foreswearing some of their own previous writings and serving as the regime's minstrels within their forms of artistic endeavor. Three Latvians — the poet Jānis Sudrabkalns and novelists Andrejs Upīts and Vilis Lācis, a member of the People's Government — fall into this group. So does Estonian writer Johannes Semper. Lithuanian poetess Salomėja Neris provides another example, especially with her now-downplayed ode to Stalin. But these readily appeared as exceptions. The majority chose silence or wrote for nonpublication. A number sought refuge in translating Russian and world classics. In spite of the frequently reiterated wishes of the Party, nothing original, apart from two poems, appeared in Lithuania to glorify the events of the Summer of 1940. The Estonian cultural monthly *Looming* presented a curious mix of fully non-Marxist works and strident Sovietese. In Latvia, a group of poets published in March, upon official suggestion, a "Writers' Promise"

> to create, within a month, a poem about the liberated Latvian people and their Great Friend, the Leader of the whole world.[44]

Results of such planned poetry rarely surpassed the level of sycophantic praise of the dictator:

> Like beautiful red yarn into our hearts we wove,
> Stalin, our brother and father, your name.[45]

Officially the churches were untouched, insofar as clerical organization was concerned. In Lithuania, all government support of religious bodies and payment of clergymen's salaries ceased; civil registration of births, deaths, and marriages was introduced. Church holidays were abolished in all three republics. Clergymen were excluded from the army, the educational system, and other government institutions. Social and informal educational church

[44] *Padomju Latvija*, 18 March 1941.
[45] V. Lukss, *Dzejas* (Riga, 1951), pp. 29-32; translation from Ekmanis 1978, p. 58.

functions were curtailed by the new laws on organizations and the reorganization of the press. In addition, harassment of church services and of the faithful by "atheist brigades," no doubt overfulfilling their plans, began to occur. Most theological institutes were closed. In Tartu, 70,000 volumes of theological literature were destroyed. Clergymen lost their pensions. They and their congregations had to pay extra taxes, rents, and utility fees.

Repression and Deportations

The significant decline in the standard of living, and the general confusion affecting the quality of life of most citizens which attended the imposition of Sovietization, were perhaps not the worst aspects of the process. Those most heavily affected on that score certainly belonged to the more enterprising elements of the Baltic populations. Left to their own devices, they would no doubt have managed to reconstruct their lives, albeit at a much lower level of material well-being than they had become used to during the relatively prosperous years of independence. Yet the Soviet system — particularly its Stalinist variant, then at a peak — was by its very nature specifically so ordered as to prevent any such development. Insecurity of the individual, irrespective of his social standing, became a cardinal element in the maintenance of social order. It affected loyal bureaucrats and party activists equally with common workers and peasants. The inculcation of fear had to be pervasive in order to fulfill its task as a method of social control effectively.

The Great Purge in the USSR had subsided by the time Soviet forces arrived in the Baltic. The dramatic events in the USSR, including the massive arrests and several spectacular show trials, were not reenacted in the newly annexed Baltic republics. Indeed, on the whole, the Soviet regime initially seemed to avoid such blatantly indiscriminate repression. That commenced only with the massive deportations initiated in June 1941, and was interrupted only by the outbreak of the war. However, these deportations had been planned for much longer and had been adumbrated by various other events during the first year of Soviet occupation.

The Soviet security organ (NKVD) arrived in the Baltic states together with the garrison troops in the fall of 1939, but its overt operations did not begin until after reinforcement by additional Soviet military in June 1940. Initially, arrests were limited to some of the more prominent figures in the old regimes plus some in special categories of Kremlin concern, like Trotskyites, who were only a handful in the Baltic countries.

The first wider arrests came on the eve of the first elections. In Lithuania, some 2,000 individuals were arrested on the night of

11-12 July 1940. Most received summary eight-year terms, although not through any personal trials, and were deported. The pace of arrests — knocks on the door, at night, of people never to be heard from again — reached an average of 200-300 per month by the end of the year. Several newly-made high Soviet officials were affected. Maksim Unt, Minister of the Interior in the People's Government of Estonia, who had been Acting President while his colleagues were in Moscow petitioning the Supreme Soviet to admit Estonia into the USSR, disappeared in early 1941 and was executed later for acts committed in 1920. Other arrested members of the People's Governments included Julijs Lācis (who died in 1941) and Pēteris Blaus in Latvia, and Juhan Narma-Nihtig in Estonia. No ethnic group was spared. Among others, the future Prime Minister of Israel, Menachim Begin, was arrested in Vilnius, six weeks after Soviet annexation, and was sent to the Soviet Arctic.[46]

The possibility of wider deportations appeared sporadically as a topic of private discussion from Midsummer 1940 on. The rumor might have been used as added insurance for smooth performance of the necessary electoral and legislative shows of July and August. Lithuanian Acting President Justas Paleckis supposedly told an acquaintance at that time about consideration of the deportation of 50,000 which could be triggered by a bad move.[47] Such arguments might have had some effect on those among the Lithuanian public who considered Paleckis, not yet formally a Communist, as an alternative preferable to some satrap imported from Russia.

Deportation rumors and actual arrests enhanced interest in evacuation among those who could claim any faint German ties. The Soviets and the Nazis agreed on such a "repatriation" in January 1941. Most Latvian and Estonian Germans had left in late 1939, but 16,000 people made use of the new opportunity, bringing the total to 80,000, compared to a total prewar declaredly German population of 78,000. Lithuania, which had 35,000 declared Germans left after Hitler's seizure of Klaipėda, saw 50,167 people leave for Germany in January 1941.[48]

Soviet documents which became known as a result of dislocations caused by the sudden German attack seem to indicate Kremlin interest in massive population shifts, especially from Lithuania,

[46] Myllyniemi 1979, pp. 135 and 145; Herbert-Armin Lebbin, *Sotsiaaldemo-kratismi pankrot Eestis* (Tallinn, 1970), pp. 319-320; Lithuanian Security Office Order of 7 July 1940 regarding arrests is translated in *Third Interim Report*, pp. 468-470. Menachem Begin, *White Nights: The Story of a Prisoner in Russia* (New York, 1979).
[47] A. Merkelis, "Masinis lietuvių išvežimas į SSSR," *Lietuvių archyvas*, II, p. 16.
[48] Seppo Myllyniemi, *Die Neuordnung der baltischen Länder, 1941-1944* (Helsinki, 1973), pp. 44-45, 161, and 293.

situated on the German border. One such document, numbered 0054 and signed by People's Commissar for the Interior of the Lithuanian SSR Aleksandras Guzevičius on 28 November 1940, lists 14 categories of individuals slated for deportation:

1. members of leftist anti-Soviet parties
2. members of nationalist anti-Soviet parties
3. gendarmes and jail guards
4. Tsarist and White Army officers
5. officers of the Lithuanian and Polish armies
6. White Russian volunteers
7. those who had been expelled from the party or the Komsomol
8. all political émigrés and unstable elements
9. all foreign citizens and individuals with foreign connections
10. all those with personal foreign ties, viz., philatelists, Esperantists, etc.
11. high civil servants
12. Red Cross officials and refugees from Poland
13. clergymen
14. former noblemen, estate owners, industrialists, and merchants[49]

The chief handicap of the NKVD in carrying out instructions like these to draw up lists of candidates was a poor and not necessarily accurate system of intelligence based of necessity on native informers. The archives, including those of the Foreign Affairs ministries which had been specifically carted to Moscow during the Summer of 1940, were mostly in the local languages. The circle of natives suitable for this kind of NKVD work was extremely circumscribed. It is doubtful whether considerable, systematic, and accurate classification could have made significant progress by the Summer of 1941. More likely, NKVD officials were fulfilling their tasks haphazardly. While the appropriate numbers of individuals did appear on their lists, the rationales for their inclusion could have been arbitrary.

Massive deportations according to prepared lists began on the night of 13–14 June 1941. A series of practical difficulties in execution prevented completion of the planned deportation. It is very likely that all listed individuals could not be readily located. Some of them, realizing their situation, began to filter to the woods or to move around frequently, maneuvers with which the still largely alien NKVD personnel could not adequately cope.

It is difficult to determine the number of persons actually

[49] *Third Interim Report*, p. 471.

deported. Figures vary according to methods of calculation and estimation. One Latvian study concludes that specifically 662 boxcars of persons with 15,081 individuals (3,332 children under 16) were dispatched from Latvia before the outbreak of the war; for Estonia, the figures were 490 boxcars and 10,205 persons (including 3,018 under 16), of whom 28% were workers and 26% salaried personnel (or their family members). A Lithuanian calculation posits a total figure of 34,260 persons deported from Lithuania between 14 and 18 June 1941.[50]

The full scope of the number of persons involved, however, must in all likelihood have been greater. Many had been arrested and deported earlier. Others were still in detention at the outbreak of German-Soviet hostilities. Some massacres of prisoners by NKVD personnel are known to have taken place shortly after 22 June. The general estimates of population losses from all causes — deportations, mobilizations, massacres, and unexplained disappearances during the first year of Soviet rule — hover around 60,000 for Estonia, where Soviet forces stayed the longest and where some conscription into the Red Army could be effected; 35,000 for Latvia; and 34,000 for Lithuania.[51] If these figures are accurate, Estonia can be said to have lost about 4% of its pre-war population, and the other two Baltic states about 1.5 to 2% each. It should be remembered that, had the outbreak of the war not intervened, the deportation figures would in all likelihood have been considerably higher. Jurgis Glušauskas, People's Commissar for Communications of the Lithuanian SSR who did not leave for Russia during the Soviet retreat, claims to have seen a document envisaging deportation of 700,000 from Lithuania.[52] There is no documentary evidence to substantiate such a claim. However, in view of the massive relocations attending collectivization during the 1930s and the national deportations actually effected elsewhere in the USSR in 1944-45, such a figure, roughly one-quarter of the pre-war population, does not appear unlikely.

The deportations served as a massive shock to the citizens of the Baltic republics; such no doubt had been the intent. Now it was no longer select individuals whose disappearance without a trace

[50] *Latvju enciklopēdija*, I, pp. 476-477; Arveds Švābe, *Lettlands historia* (Stockholm, 1961), p. 171; Uustalu 1970, p. 320; M. Kuldkepp, "Inimkaotused punasel aastal," *Eesti riik*, III, pp. 230-234; Brazaitis, "Pirmoji sovietinė," p. 369. According to these figures, deportations affected 0.9% of the population in Estonia, 0.8% in Latvia, and 1.1% in Lithuania. About 46,000 deportees from Lithuania are estimated, with 19,000 names actually listed, by Leonardas Kerelis (ed.), *Išvežtųjų lietuvių sąrašas: Stalino teroras, 1940-1941* (Chicago, 1981).
[51] Uustalu 1970, p. 323; Spekke, p. 396; Brazaitis, "Pirmoji sovietinė," p. 369.
[52] Brazaitis, "Pirmoji sovietinė," p. 369.

could be explained by some system of logic, but large groups representing various cross-sections of the population. Many of the deportees perished on their way to exile during the several-weeks trips to northern Russia or Siberia. The crowded conditions in the boxcars, and the minimal sanitary and eating arrangements, naturally had this effect on the more frail members of the groups. Families had been separated. Men were sent to one location, women and children to another. While the men were considered under arrest and, as such, destined for labor camps where many perished, women and children were as a rule merely exiled. Eventually, relatives did get some news from those in the latter category, but only after the war.

The deportations, coming as they did on the eve of the outbreak of the German-Soviet war, no doubt had an effect opposite from that intended by those who conceived them. While they did doubtless instill fear in the population, they also heightened hatred for the regime, especially among those who might otherwise have remained neutral. In spite of the efforts of the regime's propaganda in heralding popular Soviet resistance to the German onslaught, there are virtually no known instances of spontaneous native Baltic opposition to the German advance. Such developed only as the negative side of the German occupation came in time to be felt.

Resistance to Sovietization

The period of independence, 1918 to 1940, had successfully entrenched among the Baltic peoples a strong sense of national identity, as well as the corollary that this could only be properly expressed and preserved through maintenance of an independent state entity. The Soviet preservation of a formal national political existence, albeit at a "higher" level of sovereignty, failed to satisfy national aspirations. Coupled with a rapid and marked decline in the standard of living, plus the high-handedness of Soviet officials and the system of terror which they represented, this served to foster opposition to Soviet rule. Such anti-Soviet feelings were bolstered by expectations of an imminent Soviet-German conflict as well as by the refusal of the Western powers to recognize the incorporations.

The most widespread resistance was passive, primarily through boycotts of the formal political activity of the new regimes, such as the elections, and through verbal ridicule of the system and of the Russians. The old holidays, even though formally abolished, continued to be observed by the populace. In Lithuania, graves of soldiers who had fallen during the 1918–20 independence struggle were as usual fully decorated on All Souls' Day (2 November).

Christmas 1940 was still a *de facto* holiday.

In several instances, some acts of spontaneous symbolic opposition went beyond mere passivity. In Lithuania, the Teachers' Congress of 14–15 August was held soon after incorporation and planned as a demonstration of loyalty to the new system. At one point during the proceedings, someone intoned the old national anthem and the teachers joined in. Even some of the ranking members of the new government on the podium are said to have instinctively risen only sheepishly to sit down again.[53]

A variety of organized resistance groups formed soon after the coming of the Soviets. As early as July 1940, leaflets phrased in extremely emotional language appeared in Lithuania, urging a boycott of the elections. Several distinct opposition groups are known for their activity during the second half of 1940. The most widespread was the Lithuanian Activist Front (LAF), some of whose cells were formed as early as October 1940. Later, beginning in December, these managed to establish contact with the foreign cell established by the erstwhile Lithuanian Minister in Berlin, Colonel Kazys Škirpa, with German approval. Geographical difficulties prevented contacts with the West. The group in Germany included intellectuals, officers, and politicians who had managed to escape from Lithuania at various stages of Sovietization or who had been abroad in mid-June 1940 and never returned. It did not include President Antanas Smetona, who had by then left Germany for the United States.

The LAF worked out systematic rules for a widespread underground organization as well as a political program for reestablishment of a Lithuanian state. It was considering plans for an armed uprising at a favorable moment — the outbreak of a Soviet-German war — and establishment of a provisional government. The German agencies which approved of the Berlin existence of the LAF did not sanction its plans for a provisional government. A network of LAF cells combed Lithuania; membership is estimated to have reached 36,000 by 1941. Although somewhat impaired by the June 1941 deportations, the LAF did manage to rise in force upon the outbreak of the war.[54]

The resistance was more limited in Latvia and Estonia. Unarmed underground groups formed in several Estonian towns, and by March 1941 some of them had begun to interact. Armed guerrilla

[53] Zenonas Ivinskis, "Lithuania During the War," in V. Stanley Vardys (ed.), *Lithuania Under the Soviets, 1940–1965* (New York, 1965), p. 63; Iu. Paletskis [Paleckis], *V dvukh mirakh* (Moscow, 1974), pp. 353–354.
[54] Ivinskis, pp. 64–65.

resistance in the forests was triggered by the mid-June 1941 deportations.

WAR AND REVOLT

The German attack on the USSR came during the early morning hours of 22 June 1941. Lithuania, situated astride East Prussia, was immediately affected. Within three days, the Red Army had been pushed out. The German columns reached Daugavpils in Latvia on 26 June, and Riga fell to them on 1 July. By the ninth, the German armed forces were already in Pskov, and by 21 July a thrust east of Lake Peipsi nearly cut Estonia off from Russia. The rapid advance, which had taken place with a minimum of fighting, was halted for two weeks along a line running through mid-Estonia. Soviet reinforcements sent to that area during this lull stiffened opposition to the renewed German advance in late July. As a result, considerable fighting took place in northern Estonia. Tallinn fell on 28 August, but some Soviet detachments held out in the islands of Saaremaa and Hiiumaa until October.

If the goal of Soviet diplomatic pressure on the Baltic states since 1937 and military action in 1939–40 was to insure its northern flank against German attack, the results were counterproductive. The speed of the initial German thrust through the Baltic states (480 kilometers from East Prussia to Pskov, in 17 days) surpassed that of most German offensives during World War II. This advance could not possibly have been much faster in face of the weak Baltic armies defending their homelands against the traditional German enemy, and it could have been slower. In any event, the Soviet forces now trapped in the Baltic states would have been spared for the defense of Leningrad. The unusual speed of the German thrust is at least partially explained by the Stalinist feat of making the Baltic populations friendly toward the Germans.

The German attack came during the first period of massive arrests and deportations undertaken by the Soviet regime. That, taken together with the other experiences of Sovietization, tended to identify Germany with the West in the minds of the Baltic man on the street. The feeling seems to have been pervasive that the overthrow of the Soviet yoke by the Germans would enable the Baltic peoples to reassert their national independence. The majority of the native populations welcomed the arrival of the Germans at least passively. In some instances, the *Wehrmacht* was greeted with flowers. From the beginning, the German actions did nothing to preserve such feelings among the Baltic populations.

A revolt against the Soviet system broke out in Lithuania on the first day of the war. A detachment of insurgents took over the Kaunas radio station and broadcast a proclamation of the reestablishment of independence and formation of a Provisional Government, as had been envisaged in LAF plans. The Provisional Government, an *ad hoc* coalition of individuals from every major political trend in the independent state, claimed, as such, to represent the will of the nation. Units of the former Lithuanian army are also reported to have mutinied against their Soviet command and to have gone over to the Germans en masse. Local uprisings in various parts of Lithuania harassed retreating Red Army columns. It has been estimated that some 100,000 insurgents were active. Casualties reached some 2,000, with 200 in Kaunas alone.[55] While much of this activity had been planned by the LAF, many instances, especially those in the countryside, proved spontaneous.

The Provisional Government officially reinstated the administrative structure which had existed on 15 June 1940 and began to appoint personnel to fill the posts. The German occupation authorities did not welcome the appearance of such a body, which had not been planned in their designs. The designated head of the Provisional Government, the former Envoy to Berlin, Colonel Škirpa, was not allowed to return to his country. In his absence, Juozas Ambrazevičius, a literary scholar, became Acting Prime Minister and chaired the daily cabinet sessions.

The *Wehrmacht* entered Kaunas almost in parade formation on 25 June and found the Provisional Government in control. Hoping to secure recognition from Germany as the government of an independent state, albeit one allied to Germany, the Provisional Government cooperated fully with the transient German military administration. The German commandant of Kaunas, however, was not authorized to deal with any government. Still, General Robert von Pohl was an Austrian and perhaps appreciative of the Lithuanian striving for a national state identity. He took no action against the reconstituted Lithuanian authorities as long as they were not in his way.

Coexistence became more problematic as the Germans sought to reestablish civilian control. The Provisional Government continued to cooperate; indeed, this was its only choice for survival. German plans, although never clearly formulated, did not however envisage any independent or semi-independent status for the Baltic countries. It would have proved needlessly unpopular in Lithuania, and possibly detrimental abroad, to disband the Provisional

[55] *Ibid.*, pp. 67–68.

Government by force. Rather, the decision was to effect a quiet removal by forcing the authorities either to disband of their own accord or to reconstitute themselves into the *Zivilverwaltung* which the Reich leadership had envisaged for the area. The Provisional Government was denied access to the press, the radio, and other means of communication. But ties to the provinces were dependent on the couriers which had been used by the underground during the Soviet period, and thus Provisional Government decrees were on occasion published in some provincial papers not subject to German military censorship.

German designs to change, by force or deceit, the Provisional Government into its planned civil administration proved unsuccessful. A Gestapo attempt to foment a split within the LAF ranks through the use of some extreme nationalists also proved abortive. Goodwill efforts such as the release of Lithuanian army personnel in Soviet uniform who had gone over to the Germans were equally of no avail. The Provisional Government refused to compromise on its goal of an independent state which the Reich was not willing to recognize.

While it was not ready to metamorphose into an open instrument of German domination, the Provisional Government had neither the will nor the means to confront the Germans. And it was internally split over the extent to which collaboration was advisable. In early August, after a public declaration of inability to pursue its functions, the Provisional Government was disbanded. On the whole, it had not been able to influence German occupation policies. Its annulment of the confiscatory Soviet nationalization laws was stillborn. Its only concrete achievements came in areas of least immediate interest to the German authorities, such as reorganization of the educational system. However, the six-week existence of the Provisional Government was testimony of the striving by the Lithuanian population for national independence, and it inspired continued passive resistance.[56]

In Latvia and Estonia, insurgency against the Soviet administration and Red Army presence also broke out prior to German arrival. On 28 June an insurrection took place in Riga, and its radio station announced the formation of a Latvian government. The Soviets regained control the next day. Some Latvian military units managed to reorganize themselves after the outbreak of war, but they were dissolved soon after the arrival of the Germans, who reached Riga on 1 July. Two separate quasi-governmental bodies had meanwhile been formed: the Central Organizing Committee for Liberated Latvia, and the Provisional State Council (led by

---

[56] *Ibid.*, pp. 68–72.

former Transport Minister Bernhards Einbergs). The Germans avoided direct contacts with them, but used them to get the economy going again. Former Finance Minister (1938–39) Alfreds Valdmanis emerged as the strongest Latvian figure. Much to the dismay of the German administration advance men, he succeeded in facing them with a reopened Riga University and Opera — national institutions the Germans preferred closed.[57]

Guerrilla units of varying size and organization were especially active in Estonia. Some numbered several hundred men and were organized into fairly disciplined units by former army officers. In major parts of southern Estonia, Soviet local administration was replaced by an Estonian one, days and even weeks before the arrival of German main forces. Tartu was under full or partial Estonian control from 10 to 28 July. The last pre-occupation Premier, Jüri Uluots, convened a council which met repeatedly but never proclaimed itself a government. They had learned from Lithuanian and Ukrainian precedents that such an act would lead to direct confrontation with the Germans, and possibly to arrests (as in the Ukraine, on 30 June). In northern Estonia, the guerrillas amounted to 5,000 active fighters, with 1,500 in a single armed forest base in Kautla (near the present Ardu, 50 km northeast of Tallinn). Country-wide losses by the guerrillas amounted to 541 dead and missing, with comparable losses inflicted on Soviet forces during two months of fighting.[58] The Germans disbanded all Estonian units as soon as a firm German central control was established. Attempts by Uluots to present a memorandum arguing for the reestablishment of Soviet-quashed sovereignty were brushed aside by the new masters.

THE GERMAN OCCUPATION

It is quite clear from the documents in German archives that the long-range goal of the Nazi leadership was to annex the Baltic region to the Reich, to expel two-thirds of the population, and to fuse the remainder gradually with German immigrants. The competing plans by various staffs all agreed on this broad outline, and alteration of details by the top leaders always tended to make the plans even harsher. *Ostminister* Alfred Rosenberg's favorite version in 1941 was to double the size of the Baltic republics at the expense of Russia and Belorussia, and then deport most Balts into the newly annexed areas. SS Chief Heinrich Himmler's

[57] Bilmanis 1951, pp. 403–404; Myllyniemi 1973, pp. 78 and 84.
[58] K. Talpak, "Eesti metsavendlus 1941.aastal," *Eesti riik*, IV, pp. 25–27.

Generalplan Ost (1942) foresaw the deportation of almost 50% of Estonians, all Latgalians, over 50% of other Latvians, and 85% of Lithuanians. The remaining fraction was evaluated racially Nordic (and thus worth Germanization) by a 1942 Anthropological Commission field study. Due to the limited number of Germans available, immigration was expected to be rather slow: 520,000 in 20 to 25 years after the end of the war.[59]

The immediate goal of Nazi Germany, however, was to win the war. Major deportation, immigration, and denationalization were to start only after military victory. Meanwhile, such plans were ordered to be kept strictly secret so as not to upset the Baltic populations, whose maximum support for the "anti-Bolshevik struggle" was desirable.[60] On the other hand, absolutely no independence or meaningful autonomy were to be given or promised to the Baltic nations, so that Germany would not have to break its Germanic word of honor during the postwar reckoning. The Baltic states were to be treated as just another piece of the USSR, with no regard to their independence only one year earlier. The more immediate German goal was to exploit the area economically as part of the war effort.

German Administration

On 17 July 1941, Alfred Rosenberg, a Baltic German, was appointed Reich Minister for the Occupied Eastern Territories. One of his deputies, Gauleiter of Schleswig-Holstein Hinrich Lohse, became Reich Commissioner for the *Ostland*, with his seat in Riga. His fief, which came into administrative existence on 28 July 1941, included the three Baltic countries and Belorussia, each of which constituted a General District headed by a General Commissioner resident in their respective capitals (see list in Appendix A). Various lower-level officials — Area Commis-

---

[59] See Alexander Dallin, *German Rule in Russia, 1941-1945: A Study in Occupation Policies* (London, 1957), pp. 182-198, for broad outline of German Eastern policies. For details regarding the Baltic states, see Myllyniemi 1973, esp. pp. 57-59, 69-70, 89, and 146-160. See also Ekmanis 1978, pp. 82-83; Spekke, pp. 398-400; Uustalu 1970, p. 328; and Ivinskis, pp. 74-75.

[60] Settlement of 16,300 German colonists in southwest Lithuania has been reported by J. Dobrovolskis, "Lietuviškųjų buržuazinių nacionalistų antiliaudinis veikimas okupaciniame hitlerininkų valdžios aparate, 1941-1944 m.," *LTSR Mokslo Akademijos Darbai*, ser. A-2(13), 1962, p. 162. Actually this was part of the return of 30,000 Lithuanian residents from among those who had left during the January 1941 evacuation of Germans to the Reich. They received large farms and were meant to be the first link in a "land bridge" connecting East Prussia to Courland. Also, 400 Dutch farmers were settled in the Vilnius area. The Jelgava district commander in Latvia reported confidentially, in March 1942, that he had already reserved 1,100 farmsteads for German front soldiers. See Myllyniemi 1973, pp. 161-175 and 97.

sioner, County Head, and a host of special-interest officers
(*Sonderführer*) — filled out the formal German administrative,
structure. Paralleling the Soviet pattern, two other elements, the
party and the police, were also actively present, and reported to
Himmler. As had been the case under the Soviets, both were
capable, under various circumstances, of wielding greater power
than the administrative apparatus. Furthermore, the economy was
handled by Hermann Göring's *Wirtschaftsstab Ost*. Although the
manpower was frequently at a level below that required for optimal
performance, the presence of several agencies transferred aspects
of the wide-scale Berlin intra-agency rivalry, apparently tacitly
favored by the Führer as a practical means for rule, into the realm
of the Ostland operations as well. Rosenberg gradually lost most of
his power to Himmler.

In addition to the administrative apparatus introduced from
above by the Reich, German plans also included indigenous
"Directorates" or "Self-Administrations" (*Selbstverwaltungen*).
They consisted of 5 to 12 "Country Directors" (*Landesdirektoren*)
in Estonia, "General Directors" (*Generaldirektoren*) in Latvia,
and "General Counselors" (*Generalräte*) in Lithuania. These
entities were endowed only with a narrowly administrative and
advisory function. They were headed by a First Director (*Erster
Direktor*) or First General Counselor (*Erster Generalrat*) respectively, and consisted of a group of experts each of whom was
responsible for administrative functions corresponding to the
ministries of independent states.

Efforts were made to find prominent individuals to fulfill these
roles. After Theodor Adrian von Renteln, the newly appointed
General Commissioner for Lithuania, failed to convince the
Lithuanian Provisional Government to turn itself into such a body
of counselors, he was forced to appoint one himself. General
Petras Kubiliūnas, a man of extreme nationalist views who had led
an unsuccessful coup in 1934, became First General Counselor.
Three of the other 11 Lithuanian Counselors had been members of
the Provisional Government.

The selection of retired General Oskars Dankers as Latvian First
Director was not a smooth operation, either. Dankers had left for
Germany in January 1941, and had become a German citizen. The
Germans wanted yes-men, but also realized that such people would
be useless unless they enjoyed some popular prestige. In
November, Alfreds Valdmanis was accepted as Director of Law
Administration, despite misgivings by several German factions,
some of whom even opposed the whole notion of a native body
dealing with all of Latvia: they recommended separate "self-
administrations" for Courland, Livonia, and Latgale, and felt that

none of the Latvian Directors was "German-minded." The city of Riga actually was put under direct German control, with a Baltic German mayor, and was completely excluded from the reach of the Latvian Directorate. This dismemberment of the national territory remained a sore point about which the Latvian Directors never stopped protesting on the cautious grounds of administrative efficiency.[61]

Estonia's Directors were mostly picked from among those who had gone to Germany during the repatriation of January 1941. First Director Hjalmar Mäe, belonging to this group, had spent time in prison, before the war, for pro-fascist subversion. No nationally known pre-war politicians agreed to serve. The Germans felt that the rapid self-restoration of Baltic institutions had made them accept too many untrustworthy elements into the Latvian and Lithuanian self-administrations; in Estonia they took their time, and felt much more satisfied with Mäe and his team than with Dankers or Kubiliūnas. The city of Narva remained under military administration, largely outside Directorate influence.[62]

As advisory and administrative bodies, the Directorates had little if any say in formulation of the important decisions governing the daily lives of the people which they were called upon to administer. In this sense, their position was similar to the governments of the Soviet Baltic republics in 1940–41. On occasion they did manage, through bureaucratic interpretation as well as through the utilization of opportunities presented by rivalry among German officials, to blunt some of the more detrimental features of German occupation exactions. The existence of the Directorates, however, allowed the Germans to channel their demands through native bodies, thus somewhat masking the fact of occupation. The price which the Directors had to pay for their limited ability to soften the German occupation regime was public identification with, and thus in a sense a share in, the onus of all German occupation measures, even those in which they had no say or whose severity they were unable to soften. Their role, alternating between being tools of German rule fleecing their own countries and patriots trying to keep the worst from happening, was often unenviable. It is not surprising that, under such circumstances, appearances could and did prove deceptive. For instance, Pranas Germantas, the Lithuanian Counselor for Education, seemed to be close to the Nazis. However, this image facilitated his reintroduction of the old educational system which indirectly fostered the growth of resistance. In mid-1943, as the institutes of higher

---

[61] Myllyniemi 1973, pp. 107–115 and 137.
[62] *Ibid.*, pp. 109–110.

education were being closed by the German occupation authorities, Germantas was enroute to the Stutthof concentration camp.

Formally, the Directorates headed reestablished pre-war administrative and judicial systems, including some police power. These could operate fairly normally as long as questions of little concern to the German authorities were involved. The pre-war legal codes regained validity, though Germans on the one hand and Jews on the other were specifically excluded from coverage. In practice, there was generally a preference in the administration of justice for using the police, at times even military units, as well as administrative measures, rather than the courts.

Economic and Cultural Life

In the short run, the Germans considered Baltic territory as an occupied region open to maximum exploitation of its resources for the general pursuit of the war effort. The Baltic peoples were primarily viewed as providers of agricultural products and labor. This attitude was clearly reflected in the socio-economic policies of the occupation administration.

The first key economic measure radically affecting the everyday life of the populace was introduced during the short initial period of German military administration. On 26 June, the German mark was officially valued at 10 rubles. The Baltic peoples, already stung by the earlier Soviet fiscal reevaluation, were totally fleeced by this second round. For instance, the pre-war Lithuanian *litas* had been worth more or less a German mark. After the two confiscatory currency exchanges coming during the space of a year, the holder of a litas was left with roughly 9 pfennigs in a special *Ostmark* currency.

Private property was not restored. All enterprises expropriated by the Soviets were taken over by German firms specially created for the purpose. Some were extensive companies like the *Zentralhandelsgesellschaft Ost*, which ran all slaughterhouses, sugar and flour mills, and breweries, or the *Landbewirtschaft-ungsgesellschaft Ost*, which took over all the land which the Soviets had expropriated. Other industrial enterprises such as textile and paper mills and cigarette factories functioned as share-holding companies run by a German trustee whose position was usually one of patronage due to NSDAP (Nazi Party) membership.

Some reprivatization was effected on the basis of an 18 February 1943 order, as part of propaganda and morale-boosting campaigns when the tide of war had shifted against the Reich. In Lithuania, for instance, 50 farmers, on 11 May 1943, received land which had been expropriated by the Soviets. Such measures were frequently coupled with increased requisitions and harsher penalties for failure to carry them out. On the whole, they remained entirely token moves. Most owners of expropriated industrial and commercial property did not even undertake the petty and demeaning application procedure (which included a written promise to support Germany). Of those who did, only a quarter in Latvia and Estonia and 4% in Lithuania saw their property returned. The outcome for farms was similar.[63]

Rationing of food and goods was introduced in the cities in July. Practically, the black markets which had appeared under the Soviets continued under the Germans. City wages and prices for obligatory farm-produce deliveries were set at 60% of those in East Prussia, the closest German area.

On the whole, cultural life was the area of national existence least affected by the German occupation. Although cultural and religious affairs were strictly supervised, the Nazis, unlike the Soviets, did not act on a perceived need to infuse them immediately with a particular ideological aura. The requirements of waging war obviously took precedence over those of eventual Germanization, and so these areas were left largely in the hands of the local authorities.

This does not mean that the conditions of occupation and the economic exactions which went along with them did not affect cultural life. Riga University, reopened by the Latvians in Summer 1941, was ordered closed on 15 September, and was reluctantly reopened only in early 1942, along with Tartu University. Kaunas and Vilnius Universities, opened in Fall 1941, were closed in early 1943. School textbooks on history and biology were subject to direct German control, and Nazi tenets were introduced. Censorship combined with paper shortages to decimate the press. Even *Faust* in Latvian translation was forbidden; it was not for peasants who could not read German. Newspapers and periodicals were few in number. Few worthwhile books appeared. The absence of individual security in the face of the repeated manpower mobilizations directly affected educational and cultural institutions. These bore the brunt, especially in Lithuania, of German reprisals for mobilization failures. The performing arts were somewhat less affected. The theatre and opera functioned more or less as could be expected during wartime conditions. New youth organizations were created in Latvia and Estonia under district-level German control, with Directorates strictly kept out.

In the absence of any widespread armed anti-German resistance

---

[63] Juozas Brazaitis, "Vokiečių okupacija (1941–1944)," *Lietuvių enciklopedija* (Boston, 1968), XV, p. 375; Myllyniemi 1973, pp. 223–226.

which could have been based on the religious establishments, the German authorities, for the most part, did not interfere with organized religion. The significant exceptions concerned individual clergymen, some of high rank, who had become involved in anti-German activities and were therefore subject to repression. Theological institutes were allowed to function in Tartu and Kaunas, but not in Latvia.

German Mobilization of Manpower

The first German attempt to utilize Baltic labor resources came in mid-July 1941 in Lithuania. Invitations were issued for voluntary work in East Prussia. For the most part, this opportunity was utilized by individuals who had in some way been compromised during the Soviet occupation and who desired to be away from their home areas.

Compulsory drafts for labor service took on a more extensive as well as a more coercive scope when on 19 December 1941 Rosenberg decreed a general work obligation for those aged 18 to 45. Failure to register would be punished by three months' imprisonment and a 1,000-mark fine. Later, in 1942, university freshmen were required first to serve a year in the German youth labor force (*Reichsarbeitsdienst*), which in 1942–43 recruited 950 Estonians, 4,576 Latvians, and 1,645 Lithuanians. About 30% of the applicants were refused for racial reasons.[64]

Decreed exactions on the labor force continued in various forms throughout the German occupation. By early 1944, it was announced in Lithuania that each 15 ha. of farmland could only be worked by one individual. Surplus farm labor was to be sent to the Reich. The quotas were lower in labor-short Latvia and Estonia, but still 30,000 had been conscripted by February 1943.

Efforts to sabotage these drafts greatly diluted their value to the German economy. In Lithuania, only 5% of a first quota of 100,000 in early 1942 was actually filled. Various ways of evasion were soon discovered. At the lower levels, the administrators as well as the police were staffed by natives not eager to carry out their tasks conscientiously. At higher levels, officials, even Germans, could be bribed. Furthermore, the Directorates found ways of convincing order-minded German bureaucrats to somewhat limit the coercive aspects of the mobilizations by arguing that such activities would introduce disorder into a smooth functioning of the local economies, which also was deemed of interest to the Reich. A demand for 3,000 Estonian and 10,000 Latvian women in April 1943 was very strongly opposed by the Latvian Directorate, and

[64] Myllyniemi 1973, pp. 191–192 and 294.

was abandoned. The failure to meet set quotas usually led to an imposition of new and higher figures. And the cycle began anew as the Directorates managed to renegotiate these downward to figures which still could never be met. In early 1944, for instance, the Lithuanian quota of 100,000 (about 5,000 weekly) was reduced to 80,000. About 8,000 were actually provided.[65]

Conscription methods grew harsher as resistance increased. In Fall 1942, 8,000 Latgalians were forcibly dispatched to Germany. The Gestapo encircled selected villages, and all able-bodied adults were taken by truck to the nearest railway station. According to the postwar report by First Director Dankers, families were often separated, and only under-age children were left behind. Beginning with the Fall of 1943, the German authorities in Lithuania also began to bypass the Directorates in their quest for laborers. The church at Žiežmariai was surrounded on Sunday morning, 10 September, to gather able-bodied men, and such "church actions" became almost weekly occurrences thereafter. In all, it is estimated that some 75,000 Lithuanian forced laborers were netted in this manner.[66]

According to a Rosenberg memo to Himmler on 20 July 1944, a total of 126,000 Baltic workers had been sent to Germany. The national breakdown may have been 75,000 Lithuanians, 35,000 Latvians (especially from Latgale), and 15,000 Estonians. Conscription caused flight to the woods and decreased local production, especially in Lithuania. The above figures do not include those sent to the concentration camps. The total killed or deported by the Nazis from Latvia alone has been estimated at 120,000, half of them Jews (see next section) and half mainly ethnic Latvians.[67]

The German mobilization of Baltic manpower was also designed to provide recruits for military and para-military units. Although such activity clearly conflicted with international law, the measures were so couched as to render the draftees "voluntary associates." The first such units consisted of the so-called Defense Battalions ("Security Units" in Estonia), later renamed Police Battalions, which were largely staffed by volunteers. A variety of motives induced individuals to sign up. A few were genuinely pro-Nazi in orientation. Others sought revenge against Bolshevism for the deportations or murders of close ones and the indignities which had been inflicted on their homelands. Some tried to cover up their

[65] Brazaitis, "Vokiečių," p. 375; ibid, pp. 239–242.
[66] Ibid.
[67] Ibid.; Ekmanis 1978, p. 83.

earlier collaboration with the Soviets or tried to escape false accusations to that effect.

In Lithuania, where almost the entire pre-war army which had been turned into a Soviet unit surrendered en masse during the first days of the war, recruitment for the Defense Battalions was frequently presented to such soldiers in the form of a choice of joining or being sent to a POW camp. It is not surprising that many joined. It has been estimated that during the period of their operation some 20,000 Lithuanians served in these Battalions; their manpower averaged around 8,000 at any one time. In August 1941, there were 20 Lithuanian Battalions with 8,388 officers and men; in March 1944, the figure stood at 8,000.[68]

The Sovietized old Latvian and Estonian armies also surrendered en masse to the Germans. The Latvian Defense Battalions included about 15,000 men. At first, 27 undersized Battalions were formed in Estonia, later to be consolidated into 13, with a total of approximately 10,000 men.[69]

According to official pledges issued in all three countries, these Battalions should have been used only within their homelands, principally for duty against Soviet stragglers, parachutists, and escaped POW's. This promise was soon broken, and virtually all the Battalions were sent east for support duty behind the German lines, and later on the front. Some eventually even saw service in Poland, Yugoslavia, and Italy. As tactical rather than combat units, they were frequently given unpleasant tasks of civilian population control or anti-guerrilla operations. Elements from among them have been reported doing ghetto guard duty in Poland. Overall, their rate of attrition was high. Estonian Police Battalion 36 was sent to Stalingrad with 450 men, and returned with 72.[70]

A second attempt at raising military personnel was the creation of the Waffen-SS National Legions from the Fall of 1942 to the Spring of 1943. In Latvia and Estonia, recruitment for such units was again connected with compulsory labor drafts; in theory, individuals had a choice. The widely-known poor conditions in the Labor Battalions, combined with various pressures exerted by local recruitment officers, induced over half of the "volunteers" to

---

[68] Brazaitis, "Vokiečių," p. 376; *Masinės žudynės Lietuvoje: dokumentų rinkinys* (Vilnius, 1965), I, p. 323; A. Rakūnas, "Lietuvos liaudies kova prieš mobilizaciją į hitlerinę kariuomenę ir jos sužlugdymas, 1941-1944 m.," *Istorija*, VII (Vilnius, 1965), p. 41.

[69] Latvia: Myllyniemi 1973, p. 228; Estonia: Arnold Purre, "Eesti sõda Nõuk. Liiduga," *Eesti riik*, VII, pp. 25-26.

[70] Brazaitis, "Vokiečių," p. 376; *Masinės žudynės*, I, p. 323; Purre, "Eesti sõda," p. 26.

choose Legion service. The Estonian Legion at its peak size was one division numbering some 11,000 men, while the Latvians eventually manned two divisions. By August 1943 the German Security Service reported heavily anti-German attitudes in the Latvian Legion, especially among officers.[71]

Attempts to form a Lithuanian Legion floundered, along with most of the other German manpower-mobilization efforts in that country. On 17 March 1943, SS recruitment efforts in Lithuania were stopped, and Lithuanians were declared unworthy of wearing the SS uniform. The brunt of German reprisals which followed fell on the intelligentsia, and 3 incumbent General Counselors — Pranas Germantas, Mečislovas Mackevičius, and Stasys Puodžius — were among the 46 prominent individuals sent to the Stutthof concentration camp. All institutes of higher learning were closed, with the exception of several branches which the Directorate managed to save through an argument based on the letter of the German instructions rather than on its spirit.

In Latvia and Estonia, the Germans called for a new mobilization in October-November 1943. Latvia's Directorate was not even consulted. A mobilization appeal was published under the name of Latvian General Rudolfs Bangerskis, without his knowledge. He protested in writing, and refused to supervise the draft. Estonia's Directorate refused to discuss a mobilization under conditions of non-sovereignty, but Mäe published the order under his name alone, and the other Directors yielded.

New attempts to form Lithuanian military units followed the abortive Legion. An "All Lithuanian Conference" sponsored by the German occupation authorities was convened in the summer of 1943. A *Taryba* (Council), linguistically evocative of the body which had in 1918 declared Lithuania's independence, was formed and attached to First General Counselor Kubiliūnas. It was hoped that such mollification might smooth the new mobilization efforts which soon followed.

An agreement was reached between high officials of the SS in Lithuania and General Povilas Plechavičius of the former Lithuanian army, on the formation of "Local Detachments," announced on 16 February 1944, the anniversary of Lithuanian independence. These were to be Lithuanian military units, manned and officered by natives. Their use was to be restricted to the Baltic area, from Narva to Vilnius, and their operations would be

---

[71] In Latvia, 14,800 chose the Legion and 5,600 went to Labor Battalions; in Estonia, the numbers were 5,300 and 6,800. For 1942–43 mobilizations, the most detailed source is Myllyniemi 1973, esp. pp. 433–438 and 252. See also Ivinskis, pp. 79–80; and Purre, "Eesti sõda," pp. 19–40.

directed against Soviet partisan and bandit activities. This effort, unlike previous mobilization efforts, enjoyed the blessing of many native notables who saw in it the nucleus for a reestablished Lithuanian army at a time when the Soviets were approaching; and the not inconsiderable personal magnetism of General Plechavičius added another dimension of attraction. The actual level of volunteers exceeded expectations: some 30,000 came forward, and the originally planned number of battalions was somewhat increased.

Experience showed that it was naive on the part of the organizing officers to trust German assurances. Manpower demands on the eastern front overruled any promises, which may not have been made in good faith anyway. In May, the transfer of the new units into the Auxiliary Police Services of the SS was initiated. However, it triggered an immediate self-demobilization of the remaining units, most of whose personnel managed to slip away into the woods. General Plechavičius and his staff were arrested on 15 May, and some 100 of his men were indiscriminately shot. Those who did not succeed in escaping (about 3,500) were transferred for *Luftwaffe* ground duty in Germany and Norway. All later German recruitment efforts in Lithuania failed.[72]

In Latvia, military mobilization efforts continued to center around the Legion. The Soviet advance toward the Latvian border made the native administration reconsider its stand of no mobilization without autonomy. A conference of Latvian administrators (including those on the district level), called on 15 November 1943, reluctantly decided to support mobilization anyway, and the total strength of Latvian units jumped to 40,000. The peak strength, around mid-1944, has been estimated at 60,000, but may have been higher. Throughout the German occupation, up to 150,000 were inducted or recruited. At least 50,000 were killed, wounded, or missing in action. About 80,000 men were captured by the Soviets, mainly after the collapse of the Courland front in May 1945. About 20,000 reached the West at the end of the war.[73]

In Estonia, pre-war Prime Minister Uluots (whom the Germans alternatively ignored and tried to co-opt) switched his stand on mobilization in February 1944 when the Soviet army reached the Estonian border. At that time the Estonian units under German control had about 14,000 men. Counting on a German debacle, Uluots considered it imperative to have large numbers of Estonians armed, through any means, and grouped in Estonia to guard

---

[72] Ivinskis, p. 84.
[73] King, pp. 87–89, based on *Latvju enciklopēdija*, II, pp. 1317–1318; Ekmanis 1978, pp. 84–85; Myllyniemi 1973, pp. 254–255 and 276.

against Soviet invasion, and to wrench independence from the retreating Germans. It was a desperate ploy of a weasel facing two wolves — the only alternative to passive surrender. Uluots even managed to tell it to the nation through the German-controlled radio: Estonian troops on Estonian soil have "a significance much wider than what I could and would be able to disclose here." The nation understood and responded. The Germans had set an upper limit of 15,000, but 38,000 registered and 28,000 actually received poor arms and hasty training. Six border-defense regiments were formed, headed by Estonian officers, and the SS Division received reinforcements, bringing the total of Estonian units up to 50,000 or 60,000 men. Throughout the German occupation, at least 70,000 Estonians joined the German army, and more than 10,000 may have died in action. The Estonian Division was reorganized in Germany after Soviet conquest of Estonia. About 10,000 men reached the West after the war ended.[74]

Unlike their confreres to the south, Estonians facing the German draft had the alternative possibility of flight to Finland. The Gulf of Finland could be crossed overnight in a boat. A sentence of hard labor waited for those caught trying to flee. Nevertheless, mostly between April and December 1943, some 5,000 men, some of them with their families, succeeded in making the crossing. About 3,000 of these were persuaded to volunteer for the Finnish armed forces, and a special Estonian regiment saw service on the Karelian front. In August 1944, in the face of a new Soviet invasion of Estonia, 1,800 agreed to a German amnesty arranged through Finnish mediation and returned to their homeland to join local units.[75]

The Fate of the Jewish Population

The Reich's policy toward the Jewish population of areas which fell under its control is well known, and the Baltic region was no exception. While the Jewish community of Estonia was minuscule (5,000), in 1939 Lithuania, including Vilnius, had over 200,000 and Latvia 93,000 Jews.

Some outbreaks of indiscriminate killing of Jews occurred in Lithuania soon after the German attack. Several bands of *ad hoc* executioners are known to have perpetrated such massacres. The connection between their activity and the LAF's organized uprising is spotty, with no indication of any definite relationship except in

---

[74] Text of Uluots radio speech in *Eesti riik*, VIII, pp. 45–46; military detail from Richard Maasing, "Katseid Eesti sõjaväe uuestiloomiseks," *ibid.*, VII, pp. 17–51; Myllyniemi 1973, p. 276. The total number in the German army and casualties are our estimates.

[75] Evald Uustalu, *For Freedom Only: The Story of Estonian Volunteers in the Finnish Wars of 1940–1944* (Toronto, 1977).

time and circumstance. However, Soviet destruction of national elites had eliminated one element of social control over the most primitive segments of the population.

A German task force of 1,000 men (*Einsatzgruppe A*) was charged with liquidating Jews and Communists in the Baltic lands.[76] Its first groups went into action in Kaunas on 28 June — four days after the entry of German armed forces. The Germans made conscious efforts in Kaunas and Riga to take photos and films that would suggest popular initiative in the pogroms, and they urged the new local auxiliary units to participate, with some success. Nonetheless, the German *Sicherheitspolizei* reported that incitement was surprisingly difficult in Lithuania, and even more so in Riga. Altogether, German confidential reports in July estimated 7,000 Jews murdered in Kaunas, and 400 in Riga, by German *Einsatzgruppen* and local henchmen. By 15 October, one of the *Einsatzgruppen* reported having killed 71,105 Jews in Lithuania and 30,025 in Latvia, in addition to 3,387 non-Jews. Protests by people like Latvian Lutheran Archbishop Teodors Grünbergs were of no avail.[77]

The introduction of formal anti-Jewish measures followed the German advance. As long as the front-line military administration functioned, these were quite circumscribed. The establishment of civil government was accompanied by specifics regulating the lives of the Jewish communities. At first these were relatively minor, such as prohibitions on the use of parks or sidewalks by Jews, or the regulation that they wear the identifying yellow Star of David. Within a month, however, ghettos, paralleling those in other German-occupied East European areas, had been established in Lithuania. As elsewhere, these proved to be but a temporary stage in the so-called final solution. With time, ghettos were liquidated and their residents either executed or transferred to the death camps for eventual extermination. In comparison with the better-known SS death factories erected on occupied Polish territory, the camps established in the Baltic region were of modest proportions. The largest of them was at Salaspils, near Riga; another at Klooga, near Tallinn. The Ninth Fort outside of Kaunas, one in a ring of fortifications dating from Tsarist times, and Aukštieji Panėriai, outside Vilnius, were also turned into notorious locales for mass executions.

---

[76] *Einsatzgruppe A* also operated in northern Russia (Pskov, Novgorod), while eastern Lithuania (including Vilnius) was part of the territory assigned to *Einsatzgruppe B*.

[77] Myllyniemi 1973, pp. 76–78, based mainly on *Trials of the Major War Criminals before the International Military Tribunal* (Nuremberg, 1947–1949; 42 vols.), 180-L, XXXVII, pp. 670–683; Spekke, p. 402.

In their capacity as fronts for the German occupation, the Directorates have later acquired a "guilt by association" with all German policies perpetrated on their territory, whether they had any say in them or not. Soviet propaganda has been quite active in equating any anti-Soviet activity pursued by Baltic political bodies with concurrence in the Reich's genocide policy. Such charges imply participation and approval. While participation of the Directorates in the administration of German measures against the Jews cannot be questioned, it is somewhat more difficult to establish wholehearted concurrence. Doubtless some of their members agreed with the moves, but it is hard to say that all, or for that matter even a majority, in the three Directorates were so disposed.

As in most East European areas under German control, a handful of local rabble actively joined in carrying out the Nazi genocide policy. A complex series of circumstances can be said to have motivated such activity. Among them two were paramount. The first was anti-Semitism inherited from the Tsarist period, though its manifestations in Latvia and Lithuania were far milder than in other areas of the former Pale of Jewish settlement. Although some of their policies, aimed at development of an ethnically Baltic professional and middle class, by their very nature tended to discriminate against the Jewish urban population which was disproportionately represented in these groups, neither the Ulmanis nor the Smetona regime can be accused of anti-Semitism. Conditions for the Jewish minorities in pre-war Latvia and Lithuania were among the best in Eastern Europe of that time. The same applies to the tiny Jewish population in Estonia.

The second and by far greater impetus for violent anti-Semitism was provided by the socially disruptive first year of Soviet domination, which introduced a syndrome of murder and revenge accompanied by destruction of the normal structure of social control. The pent-up native hostilities naturally directed against Communists and their sympathizers were in many cases deflected onto the Jews. The Lithuanian and Latvian Communist Parties, extremely small in number, were disproportionately composed of individuals of Jewish background. While Lithuania's population was about 7% Jewish in early 1941, about 15% of the local Communist Party consisted of Jews.[78] This small number could not in any logical way be reflective of the Jewish community as a whole, but the visibility of such Communists as well as of the numerous newly installed

---

[78] The number of Jews in the Lithuanian CP on 1 January 1941 is given as 412 in *Lietuvos Komunistų Partija skaičiais*, p. 55, and as 479 (including candidate members) in *Mažoji lietuviškoji tarybinė enciklopedija*, II (Vilnius, 1968), p. 386. Either figure is about 15% of the total.

non-party officials who were Jewish led some who were personally affected by the trauma of the deportations to identify "Soviet" with "Jewish".[79] The more actively inclined among these individuals joined the terrorist bands which formed, on the first days of the war, to execute any real or imagined collaborators. Many in these small circles automatically placed all Jews in such a category. It is difficult to estimate the numbers of participants or of victims. These bands should not be summarily identified with the wider national resistance forces, which had no means to discipline terrorists supported by the Germans.

While the social circumstances which surround such activity can be explained, it does not condone indiscriminate murder. It is perhaps somewhat easier to understand the predicament of those who had joined the various German-sponsored military units with the intention of fighting the Soviets and who found themselves transferred away from their home countries to carry out aspects of the German genocide operations, under circumstances where disobedience to orders would entail courtmartial.

The Jewish communities of the Baltic states suffered tremendous losses. It is estimated that at least 170,000 from among the Lithuanian Jewish population perished. The exact pre-war figure is difficult to ascertain: the 1923 census indicates 153,743, but this of course includes neither the natural increment to 1940 nor the sizable Jewish population of Vilnius, which came under Lithuanian control in 1939. It is not unlikely that at the time of the Soviet takeover there were over 200,000 Jews in Lithuania.

In 1939, the Latvian Jewish population stood at approximately 93,000. Up to 5,000 were affected by the Soviet deportations of June 1941. About 18,000 Latvian Jews were either drafted into the Red Army or evacuated by the Soviets. The arrival of the Germans occasioned mass murders of allegedly pro-Soviet elements. About 3,500 ethnic Latvians perished, along with several thousand Jews.

---

[79] Most people in the Baltic countries did not realize that the Jews, overwhelmingly city-dwellers and often relatively well off, were also more heavily affected by Soviet deportations than the majority nationalities. The number of Lithuanian Jews deported could have been 5,000, as given in *Kniga o russkom evreistve, 1917–1967* (New York, 1968), p. 97, or even 7,000, as claimed by Dov Levin, "Participation of the Lithuanian Jews in the Second World War," JBS, VI/4 (Winter 1975), p. 310. Even if the number were 3,000, this would still mean close to 1.5% of the total Jewish population of somewhat over 200,000, while the deportation losses of the country as a whole were about 1.1% (34,000 out of 3,100,000). A figure of approximately 5,000 Latvian Jews deported (i.e., 5% of all Jews) has been given by Max Kaufmann, "The War Years," in Mendel Bobe et al. (eds), *The Jews in Latvia* (Tel Aviv, 1971), p. 351. This seems high, compared to even the highest estimates for Lithuania. However, even 1,000 Latvian Jews deported would lead to a higher percentage (1%) than for the country as a whole (0.8%).

The *Einsatzgruppen* liquidated 30,000 more before the German occupation regime concentrated the remaining Jewish population in ghettos, in October. By the end of 1941, about 30,000 of these were slaughtered. In late 1943, the Latvian ghettos were liquidated and their surviving residents sent first to Salaspils and later, as the German occupation drew to a close, to the Stutthof concentration camp. Of approximately 70,000 Jews who remained in Latvia after the Soviet retreat, only about 4,000 survived.[80]

Estonia had fewer than 5,000 Jews in 1939. Of these, only about 1,000 remained after the Soviet retreat. Most of them perished. In total about 250,000 Baltic Jews, of whom only about 10,000 survived, were deported or killed during the German occupation. Among the ethnic Lithuanians, Latvians, and Estonians, an estimated 25,000 were killed in local camps, and 10,000 were transferred to concentration camps in Germany.[81]

Resistance to the Germans

During the occupation, the rump press of the three countries was filled with exhortations for greater gratitude toward Germany as the liberator from Bolshevism. On the whole, such a mood prevailed among the majority of the native populations during the first months of the war. German occupation policies soon dissipated this reservoir of goodwill, rendering the mood either resignedly indifferent or actively hostile. Hopes among many leading elements for reattaining formal sovereignty if not real independence were quickly proven illusory. The majority might have settled for some sort of quasi-independence along the lines of Slovakia. The clear German refusal to satisfy the strong yearning for statehood, even as a formality, on the whole sealed a negative relationship between the new occupiers and the occupied. A Dutch Nazi visitor (to whom the "self-administration" officials may have talked more frankly than to Germans) reported in June 1942 that "chauvinist national consciousness" dominated in all population layers in Latvia and Estonia, and that he encountered no genuinely Germanophile circles or persons; the apparent differences in attitudes merely reflected varying ability to hide one's thoughts.[82]

An underground press began to sprout, answering the German demands of gratitude for liberation with observations on the initial

---

[80] Our calculations, based on indirect figures given by Kaufmann, pp. 353-367, and King, p. 83.

[81] See Tõnu Parming, "The Jewish Community and Inter-Ethnic Relations in Estonia, 1918-1940," JBS, X/3 (Fall 1979), pp. 257-259; and Spekke, p. 402.

[82] Myllyniemi 1973, p. 156, based on Rost van Tonningen's report in Bundesarchiv R6/441.

complicity of the Reich in the Soviet invasion. The incessant severity of economic exploitation, and in particular the attempts at mobilization of manpower, eventually gave rise to an active opposition in all population groups. When the Germans invited the Latvian Directorate to ask for "permission" to form a Latvian SS Legion, Valdmanis responded with a memo on *The Latvian Problem* to Latvia's German SS Commander, saying that the situation of Latvians was unbearable:

> Every Latvian, including those who have never given any thought to politics, is clearly faced with the question of what is actually happening. Have the Germans effectively come as liberators or as conquerors?[83]

By the middle of 1943, the influential Lithuanian underground newspaper *Nepriklausoma Lietuva* wondered whether the Nazis or the Bolsheviks "were the more inveterate murderers of innocent people."[84] The organized anti-German oppositions did not encourage armed resistance, which could only help the Soviets. Rather, the aim was one of sabotaging German occupation measures and of keeping alive an organized national political body capable of representing each nation's interest during the postwar settlement. Hope was placed in the Western powers. As one of the underground Lithuanian papers expressed it on 16 February 1944, the anniversary of Lithuanian independence:

> We are convinced that the Western nations who have formed the Atlantic Charter . . . will help us, at the right time, to secure and to defend from National Socialism as well as from Communism that for which we are prepared to sacrifice all.[85]

In Lithuania, a formal resistance began to crystallize by the Fall of 1941. The LAF had organized the Provisional Government, disbanded in early August. Later that Summer the LAF presented Hitler, through the German military command, with a memorandum on Lithuania's independence. In September, LAF Chief Leonas Prapuolenis was deported to Dachau and the organization was suppressed. One of its factions, the extreme right-wing Lithuanian Nationalist Party which had crystallized in late June, attempted to achieve some independence through collaboration and participation in the Directorate. By late October, it too had been proscribed for criticism of certain faults in the

[83] Alfreds Valdmanis, "Das Lettische Problem" (November 1942), in Bundesarchiv R6/5, as reported in Myllyniemi 1973, p. 210.
[84] *Nepriklausoma Lietuva*, nos. 11–12 (1943), as cited by Ivinskis, p. 76.
[85] Brazaitis, "Vokiečių," p. 379; taken from *Laisvės kovotojas*, 16 February 1944.

Zivilverwaltung system. From then on, organized political life continued only in the underground.

The Lithuanian resistance movement formed principally along two axes, a Catholic-oriented Lietuvių Frontas (Lithuanian Front) and a more secular Laisvės Kovotojų Sąjunga (Union of Freedom Fighters). Both published their own underground newspapers and maintained a liaison with the outside world. In early 1944, the latter even operated a clandestine radio station. By late 1943, these groups united in a Supreme Committee for the Liberation of Lithuania organized along the lines of the pre-war political parties. The Supreme Committee functioned as a center of the Lithuanian resistance until the Summer of 1944, when one of its couriers, enroute to Stockholm, fell into a Gestapo net aimed at the Estonian underground. His arrest led to others throughout Lithuania, affecting the Supreme Committee's leadership. Although alternates took the places of those arrested, the activities of the body were severely restricted and it faded soon after the return of the Soviets. Although the Supreme Committee was obviously intended eventually to become a Provisional Government, the experience of the Summer of 1941 must have dissuaded the Lithuanians from any renewed attempts at establishing such a body under the conditions of German occupation.[86]

Latvian attempts to form a Provisional Government arose from two quarters. The first emanated from within the Latvian Directorate. In his memo on *The Latvian Question*, Valdmanis proposed the formation of a Latvian army to fight the USSR in exchange for the establishment of a formally independent state entity, albeit one with somewhat circumscribed sovereignty. The Latvian Directorate declared its support for the memo. Otto Drechsler, the German General Commissioner for Latvia, admonished Valdmanis, but confidentially suggested autonomy along Slovakia or at least Bohemia-Moravia lines to his superior, Lohse, on 7 December 1942. Contrary advice came from Ostland Political Section Leader Friedrich Trampedach:

> The politically leading circles of the Baltic people . . . would use an increased independence not for rapproachment with the Reich but with the Anglo-Saxon powers.[87]

Nonetheless, the German armed-manpower problem was becoming so severe that by 26 January 1943 Rosenberg himself drafted a proposal to Hitler, covering all three Baltic states: (1)

86 Ivinskis, pp. 76–83; Myllyniemi 1973, pp. 81–83 and 265.
87 Drechsler to Lohse, 7 December 1942; Trampedach memo, 19 November 1942.

total and rapid restoration of private property; (2) creation of autonomous governments; and (3) national troops based on general mobilization. These proposals, which reflected the minimal demands of Valdmanis, met Hitler's uncompromising veto on 8 February (except for reprivatization), and again on 5 May: "Subjected peoples cannot be used as allies." Meanwhile, Lohse accused the Latvian Directors of anti-Germanism, and reminded them that 80 prominent Dutchmen had been shot for such behavior. In mid-1943, Valdmanis resigned from the Directorate. Failure also met various later attempts in Germany by members of the former Directorate who in late 1944 and early 1945 envisaged the establishment of a Provisional Latvian Government in Courland, which remained under German control until the end of the war.[88]

The second Latvian approach avoided collaboration. It centered around the seven-man Latvian Central Council (founded on 13 August 1943), an underground body representing the four largest political parties of the pre-war Parliament as well as some individuals from its presiding board. The presupposition for its existence was that the end of the war would leave both Germany and the USSR weakened, allowing Latvia to regain its independence with the aid of the Western powers. The Council had contacts in the West, and it published an underground newspaper, *Independent Latvia*. A Lithuanian-Latvian resistance conference took place in January 1944, and there were two all-Baltic ones in April, all in Riga. The Germans discovered the Latvian Council's existence in the Fall of 1944, and arrested and deported most of the leaders. The Council's leader, the Liberal Konstantins Čakste, died during deportation in 1945. A Latvian unit of the German army had 8 officers shot and 545 men sent to the Stutthof concentration camp. On 7 May 1945, as the German power in Courland was collapsing, the National Council, consisting of 73 elected members, endorsed a Provisional Government led by Colonel Roberts Osis. During the following days, the Soviet forces occupied all Courland.[89]

In Estonia, the Directorate was rather submissive. Still, Director for Internal Affairs Oskar Angelus recommended in March 1943 a declaration of independence to facilitate mobilization:

The average Estonian is saying: If I am treated badly in my own

---

[88] Rosenberg, "Entwurf einer Führervorschlag," 26 January 1943, in Bundesarchiv R6/35. Full documentation in Myllyniemi 1973, pp. 207–218 and 243.
[89] Ekmanis 1978, p. 85; Myllyniemi 1973, p. 267; Bilmanis 1951, pp. 405–406; Uustalu 1970, p. 338.

homeland now, during an exhausting war, then what will they start doing with me when peace comes?[90]

Karl Litzmann, the German General Commissioner for Estonia, also supported Slovakian-type autonomy, an idea vetoed by Hitler. By February 1944 even Mäe started to ask for sovereignty, and came to be considered a masked Anglophile by some Germans.[91]

Estonian resistance was more favored, by geographical proximity to Finland and Sweden. Traces of organized political resistance formed around underground circles in Tartu and Tallinn which were able to maintain contact with the still-resident Estonian Envoy to Finland, and through him with Stockholm and London. These circles were instrumental in the creation in early 1944 of a blanket underground organization — the Republic National Committee — a coalition of all pre-war political tendencies which in many ways resembled the Latvian Central Council. Co-optation attempts by the Germans had began in 1943; they were countered by demands for military autonomy which the Germans refused. The increased Estonian underground activity resulted in 200 arrests by the Gestapo in April, which impaired operations until mid-June 1944. At that time, foreign connections were beginning to play a significant role in the activity of the Committee. Traffic by fast motorboat was organized more or less twice a month between Tallinn and Stockholm, where August Rei, a leading Social Democrat, was active. The ability to maintain a foreign connection gave the Estonian Committee some visibility abroad. On 23 June it released, in Stockholm, a manifesto which caught the attention of foreign correspondents and the ire of German occupation authorities.

The aim of the Committee was the installation of a Provisional Government during the interval between the German retreat and the Soviet arrival. It managed to do so on 18 September, despite German opposition. It was not possible to organize any potentially successful resistance. Some Estonian units clashed with retreating Germans and set up defense positions east of Tallinn. On 22 September 1944, Soviet troops broke through these defenses and occupied Tallinn. The government decided to withdraw to Sweden; only Acting President Uluots succeeded.[92]

In all three countries, then, the bulk of anti-German resistance

---

90 Angelus memo, 15 March 1943, in Bundesarchiv R6/76.

91 Litzmann to Himmler, 31 March 1943; Mäe to Himmler, 9 February 1944. Full documentation in Myllyniemi 1973, pp. 213–214 and 269.

92 Johannes Klesment, "Kolm aastat iseseisvuse võitlust võõra okupatsiooni all," Eesti riik, VIII, pp. 7–33; Evald Uustalu, "The National Committee of the Estonian Republic," JBS, VII/3 (Fall 1976), pp. 209–219.

was channeled along the lines of political organization and sabotage of occupation exactions. Armed resistance was minimal, as it had been against the Soviets in 1940-41. Some Soviet partisan activity, although greatly inflated by Soviet historiography, did exist. Its ties with the indigenous populations were extremely circumscribed. The greatest concentration seems to have been in the eastern Lithuanian woods, where contact with the genuinely widespread Belorussian partisan activity was easiest. The earliest groups consisted of stranded Red Army personnel as well as some Communists who had not succeeded in withdrawing to the interior of the USSR. Later, these were joined by some Jews who had managed to escape from the ghettos or from train convoys enroute to concentration camps. Eventually some Soviet parachutists also joined.

The activities of the Soviet partisans provided one of the reasons for German reprisals, at times indiscriminate, against the country-side. In Latvia's Rēzekne district, all 235 inhabitants of Audrini village were executed, some of them publicly in the Rēzekne marketplace. Perhaps there was a rationale on the part of the Soviet planners that provocation of German reprisals could engender a genuine armed anti-German resistance in the country-side. The tragedy of the village of Pirčiupis, the Lithuanian Lidice, where 119 peasants were burnt to death by the Germans, was triggered by a Soviet partisan attack on 3 June 1944.[93]

In Russia, the Soviet Baltic institutions headed by their evacuated local leaderships continued a shadow existence. Most of the Baltic Red Army conscripts were considered unreliable and were sent to perish in labor camps. Later (in early 1942), specifi-cally Baltic combat units were established. Toward the end of the war, native Balts tended to be a minority in those units which saw some symbolic use during Soviet re-occupation of the Baltic states. The peak number of native Balts in the Red Army combat units may have been 18,000 Estonians (800 of whom surrendered to the Germans at Velikie Luki in December 1942), 10,000 Latvians, and 5,000 Lithuanians.[94]

Compared to most occupied nations of World War II, the Baltic nations were in the unenviable situation of facing not one, but two occupying powers. Of these, the one coming second had an unfair

[93] Myllyniemi 1973, p. 141; Brazaitis, "Vokiečių," p. 377.
[94] For Estonia: estimates based on Lembit Pärn, Sõjakeerises (Tallinn, 1968), pp. 88-118; Arnold Purre, "Eesti rahvastik okupeeritud Eestis," in Richard Maasing et al. (eds.), Eesti saatusaastad, 1945-1960 (Stockholm, 1963-1972; 6 volumes) [henceforth cited as Eesti saatusaastad], V, pp. 12-15. For Lithuania: Levin, "Participation," p. 310, note 14. For Latvia, very approximately: King, p. 83.

advantage: it did not have to destroy the national elite, because the first had done the dirty work. Therefore it generated relatively little resentment. The Baltic people could suspect Hitler of wanting to deport them east, but Stalin had actually started doing so. They saw no advantage in weakening Hitler against Stalin.

THE RETURN OF THE SOVIETS

The return of the Soviets in 1944, unlike their orderly arrival in 1940, was a nightmare for the Baltic populations. Occasionally it was preceded by severe military action, as the Germans made several attempts at stabilizing the front lines on Baltic territory.

The reappearance of the Red Army can be said to date from 20 January 1944 at Narva. The front there, however, remained immobile until Summer. The collapse of the German Army Group Center in Belorussia in June led to Soviet reoccupation of most Baltic territory by Fall. The eastern border of Lithuania was crossed in early July. Vilnius fell on 13 July; by 1 August, Kaunas had been abandoned by the *Wehrmacht*. A German counterattack temporarily halted the Soviet advance and secured German control over the Klaipėda area until January 1945. Further north, the Red Army had reached the Gulf of Riga in late July 1944, temporarily severing German land connections with Estonia. These were restored, allowing relatively orderly withdrawal, in September. Riga fell on 13 October. By late October, only Courland was still occupied by German forces, which remained bottled up there until the end of the war.

The passing of the front was immediately followed, as later in Germany, by a wave of robbery, looting, and rape. Summary executions of 400 to 700 people have been reported in Kaunas, Zarasai, and Šiauliai in Lithuania.[95] However, such occurrences appear exceptional in the immediate aftermath of Soviet reconquest.

Effective Soviet control was initially patchy and superficial. The forests were full of dispersed Germans, Baltic units of the German army, and Lithuanian nationalist guerrillas, as well as Estonian Finnish army veterans opposing both Germans and Russians. There were also people simply hiding from the war, uncertain about Soviet intentions. Roads were crowded with refugees returning home. Soviet patrols stopped younger men, but in general did not try to find out who had been evacuated by the Germans and who had tried to flee Soviet rule on their own initiative.

[95] E. J. Harrison, *Lithuania's Fight for Freedom* (New York, 1952).

Even in the partly destroyed cities, the establishment of effective control was hampered by an extreme shortage of trustworthy personnel. The pro-Soviet activists and careerists of 1941 were either dead, evacuated to Russia, or mobilized into the Red Army. A large portion of the active population had fled to the West, been evacuated by the Germans, or gone into hiding. Those who remained tended to be passively hostile or apprehensive and could not be trusted.

The Soviet response was a gradual tightening of control. Red Army rule was replaced with civilian administration as the front moved west. People willing to cooperate were initially accepted with few questions, in order to reactivate the basic food distribution, transport, and production systems. Food rationing cards were issued in the cities through places of work and the Bureau of Employment. German money was collected from among the population against receipts rather than being exchanged for rubles. For a short moneyless period, barter trade prevailed, especially for foodstuffs, along with earning vouchers issued by enterprises. Consumer goods were shorter in supply than ever before. Although much housing had been destroyed, city living was not overcrowded, since many people had left and few had arrived. But the fuel shortage became extreme during the winter of 1944–45. In buildings with central heating systems, people slept in their winter clothes. Courland, conquered only in May 1945, seemed to be especially hard-hit by ruin and hunger.

The general mood can perhaps be best described as one of wait-and-see. In Fall 1944, a dozen Moscow-located foreign correspondents were permitted a unique trip to Tallinn, and could walk around unattended. A British newsman later wrote:

> The Estonians, it soon became evident, despised and feared the Russians. . . . I don't think a single one of us spoke to a single person during the whole trip who had a good word to say for the Russian re-occupation — except, of course, the spokesmen produced by the Russians. . . .[96]

There was some relief that the worst expectations, based on Soviet behavior in 1941 and on German propaganda, did not fully materialize immediately. Some joyfully discovered that relatives evacuated to the USSR in 1941 or mobilized had not, after all, perished. The Soviets promised to maintain private farming and promoted the use of some secondary national symbols. Physical hardship could not become any worse, as bombing and military activity had ceased. The rumor mill even promised an eventual

---

[96] Paul Winterton, *Report on Russia* (London, 1945), pp. 85–86.

Soviet withdrawal under pressure from the Western Allies.

The reestablishment of Soviet control was accompanied, however, by political police (NKVD, renamed MVD in 1946) activity. The agency rapidly established branches down to the township level. These were frequently headed by experienced Russian personnel, symbolically supervised by native Balts at the ministerial level. Three-to-four-member screening commissions investigated the past and the political views of every inhabitant above the age of 12 in order to decide whom to deport and whom to arrest. Formal charges fell into two categories: "war criminal" and "enemy of the people." Presumably the first category involved Nazi collaborators, and the second, anti-Nazi Baltic patriots.

The first major wave of deportations involved mainly Baltic members of the German army sent to "labor service" outside the labor-short Baltic republics. A figure of 30,000 was mentioned in Soviet Estonian radio in late 1944, and 38,000 in Soviet Latvian sources of early 1945, before the capture of Courland.[97] We may assume larger figures for more populous Lithuania. These figures were increased by numerous captures in 1945 of Baltic soldiers in the German army. Few direct executions can be documented; starvation and death from cold and disease seem to have been the prevalent methods.

Some retribution against people serving with the competing occupation forces could be expected. But the war against the Baltic population continued and escalated, due in part to guerrilla resistance, in part to deliberate passive resistance, and to a large extent to sheer inability of a Western-oriented population to adjust in a matter of a few years to the Stalinist Soviet system.

In August and September 1945 an estimated 60,000 men, women, and children were deported from Lithuania, followed by 40,000 in February 1946, and the worst was still to come. About 60,000 people may have been deported from Latvia in 1945–46.[98]

If the goal of the deportations was to break national resistance, the results were mixed. Expectations of being next in line for deportation made many desperate people join the guerrillas in order to die fighting on native ground rather than of starvation in Siberia. Instead of slowly subsiding after the war, the guerrillas continued to gather strength in 1945 and 1946.

The reestablishment of Soviet rule was also accompanied by Red

---

[97] Tönu Parming, "Population Changes in Estonia, 1935–1970," *Population Studies*, XXVI/1 (March 1972), p. 56; Bilmanis 1951, p. 406.

[98] Thomas Remeikis, "The Armed Struggle Against the Sovietization of Lithuania After 1944," *Lituanus*, VIII/1–2 (1962), p. 38; George Carson (ed.), *Latvia: An Area Study* (New Haven, 1956), p. 82.

Army mobilizations. Estonia, which had been cleared of Germans earliest, was most affected. In August 1944, men aged 18 to 33 were called up. Success was apparently only partial, in that the call was repeated in March 1945. This time the age span was extended, from ages 18 to 37. Many of the draftees had previously served in the German army, but backgrounds tended not to be fully checked. Those who admitted to front-line German service were sent to hard-labor battalions in Russia. Those with auxiliary non-armed service with the Germans were deemed redeemable and faced labor duty in Estonia. Those claiming no German ties were sent to the Courland front and suffered heavy casualties. It is not surprising that as time passed some reportedly preferred to claim non-armed German service. The extent of the mobilization in Estonia is unclear; most likely under 10,000 were so affected. As the effective Soviet reoccupations of Latvia and Lithuania came later, the scope of mobilizations there was less extensive.

Estonia and Latvia suffered some formal territorial losses. In January 1945, the right bank of the Narva River, along with most of the Petseri district in southeastern Estonia, were ceded to the Russian Soviet republic. The area involved 5% of Estonia's pre-war territory and 6% of its population. The Latvian loss was smaller, involving the detachment of a part of the Abrene district in the northeast, about 2% of the pre-war territory and population. The Klaipėda (Memel) region, which had been forcefully taken from Lithuania by Germany in March 1939, now reverted to Lithuania.

All three states emerged from the war with considerable population and property losses inflicted by Soviet as well as German policies and activities, by internal reactions, and by the course of warfare. Material losses were difficult to overcome. In Estonia, industrial capacity was down to 55%, means of transport to 7%, city housing down to 45%, and area under cultivation down to 60% of the pre-war figures. Per-capita losses were estimated at around 6,000 rubles in Lithuania, 10,000 rubles in Latvia, and 15,000 rubles in Estonia. There is little reason to doubt Soviet estimates on destruction, which claim that by 1944 in Lithuania, 21 villages had been burned by the Germans; 86,300 buildings destroyed; 56 electric stations and 1,148 bridges blown up.[99]

Psychologically, the population losses due to the war were perhaps not as devastatingly unexpected as the deportations during the first Soviet occupation. In real terms, however, they proved far

---

[99] Leonid Lentsman (chief ed.), *Eesti rahvas Suures Isamaasõjas* (Tallinn, 1977), II, p. 439; K. Meškauskas, *Tarybų Lietuvos industrializavimas* (Vilnius, 1960), p. 124.

greater. The blame is often hard to place on any particular quarter. Estimates have to be based on weak grounds, as those best placed to know certain figures are also those most interested in hiding them. Soviet sources have never given any estimates on the number of deportees to the USSR, even though the deportations have been acknowledged. Their overviews of population losses tend blithely to ignore this category or possibly to reassign it to German deportation. Some Baltic refugee sources tend to underestimate the voluntary evacuation to the USSR and the extent of German-sponsored executions and deportations. The latter cannot be evaluated separately from the anarchistic executions by Baltic gangs who, in Summer 1941, operated outside any German (or Baltic) organized control.

The very approximate estimates in Table 2 suggest that the Baltic states lost about 20% of their population during World War II, partly due to flight to the West and 1945 territorial cuts. About 9% of the population, as shown in Table 3, suffered premature deaths caused by war and occupation. Again, these estimates are very imperfect.

How do the Baltic war and occupation death rates compare with those of other European countries? A French overview presents the following list of undefined "human losses" as a percentage of total population:[100]

Poland	20%
Yugoslavia	12
USSR	9
Greece	7
Austria	6
Germany	5
Hungary	4
Romania	4
Netherlands	2.1
Czechoslovakia	2.1
France	1.5
Belgium	1.2
United Kingdom	0.8

---

[100] Larousse, *La Seconde Guerre mondiale* (Paris, 1951), p. 232; civilian losses surpass the military ones for most countries in this list, as is the case for the Baltic states. The Soviet losses clearly include deaths in Stalin's labor camps and prisons, and many countries may have listed nonreturned refugees and prisoners of war, as of 1951, among the losses.

| Italy | 0.5 |
| Bulgaria | 0.2 |

Even assuming that all these losses represent deaths, Baltic losses figure among the largest in Europe.

CHAPTER III

POSTWAR STALINISM: 1945–1953

ADMINISTRATION

The Reestablishment of Soviet Control

The Soviet Baltic leaders returned from Russia as soon as it became possible to reestablish even symbolic control. The first sessions of the Supreme Soviets of all three republics were held between August and October 1944 in the portions of each recaptured by the Red Army. Symbolic legitimation of the regimes through the standard one-candidate elections with upper-nineties percentiles of "yes" votes had, however, to be delayed. USSR Supreme Soviet elections were held in February 1946, the Baltic republics' Supreme Soviet elections in February 1947, and local Soviet elections only in January 1948. Official explanations of the delays mention remnants of the exploiting classes; one can only wonder where these had been in 1940. We may assume that only by 1946–48 did the regime feel it safe enough to proclaim inflated results without the threat of open challenge. Resistance estimates claim less than 50% turnouts in Lithuania.[1]

Overall control from Moscow was exerted mainly through the Lithuanian, Latvian, and Estonian bureaus, which were formed on 11 November 1944 at the Central Committee of the Communist Party of the Soviet Union (CPSU CC). This seemed to be the main policy-making level for Sovietization of the Baltic countries. (See Appendix A for names of various powerholders.) The ranking native executors of these policies were the First Secretaries of each republic's Communist Party (CP) organization. Jānis Kalnbērziņš in Latvia, and Antanas Sniečkus in Lithuania, had occupied this post since 1940. In Estonia, Nikolai Karotamm replaced Karl Säre, who had been captured by the Germans and declared a traitor by the Soviets for divulging information to the Germans. Karotamm had emigrated to the USSR in 1930, and returned in 1940 as Second Secretary of the Estonian CP. Despite their spotless party records ever since underground days, the native First Secretaries were

---

[1] K. V. Tauras, *Guerrilla Warfare on the Amber Coast* (New York, 1962), p. 58.

now assigned Russian Second Secretaries to act as Moscow's watchdogs.

Next in rank were the Chairmen of the Councils of People's Commissars (renamed Councils of Ministers in 1946). These were native Communists: Vilis Lācis in Latvia, and Mečys Gedvilas in Lithuania, who continued from 1940; and Arnold Veimer in Estonia, replacing Johannes Lauristin, who perished at sea during the 1941 evacuation. The ceremonial figurehead position of Chairman of each republic's Supreme Soviet Presidium continued to be held by the 1940 incumbents. Johannes Vares either committed suicide or was murdered by the NKVD on 19 November 1946, and was replaced as Chairman in Estonia by former linguist Eduard Päll, who had grown up in Russia.

The top leadership of the Lithuanian party had changed slightly. A Russian, A. N. Isachenko, occupied the position of Second Secretary; the office had previously been held by a Lithuanian, Icikas Meskupas-Adomas. In practice, the Lithuanian leadership became an adjunct to the CPSU CC Special Bureau for Lithuania, which was headed by Mikhail Suslov until Spring 1946.[2] Suslov — who was to become CPSU CC Secretary in 1947 and Politburo member in 1955 — may also have supervised the heads of the other two special Baltic bureaus.

Although there is no concrete evidence, as in Lithuania and Estonia, the existence of a Special Bureau of the CPSU CC for Latvia may be indirectly inferred. During the immediate postwar period, two representatives of the CPSU CC, V. F. Riazanov and S. G. Zelenev, were dispatched to Latvia to keep a close watch on developments there. Throughout 1946, the Latvian press documents their presence at all significant public and party functions. Riazanov's listing seems to imply a position superior to that of Second Secretary Ivan Lebedev and following those of First Secretary Kalnbērziņš, Chairman of the Council of Ministers Lācis, and Chairman of the Presidium of the Supreme Soviet Kirhenšteins. Both Riazanov and Zelenev disappeared from press accounts in early 1947.[3]

Rule remained arbitrary, even by Soviet standards, and, as Sniečkus admitted in 1961, it had to be exercised by force and terror.[4] On the local level, officials were appointed by the Presidium of the Supreme Soviet. There was a shortage of qualified

[2] *Lietuvos TSR istorija*, IV, pp. 145–146; Z. Zalepuga, "Lietuvos KP veikla atkuriant tarybinius organus respublikoje," *LKP istorijos klausimai*, XII (Vilnius, 1973), pp. 50–52.
[3] Michael Widmer, *Nationalism and Communism in Latvia: The Latvian Communist Party Under Soviet Rule* (Ph.D. diss., Harvard, 1969), pp. 177–178.
[4] *Tiesa*, 24 October 1961.

and politically reliable personnel. Complaints over inefficiency, especially in rural administrative control, appeared endemic during the immediate postwar years.[5] "Enemies of the people" were continuously discovered and weeded out from the ranks. The peak of such activity came with the Estonian purge discussed in the next section.

The Soviet rulers clearly distrusted anyone who had not undergone the 20 years of Sovietization in the USSR. This distrust also applied to the local Communists, whose small number had been further decimated during the war. On the other hand, the need to know the local language restricted the usefulness of imported Russians. A large pool of suitable personnel was available in the form of Latvians and Estonians whose families had emigrated to Russia during the half-century preceding the Baltic independence period. Some of them had been dispatched to their ancestral lands already in 1940–41. After the war, tens of thousands returned at the command of Soviet agencies, or because of superior living conditions and major advancement opportunities. These "Russian Latvians" and "Russian Estonians" were often considered uncouth and arrogant by the local population. In Estonia they were at times called *jeestlased* (which might be translated as "Yestonians"), because that was how their Russian accent made them pronounce the word *eestlased* (Estonians).

Few Lithuanians resided in Russia before the war, and thus thousands of completely non-native cadres were imported at all levels. They included one-third of the ministers (32% in 1947, plus 13% who were Russian Lithuanians), most of the deputy ministers, and various supervisory assistants to Lithuanian functionaries. Russian officials were used heavily even in Latvia and Estonia; in Estonia, 376 "leading cadres" were imported as early as 1945: the Vice-Chairmen of the Council of People's Commissars and of the republic's Planning Committee, the Second Secretaries of the Estonian Communist Party (ECP) and of the Komsomol (Communist Youth), and the 3 ECP Acting Secretaries were all Russians.[6]

The pre-war territorial administrative units (which had not undergone change in 1940–41) continued to be maintained long into the postwar period. As a result, the Baltic subdivisions for both government and party institutions differed from the rest of the USSR (see Table 9). From March 1945 on, Soviet-type "village

---

[5] *Sovetskaia Latviia*, 30 May and 29 June 1946; *Sovetskaia Estoniia*, 28 September 1946.

[6] Thomas Remeikis, "Berücksichtigung der nationalen und verwaltungsmässigen Interessen . . . ," AB, X (1970), p. 142; Lentsman, p. 447.

council areas'' were gradually superimposed on the existing units. Traditional districts were at times subdivided, and cities were separated from them. The townships and districts (some of them with folklore-hallowed names going back to the pre-Christian era) were abolished in 1950. The new *raions* (the Soviet term for district) were much smaller than the previous districts, and their large number (39 to 87 per republic) presented a rationale for dividing the republics into a few provinces or *oblasts* (4 in Lithuania, 1950, and 3 each in Latvia and Estonia, Spring 1952). These larger units seemed seriously to undermine the administrative significance of the national republics. In April 1953, however, the oblasts were liquidated. The constant revamping of administrative units increased confusion, but made for great office politics.

The Communist Parties and the Estonian Purge

Party membership continued to be heavily non-indigenous long into the postwar period, and the proportion of party members among the populations of the three republics stayed well below the USSR average. Membership grew slowly (see Table 6). Recruits who had lived under German occupation were distrusted, and the majority of the population considered the Communist Party as alien. During the last quarter of 1944, only 56 new party members were enrolled in Estonia, and local recruitment during 1945 probably totalled a few hundred. In early 1944, the ECP and the Communists in the Red Army Estonian Corps (who were not administratively part of the ECP) numbered around 7,400. By January 1946, after demobilization and disbanding of the Corps, the ECP counted 7,139 members, 52% of them Russian, about 21% Estonians from Russia, and only about 27% (1,900 members) home-grown Estonians.[7] The ECP was not only taking its orders from the outside; it also consisted largely of outsiders.

The Lithuanian CP (LiCP) emerged from the war with 8,060 members in January 1946 (as opposed to 1,500 in June 1940). By January 1949 the figure had risen to 24,000, the majority of its membership non-Lithuanian. Indeed, even 46% of its Central Committee (CC) was staffed by non-indigenous elements. Such a low numerical strength of locals was grossly inadequate for effective exercise of control over the country. The dominance of the Special Bureau of the CPSU CC was paralleled at the lower levels by political control exercised by thousands of non-native cadres and government officials specially imported for the

---

[7] Lentsman, p. 447; Jaan Pennar, "Soviet Nationality Policy and the Estonian Communist Elite," in Tönu Parming and Elmar Järvesoo (eds.), *A Case Study of a Soviet Republic: The Estonian SSR* (Boulder, Colo., 1978), p. 118.

purpose. In 1945, Lithuanians made up less than 31% of the LiCP, a figure which rose to 38% by 1953.

On 1 January 1946, the Latvian CP (LaCP) had 10,987 members, about half of whom were of Latvian origin. The pre-war underground members still alive probably numbered a few hundred. Of those who joined in 1940–41, up to 2,000 may have survived the war. A third group consisted of those who had joined during the war, from among the evacuees and army units. They probably numbered less than a thousand. The rest of the Latvian half of the LaCP was accounted for by the "Russian Latvians." From early 1945 to early 1951, at least 9,000 Communists were transferred to Latvia from elsewhere. In early 1950, the membership figure stood at 34,224 (about 1.5% of the population). In 1949, Latvians maintained a narrow majority of 53% in their party membership. As descendants of emigrants to Russia are included in these figures, home-grown Communists formed only about a quarter to one-third of the total membership. During the period between 1945 and 1950, only 9,561 individuals from within the republic were accepted for party membership. In late 1945, the great majority of those who served in district party organizations had come from the outside. Most could not have been proficient in Latvian. In March 1949, of the 30 non-staff lecturers in the Agitprop Department of the City of Riga Lenin District Committee, only 8 knew Latvian — and these were people whose task it was to spread Soviet ideology among the population.[8]

The preponderance of non-native elements was similar in the Estonian party, which in 1946 was 48% Estonian (including "Yestonian" immigrants from outside the republic), and which in January 1949 numbered about 17,000. These low figures suggest a reluctance of the population, as in the other two Baltic republics, to join in the occupation regime politically at this early date of Soviet control. They also most likely indicate a preference by the regime for importing a new ruling elite rather than recruiting it from among an untrustworthy population.

Home-grown Communists in all three countries represented only about one-third of the total membership around 1949. Despite the career opportunities involved, only 0.3% of the Lithuanians and 0.7% of the Latvians and Estonians had joined the CP after five years of continuous Soviet occupation. This rate was 5 to 10 times less than the USSR average at that time.

In 1950–51, nearly all home-grown Estonian CP leaders lost

8 *Sovetskaia Latviia*, 26 January 1949; Widmer, pp. 123 and 552; King, p. 183; Carson, p. 354. See also sources in Table 6.

their positions, and some vanished without a trace. They were replaced by Yestonians. Unlike other upheavals like the collectivization of agriculture (to be described later), which simultaneously affected all newly acquired Soviet western territories, the leadership purge did not spread to Latvia or Lithuania, and it is still unclear what triggered it in Estonia.[9]

It may be that of all three Baltic Communist leaders, Karotamm most actively pleaded for a slower pace of collectivization, for moderation in the deportation of farmers, and for keeping the deportees within Estonia, where the oil-shale mines needed labor. Once Stalin's suspicion had been aroused, Karotamm's obedient execution of collectivization through deportation might actually have worked against him. Estonia's record-breaking pace in this regard may have only suggested to Stalin that Karotamm had been timorous and could have achieved a breakthrough even earlier. Once Karotamm was demoted, every underling whom he had at times praised became suspect in turn. The sequence of events was the following:

In February 1950, a very eager Estonian Minister of Security was nonetheless replaced by a Ukrainian from Siberia. In March, the Soviet Politburo passed a resolution on "The Shortcomings and Errors in the Work of the Estonian Communist (Bolshevik) Party CC." This resolution, which was presented at an Estonian party plenum, "helped to unmask a bourgeois nationalist anti-popular group who had forced their way into the party and caused great harm, especially on the ideological front."[10] CC member Lembit Lüüs was declared "dangerous to the Estonian people," expelled from the party, and sentenced to 25 years of forced labor; so was Trade Minister August Hansen (who died in 1952). Hans Kruus, Foreign Minister and President of the Academy of Sciences, was expelled but not deported (although some of his fingerbones were broken during torture in Leningrad).

The charge against Karotamm was that he

did not ensure implementation of the correct political line regarding the most important issues of ideological work and socialist

[9] A possible connection with the purge of supporters of Zhdanov in nearby Leningrad has been suggested by Benedict Mačiuika, *The Baltic States Under Soviet Russia: A Case Study in Sovietization* (Ph.D. diss., University of Chicago, 1963), pp. 266–269. However, there is no evidence that Zhdanov maintained any special influence in Estonia after July 1940, and a power struggle among basically Russian factions in the CPSU leadership would not explain the heavy purge of non-party intellectuals in Estonia.
[10] *Rahva Hääl*, 4 April 1951. The major source on Estonian purges is Arnold Purre, "Teine punane okupatsioon Eestis: Aastad 1944–1950," in *Eesti saatusaastad*, II, pp. 7–65.

reconstruction, committed rightist opportunist errors, and guided the party organization toward peaceful coexistence with class-hostile elements.[11]

Karotamm was dismissed and finished his days as an economics researcher in Moscow. He was replaced by Ivan Käbin, whose family had emigrated to St. Petersburg in 1910. The thoroughly Russianized Käbin, who had become a professional party organizer, was sent to Estonia in 1941 and had become one of the ECP secretaries in 1948. He was fully prepared to implement the denationalization of culture, appointment of Russians to key positions, extended use of the Russian language, and subservience to everything Russian; or, in the words of *The History of Soviet Estonia*:

> fight against the bourgeois nationalist ideology, for the imple-mentation of the Leninist policy of cadres, and for the education of all workers in the spirit of Soviet patriotism and proletarian internationalism.[12]

Among those active in condemning Karotamm was Vice-Chairman of the Council of Ministers Hendrik Allik, who had been sentenced to 25 years prison in 1924 for subversive Communist activities against the Republic of Estonia. In July 1950 he received the Order of Lenin, but in December he received his second 25-year sentence, this time for alleged bourgeois nationalism. Chairman of the Council of Ministers Arnold Veimer, with a similar back-ground, was dismissed in April 1951, but maintained some public functions. Major officials deported or vanished in 1951 included Party Secretaries Villem Kuusik (who apparently died in a labor camp) and Aleksander Kelberg. Hundreds of other functionaries and intellectuals were deported. The purge extended from Tallinn to Tartu University and to minor cities. The Estonian share of ECP membership fell to 41% (including Yestonians). By late 1952, not a single home-grown ethnic Estonian was left among the 4 ECP secretaries and the 26 ministers.

Meanwhile, Baltic CP membership continued to grow, nonethe-less. By the early 1950s it was becoming evident that Soviet power was likely to stay and that career opportunities required party membership. Guerrilla activities (to be discussed in the next section), which had at times made such membership dangerous, were subsiding. Moral condemnation of collaboration with the enemy also became muted, as deportations made people shut up.

---

[11] *Rahva Hääl*, 23 March 1953.
[12] *Eesti NSV ajalugu*, III, p. 684.

At Stalin's death in March 1953, total CP membership was 36,000 in Lithuania, 42,000 in Latvia, and 22,000 in Estonia. In their own republic, Lithuanians formed 38% of the members, and the percentage was probably slowly increasing. The Latvian figure was around 50%, and probably decreasing. The Estonian share stood around 42%, slowly recovering from the purge.

GUERRILLA WARFARE AND COLLECTIVIZATION

Guerrilla Resistance

"Forest Brothers" was the name by which the population called the guerrillas in all three countries and languages. At peak size they involved 0.5 to 1% of the total population. This is comparable to the peak Viet Cong strength in South Vietnam (discounting the North Vietnamese supplements) of about 170,000 fighters and supply runners out of a population of 20 million. Lithuania emerged from the German occupation with a strong national resistance movement. By the spring of 1945, some 30,000 armed men roamed the woods (see Table 4), although a unified command was not to emerge until 1946. In Latvia, indirect evidence suggests that 10-15,000 individuals were in the forests during the peak period; *The History of the Latvian SSR* reports over 1,000 surrenders in the Rēzekne district alone. In the Madona district, about 780 guerrilla fighters were reported killed or captured in 1945-47.[13] No unified command emerged. The situation was similar in Estonia, where the forest brotherhood may have at times reached a strength of 10,000.

Why did people join the forest brotherhood now, although they had submitted peacefully to the Soviet invasion of 1940? Why did they decide to resist under the much less favorable postwar occupation conditions? Patriotic idealism was an important motive. In 1940 it had been tempered by the desire not to die, but by 1945 war and both occupations had engendered a feeling that one might die soon anyway. Fugitive life had become familiar to many, and scattered arms had become plentiful. However, the prime direct reason for resistance was the Soviet terror during the 1940-41 occupation, and its reintroduction after re-occupation. Terror affected many more than just the wealthy or the German collaborators. Anyone with democratic views was a likely target, including Social Democratic workers. Anyone who had voiced a preference for national independence instead of Russian or

---

[13] Vietnam: *The Economist*, 16 August 1969, p. 26. Latvia: *Istoriia Latviiskoi SSR*, III (Riga, 1957), p. 596; Carson, p. 499.

German domination was a target. Anyone complaining about some aspect of Soviet bureaucracy or unable to adjust to its demands (such as farm grain deliveries) was a target. The sloppy randomness of the MVD and MGB repression units, and lack of due process, in fact made practically everyone a potential target, the more so since the Soviets considered everyone who had survived the German occupation a Nazi collaborator of sorts. People went to the forests mainly when they could no longer take the insecurity of civilian life.

Different groups and individuals reached that point at different times, depending on personal and societal circumstances of the moment. The first wave consisted of willing and unwilling German collaborators and draftees, anti-German national underground members (chiefly in Lithuania), and ex-members of the Finnish army (in Estonia). Men avoiding the Soviet draft and Red Army deserters soon followed. Soviet land redistribution and other social restructuring measures produced new waves, as did Soviet screening and deportation campaigns. The last major wave was to come during the 1949 farm-collectivization process.

In Lithuania, religion added a particular facet to resistance. Catholic parishes represented a grass-roots institution encompassing the majority of the population. The Soviet threat to their existence in itself fostered resistance. The Lutheran Church in Latvia and Estonia offered no comparable spiritual and national rallying point due to its century-long association with Baltic Germans. This difference may explain the relative strength of the Lithuanian guerrillas. Some clergymen and sacristans figured among guerrilla leaders in Lithuania, but there is only one claimed instance of their participation in the Latvian guerrilla effort,[14] and none in Estonia.

While pushed by despair, people were also pulled into the forest brotherhood by expectation of an imminent Western-Soviet war. This prognosis was not unreasonable on the part of those who through bitter experience had learned Stalin's attitudes toward the Western way of life and now observed a sharp increase in Soviet anti-Western propaganda. From such a viewpoint, it was only a matter of holding out for a few years, thus minimizing the risk of deportation and the harm done to the nation's social fabric. While such an outlook boosted morale, it also led the guerrillas to overstress the military aspect of the struggle and to neglect political education and planning. Even military action was to be directed only at the MVD units, their local auxiliary units, and other real or perceived collaborators; regular Red Army units were not to be

[14] *Cīņa*, 2 November 1966.

needlessly provoked any more than their German predecessors had been.

Russian deserters and escaped German POWs occasionally found their way into Baltic forests. At times they were accepted into guerrilla groups, but they rarely played a leading role. There is also little documentation identifying any of the guerrilla leaders as previous German collaborators of any magnitude. Such people fled to Germany or switched to collaboration with the Soviets, often under new identities. Prior to their defeat in 1945, the Germans (who still held Courland) tried to make use of the Baltic guerrillas. In Lithuania an anti-German underground group called LLA (Lithuanian Freedom Army) reoriented itself in 1944 as the Soviet front reached Lithuania, and received limited amounts of German arms. [15] There is no evidence that such supplies bought the Germans any more influence than British supplies had achieved in the case of Tito. Guerrilla groups also tend to attract adventurers, criminal elements, and romantic rebels against any authority; but in the Baltic case there were factors reducing this component. The business was too deadly, dull, and devoid of booty. Joining the Soviet-organized militia offered more feeling of power and import-ance, looting during arrests and deportations, and feeling of rebellion against one's own society's established values.

Forest brotherhood groups ranged in size from 800 men down to individuals in bunkers near their home farms or even underneath the family home. Many of the individual underground people were merely hiding, did not take any action against the Soviets, and had little contact with others. Some married couples or small groups of friends would circulate from one acquaintance to another, never spending more than a few weeks in one spot. Many others joined larger armed groups. An even larger segment of the population supported and supplied individual fugitives and guerrilla groups while remaining in the cities and on farms. Some "forest brothers" would return to the cities with forged papers to carry out intel-ligence and passive resistance work, or to try to give up forest life for good. As terror temporarily relaxed, people would drift back to civilian life. As organized guerrilla units suffered casualties, some supporters would shift to an active role. Members of decimated guerrilla units might become individual fugitives. It is thus impossible to draw a firm line between guerrilla and non-guerrilla.

The average lifespan of a forest brotherhood career has been

---

[15] Thomas Remeikis, *Opposition to Soviet Rule in Lithuania, 1945-1980* (Chicago, 1980), p. 60. The Soviets have published a series of former LLA member testimonies to Soviet interrogation authorities, in *Hitleriniai parašiutininkai* (Vilnius, 1966), pp. 63ff.

estimated to be two years, due to casualties, disease, and return to civilian life. Thus over the 8 years of intense guerrilla activity (1945–52), about 100,000 people may have been involved in Lithuania. This estimate is in line with estimated guerrilla casualties of 20,000 (Soviet estimate) to 50,000.[16] The Latvian and Estonian forest brotherhoods may have involved a total of about 40,000 and 30,000 people, respectively, at one time or another.

Forest brotherhood living conditions were primitive. Housing tended to shift from use of outlaying haybarns in 1944 to above-ground huts in 1945 and underground bunkers later on. The latter rarely fitted more than 3 people, had poor ventilation, one entrance, and were suitable for hiding, but unsuitable for self-defense when discovered. Bunkers were located in forests, farms, and even under village roads. Humidity was the main enemy in the long run, and lack of medical aid made every disease and wound deadly. Food and clothing supplies from the population were adequate, especially before collectivization. After that time, attempts to build up forest reserves of grain and fat were made. Large quantities of arms were abandoned by the Germans, but ammunition soon ran out or rotted. By 1948 most guerrillas had shifted to Soviet arms obtained by battle and by raids, but ammunition remained a problem.[17]

Compared to the German occupation, the Soviet one confronted the national resistance with more difficult operating conditions. A Council for the Liberation of Lithuania formed in Fall 1944 was broken up by arrests by May 1945, as were several subsequent centers. Consolidation finally was achieved from the bottom up, with individual groups of ten to several hundred men coordinated at the county level. Thus on 25 August 1945, all detachments in the Suvalkija region (south of the Nemunas River) merged into a Tauras guerrilla district. A central organization for Lithuania was finally restored in 1946, and was to last until 1951. The United Democratic Resistance Movement (Bendras Demokratinio Pasipriešinimo Sąjūdis, or BDPS), formed on 10 June 1946, sought to coordinate armed units, passive resistance groups, and political organizations. The armed forces were called Freedom Fighters. The declaration of the founding conference rejected narrow-minded nationalism, spoke of the need for far-reaching

[16] George Weller, *Chicago Daily News*, 17 August 1961, p. 21, based on an interview with Soviet Lithuanian official Romas Šarmaitis; Remeikis 1962, p. 32. On lifespan: V. Stanley Vardys, "The Partisan Movement in Postwar Lithuania," in *Lithuania Under the Soviets*, p. 95.

[17] Eerik Heine, "Metsavennad," in *Eesti saatusaastad*, II, pp. 68–70; Tauras, p. 40.

socio-economic reforms and a world government, and proposed creation of an international democratic welfare state. The BDPS seemed to have the format of an underground government, with a President and a Council of the Republic.[18]

The guerrillas later split with the passive resistance and formed a separate Lithuanian Freedom Fight Movement (Lietuvos Laisvės Kovų Sąjūdis, or LLKS) on 16 February 1949. Nine separate guerrilla districts were fused into three military regions (Northeast, Northwest, and the Nemunas area), with common military and political staff. Leadership of the guerrilla groups was as diverse as the membership. In June 1945 the staff of the Skardupiai unit (50 km southwest of Kaunas) consisted of a carpenter, a church janitor, an education student, a farmer, a policeman, and a priest. Leaders of primary groups were elected by the ranks, and they in turn elected higher commanders. Leadership gradually passed into the hands of former officers of the Lithuanian army, who tended to underestimate the importance of political struggle.[19]

The underground press ranged from irregular mimeographed leaflets and posters to printed periodicals such as *Laisvės varpas* (*The Bell of Freedom*), consisting of 127 issues by 1947 and continuing at least until 1951. Apart from BDPS's *Kovas*, publication was decentralized to district level, with a distribution of about 1,000 copies. The press carried local and international information, using foreign-radio monitoring sites and "correspondents" in the administrative offices of the occupation regime. It warned, advised, and encouraged the population. Articles were often written by civilians. Anti-Soviet posters in public places were sometimes used as mine triggers in order to discourage removal by collaborators. Manufacture of forged Soviet documents was another aspect of the guerrilla press.[20]

A country-wide 17-day officer training course was successfully carried out in Summer 1947, with 72 graduates. The second course in September 1948 was interrupted on its last day by a random MVD or MGB search group, which lost half of its 70 men.[21]

External contacts of the Lithuanian guerrillas were limited. Some cooperation with Latvian guerrillas occurred. Western agents apparently established contacts with Lithuanian guerrillas as early as 1945, and a prominent guerrilla leader, Juozas

---

[18] Remeikis 1962, p. 34; Vardys, "The Partisan Movement," p. 97; Tauras, p. 34; Stasys Žymantas, "Twenty years of Resistance," *Lituanus*, VI/2 (September 1960), p. 44.
[19] Remeikis 1962, pp. 31 and 35; also Vardys, "The Partisan Movement," pp. 100–101.
[20] Tauras, pp.43–46; Žymantas, p. 44.

Lukša-Daumantas, reached the West in 1948 to request help and to write a book on *Partisans Behind the Iron Curtain*.[22] No material help was forthcoming, but American intelligence parachuted Lukša and several other guerrilla representatives back to Lithuania in 1949-51, where Lukša soon died.

Guerrilla military activity largely consisted of surprise raids by small groups against the Soviet MVD repression units in order to keep them on the defensive. In Summer 1946, the MVD office in Šiauliai was reportedly blown up. More ambitious enterprises occurred occasionally. In February 1948 a 250-man MVD garrison in eastern Lithuania was unsuccessfully attacked by 120 guerrilla fighters. Major engagements took place when MVD tried to penetrate the guerrilla territory. An underground report of 7 June 1946 lists 6 major battles within 13 months, with the following median figures: 2,000 MVD troops attacked 100 guerrillas; 174 Russians and 24 Lithuanians died.[23] While the absolute numbers are to the Lithuanian advantage (and may be exaggerated), it should be kept in mind that the Lithuanians tended to lose one-quarter and the MVD only one-tenth of forces engaged.

Major guerrilla and passive-resistance efforts went into disrupting the administration and social structuring by the occupation forces. Local Soviet-appointed officials were intimidated, forced into being double agents, and — in case of excessive collaborationist zeal — murdered. From 1945 to 1952, an estimated 4,000 to 13,000 Soviet collaborators and suspects were executed.[24] The terror tactics of Soviet repression placed many uninvolved individuals into unbearable positions. The guerrillas and the occupation regime agreed on one point: no one must stay neutral. At the same time, the guerrillas did enjoy success in protecting the population against robberies committed or tolerated by Soviet officials. They also tried to warn of impending deportations as well as to liberate prisoners and deportees. However, the heavy MVD supplements brought in for deportations largely foiled such attempts. In the Spring of 1946, an effort was also made in southern Lithuania to limit moonshining and drinking. Throughout the period 1944-46, Soviet land-redistribution measures were opposed with force.

The active opposition presented to the Soviet elections of 1946-47 forms a special chapter in the history of Lithuanian guerrilla activity. They countered Soviet propaganda and threats

[21] Tauras, p. 36.
[22] Juozas Daumantas [Lukša], *Partizanai už geležinės uždangos* (Chicago, 1950).
[23] *Ibid.*, pp. 305-306; Žymantas, p. 43.
[24] Low estimate by Tauras, p. 52; Soviet estimates are on the higher side.

designed to achieve a total turnout by destruction of communications, attacks on armed guards at polling stations, and collection of passports (where proof of voting was to be entered) from among the rural population. The last measure both intimidated the prospective voter and provided him with an alibi for not voting.

Dogged Lithuanian efforts at establishing and maintaining unified command apparently had few parallels in the other two countries. A systematic account by a presumable participant (Eerik Heine) discusses arms, local intelligence, tactics, and group leaders, but the very idea of even district-wide cooperation is absent. There is no evidence of mimeographed guerrilla publications, of active contact attempts with the West, of organized officer training, of city intelligence activity, or of concerted campaigns against elections. A Soviet source reports destruction of an Estonian National Committee with numerous branches. In Latvia, a Soviet source names three regional guerrilla associations which had their own commanding staffs. Furthermore, a nationwide Latvian Partisans Communications Staff seems to have operated until 1947 in Riga itself, on Matiss Street.[25]

At the local level, fighting was as hard as in Lithuania. The forest brotherhood operated in practically every Latvian and Estonian county. Whole townships were for weeks outside Soviet control, and church towers flew national flags. However, it seems not to have occurred to the guerrillas to make positive use of this power base in order to inform and organize the population. At night the guerrillas ruled wide stretches, with Soviet occupants and quislings retrenched in stone buildings or moving in armed convoys. Offices and railroad bridges were blasted. In 1945 a 100-man group attacked the central prison in the city of Tartu, and an 800-man guerrilla unit allegedly fought it out with a Red Army division in Tartu district. In October 1946 the forest brotherhood occupied the townlet of Kilingi-Nõmme in southwest Estonia. October Revolution celebrations in that area were blocked by guerrilla posters threatening to blow up the buildings. Collaborators were forced to turn in their Communist Party or Komsomol (Communist Youth) cards and to go easy in their jobs, or give them up under threat of death. Giving in to the guerrilla threats could mean arrest by the

---

[25] Heine, pp. 66-75; Purre, "Teine punane," p. 37; J. Vēvers, *Indīgas saknes* (Riga, 1970); Ādolfs Šilde, *Važu rāvēji* (Stockholm, 1960), p. 102, and *Resistance Movement in Latvia* (Stockholm, 1972), p. 9; A. Pork, "Na strane zavoevanii Oktiabria," *Kommunist Estonii*, 1967/12, p. 10. For further Soviet views, see Rein Taagepera, "Soviet Documentation on the Estonian Pro-Independence Guerrilla Movement, 1945-1952" [henceforth cited as "Guerrilla"], JBS, X/2 (Summer 1979), pp. 91-106.

[26] *Eesti NSV ajalugu*, III, pp. 588 and 592; Purre, "Teine punane," pp. 35-38.

Soviets. The population faced double terror regardless of their personal preferences. *The History of the Estonian SSR* says "several hundred Soviet people were killed" by the guerrillas in 1948 and early 1949, although "the backbone of banditism was broken by the end of 1946." Hence close to 1,000 collaborators must have been murdered in Estonia from 1944 to 1952.[26]

The Decline of the Guerrilla Movement

The occupation regime countered the national guerrilla movement with overwhelming brute force, coupled with sophisticated political measures to drive a wedge between the guerrillas and at least a part of the population. Defending themselves against brute force kept the guerrillas so busy that they lost the political struggle through default without even noticing it.

The Kremlin's dispatch of top cadres to organize repression indicates the seriousness with which it viewed the guerrilla challenge to the Soviet occupation. Beria's deputy and successor Sergei Kruglov was placed in charge of NKVD operations in Lithuania. In July 1944 he was assigned the special troops which during the preceding month had carried out the deportation of the Crimean Tatars. In September, he urged them to abandon their "sentimental approach," to shoot unarmed people who try to run, and to burn farms and villages in which such people take refuge.[27]

The forces massed to break the Lithuanian guerrilla activity in 1948 included at least 70,000 MVD and MGB troops. The eight regular Red Army divisions, as well as some Air Force units stationed in Lithuania, were also sometimes used against the guerrillas. To these figures it is necessary to add the locally-formed militia, which often proved unreliable, as well as "special extermination squads" consisting of Lithuanian Komsomol members commanded by Russian MGB officers. In 1948, some 300 such groups involving about 7,000 individuals were active. Losses by repression forces have been estimated to 20,000 by the Soviets and to 80,000 by the guerrilla sources.[28] During 1950–51, repression was handled by the MVD 2nd and 4th Special Task Divisions, from which many soldiers and officers deserted in disgust. On a smaller scale, the pattern was similar in Latvia and Estonia. During deportations, election campaigns, and major forest searches, massive repression forces could be concentrated, including Russian units temporarily brought in from Russia and Poland, while

---

[27] Testimony to the U.S. Congress by former Soviet Border Guard Colonel Burlitski, in *Fourth Interim Report of the Select Committee on Communist Aggression* (1954); also reproduced in *Lituanus*, VIII/1–2 (1962), pp. 52–55.
[28] Remeikis 1962, pp. 32–33; Tauras, pp. 50 and 77; Weller, *Chicago Daily News*, 17 August 1961.

guerrilla units had little mobility beyond the district level. Most casualties occurred in small-scale raids and searches.

Provocateurs were trained by a special MVD school in Vilnius to infiltrate the guerrilla groups and locate their civilian supporters. In 1946, whole pseudo-guerrilla bands were formed to plunder and murder civilians in an effort to prove that the guerrillas were bandits. Soviet sources confirm the use of fake guerrilla groups to catch the real ones. In response to such tactics, some guerrilla units assigned newcomers to execute local collaborators.[29]

Mass deportations of the civilian population in guerrilla-frequented areas affected guerrilla activity severely. They lost not only potential recruits but also their all-important food-supply system, and the remaining population was scared away from supporting the forest brothers. Soviet Baltic literature contains descriptions of entire grown-over villages where not a single farm-hand remained after the "kulaks" had been deported for supplying the guerrillas, but as has been mentioned, deportations also back-fired by forcing people to flee to the forest.

Amnesties to guerrillas were repeatedly offered. In Estonia the offers in October 1944 and Spring 1945 were followed by two more, but the Soviets destroyed their effect by deporting most returnees after a few months of showcasing. Only the fifth amnesty, in 1955, was to be largely genuine. In Lithuania the occupation forces invited the clergy to join the 1945 and 1946 surrender appeals, but spoiled the show by arresting bishops. The 1946 amnesty proclamation threatened to deport families of guerrillas and passive-resistance members, and announced that people who did not report guerrilla bunkers on their property would be tried as bandits.

The Soviet land redistribution (described in the next section) presented the forest brotherhood with its most sophisticated political challenge. Redistribution pitted those who lost against those who received land. The latter now had an apparent economic stake in continuation of the Soviet regime (as long as collectivization was soft-pedalled), in conflict with their national and, in Lithuania, religious feelings. Land-losers were motivated to join the guerrillas, and tilted the guerrilla policy, at least in Lithuania. "The resistance came out strongly against this land reform. . . . This was exactly what the Soviet regime desired. First of all, the Soviet regime expected to create a 'class struggle' with the land reform, and partly succeeded."[30]

The power for positive action was in Soviet hands. Opposition to

---

[29] Remeikis 1962, p. 38; Tauras, p. 79; *Noorte Hääl*, 30 March 1957 and following issues, as reported by Purre in "Teine punane," p. 37; Heine, p. 73.
[30] Remeikis 1962, p. 37.

every Soviet measure may have looked supremely patriotic at first, but as the years went by, it became indistinguishable from social obstructionism. The Soviet viewpoint, spread massively through schools, newspapers, and meetings, may have been largely discounted, but even minor successes outweighed the meager information flow by the guerrillas. At the Soviet regime endured, more and more people came to believe that stable jobs and careers were better assured by collaboration. As more people collaborated, more became targets of guerrilla counter-terror, with a pro-Soviet effect on the victims' families. More people joined the Komsomol and the Soviet militia. As the outlook for guerrilla triumph (with Western help) faded, their national-liberation aura was increasingly transformed into an image of rebels who hit and ran, leaving the civilian population to face the wrath of those in power. People were tired of living between two terrorisms.

The deportation and collectivization drive of 1949 (discussed in a later section) gave the guerrilla war its last Pyrrhic boost. A new wave of escapees flowed into the forest, but the guerrilla supply-system was wrecked. Even worse, their relations with the farm population received a new antagonistic turn. Voluntary donations by farmers were replaced by raids on collectivized cattle and grain which the guerrillas blithely considered Soviet property. The peasants, however, were still forced to try to survive and to meet the unrelenting state-delivery norms. By raiding stores, the guerrillas felt they robbed only the illegal Soviet state; but the civilian population was left without scarce consumer goods. Increasingly reduced to struggle for their personal subsistence, the Freedom Fighters started to fit the "bandit" label the occupation forces tried to pin on them.

By 1949, the Lithuanian guerrilla groups could no longer paralyze the functioning of local Soviets. In Latvia and Estonia this ability had been largely lost by the end of 1946. By the end of 1949 the Latvian guerrilla resistance was largely crushed, although even in February 1950 a battle near Okte in Courland is said to have involved some 50 guerrillas. In Estonia, fighting continued well into 1953.[31]

Lithuanian guerrilla numbers fell to 5,000 by the end of 1950 and to 700 by the end of 1952, when unified command ended after calling for "demobilization" in favor of passive resistance. Most remaining guerrillas re-entered civilian life with forged documents,

---

[31] Jānis Rutkis (ed.), *Latvia: Country and People* (Stockholm, 1967), pp. 260 and 275; Šilde 1972, pp. 12–13. Armed underground activities in Estonia were, according to the ESSR KGB chief Ado Pork, largely crushed by early 1953; see Pork, p. 11.

and many made use of the 1955 amnesty. A 1956 amnesty offer indicated some continuing guerrilla existence.[32] Isolated arrests and executions continued into the late 1950s and even much later. A typewritten guerrilla prayerbook dated 1956 was on display at the Vilnius Museum of the History of Religion and Atheism in 1968. The capture of a guerrilla group was reported in *Tiesa* in 1961. As late as 1978 a guerrilla survivor, August Sabe, drowned rather than surrender in the south Estonian woods. The last leader of the Lithuanian movement, Adolfas Ramanauskas-Vanagas, was arrested and murdered in 1956.[33]

It seems that Western interest in Baltic guerrilla activity rose during the Korean War, but it was too late. The forest brotherhood was disillusioned with the West, literally sick of living years in the forest, facing a tired and decimated population, outwitted politically, and — above all — outgunned by vastly superior occupation forces.

Successful guerrilla fighting requires both extensive popular support and foreign supply and rest bases. In the 1970s, the world observed the sudden collapse of the rugged and widely popular Kurdish guerrilla effort in Iraq the moment Iranian support was withdrawn. The Baltic guerrilla movement received from the West nothing beyond a few dozen liaison men and their handguns. It is pointless to ask why it failed, in the face of such heavy odds. Its persistence for 8 years defies imagination, even with obviously extensive popular support.

Land Redistribution and Taxation

Land redistribution received high priority on the Soviet agenda. Given their overall shaky hold over the countryside after the war, the Soviets had to reassure owners of middle-sized farms that their property was safe. They also had to distribute the land of large farms among peasants with little or no land in order to build up a group with a vested interest in the new regime.

The 30-hectare upper limit on farm size imposed in 1941 was reasserted, with a new stipulation: this allotment could be reduced to 20 ha., "taking into account the quality of the soil and the situation of the land."[34] The farmsteads of "active supporters" of

---

[32] *Sovetskaia Litva*, 22 March 1956.
[33] Žymantas, p. 45; Tauras, p. 96; *Sōnumid*, no. 71 (March 1979), pp. 3–5; Remeikis 1962, p. 39. Guerrilla prayerbook was seen by R. Misiunas.
[34] Pranas Zundė, "Lithuania's Economy: Introduction of the Soviet Pattern," in Vardys (ed.), *Lithuania Under the Soviets*, p. 145; Jānis Labsvīrs, *A Case Study in the Sovietization of the Baltic States: Collectivization of Latvian Agriculture* (Ph.D. diss., University of Indiana, Bloomington, 1959), p. 64; Edgar Tõnurist *(ed.), Eesti NSV Põllumajanduse kollektiviseerimine* (Tallinn, 1978), p. 48.

the German occupation were cut to 5–7 ha. As in many other areas of Soviet legislation, the definition allowed flexible interpretation. Even those who had fulfilled German requisition norms under threat of execution could, if it suited officials, fall into the collaborator category. All refugeeş to the West apparently were declared "traitors to the fatherland," and their farms were redistributed. From mid-1945 on, similar treatment was applied to supporters of the guerrilla resistance.

The result of such measures was the creation of state-land funds which were considerably larger than those in 1940. The Latvian state-land fund increased from 875,252 ha. in 1940 to over 1,500,000 in 1944. According to 1948 statistics, the Lithuanian state-land fund consisted of 1,575,094 ha., and it included about one-third of the republic's farm implements: 33,400 horses, 55,600 cattle, 126,600 farm machines, 116,400 farm buildings, and 47,200 farmsteads; 96,330 recipients received 688,466 ha. of land. In all, 17,133 horses, 24,238 cattle, 50,162 farm machines, 60,565 farm buildings, and 26,095 farmsteads were given out to smallholders *and* to their cooperatives. Presumably, the rest went to state farms.[35]

In practice, however, the redistribution worked slowly because, for a variety of reasons, there were initially few applicants among the landless and small farmers. Some plainly disliked Russian rule, felt that the Soviets had no legitimate authority to carry out land redistribution, and saw in it a device to divide-and-rule the countryside. Others knew that this was how the situation was perceived by the previous owners, who were ready to work retribution on those who accepted land from the conquerors. While expropriation was formally carried out in 1945, redistribution was slower. In Latvia, 42% of the land fund remained undistributed by the end of 1945. In Estonia, 32% remained so even by July 1947, when the program was declared completed. In Lithuania, the process continued into 1948, and 19% remained undistributed.[36]

Implementation of the land-reform measures was also accompanied by creation of a "socialist sector" in the countryside consisting of state farms, MTS (machine-tractor stations), and MKPP (machine-horse-renting points). Established on sequestered larger farms, these ostensibly sought both to serve as examples of large-scale mechanized cultivation and to provide traction power for the newly-established smallholder farms. During the period of 1944–46, 41 state farms, 50 MTS, and 445 MKPP appeared in

---

[35] *Istoriia Latviiskoi SSR*, III, pp. 503 and 594; *Tarybų Lietuvos valstietija*, p. 80.
[36] Labsvīrs, p. 66; Tõnurist, p. 134; Pranas Zundė, "Die Kollektivierung der Landwirtschaft Sowjetlitauens," AB, II (1962), p. 99.

Latvia. The figures for Lithuania were 101, 58, and 279; for Estonia, 70, 24 and 240. Official complaints about the low profitability levels of the state farms and the poor functioning of the MTS suggest that their impact on the countryside at this time was minimal. The MTS were hampered by a lack of tractors; in 1946, only 1.5% of the total arable land in Estonia was worked by the republic's MTS. At the end of 1945, the 48 Lithuanian MTS possessed a mere 342 tractors, and the 50 stations in Latvia had 400 tractors.[37]

Equality of farmsteads was not among Soviet goals. Soviet analysts agree that the express purpose of redistribution was a parcelling out of the land in unviably small patches:

> By redistributing land and other means of production . . . the
> ECP agrarian policy, including land reform, did not aim at all at a
> blooming of individual small farms. . . . Already by 1947 the wide
> masses of the working peasantry in the Estonian SSR could
> convince themselves through their own experience that their
> individual farms would not enable them to reach a prosperous and
> cultured life.[38]

The initial strategy for supplying such experience consisted of gradually increasing taxes and obligatory deliveries. Nonetheless, the farmers did relatively well in 1946-47. Obligatory farm-product deliveries were not as sharply differentiated as they had been in 1941, and were light compared to those in force toward the end of the German occupation. The amounts represented about one-fifth of a farmer's produce, and were generally delivered early and completely in order to avoid further trouble with the authorities. Plenty remained for farm consumption (including guerrilla needs) and for the free market in the cities, where a sellers' market prevailed — especially in Estonia, where local inhabitants had to compete with hundreds of wholesale speculators from Leningrad. In addition to black-market industrial goods, many farmers with new land needed money to pay high interest on state loans for construction and inventory purchases. A major rural nuisance consisted of swarms of beggars from Russia ("the bagmen," as they were called in Estonia), who were inclined to steal anything and at times even murdered whole farm families.

Soviet land redistribution had by 1947 cut many farms to economically inefficient size, and created new ones that were

---

[37] Mačiuika 1963, pp. 141-142; *Tarybų Lietuvos valstietija*, p. 85. There are some minor discrepancies in the data presented in these works.
[38] Ervin Kivimaa, "Eesti NSV Põllumajanduse kollektiviseerimine aastail 1947-1950," in Edgar Tõnurist (ed.), *Sotsialistliku põllumajanduse areng Nõukogude Eestis* (Tallinn, 1976), p. 71.

purposely so small that they could not flourish. The "policy of restricting and expelling the kulaks" made doubly sure that efficient private farming would become impossible. People somehow continued to belong to the wealthy *"kulak"* category even after their farms were cut to size and paid labor was prohibited. State credit (i.e., the only credit available) was denied to them. They were forced out of voluntary agricultural cooperatives, a heritage of independence time which flourished, in contrast to western Belorussia and Ukraine, in the postwar Baltic republics. In late 1947,

> an offensive through taxation policy . . . undermined prosperous farms and demonstrated to wide peasant masses, also including medium farmers, that the past traditional road to prosperity was permanently blocked, that the Soviet regime follows a firm course toward liquidation of exploitive households.[39]

For the average "kulak," income tax was 40% of his estimated income in 1947 and 75% the following year. The income estimates tended to be on the high side, so that "the total taxes started to surpass the money income of the kulaks." Taxes on other farms also went up steeply — to about 35% of estimated income in 1948, for larger farms, and close to 30% even for the small ones.[40] For example, a 5-ha. farm in Lithuania was annually assessed 60 kg of rye, 50 kg of potatoes, 200 liters of milk, 20 kg of meat, 70 eggs, and 0.5 kg of wool at exceedingly low official government-delivery prices.[41]

Confiscatory taxation was accompanied by collectivization propaganda. Whereas during the first two years of reoccupation the Soviet authorities appeared reticent to talk about collectivization, as they had been in 1940, by the end of 1946 the tone changed. Increasing space in the local press came to be devoted to discussion of collective-farm operations elsewhere in the USSR, along with glorious depictions of collective rural well-being. "Fact-finding" visits by delegations of Baltic peasants to various havens of prosperity became increasingly frequent objects of news reporting. From 1948 on, various party directives and government decrees were aimed at facilitating "spontaneous" efforts by peasants to establish *kolkhozes* (collective farms). The results were not only meager but also disconcerting to the Soviets. Contrary to

---

[39] *Ibid.*, p. 72. The remainder of this section is based mainly on Rein Taagepera, "Soviet Collectivization of Estonian Agriculture: The Taxation Phase" [henceforth cited as "Taxation"], JBS, X/3 (Fall 1979), pp. 263–282.

[40] Kulak taxes: Kivimaa, p. 83; other farmers: Zundė, "Die Kollektivierung," 1962, pp. 97 and 101; and Taagepera, "Taxation," p. 276.

[41] Mačiuika 1963, p. 139.

ideological presuppositions, some of the larger farmers were more willing than the smaller ones to join kolkhozes, hoping thereby to escape high taxes and the deportation-prone label of "kulak."

Collectivization of agriculture was carried out according to a unified pattern and timetable not only throughout the three Baltic republics, but also throughout all western areas annexed by the USSR in 1939-1944. The percentage of Baltic, Moldavian, and western Belorussian and Ukrainian farms collectivized grew in a similar way, with a very sharp increase in 1949. Policies visibly formulated in Moscow were little adjusted to local conditions and moods. The same periodization thus applies throughout this area:

> softening the ground for collectivization through taxation (1944-48)
> deportation-induced mass collectivization (1949-50)
> completion and consolidation (1951-53)

The first postwar kolkhozes were formed in Latvia in November 1946, in Lithuania by February 1947, and in Estonia in September. Meanwhile, Moscow issued a short decree on collectivization in the Baltic republics on 21 May 1947. It first told the Baltic lieutenants that "no hurry must be shown; no extensive plans must be made regarding this endeavor; the kolkhozes must be created on a completely voluntary basis." Then, in a masterful turnabout, it "recommended" that the Baltic lieutenants hand in detailed plans within twelve days. They did. Nonetheless, progress was slow. Published Soviet documentation shows extreme reluctance by most farmers. Even among the party members, 67% in Estonia were not yet collectivized in January 1949. Most kolkhoz chairmen were appointed from outside the village, and the process was rigidly centralized and run from the cities.[42]

Advances made were achieved mainly through the confiscatory tax squeeze: the percentage of farms collectivized tended to be higher in districts where the normal (non-kulak) taxes were higher. Rich farmers' counterpropaganda, which is stressed by Soviet accounts, did not seem to have an effect: if anything, collectivization advanced faster in districts with a larger percentage of farms classed as kulak. Thousands of farmers (medium and kulak) were unable to pay their taxes and saw their farm tools auctioned away.

---

[42] CPSU CC decree on the formation of kolkhozes in the Lithuanian, Latvian, and Estonian SSRs, 21 May 1947. Full text in *Resheniia partii i pravitelstva po khoziaistvennym voprosam v piati tomakh*, III (Moscow, 1968), pp. 427-428; also in Tõnurist 1978, p. 239. On party members' not joining kolkhozes: Evald Laasi, *Eestimaa Kommunistlik Partei ellu viimas V.I. Lenini kooperatsiooniplaani, 1944-1950* (Tallinn, 1980), p. 157.

Thousands of others liquidated their households, abandoned the land, and fled to the cities. Cattle slaughter took on massive proportions, despite fines ten times the value of the cattle.

Farmers had accurate information about the miserable life on long-standing Russian kolkhozes, and most of them tried to postpone for as long as possible a capitulation which by that time must have looked inevitable in the long run. As 1949 started, only 3.9% of the Lithuanian and 5.8% of the Estonian farms were collectivized; in Latvia the figure was around 8%.[43] Due to tax pressures, the percentage was starting to rise relatively rapidly (to 8.2% in Estonia by 20 March), and collectivization could be expected to be fairly complete in a few years, with no new types of pressure needed. Nonetheless, more brutal methods were introduced.

Collectivization Through Deportation

The decisive stage of Soviet rural rearrangement started at the end of March 1949 when, in the words of a Soviet scholar, Ervin Kivimaa,

> The collectivization process acquired a massive character.
> Peasants joined by entire villages and townships. It coincided with the liquidation of the kulaks as a class, by methods . . . similar to those which had been used in the older Soviet republics: expropriation and deportation.[44]

In a few days after 20 March 1949, about 60,000 individuals were deported from Estonia and at least 50,000 from Latvia. In Lithuania, where 70,000 had been deported in late 1947 and another 70,000 on 22 May 1948, 40,000 joined the earlier groups on 24–27 March 1949 and another 40,000 in Summer. During the last ten days of March 1949, the Baltic nations lost about 3% of their native populations.[45]

---

[43] *Lietuvos TSR istorija*, IV, p. 206; Taagepera, "Taxation," p. 265; also calculations based on Carson, pp. 530–531, and Walter Hanchett, "The Communists and the Latvian Countryside, 1919–1949," in Adolf Sprudzs and Armins Rusis (eds.), *Res Baltica* (Leyden, 1968), p. 109.

[44] Kivimaa, p. 85.

[45] Most of this section is based on detailed analysis of Soviet documentation, in Rein Taagepera, "Soviet Collectivization of Estonian Agriculture: The Deportation Phase," *Soviet Studies*, XXXII/3 (July 1980), pp. 379–397. The number of Estonian deportees is based on a decrease in the number of inhabited farms (about 20,000, from 20 March to 5 April) which can be calculated from Soviet data, e.g., in Kivimaa, p. 87, or Tõnurist 1978, pp. 521 and 568. This number agrees with a figure of 80,000 people on the deportation list, as leaked from the Soviet Estonian Trade Union Council. Of these, about 20,000 escaped into the forests. The Latvian figure is a very conservative estimate reported in King, p. 83. It can be calculated from data in Carson, pp. 530–531, that the number of inhabited farms decreased by about 30,000. The Lithuanian estimates for 1949 are also based

Preparations had begun in late 1948. In December, numerous Communist Party and Komsomol members received special training in secret. Many of them were postwar immigrants. In January 1949, they were sent throughout the countryside to "enlarge" kulak lists, to prepare deportation schedules, and to find suitable candidates for kolkhoz chairmen. During the Spring months of 1949, the number of Communists in the rural areas of Lithuania almost tripled. The Lithuanian CC and its district committees sent over 1,050 party members into the countryside.[46] The actual deportations were carried out with the help of special MVD troops from Russia. As a Soviet Estonian newspaper put it: "When collectivization started in our country, the Russian working class gave tens of thousands of its best representatives, who helped to create a new happy life in our villages."[47]

Although a background of wealth was not an absolute requisite for inclusion in kulak lists, it helped. According to official definition, only kulaks objected to any aspect of Soviet farm policy or practice; therefore, any farmer who displeased Soviet authorities was a kulak. Moreover, the criteria of wealth referred only to the past; land reform had reduced all farms to 30 ha. or less. Some kulaks now owned 5-7 ha. Laws against hired labor were also applied retroactively, cutting a wide and arbitrary swath into villages where even small farms occasionally used to employ some hired help. The Lithuanian CC definition of "kulak" issued on 12 December 1947 included seven categories of farms:

1. Those which employed agricultural workers or craftsmen for pay in either cash or goods
2. Those which had employed hired help during the German occupation
3. Those which had taken in unpaid outsiders as "members of the family"
4. Those which systematically employed seasonal help
5. Those which rented out animals or equipment
6. Those which owned any complex machinery
7. Those which systematically purchased agricultural goods for resale[48]

---

on a decrease in the number of farms: 12,000 from 1 January to 1 April, and another 12,000 from 1 July to 1 October, as can be calculated from *Lietuvos TSR istorija*, IV, p. 206. The Summer deportation seems to have occurred in July (Remeikis 1962, p. 38, even says June), and by I October many emptied farms would have found new occupants — see specific case in Taagepera, "Guerrilla," p. 101.

[46] Mačiuika 1963, p. 154, based on A. Sniečkus in *Pravda*, 21 July 1949.

[47] *Rahva Hääl*, 30 December 1952.

[48] Zundė 1965, pp. 148-149, based on Gregorauskas, p. 137; Tõnurist 1978, p. 231, has the text of a similar decree by the ESSR Council of Ministers, 30 August 1947.

The categories were similar in Latvia and Estonia.

The first kulak lists had been compiled in 1945. Under pressure from higher authority, these were gradually expanded. The last drastic revision was carried out in early 1949 by outsiders, in preparation for the deportations — haphazardly, frequently on the spur of the moment, and with quotas to fill. In a 17 January letter to Stalin, ECP First Secretary Karotamm said there were 5,500 kulak and German-collaborator farms in Estonia,[49] but nine weeks later the number of inhabited farms dropped by at least 19,000. Many people on the final deportation list must not have fitted the official criteria for kulak — otherwise they would have been found out and listed much earlier. By 1949, all the formal criteria applied solely to the past, anyway. The only property which had not been confiscated was the kulaks' possibly higher education and spirit of initiative. In the case of younger children, the kulak label applied to the time before their birth. A regime which did not recognize hereditary wealth applied hereditary criteria of guilt. An entire population category was destined to slow extinction in the Siberian woods. Whether this was genocide depends on a definition of the term.

A report by a township CP secretary describes the deportation in the following terms, a week later:

> Following the [party] meeting, the deportation of kulaks and of
> German collaborators in the Ruusmäe township was carried out.
> Altogether it was planned to send away 13 families. Sent away: 8
> families, 31 persons in total. Five families who had been listed for
> deportation had fled from home. Most of those families of
> German collaborators who were not listed for deportation also
> had fled from home. Of these, Tigane and Minnat have not
> returned up to this time. The rest have returned. Four explanation
> meetings have been carried out.[50]

The farmer and his family typically were only told, often in the middle of the night, that they were to "settle elsewhere." They had to pack their things in ten minutes to two hours, depending on how heavy the deporter's schedule happened to be. Trucks took them to railway stations where they were packed into cattle wagons with barred windows. The destination apparently was western Siberia (Novosibirsk) or northern Kazakhstan (Semipalatinsk). About a quarter of the people on the deportation list managed to avoid the

[49] ECP CC First Secretary's report to the Chairman of the USSR Council of Ministers, J. V. Stalin, 17 January 1949. Full text in Tõnurist 1978, pp. 489–494.
[50] A report (31 March 1949) by Secretary Shilkin of the Ruusmäe township party organization in Võru district, Estonia; partly reproduced by Tõnurist 1978, pp. 523–524.

dragnet by hiding in the forests until the chase was over.

After one-tenth of Latvian and Estonian farmers had been deported, the remainder decided voluntarily to collectivize. In Latvia, the percentage of farms collectivized jumped from about 11% on 12 March to more than 50% on 9 April. In Estonia it rose from 8% to 64% within a month (20 March to 20 April), according to detailed Soviet data. By the end of the year, 93% of the Latvian and 80% of the Estonian farms were collectivized. This speed exceeded by far the projections of the party and the rate of Soviet collectivization in 1929. In Lithuania the process was slower. By the end of June the figure was 34%, and new deportations occurred. Even by the end of 1949, a figure of only 62% had been reached. It is possible to attribute the slower rate to guerrilla activity. In the Varėna district, for instance, only 3% of all farms had been collectivized by 1950. The surrounding forests were guerrilla strongholds. There was a similar delay in the southeast Estonian guerrilla stronghold of Haanja, which was only 30% collectivized by July 1950. However, it should be noted that western Belorussia also reached 60% only by mid-1950, and there is no indication of extensive guerrilla activity in that region.[51]

Soviet and Western historians now seem to agree that deportation started a stampede into kolkhozes, but there is disagreement regarding the motives. Were farmers afraid of being deported unless they joined? Or were they, as claimed by Soviet historians, eager to join kolkhozes the moment they were freed from the threats and scare stories spread by the "kulaks"? The very suddenness of the rush argues strongly against the liberation-from-pressure scenario. The strongest physical threats against collectivization would have come not from farmers still living on their farms, but from the guerrillas, whose strength was affected by deportation only indirectly and slowly. As for scare stories regarding kolkhozes, their effect could not have vanished within a few weeks after deportation of presumed propagators, especially since they were supported by factual knowledge about "the difficult situation of the USSR agriculture as a whole and by the peasantry's fairly deep attachment to their small property."[52] Moreover, the previously wealthy farmers were far from presenting a united front against collectivization: under the pressure of confiscatory taxes, many had sold out or were willing to join kolkhozes. The deportations affected not only those who retro-actively

---

[51] Taagepera 1979, "Taxation," p. 265; Carson, pp. 530-531, and calculations based on it; *Lietuvos TSR istorija*, IV, p. 206; Kivimaa, p. 88. The Estonian figures are based on extensive documentation in Tõnurist 1978.

[52] Kivimaa, p. 73.

fitted the "kulak" criteria, but also "other elements hostile to the people." The only possible explanation for the sudden panic-speed rush into kolkhozes is the fear of deportation.

After a slowdown in early 1950, collectivization of the remaining Latvian and Estonian farms speeded up in the Fall when the state deliveries and taxes became due. Taxes had been meanwhile "regulated" to confiscatory levels even for small farms. By the end of 1950, only 4% of Latvian and 8% of Estonian individual farms survived. In December 1951, 98.4% of Latvian farms were collectivized. Throughout the process, the smaller farmers and recent land recipients showed the most reluctance to join, or the most ability to avoid joining. In the words of a district supervisor's report:

> The greatest activity and rush into the kolkhozes is shown by the medium peasants; the farmhand and the poor peasant are slower to join.[53]

This observation, which goes against conventional wisdom, is borne out by statistical analysis: the average sown area of Estonian farms remaining private decreased from 6.2 ha. in 1948 to 4.4 ha. in 1950, and to 2.5 ha. in 1951.

In Lithuania, the collectivization process was appreciably slower than in Latvia or Estonia, and came almost to a halt in Spring 1950. Even by July 1950, 27% of farms were still private; but the figure dropped steeply to 11% by the end of the year, possibly due to new deportations.[54]

Meanwhile, several hundred thousand deportees, who had left on short notice with scant baggage, were cut off from their homeland and had to adapt to new surroundings and a new language. There were no native-language books, newspapers, or schools. Most often there was a dire lack of food and shelter. Many, and possibly more than half, died of cold and hunger. Families were systematically torn asunder. Men typically were sent to labor camps, ranging from coal mines in Karaganda (Kazakhstan) and Vorkuta (beyond the Arctic Circle) to lumber camps throughout Siberia. Women and children typically were brought to Siberian

---

[53] Control Brigade member M. Dorogov, report to N. Karotamm (October 1948), reproduced in Tõnurist 1978, pp. 411–412, translated in Taagepera, "Taxation," p. 277. Statistics in this paragraph are based on *Eesti NSV ajalugu*, III, pp. 583 and 586; Kivimaa, p. 87; and *25 aastat Nõukogude Eestit: statistiline kogumik* (Tallinn, 1965) [henceforth cited as *25 aastat*], pp. 49–50.

[54] On 1 April 1950, 71.9% of Lithuanian farms were collectivized, on 1 July the figure was 72.8% and on 1 January 1950 it was 89.1%, according to *Lietuvos TSR istorija*, IV, p. 208, and *Mažoji lietuviškoji tarybinė enciklopedija*, II (Vilnius, 1968), p. 177.

kolkhozes and left to fend for themselves: to build cave-like earthen huts, try to tear up ground to grow food, and to survive somehow until this miserable crop ripened.[55]

Stalin's lieutenants in the Baltic area were concerned with nominating supervisors for the kolkhozes, establishing a system of political propaganda on the new units, and reading reports. The pressing economic issues resulting from the switch to collective farming received little attention. Local farmers with some organizational experience had been largely deported. The pre-war voluntary cooperatives which had successfully operated until 1949 had been totally dismantled instead of being utilized for gradually increasing cooperation. Terse orders from Moscow "paralyzed local initiative and creative attitudes toward building up the kolkhozes," and official denial of the "principle of material interest" as an incentive for farmers made the situation "rather difficult."[56] Production decreased, and along with it the farmers' standard of living.

The human and economic costs of collectivization can only be estimated. A 1970 prize-winning Soviet Estonian novel *Tondiöömaja* (*The Spook Hostel*) by Heino Kiik provides a wealth of vivid detail from those years.[57] His description of wasteful management, poor organization, and petty interference by Moscow can in a general way be said to typify conditions in all three republics. Prevented from farming individually, Baltic farmers were not allowed to form a really functioning collective either. They seem to have been kept in a halfway house gradually wrecked by order-spewing spooks from township, district, raion, oblast, republic, and Moscow offices. Some examples from *The Spook Hostel* follow.

With masterful disregard for climate, Estonian kolkhozes in 1949 were ordered to start deliveries to the state before normal harvesting time, so as not to fall behind the more southerly Latvia.

---

[55] See, e.g., eyewitness descriptions by Maria Jürimäe, as written down by Johannes Kaup, *Hauatagune Siber* (New York, 1963); and by Barbara Armonas, as told to A. L. Nasvytis, *Leave Your Tears in Moscow* (Philadelphia, 1961). A condensed version of the Armonas experience appeared as "A Brave Woman's Ordeal in Siberia," *Life*, L (28 April 1961), pp. 84–88. Camps with Baltic prisoners have been described in some detail by Ādolfs Šilde, *The Profits of Slavery* (Stockholm, 1958).

[56] Kivimaa, p. 90.

[57] Heino Kiik, *Tondiöömaja* (Tallinn, 1970); review by Ilse Lehiste, "Where Hobgoblins Spend the Night," JBS, IV/4 (Winter 1973), pp. 321–326. Some similar, though not as extensive, descriptions of Lithuania can be found in J. Avyžius, *Kaimas kryžkelėje* (Vilnius, 1964), also available in Russian translation, *Derevnia na perepute* (Moscow, 1960); the bulk of the novel, however, concerns the later 1950s.

But in 1951 they were forbidden to harvest barley which had ripened before the planned date. They also wasted critical hay-making weather on cutting reeds for "silage," which became a gooey mess, and in 1954 they had to sow corn, which does not ripen so far north. In 1951 women were forced to pick potatoes from chilly flooded fields, in disregard of health and economics, because "the state cannot allow a single hectare to remain unharvested."

City-bred district officials and kolkhoz chairmen imposed grotesque orders, with ignorance and contempt for agricultural realities. Kolkhozes were ordered to deliver teenagers for work in oil-shale mines. "Making kulaks" continued: farmers who displeased the party, or whose homes were coveted by the kolkhoz chairmen, were expelled, in spite of contrary votes by the kolkhoz general meetings, and they vanished, presumably to Siberia. The farmers eventually learned to vote in favor of every mild suggestion from higher up. They even elected total strangers for kolkhoz chairman on an hour's notice. Kolkhozes which still managed to cope with this *diabolus ex machina* show were in 1950 ordered to fuse with several failing ones, as if to ensure that failure be general.

While individual farmers paid 6,000 rubles yearly tax, the collective farmers paid only 600 rubles. But the pay per day for collective work in the kolkhoz amounted to 4 pounds of potatoes and 3 rubles (the price of a pack of cigarettes) in 1952, and to 3 kopeks (0.03 rubles) in 1953. Obligatory state deliveries amounted to confiscation: farmers received 2 kopeks per liter of milk, and could not buy a bottle of state-sold vodka for the price of a bull. State deliveries left no grain for the kolkhozes, and farmers competed with city people in buying scarce but cheap bread from city stores. One state official threatened to fire a collective farm's agronomist for using substandard seed because another had seized seed-grain for state deliveries. People (including kolkhoz chairmen) started to compare their units to the despised nineteenth-century estates of the Baltic barons. By 1952, villages looked as if they had undergone three years of warfare. Farmers avoided unpaid kolkhoz work, subsisting on their private patches and on work outside their farms. Some fled to the cities, abandoning their theoretical share of common ownership. Harvesting sometimes lasted until December; rotten grain was gathered. By the Spring of 1954, cows had to be carried out of stables. Drinking moonshine had become rampant.

This is how the Soviet Estonian novel describes this period. The truthfulness of the picture painted in the novel is confirmed by reminiscences of the participants and by statistics published later on. In the words of a kolkhoz chairman:

In Spring 1953 we gave one sturdy collective farmer the special job to lift up cows blown over by the wind. The cows were so weak they could not get up by themselves. That man got his norm days calculated on the basis of this work. Now this story makes one laugh, but then we were far from laughing.[58]

As for statistics, Table 8 shows the drastic decrease in total agricultural output and in cereal-crop yields in all three countries from 1950 to 1955. The 1950 production itself was already much below that of 1940, and probably also below that of 1948 (a year on which the Soviets have not published any data). The decrease extended to most aspects of agriculture, and took place gradually over the years. Sown area tended to decrease up to about 1958. Total grain production in Latvia dropped from 1,372,000 tons in 1940 to 732,000 in 1950, and to 436,000 tons in 1956. In Lithuania, dairy cattle dropped from a pre-war figure of 848,000 in 1939 to 504,000 in 1951 (after a major decrease during the preceding two years); there was a slight rise to 531,000 only by 1957. In Estonia, the total number of cows dropped from 294,000 in 1949 to 263,000 by 1953 and stayed at that level for many years. Milk production per collectivized cow kept steadily decreasing between 1950 and 1955, while that of private cows increased by 38%.[59]

Collective farm operations were furthermore hampered by reorganizations. The original units had generally been small, involving an average of 48 households in Latvia, 38 in Lithuania, and 34 in Estonia at the end of 1949. In accordance with a Union-wide decree of 1950, the regime began a consolidation which hit the young Baltic kolkhozes at a particularly vulnerable stage. The number of Latvian kolkhozes decreased from a peak value of 4,169 in May to 1,792 by the end of 1950; Lithuania's decreased from 6,032 to 1,795 in 1955. The number of households per kolkhoz was multiplied accordingly, and so were problems of internal work-force management.

---

[58] *Sovetskaia Estoniia*, 26 October 1963. Prices of 0.58 to 1.64 kopeks per kilogram of grain, 3.33 kopeks per liter of milk and 10 kopeks per kg of live cattle can be calculated from M. Rubin, "Varumishinnad ja kolhooside rahalised sissetulekud Eesti NSVs aastail 1950-1960," *Eesti NSV Teaduste Akadeemia Toimetised — Ühiskonnateadused*, XXX/4 (1981), pp. 350–361. The price/production-cost ratio for the Estonian kolkhozes decreased from 0.55 in 1950 to 0.46 in 1952. Rubin comments: "The obligatory sale to the state effectively represented taxation in kind, since the state was paying the kolkhozes only a symbolic price."

[59] Andrivs Namsons, "Die Umgestaltung der Landwirtschaft in Sowjetlettland," AB, II (1962), p. 75; Zundė, "Die Kollektivierung," p. 105; and calculations based on: *Eesti NSV ajalugu*, III, p. 586; *25 aastat*, pp. 53–63; and *Nõukogude Eesti saavutusi 20 aasta jooksul: statistiline kogumik* (Tallinn, 1960) [henceforth cited as *20 aasta*], pp. 41–52.

Improvements in some aspects were cancelled out by further set-backs and demoralization in others. In 1952, parents and adult children crowded under the same roof were declared to be a single household, thus reducing the total number of private cattle they could own; the excess cattle were confiscated. Calves and pigs were also collectivized, and yet every household was required to deliver 30 kg of meat annually, out of their single private cow.[60] A vicious circle formed between state demands and farmer productivity. Collective farmers who at times were not paid for their collective work for two years in a row lost virtually all interest. They con-centrated on their private patches, bringing collective farming to a nearly complete standstill.

ECONOMY AND CULTURE

Immigration and Industrialization

Reconstruction and expansion of industry were high on the Soviet priority list in the Baltic states for a series of economic and political reasons. From a pragmatic economic viewpoint, Latvia and Estonia represented a skilled-labor reserve unlike any other in the Soviet Union. They also had a very substantial physical infrastruc-ture which had not been destroyed during the war, or which could be reconstructed fairly easily compared to, say, Belorussia. The existing network of roads, factory buildings, housing, and schools could, from the Soviet viewpoint, be used more intensively. New workers could be crammed into existing apartments, and night shifts could be added to existing factories. The infrastructure was also very attractive for placement of new plants. Precisely because there had been previous development during independence, further investment was, in a sense, encouraged.

There were also non-economic reasons. Ideologically, the indus-trial proletariat was considered superior to the peasantry and was expected to be more supportive of the Soviet regime. From a colonial imperialist viewpoint, industrialization offered a path for settling large numbers of Russians among a reticent local population. At times, such colonization seems to have become a goal in itself rather than a means of industrialization. In particular, it made little economic sense to deport Baltic farmers to Siberia, and then import Russian labor to the Baltic cities.

---

[60] Labsvīrs, p. 96; Taagepera, "Taxation," p. 265; Carson, p. 531; Arnold Purre, "Kommunistlikus haardes," in *Eesti saatusaastad*, III, pp. 51–53. By law, farmers could own two cows, but in Soviet practice they were limited to one — see Tõnurist 1978, p. 89.

By early 1945, most undestroyed industrial facilities were back in operation, and "socialist competitions" between plants had started. City streets were cleared of bombing rubble, largely with the help of unpaid "Sunday sessions" by citizenry. What private industry, mostly small servicing enterprises, had existed in 1945 was nationalized by 1947. For those not affected by the continuing sporadic arrests and deportations, city life continued on a course toward postwar normalization. Food rationing was terminated by the end of 1947, but limited food supplies resulted in huge waiting lines. Also at the end of 1947, an all-Union currency reform depleted savings: 10 old rubles were exchanged for 1 new ruble, with prices remaining the same. Designed to hit speculators, the conversion hit hard at anyone with even modest savings.

By 1948, clothing and shoes seem to have become available in stores. Black markets flourished, fed by home industry, farms, thefts from state enterprises, and leaks from special stores for party members and military officers. In early 1947 a kilogram of sugar cost 250 to 300 rubles, while a schoolteacher's pay in Tallinn was 350 to 450 rubles per month. The flood of food-seeking "bagmen" from Russia decreased around 1948, and by 1951 nightly robberies in the streets became rare. Fuel supplies also improved, but firewood remained rationed and scarce at least until 1954. In the store waiting lines, Russian-Baltic conflict flared frequently.[61]

Reconstruction of war-destroyed cities was largely completed by 1950, but insufficient allowance was made for the influx from the countryside as well as for immigration from Russia. Private construction of single-family dwellings was officially encouraged, but few construction materials were available through legal channels.

In spite of the local shortage of labor, industrialization plans and investments in Latvia exceeded the USSR average. Emphasis was placed on machine-building and metalworking. Major factories were created or expanded, mostly in Riga. The Riga Electrical Machine Plant started operations in 1947, the Riga Diesel Plant in 1949. Products included electric motors (especially for electric trains), electrical apparatus for cars, various control instruments, and diesel motors. Textile fibers were expanded in Daugavpils. Lumber-cutting in 1950 surpassed that in 1938 by 55%, resulting in serious depletion of Latvia's forest reserves. Production of textile fabrics was up by 27%, and of paper by 77%. Shoe production reportedly had increased sixfold. There is no information on quality and destination; the local market continued to be short of consumer goods. By 1947, total industrial production reportedly

[61] Purre, "Teine punane," pp. 26-27; Endel Kareda, *Estonia in the Soviet Grip* (London, 1949), pp. 59-65 and 74-80.

surpassed that of Soviet Latvia in 1940 by 28%. However, judging from data in natural production units, the 1937 level was not yet reached in 1947. The explanation of this discrepancy may lie in that the 1940 comparison figures refer, literally, to *Soviet* Latvia, and Latvia did not become a Soviet republic until August of that year. Thus "Soviet Latvia" in 1940 existed for less than five months. An index pegged to the production of the whole calendar year 1940 would be 5/12, or roughly 40% of the index pegged to Soviet Latvia of 1940. The same observation applies to Lithuania, which for 1950 claimed a 91% increase over the 1940 figures, as well as to Estonia.[62] But regardless of such index games, Baltic industry surpassed its pre-war level by a wide margin rather rapidly (see Table 7).

In Lithuania, emphasis was also on heavy industry. However, whereas industrialization was conducted at twice the all-Union rate in Latvia and Estonia, it remained below the all-Union level in postwar Lithuania, in terms of capital investment. The intense resistance and extent of guerrilla opposition may have been responsible in part. Lithuania's weaker industrial base may also have led industrial planners to favor Latvia and Estonia, where investment would yield tangible results in a shorter time period. Light industry and food processing continued to predominate in Lithuanian industrial production. Food processing retained its 1940 position of preeminence. However, while most other areas indicated growth in comparison with pre-war figures, Lithuania's 1950 indicators show a considerable decline. The emphasis on heavy industry meant that the food industry was not given adequate support in terms of machinery and equipment.[63]

In Estonia, the industrial working force in late 1944 was down to 52% of the pre-war 89,000. The gap was partly filled by Estonian Labor Battalions of the Red Army, and by German prisoners of war. There may have been 40,000 of the latter in Estonia, half of them in the Kohtla-Järve oil-shale region and one-quarter in Tallinn. There were also civilian prisoners, including women from the Baltics, Russia, Poland, and, after 1948, from Czechoslovakia. Postwar per-capita investment in Estonia exceeded the Soviet average by 54%, imports exceeded exports by 70%, and industrial production grew by more than 35% every year prior to 1949. Much

[62] Production data from Jānis Bokalders, "Die Industrialisierung Lettlands nach 1940," AB, II (1962), pp. 146–175. For the five-month year, see King, p. 19; Zundė 1965, p. 156; and Elmar Järvesoo, "The Postwar Economic Transformations," in Parming and Järvesoo, p. 136.

[63] Zundė 1965, p. 157; Thomas Remeikis, "Modernization and National Identity in the Baltic Republics," in Ihor Kamenetsky (ed.), *Nationalism and Human Rights: Processes of Modernization in the USSR* (Littleton, Colo., 1977), p. 116.

of the equipment initially came from dismantled plants in Germany.[64]

In Estonia, development of oil-shale products overshadowed machine-building. While oil-containing shale occurs throughout the world, it has been neglected because its energy content is less than that of coal, and its burning produces large amounts of ashes. Motivated by a desire to reduce dependence on imported coal, independent Estonia had become the world pioneer in oil-shale development. The Soviet regime continued and expanded this effort in order to supply Leningrad. Transport costs were to be reduced by gasifying the oil in the shale on the spot. The world's first shale-gas facility went partly operational in 1948, and oil-shale mining was increased at a rapid rate, largely with labor imported from Russia.

Continuing labor shortage was only temporarily eased by returning evacuees, demobilization, and prisoners. Local artisans, women, and youth were pressed into "social production," including mining and lumber work. Collectivization of agriculture in 1949 opened up another local labor pool. But the largest increase came from an influx of outsiders, mainly Russians. Some came on their own initiative, attracted by the relative wealth and well-being in the Baltic states, compared to areas under long-term Soviet control. But others were actively recruited. In the Soviet view:

> During the years of building socialism, the specific weight of other nationalities increased within the Estonian working class, but the identical interests and goals and common work linked the settlers from fraternal republics to the local workers. Both were formed into a single Soviet Estonian working class. . . . Political educational work was used in trying to help workers to free themselves from the influence of the bourgeois-nationalist propaganda.[65]

In other words, the Baltic workers themselves did not perceive those "identical interests and goals." It was an industry based on Russian investment and Russian labor, managed by Russians according to goals set by Russians, importing a large part of the raw materials from Russia, and exporting most of its product. The whole show was called "Baltic" industrial growth because the Soviets decided to run it on Baltic soil.

While the native population was decimated by deportations and guerrilla-war losses, large contingents of Russians and other non-Balts were brought in, along with Russianized Latvians and

[64] *Eesti NSV ajalugu*, III, p. 569–571; Purre, "Teine punane," pp. 40–43.
[65] *Eesti NSV ajalugu*, III, p. 577.

Estonians whose families had settled in Russia in Tsarist times. The most influential segment of Russians consisted of thousands of officials assigned to direct and supervise social and economic changes at republic, district, and commune levels. The numerically largest segment consisted of unskilled industrial labor. Some of them were voluntary immigrants, others were forced labor deported from other Soviet areas. Many of the latter were non-Russians forced to play a Russianizing role, since they tended to know some Russian, but not the local national language. Armed forces, ranging from Red Army units facing Scandinavia to MVD repression units designed for internal use only, were also numerous.

The peak influx period may have been 1945–47. But immigration continued later on, and its denationalizing effect was aggravated by depletion of the native farm population through the deportations of 1949. Collectivization pushed farmers into cities and thus reduced the need for immigration, in the short run. In the long run, however, the deportations reduced the local rural labor pool. Soviet industry in the Baltic states kept being expanded, in disregard of its denationalizing effect at best, or quite possibly with express imperial colonization in mind.

About 400,000 Russians and 100,000 people of other nationalities immigrated to Latvia from 1945 to 1959, most of them probably before 1953. This amounted to 25% of the pre-war population. Riga's population in 1951 surpassed that in 1939 by 149,000, or 43% (see Table 11), despite heavy war losses (including flight to the West) and little influx from the Latvian countryside. (Rural population decreased by 185,000, but war and deportation losses accounted for most of it.) The Latvians' share of their country's population was probably around 83% in 1945, but dropped to about 60% by 1953, due to immigration and deportations (see Tables 1 and 5).

Approximately 180,000 non-Estonians arrived in Estonia in 1945–47, and at least 33,000 more immigrants came in 1950–53, adding up to an increase of 19% over the pre-war population, or 25% of the reduced population of 1945. The share of Estonians in their country's population decreased from about 94% in early 1945 to 80% in early 1949, plunged to 77% during the 1949 deportations, and continued to slide to about 72% by 1953.

In more agricultural Lithuania, the local rural labor pool seemed to supply most of the relatively modest increase in the industrial work force. New immigrants could hardly be attracted to the countryside, especially under the conditions of continuing guerrilla resistance. Influx was hence largely limited to functionaries and the armed forces. Due to heavy guerrilla and deportation losses,

Lithuania's population probably decreased from about 3.1 million in 1940 (within postwar borders) to 2.6 million in 1953, about 75% of whom were Lithuanians.[66]

Given Soviet policies of massive labor transfer, a drastic increase in Soviet industrial production on Baltic soil was not surprising. The degree to which such output surpassed the pre-war Baltic output is unclear. The proper comparison point would be a year preceding major war disturbances, i.e., 1939 or even 1938, or an average of 1937–39. However, Soviet statistics invariably start with 1940 and, as mentioned before, many apparently take into account only the 5 last months, during which the Baltic states were technically part of the USSR. Both baselines are shown in Table 7, which compares production from 1940 to 1980. Since the product mix and relative prices were changing, the comparisons are perforce approximate. Furthermore, the 1940 baseline may not include production by small private shops. The median ratio of physical outputs in 1955 and 1940 in Estonia is around 3.7. The pre-war level of industrial production was certainly reached by 1949 in Latvia and Estonia, and by 1952 in Lithuania. By 1953 Baltic industrial employment was double the pre-war level, and industrial production showed at least as great an increase (see Table 7).

Aggregate industrial-production efficiency per worker was shown by the Soviets to have increased considerably above the pre-war level, in terms of non-market-determined prices. However, data on physical quantities tell a different story. For instance, Estonian oil-shale production per worker was 494 tons per year in 1939 and 482 in 1950.[67]

Education and Culture

The flight to the West had affected the educated Baltic elite especially strongly. Close to half of those with a higher education may have left.[68] In the short run, the losses weakened Baltic society considerably, but they also brought an unusual surge of upward

---

[66] For all three countries, see Rein Taagepera, "Baltic Population Changes, 1950-1980," JBS, XII/1 (Spring 1981), pp. 35-57. See also King, p. 92; Carson, pp. 174-175; *Narodnoe khoziaistvo Latviiskoi SSR v 1977 godu* (Riga, 1978) [henceforth cited as *Nar. khoz. LaSSR 1977*], pp. 6-8; Parming 1972, pp. 56-65; *Narodnoe khoziaistvo Estonskoi SSR v 1977 godu* (Tallinn, 1978) [henceforth cited as *Nar. khoz. ESSR v 1977*], pp. 12-16; Zundė 1965, pp. 155-169.

[67] ESSR Academy of Sciences, *Töös'use ja ehituse ökonoomika küsimusi*, I (Tallinn, 1959), p. 6.

[68] The percentages appear to have varied considerably, depending on the particular country and the particular profession. More writers than artists tended to leave. In Lithuania, 637 physicians and 221 dentists remained in 1946, out of a prewar total of 1,446 and 686, respectively, according to Mačiuika 1963, p. 90; this decrease may involve an appreciable number of Jews murdered by the Nazis.

mobility and thus resulted, in the long run, in a rejuvenation of the elite. This effect was most pronounced in educational and cultural fields, where the need to know the national language prevented an injection of Russians, and where even the Russianized Balts from the pre-war USSR prominent in Latvia and Estonia were at a disadvantage. In economic and technological fields, the gap left by the refugees offered Moscow a welcome opportunity to introduce outsiders.

Schools started to reopen in October 1944, largely using the existing non-Soviet-trained teachers. Some textbooks printed during the German occupation were temporarily accepted. Those published during Baltic independence were banned immediately, though some nevertheless had to be used initially. By the beginning of 1945, most grade schools had reopened (although heating remained a problem), and new textbooks had been printed. But one-third of the teaching staff had no pedagogical training. Of those teachers who had not fled, "many were scared and took an apolitical, sometimes even an hostile attitude toward the Soviet regime."[69] The Soviet response was reeducation of existing teachers, bringing in teachers from other parts of the USSR, and a gradual introduction of new local teachers, trained according to the Soviet pattern. By its very nature, such a process had to be gradual in all three republics.

The Komsomol and the Pioneers (Communist youth organizations) became an integral part of the school system. In at least some schools, youngsters were forced to attend classes preparing them for the Pioneer oath. Strong-arm tactics were sometimes used to make them take that oath, but initial results were meager. At times, children's clothing, which was extremely scarce, was made available through the Komsomol. By the Summer of 1946, about 15% of Estonia's students had joined the Komsomol or the Pioneers. The figures were hardly higher in the other two republics. However, by 1950, 28% of Lithuanian and 44% of Estonian students had joined.[70]

Higher education suffered most from faculty flight to the West.[71] Vacant posts had to be filled by assistants and gymnasium teachers. The setback in quality was only temporary; the new incumbents were well-prepared and adjusted rapidly. But posts

[69] *Eesti NSV ajalugu*, III, p. 617.

[70] *Ibid.*, p. 622; A. Bendžius, *Bendrojo lavinimo ir aukštoji mokykla Lietuvoje, 1940–1970 m.* (Kaunas, 1973), p. 228; Manivald Rästas, *Tulin kodumaalt* (Lund, 1955), pp. 20–30; Jaak Survel [Evald Uustalu], *Estonia Today* (London, 1947), p. 36.

[71] At most, 35% of Tartu University's faculty remained; see tabulation in Survel, p. 38.

won by default rather than through competition left some with a persistent feeling of inadequacy. As could be expected, scholarly activities recovered more rapidly in the natural sciences than in the humanities.[72]

The Soviet system identified the goals of ideological penetration with educational training. Mass education was accordingly expanded rapidly, and the sheer number of students in general secondary, special secondary, and higher educational institutions grew rapidly. A concerted attempt was made to offer crash education and more significant roles in society to those who could never have dreamed of such within the traditional social structure. "Rabfaks" where eight years of schooling could be had in three appeared for adults who had not been able to continue their education above the primary level. Such recruitment of a fraction of the underprivileged served both to intimidate the traditional establishment and to set up a new "elite" of faithful adherents to the new order of things, inclined to see the new and unexpected opportunities before them as an embodiment of social justice. Although this process began before the German attack, it could not have had significant effect until the postwar years.[73]

Mass culture was both developed and regimented through "culture houses." Massive indoctrination courses for their directors and inspectors were soon organized. By 1948, hundreds of political, agricultural, and literary study groups had been formed. Massive song and folk-dance festivals began to be held, with an increasing number of Russian songs and dances as well as those of other republics included. Sports were also encouraged. During the late 1940s, the Soviet basketball team was largely Baltic.

Literary activity revived, but remained low. Half to two-thirds of the recognized pre-war writers had fled to the West in all three republics.[74] Those who stayed tended to remain silent. Others tried to adjust to the new demands with pitiful results, sacrificing literary quality, yet still failing to satisfy the authorities. Most of the Communist-oriented writers who had been evacuated returned after the war, but their productivity was also kept low by increasing ideological demands.

The immediate postwar period actually proved to be one of relative relaxation. From mid-1946 on, a "struggle against apolitical

[72] For a detailed picture of the immediate postwar situation at the University of Vilnius, see Tomas Venclova, "The Years of Persistence," *Lituanus*, XXVII (1981), pp. 101–108.

[73]. Aleksandras Shtromas, "The Official Soviet Ideology and the Lithuanian People," to be published.

[74] Rolfs Ekmanis, *Latvian Literature Under the Soviets, 1940–1975* (Belmont, Mass., 1978), p. 53. [This is the major English-language source for this section.]

culture" engulfed the Soviet Union. This first wave of the so-called *Zhdanovshchina* was followed in mid-1947 by a second one "against cosmopolitanism," aimed primarily against Jews. Already on 31 August 1946 the Chairman of the Latvian Council of Ministers charged that the editorial boards of the literary periodicals *Karogs* and *Literatūra un māksla* were poisoning the minds of Latvian youth: "On the pages of *Karogs* there prevails nothing but rotten and nonsensical liberalism." Lācis attacked a dozen writers by name; charges included depicting only the past, work filled with grief or sadness, and daring to exclaim that "nothing is more beautiful than love." It could have sounded funny, except that such attacks could end with deportation. In late 1949 and early 1950, the Soviet Latvian Artists Association expelled 50 members. Waves of criticism followed each other, until even the work of Lācis himself was taken to task in *Pravda* in late 1951. This overeagerness was quashed, however, and Lācis received his second Stalin Prize in five years.[75]

Much of the scarce paper was assigned to socio-political publications, and ideological requirements strangled art. Social-realist optimism became a must. A typical description of a writer's function was given in an editorial of the Lithuanian cultural weekly *Literatūra ir menas* of 24 April 1947:

> The struggle against the bourgeois nationalists, against the bourgeois nationalist ideology and its influence, struggle against the villainous kulak bandits, against the reaction of clericalism, which is doing everything it can to poison the consciousness of youth and to insinuate itself into its spirit, sharp class struggle, the rise of a new, brave, and energetic working-man, all this is a fine ideological weapon which must be given first of all to the young people by the writer.[76]

In Latvia, Jānis Plaudis was reproached for having written the poem "The Scent of Soil" without specifying that it was Soviet soil that he had in mind. When describing love between two people, authors were enjoined to make it clear to the reader that love for a person does not mean an end of love for the whole working class. Sycophantic praise of Stalin continued:

> Your name glows for us like the flaming sun,
> Like an eternal flame that calls to battle,

---

[75] Ekmanis 1978, pp. 119–122, 151, and 384; Rutkis, p. 534; *Pravda*, 14 December 1951 and 25 February 1952.
[76] Rimvydas Šilbajoris, "Socialist Realism and the Politics of Literature in Occupied Lithuania," to be published.

Hoover Institution

The fate of the Baltic states was decided on the night of 23-24 August 1939 with the conclusion of the Treaty of Non-Aggression between Germany and the USSR. The above pictures of Stalin and German Foreign Minister Ribbentrop were taken during the signing ceremony in the Kremlin in the early hours of 24 August.

Eesti riik ja rahvas teises maailmasojas

Two facets of Soviet-Estonian relations. In 1937, visiting Soviet Chief-of-Staff Marshal A. I. Egorov was welcomed in Tallinn by Estonian President K. Päts. Egorov was purged in February 1938 and is reported to have died in prison in March 1941. Päts was deported from Estonia to Ufa in July 1940. The Soviet armored car in the lower picture appeared in front of the Tallinn Central Prison on 21 June 1940 during the course of what has been described in Soviet sources as an internal uprising.

The drama of the incorporation of the Baltic states into the USSR included staged mass demonstrations to underscore popular approval of the moves. The Soviet-organized demonstration in Tallinn on 21 June 1940 is claimed to have drawn 30,000 to 40,000 participants, though this officially promulgated picture seems to indicate a considerably smaller number.

Postwar guerrilla resistance appeared in all three republics but proved most marked and prolonged in Lithuania. This photograph from 1947 shows a group of partisans from the Kęstutis [a fourteenth-century Lithuanian ruler] Unit in the Tauras Guerrilla District which covered south-west Lithuania. The men are wearing the uniform of the army of the pre-war republic. Their weapons appear to be of diverse origins.

The bronze statue "Prince Viachko of Polotsk and Lembitu's Son Meelis at the Defense of Tartu in 1224" by the Estonian sculptor O. Männi is a prominent example of Stalinist historical canon expressed in a work of art. The elder Russian brother is helping the younger Estonian resist German invaders.

Long-term Lithuanian CP First Secretary Antanas Sniečkus at the dedication ceremony in 1972 of the massive outdoor war memorial at Kryžkalnis near Raseiniai to "The Red Army, the Liberator."

The Independence Monument, a prominent pre-war landmark in the center of Riga inexplicably survived the post-war years; during that period analogous monuments in Lithuania and Estonia disappeared.

Two facets of monumental modernist architecture in the Baltic republics. The Stalin-gothic building in Riga is the only one of its kind in the area. Begun in the post-war years as a ''House of Collective Farmers'' it became the Academy of Sciences of the Latvian SSR upon its completion in 1957. The Vilnius Opera House in the lower picture was completed in 1974 after several years of construction. Both buildings are prominent in the centers of the two cities.

Housing developments have accompanied the rapid post-war urbanization and immigration. The upper photograph, taken in 1965 in Jelgava, Latvia, shows a typical development. Attempts at incorporating such complexes into the landscape have been particularly marked in Lithuania. The lower photograph shows a panoramic view of Lazdynai, a residential suburb of Vilnius, whose construction began in the late 1960s and continued into the mid-1970s.

The Soviet Union has begun to enter the automotive age and the Baltic republics are in the forefront of this development. A new eight-pump gasoline station was front page news in Soviet Estonia's main daily *Rahva Hääl* on 29 September 1972. Driving under the influence of alcohol has become and increasingly pressing problem. The lower picture, taken in the Latvian countryside during the late 1970s, shows an overturned tractor whose driver was drunk.

Soviet authorities are proud of visible evidence of industrialization. The two pictures, taken recently, show docking facilities at Ventspils, Latvia, constructed especially for the export of locally produced ammonia, a venture involving some foreign participation.

Eesti Päevaleht, Sweden

According to a 1956 Soviet geography book "enormous ash mounds up to 100 meters in height" were a typical panorama of the oil-shale region along Estonia's north coast. Such trumpeting of pollution in a positive vein has lately abated, but the mounds continue to grow, as is shown by this recent photograph.

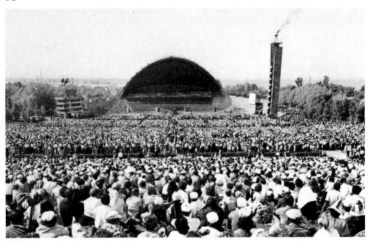

One of the visible signs of the rebirth of the national cultures of the Baltic peoples during and after the Thaw of the 1950s was the revival of the national song festivals, a tradition dating from the nineteenth century. It has been estimated that 250,000 spectators attended the 1969 Estonian Song Festival.

Public demonstration of national identity without a Soviet qualification was also noticeable during the Thaw of the 1950s. In this photo, taken at the First Spartakiad in Moscow, 1956, the Estonian participant in the center still has an earlier Russian form "ESSR" on her uniform, while the Latvian Inessa Jaunzeme on the right already sports "LATVIJA" in Latvian without the "SSR," a change emulated soon thereafter by the Estonians and Lithuanians as well.

In spite of the complaint of N. S. Khrushchev in 1961, restoration work has continued on the island fortress of Trakai, one of the capitals of the medieval Lithuanian state which had lain in ruins since the early eighteenth century. The photograph, taken in 1980, shows the restored central building.

The Church of Mary Queen of Peace in Klaipėda, Lithuania, has become a cause célèbre in Lithuanian religious dissent. Constructed between 1956 and 1962 with funds donated by Catholics from throughout Lithuania, it was confiscated by the authorities after its completion. In the summer of 1979, a petition was sent to the General Secretary of the CPSU Leonid Brezhnev with over 149,000 signatures from throughout Lithuania requesting a return of the building to its congregation. The picture on the left shows the edifice upon completion in 1962; on the right is a picture taken in 1976 after the building had been converted into the "People's Philharmonic."

Numerous churches have been converted to other uses. The photograph of the Lutheran church at Vidsmuiža, Latvia, which now serves as a grocery shop was taken in 1968 by Žanis Skudra. In 1979, he was sentenced to twelve years allegedly for transmitting military information abroad. He had given a collection of such photos to a visiting Latvian from Sweden.

The Hill of Crosses near Šiauliai, Lithuania has become a symbolic center of living Lithuanian Catholicism. In spite of persistent efforts by the authorities to weed out the crosses, new ones keep appearing on the site. According to the *Chronicle of the Catholic Church of Lithuania,* the hill has some 3,000 crosses. The upper photograph is a view from pre-war times. The middle photograph was taken during the summer of 1977. In the lower photo, the Rev. Algirdas Mocius, a former post-war deportee who has not been allowed by the authorities to serve as a parish priest and is therefore currently Altarist in Jurbarkas, Lithuania, begins a 70-kilometer cross-carrying to the Hill of Crosses on 22 June 1979.

Outward manifestations of dissent are endemic in the three republics. One such example dates from the spring of 1976 when the graffiti ''Sakharov— our conscience'' appeared stencilled in paint on Riga suburban trains.

Bishop Julijonas Steponavičius (second from left), Administrator of the Catholic Archdiocese of Vilnius, who has not been allowed to reside in his see since 1961, and Bishop Vincentas Sladkevičius (first on the left) of Kaišiadorys, who has been internally exiled since 1957, preside over the funeral on 10 April 1979 of the Reverend Karolis Garuckas, a member of the Lithuanian Helsinki Watch Committee. It is widely held that Bishop Steponavičius is the Cardinal named *in pectore,* i.e., without public revelation, by the Pope in May 1979.

On 14 May 1972, Romas Kalanta, a nineteen-year-old student in Kaunas, Lithuania, poured gasoline over himself and struck a match. The act took place in front of the theater where in 1940 the People's Assembly had staged its session to vote on incorporation into the USSR. Kalanta subsequently died in a hospital. His funeral sparked riots involving several thousand students.

The Estonian dissident Jüri Kukk died in a north Russian prison in 1981, apparently after attempted forcefeeding during a hunger strike. The family photo of the former University of Tartu lecturer in chemistry was taken in March 1980, a few days before the children last saw their father.

"Dancing in a City Square" (1972), an etching by the Estonian artist Vive Tolli, is typical of the modernism in style which has become prevalent in the artistic output of the Baltic republics. While in the course of the 1970s such art has become more frequent throughout the USSR, it was more noticeable in the Baltic republics somewhat earlier.

To all of us you are the dearest friend,
You, our conscience and our honor.[77]

As one Soviet observer later noted, while writers around 1950
supposedly sought a complete description of Soviet man,

> a tendency to smooth out many of the contradictions which life
> presents also occurred. Many superficial works were also pub-
> lished, where real conflicts were replaced by apparent and
> superficial ones, and where positive figures often suffered from
> grayness and stereotype. Vulgar sociological tendencies exerted an
> inhibitive influence.[78]

In 1949–52, literature, language, and theatrical arts faced the
pressure of increased Russification. As one apologist for the trend
observed, continuing technological development and the changing
socio-political scene required new terminology. In the past, new
words had been derived from native word-roots or borrowed from
international usage. Now Russian became the source:

> When a new term is needed which the given language does not
> have, then it must not be created anew but must be boldly taken
> from the Russian, which is the richest of languages and which in
> the Soviet Union is the international language. Enrichment of the
> vocabulary of the languages of Soviet nations with Russian words
> is perfectly natural. The influence of the Russian progressive
> culture and language enriches and develops the culture and
> languages of the other nations.[79]

Baltic writers were made to praise the master nation's tongue. In
a poem titled "People's Friendship," the roles of different nations
were strikingly disparate:

> The Russian language seems to me like a huge bridge of sunbeams
> Over which the Latvian heart will climb into high horizons.[80]

Literature, long purged of anything critical of the Soviet
occupation, now was purged of anything politically neutral or
lukewarm. Even within the politically orthodox range, any literary
techniques unfamiliar to the Stalinist leadership were denounced as
Western capitalist-formalist and bourgeois-nationalist. A look at
book covers is striking: from the contemporary European style

[77] Anna Brodele, in *Latviešu padomju dzeja* (Riga, 1952), pp. 269–270, as
translated in Ekmanis 1978, p. 164. For soil and love, see *ibid.*, pp. 122–124.
[78] *Eesti NSV ajalugu*, III, p. 642.
[79] *Bolševik*, no. 8 (1952); as reported in Purre, "Teine punane," p. 52.
[80] Janis Grots, in *Latviešu padomju dzeja*, pp. 97–98; translated in Ekmanis 1978,
p. 162.

practiced in the 1930s, Baltic book covers of the 1950s seem to be set back into the nineteenth century. So was the degree of sophistication of the contents. No Western literature could be published, not even leftists like Brecht or Neruda. Nearly all native literary groupings and trends of the twentieth century were declared decadent. Such books were removed from circulation, and any defense or imitation of them became punishable. The few classics which were republished suffered deletions and even additions.[81] The same methods applied to the theatrical and figurative arts. The Latvian cultural monthly *Karogs* and the Estonian daily *Rahva Hääl*, replete by now with attacks against national culture, still were severely admonished in *Pravda* for being nationalist:

> *Rahva Hääl* acquaints its readers extremely poorly with the friendship of peoples and with Soviet patriotism. . . . Instead of unmasking the attempt of the Estonian bourgeois literature in the past to drug its readers' awareness, it focuses its attention on the personal life of bourgeois Estonian writers. . . . *Rahva Hääl* does not unmask the rotten bourgeois culture of the West.[82]

The newly-created or re-created Academies of Sciences for the Baltic republics, too, were hampered by the "conditions of a sharply intense ideological struggle" where young ideologists were telling older specialists how to run their business.

Cultural Russification was particularly reflected in the rewriting of history through the contriving of age-old intense and friendly relations with the Russians, who always were presented as superior to the Balts. LaCP First Secretary Kalnbērziņš maintained that the ancient Latvian tribes had grown and developed "only thanks to their organic connection with the Russian principalities, to the extremely powerful influence of Russian culture."[83] It was like Nazi propaganda, with the term "German" replaced with "Russian." It was irrelevant to Marxism, and contrary even to Lenin's views about Russian imperialism. Baltic struggles against German aggression in the thirteenth century were given full coverage, and temporary alliances with Russians or East Slavs were emphasized. Wars against them, at times by the same Baltic leaders who fought the Germans, had to be ignored.

The expected behavior of the Balts toward the Russians is well

---

[81] For a detailed exposition of the process in Lithuania, see Tomas Venclova, "Translations of World Literature and Political Censorship in Contemporary Lithuania," *Lituanus*, XXV/2 (Summer 1979), pp. 10–15.

[82] On Estonia: *Pravda*, 6 July 1951; on Latvia: *ibid.*, 4 February 1952.

[83] Jānis Kalnbērziņš, *Ten Years of Soviet Rule* (Moscow, 1951), p. 21; as reported in Ekmanis 1978, p. 118.

expressed by a much-reproduced bronze statue by Olav Männi (1950), with the detailed title "Prince Viachko of Polotsk and Lembitu's son Meelis defending Tartu in 1224." The statue shows a sophisticated Russian feudal prince pointing something out to an eager but not too bright peasant boy. The boy is supposed to be the son of Lembitu, the chief leader of Estonian resistance to the Germans, who in his spare time pillaged the Russian city of Pskov — a fact ignored by Stalinist history.

As if by magic (and without any presentation of prior proof), commerce allegedly flourished whenever an area was taken by Russian rulers and wilted if they had to withdraw. The Lithuanian expansion in Belorussia and the Ukraine during the fourteenth century was labelled "feudal aggression," while subsequent comparable Russian expansion was not. Swedish rule (1600-1700) in Estonia and northern Latvia, which had been somewhat overly praised by Baltic historians reacting to German as well as Russian views of their history, was now over-vilified. The Russian conquest of this area at the beginning of the eighteenth-century became "progressive," even though it resulted in enormous population losses in both Latvia and Estonia as well as in a tightening of the grip by German estate owners over their peasants. Likewise, the late eighteenth-century partitions of the Polish-Lithuanian Commonwealth which brought Lithuania and Courland, among other areas, into the Russian Empire, also became "progressive," as it foreshadowed their eventual inclusion into the USSR.

This re-creation of the past extended from press to school texts, though few scholarly studies had time to be written (and those which were, soon were denounced for being overly modest). It overflowed into operas and pictures about medieval and recent history, with the Marxist form continuously overridden by the Russianizing content.

Russification of history also affected the past of the Communist movement. Many Balts, especially Latvians, had been prominently active within the Bolshevik ranks, among them Jukums Vācietis, the first Commander of the Red Army; Pēteris Stučka, the creator of the Soviet legal system; and Jānis Rudzutaks, a long-time Politburo member. While a Marxist approach to Baltic history could have been expected to emphasize such native initiative, the reverse was true under Stalin. Most of these Baltic Bolsheviks were purged during the 1930s, and their names had thus become unmentionable. But even more generally, the Russian imperialist view of history denied any initiative, even be it Marxist, on the part of the Balts. The Baltic masses were depicted as enthusiastically, albeit passively, to have followed Russian Marxist leadership.

Even the events of 1940, which in Soviet historiography are

depicted as "native revolutions" against fascist regimes, came — at least in one instance — to be partially credited to Soviet action. A 1949 Lithuanian booklet, *The Aid of the Soviet Union to the Lithuanian Nation in Its Defense of Liberty and Independence in 1939 and 1940*, appeared under peculiar circumstances.[84] In 1948, the Soviet Information Bureau responded to the American publication of *Nazi-Soviet Relations*, a collection of diplomatic documents captured during the war, with a pamphlet entitled *Falsifiers of History*. Claiming Western designs at deflecting German aggression eastward, the brochure interpreted Soviet actions in the Baltic states mainly in the context of the need to prepare for eventual Nazi aggression. They were likened to the stationing of British troops in Egypt and American landings at Casablanca. The Lithuanian author's task became one of reconciling this new line with the "spontaneous" Baltic revolutions. He did this by pointing out that the class struggle in Lithuania had reached a revolutionary level in 1939–40 which forced the regime to accept the Mutual Assistance Pacts offered by Moscow, a success which inspired the masses to greater revolutionary activity. Lithuania should then be grateful to the USSR and its party as well as to Stalin for its 1940 "revolution."

Even historians who had gone over to the Soviet side found no mercy. Professor Hans Kruus had in 1940 become Soviet Estonia's first puppet Vice-Premier. After the war, as Foreign Affairs Minister, he attended international meetings requesting UN membership for Soviet Estonia. Yet in 1950 he was thrown out of the party. As Soviet Estonia's main daily explained it, his pre-war writings on thirteenth-century history were the reason:

> Kruus adjusted his step to that of his fascist colleagues and complemented his friends' slander theory with his own contribution: Estonians supposedly defended their country against the Russians. . . . Reversing the facts, Kruus wrote that, in the eastern Baltic areas, prior to the thirteenth century, "Russians were the nearest and the most active adversaries." . . . Facts show, on the contrary, that in the fight with the "dog-knights," the Russians from the very beginning acted as the protectors and aiders of the Estonians.[85]

The Baltic cultural elite reacted to cultural straitjacketing in various ways. Some withdrew into retirement or manual occupa-

---

[84] Juozas Žiugžda, *Tarybų Sąjungos pagalba lietuvių tautai apginant savo laisvę ir nepriklausomybę 1939 ir 1940 metais* (Vilnius, 1949). This work is extremely rare in the West; insofar as we can ascertain, no major library in the U.S. shows it in its holdings.

[85] Artur Vassar, in *Rahva Hääl*, 21 October 1951.

tions or minor office work. Some writers switched to translating Russian classics. If they wrote original work, it was only "for the drawer," i.e., not for publication, but for safe-keeping in the hope of better times. Sometimes such passivity was accepted by the regime, sometimes it was not. Some cultural figures tried to cooperate with the regime's demands in order to be culturally active at all, or to avoid the image of possible hostility, or to make a career, or because somewhere between 1940 and 1944 the meandering course of history had carried them into partial collaboration with the Soviets, and there was no quiet getting-out for whomever the Soviets had identified as their activists. During the 1949-51 period, 16 members were excluded from the Lithuanian Writers' Union, 9 of them for inactivity.

In retrospect, collaboration proved no safer than passivity, since collaborators risked unwittingly committing ideological mistakes and being charged with subversion. Criticism was dished out in an erratic way, and penalties could range from public admonition, demotion, or effective house arrest to arrest, questioning under torture, and deportation. In Latvia, the prominent lyrical poet Jānis Medenis was caught in 1945 as he was trying to go to Sweden in a fishing boat. He was jailed until the late 1940s, and then was sent to the Kolyma forced-labor camp in northern Siberia. Also deported were Elza Stērste, Valdis Grēviņš, and Vilis Cedriņš (who died in 1946), to mention just some of the best-known Latvian poets. Estonian poet Heiti Talvik was arrested and died in 1947. Deported and imprisoned Lithuanian writers included Juozas Keliuotis, Kazys Inčiūra, Antanas Miškinis, Kazys Boruta, and Valys Drazdauskas, individuals spanning the whole spectrum of pre-war political persuasion. Others became "non-persons" whose names were not to be mentioned in the press.[86]

Balys Sruoga, a veteran of the Stutthof concentration camp, was attacked on ideological grounds. The immediate catalyst for the attack was provided by his camp reminiscences, *The Forest of the Gods*, which proved unsuitable for publication. As LiCP Secretary Kazys Preikšas put it in his speech to the Lithuanian Writers Congress, 1–2 October 1948 (one year after Sruoga's death):

> As a concentration camp inmate, [Sruoga] had a good
> opportunity to acquaint himself with the other inmates. He saw
> fighters against German aggression. But the description of the
> camps in his book is essentially a mockery of them, a cynical
> banter at the expense of victims of German aggression. . . . It

[86] Ekmanis 1978, pp. 215-217 and 384; *Eesti kirjanduse biograafiline leksikon* (Tallinn, 1975), p. 387; Jonas Grinius, "Literature and the Arts in Captive Lithuania," in Vardys (ed.), *Lithuania Under the Soviets*, p. 199.

> appears as if the inmates themselves are guilty for their travail, and the German fascist goons innocent.
>
> What did Sruoga see in this giant tragedy called the German camps? He only saw petty people concerned with some of their physiological functions. . . . If Sruoga's book had appeared, our enemies would be perfectly justified in claiming that the Germans were right in holding such dregs of humanity in concentration camps.

However, as Preikšas elaborated, it was not only this work which evoked condemnation. Sruoga apparently was intrinsically unacceptable to the new masters.

> In talking about Sruoga, one cannot ignore his earlier two-volume *History of Russian Literature*, slandering the Russian nation and the Soviet state system.[87]

Following a somewhat similar pattern, the prominent Latvian poet Aleksandrs Čaks, who drank himself to death in 1950, was viciously criticized in 1951, and publication of his works ceased.

In Estonia, massive personal reprisals against prominent figures on the cultural scene, starting in 1949, accompanied the aforementioned purge of native Communists in 1950. In July 1949, an article appeared in the cultural monthly *Looming* which charged several passive and collaborationist writers and artists with formalism and bourgeois nationalism. Even before, people were forced to condemn themselves publicly and in writing for formalism (e.g., composer Lydia Auster in 1948). Now people would be required to launch surprise attacks on their colleagues, or be themselves doomed. One such attack was later described by Soviet Estonian writer Enn Vetemaa: a professor's favorite student is asked to denounce him, supposedly in order to spare the professor worse attacks by others. The professor soon after dies during a police interrogation.[88]

Among major neutral cultural figures, writer Friedebert Tuglas was drenched with invective ("He tried to cover up the stench of putrefication of the bourgeoisie's corpse")[89] and banned from public life, to become a non-person. This fate was shared by

---

[87] *Už tarybinę lietuvių literatūrą* (Vilnius, 1948), pp. 22–23. Ten years after Sruoga's death, his *Forest of the Gods* was published in Lithuania. It subsequently saw considerably abbreviated Russian (1958), Polish (1965), French (1967), and Latvian (1968) translations.

[88] Lydia Auster, in *Looming*, no. 10 (October 1948), p. 1256; Enn Vetemaa, *Pillimees* (Tallinn, 1967); see review by Rein Taagepera. "The Problem of Political Collaboration in Soviet Estonian Literature," JBS, VI/1 (Spring 1975), pp. 30–40.

[89] Lembit Remmelgas, *Rahva Hääl*, 7 July 1951.

hundreds of writers, artists, and teachers. Popular playwright Hugo Raudsepp was deported in 1951 and died a year later. The collaborationist Chairman of the Writers Union, Johannes Semper, was suddenly found to be "the meanest enemy of the Soviet people and literature." Since he was the author of Soviet Estonia's pro-Russian anthem, this anthem from now on could only be played, but not sung. Marxist literary critic Nigol Andresen, a left-wing Socialist Parliament member during Estonia's independence, had become the quisling government's Foreign Minister after Soviet occupation in 1940, and later (1946-49) the equivalent of Vice-President. In 1950 he was deported as a "venomous bourgeois nationalist" who "tried to poison our adolescent youth." The most ironic casualty was Soviet Estonia's formal head of state Eduard Päll, an Estonian grown up in Russia who was to be an unreconstructed Stalinist way into the 1970s. In 1950 he was demoted to faculty member of the Pedogogical Institute, due to the following charges:

> Andresen's group directed our literature not toward the Russian and Soviet classics but toward the rotting bourgeois literature of the West. Andresen, and with him Päll too, glorified the reactionary bourgeois nationalist ideas of "Young Estonia." "Young Estonia" was created as early as 1904, and since then it has never tired of exhorting everyone to acquire a Western orientation.[90]

The notion of a "historical gap" in the development of Baltic culture around 1950 has had wide currency among the Soviet Estonian intelligentsia. Its existence has been denied in official Soviet announcements. However, the major post-Stalin Soviet Estonian anthology (1967) selects fewer poems from 1949-51 than from any other three-year period during this century (if one excludes poems by refugees in the West). A similar pattern is followed by literary works mentioned in the major English-language survey of Estonian literature (1970); the average number for 1949-53 is only a quarter of the average of the last five independence years. Even according to the Soviet criteria twenty years later, the last five years under Stalin were less creative and productive than the war years or the early postwar reconstruction years, not to mention the independence period.[91] This historical gap of 1949-53 is likely to be detected in most fields of cultural creativity in all three Baltic countries. It does not, however, seem to

[90] I. Kebin [Johannes Käbin], *Pravda*, 13 May 1950.
[91] Rein Taagepera, "A Portrait of the 'Historical Gap' in Estonian Literature," *Lituanus*, XXVI/3, (Fall 1980), pp. 73-86, based on analysis of Paul Rummo (ed.), *Eesti luule* (Tallinn, 1967), and Endel Nirk, *Estonian Literature* (Tallinn, 1970), biographical appendix.

have become a question specifically discussed by the Lithuanian intelligentsia, though some official admonition against needless denigration of the postwar period seems to have appeared.

Religion

After the war, foreign-policy considerations induced the Soviets to go softer on churches, use them for peace campaigns abroad, and reduce their domestic influence through atheistic lectures, coupled with taxation, regulation, and infiltration. Their degree of success in the Baltic states varied, depending on the historical background of the various churches.

In Lithuania, the dominant Catholic Church had deep native roots. As in Ireland, nationalism and religion were interconnected, and some priests participated in the guerrilla resistance. This nationalism made the Church a prime target of the Soviet campaign against Lithuanian national culture, but the concomitant broad popular support also made it a resilient target. The first Soviet step, started in 1944, was to try to create a "national church" forbidden to have any ties with the Vatican. Bishops who refused to condemn guerrilla violence without mention of Soviet violence were arrested. Mečislovas Reinys, Archbishop of Vilnius, a former Foreign Minister and scholar with an anti-totalitarian record, was arrested in 1947 and died in 1953 in the prison of Vladimir, Russia. Three other bishops were deported or executed in 1946, three had fled to the West, and one had died. By 1948, only one bishop was left in Lithuania — the aging Kazimeras Paltarokas — but he still refused to denounce the Pope or accept lectures on Marxism in the sole remaining seminary.[92]

The Soviets had assumed that clergymen had taken up their profession for the sake of profit. Yet most of them continued to serve even when Church property was confiscated, regular clergy salaries were discontinued, and heavy special taxes were set on income received from the congregation. Sermons were recorded, hospital and school visits prohibited, and visitors to the priests were blacklisted. From 1946 to 1949, about 350 priests were deported, especially when the Soviets failed in their attempts to induce younger clergy to form a collaborationist church. By 1954, the number of priests still held at 741 (compared to 1,451 in 1940), and 688 churches were open (1,202 in 1939). The appointment of priests was subject to approval by the regime's Director for Religious Affairs. The number of seminaries was reduced from 4 in 1944 to 1 by 1946. The allowed number of seminarians was reduced from 300

---

[92] V. Stanley Vardys, *The Catholic Church, Dissent, and Nationality in Soviet Lithuania* (Boulder, Colo., 1978), pp. 62–82.

in 1944 to 150 in 1946, and to 75 in 1954. No Catholic literature was legally published until 1956. Atheistic literature and oral propaganda expanded, but success was limited, due to a simplistic heavy-handed approach and the stigma of being connected to foreign occupation.

In Latvia and Estonia, the prevalent Lutheran Church never had become quite popular, due to its long association with the Baltic German oppression. Even during independence, the percentage of children christened in Estonia had been decreasing steeply — from 92% in 1922 to 77% in 1933, i.e., a drop of almost 2% per year. The relatively mild further decrease to 56% by 1957 — less than 1% per year — suggests that Stalinist persecution of the church may have slowed down the secularization rather than speeded it up. Latvian Lutheran clergymen numbered about 250 in 1940, and 95 by late 1944 (mostly due to flight to the West); Estonian figures were 191 and 79. Prior to his deportation to Germany in October 1944, Latvian Archbishop Teodors Grünbergs had appointed Dean Kārlis Irbe to act in his place, but Irbe was deported by the Soviets to Siberia. Two successive bishops in Estonia, Anton Eilart and August Pähn, met the same fate in 1945. Of the remaining 95 Latvian clergymen, 5 had been killed and 35 imprisoned or deported by 1950. A Soviet-sponsored new Archbishop, Gustavs Tūrs, was finally accepted in 1948. In Estonia, a bishop was appointed in 1949 as part of an accommodation which gave a Soviet agent the post of Chief Secretary of the Church Consistory. Latvia's Catholic Metropolitan Antonijs Springovičs managed to maintain his post, but one of his two auxiliary bishops, Kazimirs Dulbinskis, was deported soon after his appointment in 1947. The Baltic Orthodox Churches were attached to the Russian Patriarchate of Moscow in 1946, and a non-Estonian-speaking bishop was appointed for Estonia. The Jewish synagogues destroyed by the Nazis apparently were not reconstructed. The Free Churches were ordered in 1945 to join a single Baptist League for the entire USSR. Traditionally militant minorities, these congregations flourished until 1950 and held their own thereafter.[93]

Interaction with the World

Soviet annexation of the Baltic states had been immediately recognized by Nazi Germany and Sweden. After the war, Baltic diplomatic representatives continued to be accredited in countries

---

[93] Vello Salo, "The Struggle Between the State and the Churches," in Parming and Järvesoo, pp. 198-204; Ernst Staffa, "Religion im historischen Materialismus in Sowjetrussland und in den baltischen Ländern," AB, X (1970), p. 82; Rutkis, pp. 624-625.

such as Great Britain, the United States, Canada, and Australia.[94] France, pressured by Nazi Germany to recognize the annexation, reestablished limited accreditation after the war. The Soviet Union brought the puppet Foreign Affairs Ministers of the Soviet Baltic republics to the Paris Conference of 1946, trying to make them part of the peace settlement and to obtain United Nations seats for the Soviet Baltic republics. These attempts failed. The activities of Baltic diplomatic representatives and pre-war emigrants probably played a role. As Baltic refugees started to acquire citizenship in their new countries of residence, their opposition to recognition of Soviet annexation acquired electoral weight in those countries.

In terms of percentages of the total pre-war ethnically Baltic population, these refugees involved 6% of Estonians, 8% of Latvians, and 3% of Lithuanians, and an even larger fraction of the educated elite. The numerical basis for an émigré culture was there, and a need for such a culture was felt more acutely the more the historical-gap syndrome developed in the Baltic states. In the first postwar decade, émigré activities played a prominent and possibly indispensable role in keeping the national cultures alive. Their very existence influenced developments back home, and probably speeded up the post-Stalin cultural recovery.

The Soviet reaction to émigré culture was a mix of some clumsy repatriation propaganda and of thorough isolationism. The threat of Soviet reprisals against those with foreign ties cut even private correspondence between émigrés and their relatives back home down to near zero. Practically no printed émigré literary works reached the Baltic republics. Listening to foreign radio information was restricted and punishable. Little mention of émigrés was made in the Soviet Baltic press and literature, except in negative generalities. However, general awareness of countrymen abroad persisted among the Baltic population. In the absence of specific information, their activity frequently was even overestimated. The ideological content of Soviet policies in the Baltic republics may have been hardened by the awareness of competition from abroad. But also, the existence of the émigré culture made it harder for Stalin to toy with the idea of strangling Baltic cultural life altogether. Because of such a component abroad, even the most drastic acts within the Baltic states could not totally obliterate their culture.

Surprising as it may seem, the Baltic deportees may also have had some cultural-political impact on the Soviet Union. Forced to live

---

[94] See Lawrence Juda, "United States' Non-recognition of the Soviet Union's Annexation of the Baltic States: Politics and Law," JBS, VI/4 (Winter 1975), pp. 272-290.

in camps with Russians and other nationalities, they sometimes managed to transmit to the latter some utterly novel ideas about western democracy and practices. The best-documented case is the interaction of Aleksandr Solzhenitsyn with Arnold Susi, a member of the briefly reconstructed government of Estonia of September 1944. In his *Gulag Archipelago*, Solzhenitsyn repeatedly stressed the impact that Susi's long talks made on his incredulous mind:

> To understand the Revolution I had long since required nothing beyond Marxism. . . . And now fate brought me together with Susi. He breathed a completely different sort of air. . . . I listened to the principles of the Estonian Constitution, which had been borrowed from the best of European experience, and to how their hundred-member one-house Parliament had worked. And, though the *why* of it was not clear, I began to like it all and store it all away in my experience.[95]

There were limits to such impacts, and one cannot evaluate the total effect of Baltic inmates on other Soviet prisoners. After 1955, most of the surviving deportees were to return to the Baltic republics, often with broken health, but frequently also with steeled spirit: they no longer could be threatened with an unknown land called Siberia.

NORMALIZATION UNDER NEW NORMS: 1952-1953

In 1952 the Baltic scene changed considerably because it no longer changed appreciably. The whole period since 1944 had been a succession of shattered hopes and social upheavals. On the national level, the guerrilla resistance was broken, and hopes of Western support had to be given up. On the personal level, one had to give up hope of ability to escape terror, even if one was not a German collaborator, outspoken patriot, private farmer, intellectual, or native Communist. All these groups had been reached by the terror, one after another. Which new group was to come next? None was, but at the time no one knew. Terror had become an expected norm. In this sense, things had normalized.

Every year since 1944 (and indeed, since 1939) had brought major social changes. In 1952, for the first time, nothing changed much. The same slogans and the same type of repression continued, with occasional arrests. Toward the end of the year, rumors of new mass arrests were rife: deportation of Jews (in the wake of

---

[95] A. I. Solzhenitsyn, *The Gulag Archipelago, 1918–1956* (New York, 1974), pp. 213–214.

the alleged "doctors' plot" in Moscow), new deportations from the badly functioning kolkhozes, and purges of the remaining intellectuals. But Stalin died in March 1953, and small things unthinkable a year earlier began to occur.

Newspapers reduced threats and started to write about socialist legality. At the Estonian trade union conference, a delegate dared to declare: "Regarding improvement of workers' welfare, only promises are made. That doesn't take us very far." Such unheard-of criticism now was even reported in the press.[96]

None of the Stalinist decrees were rescinded, and some practices were even tightened. Social norms remained harsh, but at least they did not change any more. Adjustment to them became possible. And the desire for that was there. The sense of irony and resistance that met the first Soviet measures in 1940 and even after 1944 had dissipated a long time ago. Terror had outlasted any rationale for it. The Baltic populations were numb. Having stable harsh rules, and getting hit only when overstepping known bounds — that sounded like a happy dream, after years of erratic terror and shifting demands.

Some resistance still occurred in 1953 and later. However, such activity seems to have been exceptional. People who felt that they could be deported anyway might as well die fighting when it looked like a choice between death and Siberia. With terror subsiding, it became a choice between death and collaboration, and few chose death.

By 1953, the Soviet rule had come to be considered more than a momentary and superficial occupation. In this sense, it had become "legitimate" — if the Soviets were not considered morally entitled to proclaim and enforce laws, at least it was accepted that they were able to enforce their laws fully, and that one better act as if the Soviet rule were legitimate. The habit of mentally challenging every Soviet rule slowly shifted into the less strainful habit of submission. A significant change of attitude seems to have taken place — from struggle against a foreign "occupation" to working for one's own interest within a framework of foreign "rule."

Like the war period, the postwar years were ones of tremendous population loss for all three Baltic peoples. However, this was countered by an influx of colonists. Latvia lost at least 150,000 and Estonia about 100,000 natives through deportations, executions, and guerrilla warfare. Over a decade, births managed to compensate for less than half of these. The war-time and postwar losses amounted to about 30% of the pre-war population through death, deportation, and flight (see Table 5). Colonization added an equal

[96] *Rahva Hääl*, 20 February 1954.

number of newcomers. Predominantly Russians, they represented an alien colonial master-class unable and unwilling to integrate with the existing national language and culture. On the contrary, they largely expected the national population to assimilate with them. In Lithuania, guerrilla warfare resulted in proportionately higher losses, with a total of about 450,000. This was partly compensated by higher birth rates. The lower level of industrialization also kept down Russian immigration.

From the vantage point of 1953, the future of the Baltic nations looked grim. A few years earlier, terror had proceeded at a genocidal rate. The only hope had been the dictator's death. This death had come, and the system had survived. Terror had subsided, but the machinery that had perpetrated it remained intact. The new leaders could reactivate it once the power struggle was over. Hopeful signs appeared. One wanted to hope; one was afraid to hope — hope had been squashed too many times before.

The countryside was not recovering from collectivization. City life showed hardly any improvement. Culture was at a standstill. National survival had stopped being a prime concern when common resistance had been smashed and everyone's personal survival was at stake. Society was atomized. All the gains of the period of independence had been undone — political, cultural, and even economic.

It could have been worse: Russian-language schooling, as had been the case around 1900, could have been introduced; and even total deportation, like the Crimean Tatars, was not an impossibility. But the situation was already bad beyond the worst expectations of 1940. Major improvements were around the corner, but these could not be known as yet. In 1953, the future of the Baltic nations appeared grimmer than it was actually going to be.

CHAPTER IV

THE RE-EMERGENCE OF NATIONAL CULTURES: 1954–1968

THE VAIN STRUGGLE FOR POLITICAL AUTONOMY

The Thaw

The general relaxation ("Thaw") in Soviet life which followed the death of Stalin affected the three Baltic republics perhaps somewhat more than most other regions of the USSR, though not as much as the East European satellite countries. As elsewhere in Eastern Europe, the psychological impact of de-Stalinization served as a catalyst for reassertions by the local leaderships of their prerogatives within the system as well as for trends toward fundamental change which questioned the social order itself.

The struggle for succession in the Kremlin allowed a slight, gradual extension of the functions and privileges of the republics' administrations. Among the Soviet power contenders, Nikita Khrushchev proved particularly adept at exploiting such local sentiment in his advance to power. The republics' leaderships used the situation to attempt expansion of their local political machines, perhaps in hope of securing some indigenous approbation of their existence. During the 15 years after Stalin's death, the Lithuanian regime was most successful in weathering reactions and in utilizing the situation to nativize its administrative apparatus and to secure a grudging indigenous acceptance as being perhaps the lesser evil under the circumstances. The Latvian regime proved least successful in this regard, with that of Estonia falling somewhere in between.

One of the earliest reflections of the new tendency appeared in the area of party membership, which peaked throughout the USSR in 1953; the Baltic republics were no exception. The number of candidates (new probationary members) in particular dropped drastically after Stalin's death, as people adopted a wait-and-see attitude. In Estonia, the number of candidates fell from 1,903 in 1952 to 578 in 1953; the earlier figure was not reached again until 1956. The remarkably high Lithuanian figure of 9,224 candidates in 1952 was not equalled during the subsequent decade.[1]

During the postwar period, the three Baltic parties had remained small by Soviet standards and suffered from a lack of indigenous participation. Of necessity, all three parties as well as the administrative apparatuses of the three republics had to be disproportionately staffed by imported cadres. The existence in Russia of small bodies of pre-war Estonian and Latvian Communist expatriates who could be transferred back to their former homelands mitigated this situation somewhat in those two republics. The "foreignness" of the party was particularly acute in Lithuania, for which even such a limited pool had been virtually nonexistent. Moreover, as areas of recently rampant opposition to Sovietization, the three republics had been inundated with heavy concentrations of Soviet security forces and personnel who swelled the non-indigenous ranks of the party membership. By 1953, the new Soviet leadership may have decided that the number and growing seniority (and trustworthiness) of home-grown members made a moderate re-nationalization desirable in order to reduce the most glaring signs of external control. In the Summer of 1953, the Russian Second Secretaries of the Baltic party organizations were all replaced by ethnic Balts. However, Russians were soon reintroduced in Lithuania (1955) and Latvia (1956), while in Estonia a "Yestonian" lasted until 1964 (see Appendix A).

The Lithuanian party leadership used the opportunity presented by new moods in the Soviet Politburo to emancipate itself from much of the direct *apparatchik* (full-time party officials) control which had been exercised by Moscow. Rapid and evident nativization of party as well as non-party personnel seems to have taken place immediately after the death of Stalin. It was most likely connected with an effort on the part of Beria to curry favor among the national republic leaderships. The Fourth Plenum of the Lithuanian CC held in June 1953 sanctioned such nativization, though this was not mentioned in the press at the time. Wide-scale dismissals of non-natives who had not learned the Lithuanian language followed. Popular expressions of anti-Russian sentiments led, in some cases of overexuberance, to arrests. After Beria's fall, these cases were generally de-politicized through reclassification as disturbances of the peace or hooliganism, and the policies of the late Security Chief were blamed for having

---

[1] For more details on administration and party affairs in 1955–68, see Thomas Remeikis, "The Administration of Power: The Communist Party and the Soviet Government," in Vardys (ed.), *Lithuania Under the Soviets*, 1965, pp. 111–140; King, pp. 170–206; Pennar 1978, pp. 105–127; Remeikis 1970, pp. 121–156; Aleksander Kaelas, *Das Sowjetisch besetzte Estland* (Stockholm, 1958).

provoked such unacceptable behavior.[2] On the whole, however, Beria's demise did not result in a change in the policy of nativization, though it came to be pursued at a more modest pace.

Wide-scale transfers of non-native party cadres out of Lithuania are suggested by the extremely slow growth between 1953 and 1956 of the total LiCP membership, at a time when it is claimed that significant numbers of recruits were being accepted. The post-Stalin uncertainty also made some Russian party members leave Latvia and Estonia. Between 1952 and 1956, the number of non-Estonian members of the ECP decreased by over a thousand, from 13,374 to 12,138 — the first such decrease since 1945. A purge of Beria supporters may have affected Baltic Russian party members more than home-grown ones.

Khrushchev's denunciation of Stalin at the February 1956 CPSU Congress released a shock-wave which furthered the trend toward increased stature of the republics within the Soviet system. The condemnation of the "cult of personality" implicitly reaffirmed the need to observe the law, and "sovereignty" of the republics was a constitutional principle.

A series of administrative reorganizations conducive to the expansion of local prerogative accompanied the psychological atmosphere attending de-Stalinization. Abolition of the USSR Ministry of Justice rendered the important state procurators subordinate to local ministries of justice. The republics were given the right to draft their own law codes within a general all-Union

---

[2] Based on a conversation with Aleksandras Shtromas, who at the time worked as a defense lawyer in Lithuania and had close family connections with then-First Secretary Sniečkus. For the LiCP Plenum as well as an analogous Plenum in Latvia, see Borys Lewytzkyj, *Die sowjetische Nationalitätenpolitik nach Stalins Tod (1953-1970)* (Munich, 1970), pp. 25-26. Perhaps the most dramatic case of this Beria nativization in Lithuania occurred within Beria's own domain, the Security Service. Since 1945, a Russian, D. A. Efimov, had occupied the post of Minister of State Security in the Lithuanian SSR. His ministry was now merged with that of the Interior and placed under an old native Communist, Jonas Vildžiūnas. Efimov, who under normal circumstances could have been expected to head the new unit, became Vildžiūnas' deputy. Vildžiūnas had briefly worked for the Security Police after the Soviet occupation in 1940. However, since he had a brother resident in the U.S., he was not, according to Stalinist canons of eligibility, considered suitable for such service and had been sidetracked into other posts, most recently that of Chairman of the Kaunas City Executive Committee. His interview with Beria upon his new appointment forms part of the lore among high Lithuanian party personnel. In a thick Georgian accent, Beria is supposed to have answered Vildžiūnas' mention of his American brother with: "We will discuss that when we decide to appoint him minister." After Beria's fall, Vildžiūnas returned to apparently more normal preoccupations of urban management. In 1954, he was demoted to Chairman of the Vilnius City Executive Committee. For a biography of Jonas Vildžiūnas, see *Mažoji lietuviškoji tarybinė enciklopedija*, III, p. 751.

framework. Police functions were separated from the organs of state security.

Even though the precise implications of the move remained vague for some time, establishment of the *sovnarkhozy* (regional economic councils) in 1957 appeared as a tangible expansion of the role of the republics. The discussions preceding their appearance served as a forum for the expression of local interests. Aleksei Müürisepp, Chairman of the Council of Ministers of the ESSR, in a 22 September 1956 article in *Izvestiia* criticized the policy of economic interdependence for having prevented Estonian industry from using local raw materials, for having mandated export of output before the republic's own needs had been met, and for the dispersal of Estonian specialists throughout the USSR and the influx of Russians to take their places. Similar critiques also appeared in the press of the three republics.

Müürisepp's last point touched on an extremely sore issue among the Baltic population. The large influx of Russians was rationalized in Estonia by presenting it as having been inevitable to cover the loss of so many specialists who had left during the war.[3] Similar open concern over an indigenous brain-drain appeared in Latvia. The shortage of engineers in the republic was blamed on the annual dispatch of about half of the graduating specialists to the Soviet Union outside the republic.[4] Another complaint was that Latvians studying in Moscow, Leningrad, or other cities were not being sent back to their country after graduation.[5] While the temporary harvest work performed by students in the Virgin Lands of Kazakhstan was extensively publicized in 1956, publicity accompanying such "volunteer" labor dropped considerably in Lithuania during the following year.

According to the new system, each republic was to become a separate unit for the purposes of economic planning. As one observer noted in the Latvian party journal:

> The establishment of the Economic Districts and the *Sovnarkhozy*
> in the republics will contribute widely to an extension of their
> rights. The republics' organs will work out plans for the
> development of their economies and will carry out organizational
> work.[6]

The stature of local managers and planners was thus enhanced. Moreover, the reorganization necessitated some expansion in the

[3] "V bratskoi seme sovetskikh narodov," *Kommunist Estonii*, 1957/7, p. 10.
[4] *Cīņa*, 5 June 1957.
[5] *Ibid.*, 21 April 1957.
[6] "Novyi etap v ekonomicheskom razvitii strany," *Kommunist sovetskoi Latvii*, 1957/6, p. 6.

political and administrative bureaucracies. Some officials were doubtless made available by the consolidation of local government districts which took place from 1954 to 1967, with most rapid change in 1959 (see Table 9).[7] The expansion of the pools of economic administrators and managers provided an added rationale for increasing native cadres.

De-Stalinization and economic reorganization combined to nurture the mood that considerable change was necessary and beneficial. Visible expressions of native patriotism appeared which would not have been tolerated earlier. The officially sanctioned moves all fell into the pattern of a search by the local regimes for symbolic legitimation. Republic prizes were instituted for promotion of science and the arts among native cultural circles. In May 1957, a three-colored university student cap based on the pre-war student fraternity tradition appeared in Estonia. Estonian athletes began sporting "EESTI" (Estonia) on their uniforms, instead of "EESTI NSV" (Estonian SSR), in 1957. In Latvia and Lithuania, such shifts had already taken place in 1956.

A sense of communality among the three Baltic republics, apart from their membership in the USSR, made its appearance. In 1958, the first postwar Baltic soccer games were held. With time, an attempt was made to water down this growing sense of regional identity through artificial inclusions of Belorussia, the Kaliningrad Oblast, and/or the Leningrad Oblast in "Baltic" events.

At times, efforts were made to subsume focal points of native patriotism into Soviet tradition. The Brethren Cemetery in Riga, an elegant pre-war memorial to those who fell on both sides during the 1918–20 Latvian War of Independence, had been privately cared for in the postwar years. Now the authorities took over maintenance of the shrine, but in July 1958 added 22 Red Army soldiers and partisans of World War II.

Rising Expectations

The impatience for change was particularly strong among the youth, where it proved difficult to contain de-Stalinization within officially approved channels. In 1956, for instance, the students of the Tallinn Polytechnic Institute sought to form a new student organization. Their cardinal sin was not so much the move as the apolitical nature of their organization, which was not intended to be a part of the Komsomol or trade union organizations.

The psychology of rising expectations fanned incidents. On 2

---

[7] Gottlieb Ney, "Administrative Gliederung und Verwaltungsorgane der sowjetisierten baltischen Staaten," *AB*, II (1962), pp. 9–34; *Eesti nõukogude entsüklopeedia* (Tallinn, 1968–1976), II, p. 85, and IV, pp. 381 and 541.

November 1956, the All-Souls' Day tradition of lighting candles by the graves of loved ones turned into a massive demonstration in Lithuania. It was a work day, and the custom had not been sanctioned by the regime. Student riots also broke out in Vilnius concurrently with the Hungarian uprising.[8] Likewise, thousands of candles appeared that year on 25 November, the pre-war Latvian Memorial Day, by the statue of mourning Mother Latvia in Riga.

The rise in open dissatisfaction alarmed official circles, especially in view of the events in Poland and Hungary. A hardening attitude accompanied by searches for new culprits began to appear in the media in late 1956. Three villains were particularly singled out for castigation: propaganda by hostile elements abroad; bourgeois nationalism; and corruption, as well as bureaucratic inefficiency, at home. Attacks on "undue" fascination with the West and growing attention to nationalist propaganda by émigré organizations in the West increased. Arvīds Pelše, Secretary of the Latvian CC, declared in a radio broadcast on 20 July 1957:

> Bourgeois nationalists abroad croak like crows that the unfortunate Latvian nation and her future are endangered because the people are subjected to Russification. In telling these and similar fairy tales, our enemies seek to touch the national spirit and to influence hesitating elements in our republic. . . . Maybe, and quite obviously . . . we committed some mistakes, and some failures have been evident. For example, not always and not everywhere have equal rights been given to languages. Not every sign or name of a street is written in both Latvian and Russian. Not every salesman or militiaman speaks both languages.[9]

Pelše's need to make fun of national sensitivities, with the language question as a principal one, indicated their relevance. The continuing nativization of the party cadres in all three republics had evidently begun to raise a question of the possibility of "national Communism," as attested by the frequent appearance of press attacks during the Summer of 1957. The Latvian party organ *Cīņa* likened national Communism to "sophisticated bourgeois nationalism":

> The aim of the slogans of national Communism is to smash the indestructible foundations of proletarian internationalism, to split it and to make people of socialist countries fight each other in

---

[8] Thomas Remeikis, "Acquiescence and Resistance," *Lituanus*, VI/2 (1960), p. 65.

[9] Assembly of Captive European Nations, *A Survey of Developments in Nine Captive Countries* (New York, 1957) [henceforth cited as ACEN], III, p. 5, based on a Radio Riga broadcast of 20 July 1957.

order to destroy the foundations of socialism. National Communism is nothing but sophisticated bourgeois nationalism.[10]

The most forceful statement came a year later from Lithuanian First Secretary Sniečkus, in his speech to the Tenth Congress of the LiCP:

> It is important for every member of the working class to know that anyone who would stir up antagonism toward the Russian nation, anyone who would tear the Lithuanian people away from the Russian people, would be digging a grave for the Lithuanian nation.[11]

The third villain, corruption and bureaucratic inefficiency, was also faulted as a contributing cause for a loss of faith in Communism and receptivity to enemy blandishments. This was clearly enunciated by Pēteris Plēsums of the Latvian CC in his article "On the Moral Attitude of a Communist." He catalogued a whole series of negative phenomena in the party ranks:

> There are cases where particular persons who strongly believe in capitalist remnants try to join the party, not because they believe the party is right or because they want to help, but only in search of some material benefit. Because of such "Communists," it happens that good people, people doing decent work who deserve to be members, avoid the party . . . What kind of example can a Communist show who until now has not freed himself from religious prejudices? But such Communists — admittedly not many — are still to be found in our party. There are cases where Communists baptize their children, ask ministers to attend funerals of their family members, etc. . . . Among those in the republic expelled from the party in 1965, there were 39 candidate-members whose faults were mostly drinking, hooliganism, and misbehavior. . . . The largest group was expelled because of appropriations of state and private property.[12]

Widespread corruption was thus held responsible for the evident lack of ideological fervor. While it is difficult to judge how fervent belief in Communism had been among the Baltic Communists, few in number to begin with, Khrushchev's revelations on the crimes of Stalin most likely also contributed significantly to the undermining of faith in the ideology.

Such concern over the effects of ideological lackadaisicalness also proved to be a rationalization for manifestations of real

---

[10] Cīņa, 11 July 1957.
[11] Literatūra ir menas, 15 February 1958.
[12] P. Plesum[s], "O moralnom oblike kommunista," Kommunist sovetskoi Latvii, 1957/7, pp. 51–52.

dissatisfaction among the workers, due most frequently to chronic economic shortcomings. A wave of dissatisfaction apparently swept the 250-worker "Parkett" artel in Tallinn during 1957. Ivan Käbin of the Estonian CC offered the following explanation:

> No one acquainted himself with the interests of workers and personnel at the artel. . . . Hostile elements made use of this situation, misinterpreting the meaning of current events, trying to create an unhealthy attitude and dissatisfaction among people who were not firm enough in their beliefs.[13]

Discussions of the *sovnarkhozy*, which initially had emphasized local initiative, now came to be accompanied by a marked stress on the growing unity and interrelationship of the Soviet nations. The Union was presented as a giant melting-pot wherein the national groups were "freely" abandoning their identities to blend into a homogeneous Soviet people with the coming of Communism, which according to one ebullient pronouncement of Khrushchev was a scarce 20 years away. Attacks on impediments to its achievement, such as nationalism and religion, were stepped up. While the terror of the Stalin years could not be brought back — the regime had locked itself into condemnation of such a system — attempts set in to repress the national self-assertiveness that the Thaw had allowed.

The effect of the Thaw on the economy was slow, as reorganization gradually took place and transition difficulties were overcome. The change was slowest in agriculture. While Stalin's death may have saved Baltic farmers from further deportations, it did not immediately reverse the "spook hostel" syndrome. It was even deepened by Khruschev's drive to grow maize everywhere. The new emphasis on collective leadership did not extend down to the collective farms. Chairmen were appointed without any say by the collective owners. Worst of all, the farms were not allowed to own their own tractors, and remained at the mercy of the state machine-tractor stations (MTS), which faced no produce-delivery pressures and which the kolkhozes had to pay in kind. Meddling by "plenipotentiaries" dispatched from district headquarters continued to erode initiative. The first major reprieve came in June 1955, when Nikita Khrushchev declared, at an agricultural conference in Riga, that the implementation of his *agrogorod* ("agricultural cities") idea had been pursued too fast and with too many errors. Some of the largest kolkhozes were subdivided, and kolkhoz chairmen started to feel that they could ignore the most

[13] Ivan Kebin [Johannes Käbin], "Politicheskaia robota v massakh," *Kommunist Estonii*, 1957/3, p. 22.

senseless instructions from above and address the real problems at hand.

The real breakthrough in agriculture came only in 1958, when the MTS were dismantled throughout the Soviet Union. Collective farms were now able to purchase and maintain their own machinery. Baltic farmers had cooperated in the use of machinery since independence times, and they eagerly purchased the equipment from the MTS (mostly on credit, with state support). This was not always the case throughout the rest of the USSR. The complicated system for disposal of farm produce (compulsory deliveries below cost, low-price payments in kind to the MTS, and voluntary sales at higher rates) was simplified. Compulsory delivery was abolished; prices were raised to nonconfiscatory levels; and price differentials were eliminated. High taxes and compulsory deliveries from private plots were also ended in 1958–59.

The demographic pattern was markedly changed by the Thaw. Immigration of non-Balts largely stopped around 1953, as people and officials adopted a wait-and-see attitude. Forced labor brought to the Baltic republics started to leave, and so did some functionaries uneasy about the native popular mood. The outflow, in fact, surpassed the inflow in some years. In 1956–59 many Baltic deportees returned, possibly the majority of those who had managed to survive. As a result, the ethnically Latvian and Estonian percentages of the countries' population increased, recouping some of the losses inflicted by Stalin, and probably reached a peak (62.0 and 74.6%, respectively) around the 1959 census (see Table 1). Many of the returnees stayed in the cities, and scarcity of living space reached its most acute stage during the whole postwar period around 1955–56 (see Table 10). In Latvia, a sharp upsurge of immigration took place in 1956, for unknown reasons — a net influx surpassing that of the six preceding years combined.[14] This surge may have been a major motive for a nativist reaction which, in turn, brought on a severe purge.

The Latvian Purge of 1959

Khrushchev's successful purge of the "Anti-Party Group" in June 1957 marked an end to the expansion of the republics' prerogatives. Khrushchev no longer needed to court political support in this quarter. The shift proved most traumatic in

---

[14] The outflow was massive in the case of Lithuania (see Table 14). In Latvia and Estonia, the net outflow was close to 2,000 each in 1955. However, in 1956 the net influx into Latvia suddenly surged to 26,800. See Taagepera, "Baltic Population Changes," p. 36.

Latvia.[15] It coincided with difficulties in the LaCP which emerged at the Fifteenth Congress in January 1958. During the preceding two years, a considerable decrease in the numbers of party members and candidates had taken place. It is unclear whether this was the result of a massive transfer of Russian party members out of Latvia, as had been the case in Lithuania. It is clear, however, that a trend toward "national Communism" had emerged in the Latvian party organization. Its main goal seems to have been to reduce the unpopularity of the Soviet regime and of the CP by expanding the republic's autonomy and by eliminating the Russifying aspects of the regime.[16] Some speeches favored strengthening the party through admission of native Latvians, increasing the use of the Latvian language within the party, and devoting more attention to the Latvian intelligentsia and youth.

The personnel decisions announced during the Congress reflected a slight "Latvianization" of the leadership. While the percentage of Russians in the CC was not decreased, the composition of its Bureau (executive body) became markedly more Latvian. A trend toward "Latvianization" could be noted in other bodies as well. At the Twelfth Congress of the Latvian Komsomol in March 1958, V. Ruskulis, a native, replaced an immigrant Latvian from Russia in the post of First Secretary of the Komsomol. The Council of Trade Unions elected in May 1958 contained 21 Russians out of 71 members; the previous Council had had 24 Russians out of a total membership of 47. The Council's perennial Chairman, K. Voltmanis, an old Stalinist, was replaced by Indriks Pinksis, First Secretary of the Liepāja Municipal Committee, a partisan commander during the war who had been active in the extreme left trade-union movement of independent Latvia.

In August 1958, a Second Plenum of the LaCP was held. The most significant development was the return of Vilis Krūmiņš as Second Secretary, the post which he had lost in 1956 to a Russian.[17]

---

[15] For a detailed study of the Latvian purge, see Widmer, pp. 196-217. A more concise overview is presented by Juris Dreifelds, "Latvian National Demands and Group Consciousness since 1959," in George W. Simmonds (ed.), *Nationalism in the USSR and Eastern Europe in the Era of Brezhnev and Kosygin* (Detroit, 1976), pp. 138 ff.

[16] King, pp. 193-195.

[17] Many sources indicate Pelše as Second Secretary during 1958-59. However, his biography in the *Bolshaia Sovetskaia Entsiklopediia*, XIX (1975), clearly says: "March 1941 to 1959, LaCP Secretary for propaganda and agitation." King, p. 190, says an autonomist was elected, and Krūmiņš is specified as the Second Secretary by Vilis Hazners, "Who Is in Power in Latvia?" *Baltic Review*, no. 24 (March 1962), p. 10. On the other hand, Pelše is listed as such for July 1958 by Andris Trapans, "A Note on Latvian Communist Party Membership, 1941-1961,"

At that time, however, he had retained his membership in the Bureau while also becoming Deputy Chairman of the Council of Ministers. In mid-1958, Colonel-General Aleksandr Gorbatov, Commander-in-Chief of the Baltic Military District, was also dropped from the Bureau and soon thereafter transferred out of Latvia. His successor, General Pavel Batov, apparently was not co-opted into the Bureau *ex officio*, as had been the practice up to that time. As a result of these and other changes, only one Russian, Aleksandr Nikonov, remained as a full member of the Bureau, and he had been a resident of Latvia during the interwar period. Moreover, only two of the full members of the Bureau were post-1940 immigrants. The return of Krūmiņš to the position of Second Secretary left a vacancy in the Council of Ministers. His old position there as Deputy Chairman was filled by Eduards Berklāvs, who since January 1956 had been First Secretary of the Riga City Committee. Like Krūmiņš, Berklāvs was a younger native Communist.

Continuing ferment in Latvian party circles was reflected in a series of articles attacking irresponsible statements at party meetings as well as corruption. At some conferences, the party leadership came under heavy fire:

> At the party conferences at Dobele, Daugavpils, and Ogre, some faultfinders produced even irresponsible and demagogic speeches. . . . It is no secret that there are also among us Communists who do not play any advance-guard role. Some are passive, but others transgress party and state discipline, and there are those who transform themselves into petty bourgeois, drink heavily, and do not behave properly.[18]

Much of this criticism should be taken within the context of an effort to "Latvianize" the party. As it has been established that two-thirds of the LaCP membership at the time was made up of Russians, such criticism may well have been aimed at non-Latvian-speaking Communists.

The autonomists' goal of making Communism more palatable

Baltic Review, no. 26 (April 1963), p. 28. A possible explanation of the confusion may be that Pelše became Second Secretary during the January 1958 Congress, but was replaced by Krūmiņš during the August 1958 Plenum. See Appendix A for chronological list of LaCP Second Secretaries. Ādolfs Šilde, *Bez tiezībām un brīvības* (Copenhagen, 1965), p. 61, lists Filipp Kashnikov from January 1956 to April 1958 and Krūmiņš from April 1958 on. *Latvijas PSR maza enciklopēdija*, vol. III (Riga, 1970), for which Krūmiņš is a "non-person," says nothing on 1958–59. An unpublished draft study by Professor Grey Hodnett (no date) says Kashnikov was not reappointed in January 1958 and the post remained empty until April.

18 "Usilit vnimanie k vnutripartiinoi robote," *Kommunist sovetskoi Latvii*, 1959/2, p. 61.

to the Latvian population required an increase in the living standard. Medical services, housing, construction, pensions, and rural consumer goods distribution were expanded in 1957–58. More generally, the autonomists offered Moscow increased deliveries of commodities in exchange for more autonomy in ways of organizing the local economy.[19] In the words of Pauls Dzērve, Director of the Latvian Institute of Economics, the goal was

> to develop Latvia's industrial structure and specialization so that the most rational and economic use of *all* Latvian natural and labor resources would *maximize* the Latvian contribution to the development of the Soviet Union's economy as well as the living standard in Latvia.[20]

Matters came to a head during the Summer of 1959. In the middle of July, the Latvian mass media announced laconically that the Presidium of the Supreme Soviet of the Latvian SSR had, by its decree of 15 July 1959, dismissed Berklāvs from his duties as Deputy Chairman of the Council of Ministers. On 5 August, it was announced that the Plenum of the Latvian Council of Trade Unions had discharged Pinksis from his duties as Chairman and had removed him from its Presidium as well. Both were expelled from the party. It was the beginning of an extensive purge which continued for several years.

The ostensible reason for the dismissal of Berklāvs was provided by Vilis Lācis, Chairman of the Council of Ministers of the Latvian SSR. During a discussion of Latvia's contribution to the Seven-Year Plan, Berklāvs had supposedly openly opposed the general party line on the development of heavy industry. He had favored industries for which Latvia had raw materials and could supply labor, arguing that Latvian products should first satisfy the demands of local consumers before being poured into the general Soviet pool of production. Berklāvs was also one among "some leading workers who attempted to turn the development of the republic from the correct path to one which would have led it in the direction of nationalistic limitations and seclusion."[21]

No specific rationale was provided for the dismissal of Pinksis. He was known, however, to have objected to the transfer of workers, especially skilled labor, to other republics while a labor shortage existed in Latvia, and he had openly doubted the possibility of finding the 10–12,000 workers from rural districts for

---

[19] King, pp. 195 and 200–203.
[20] Summarized by King, p. 201, from Dzērve's statement in *Karogs*, no. 1 (January 1959), p. 103.
[21] V. Latsis [Lācis], "Blagotvornye preobrazovanie," *Partiinaia zhizn*, 1959/16, p. 15.

the construction projects of the Seven-Year Plan. In effect, he was implicitly criticizing the immigration of non-Latvians into the republic, which would become necessary to carry out these projects. Pinksis had also at an earlier time had a feud with Lācis: in Stalin's time, Pinksis had criticized Lācis' novel *Towards New Shores*, and had received a rebuke in *Pravda*. Lācis had been awarded the Stalin Prize.

Initially, the majority of the Latvian CC apparently opposed the measures. Lācis supposedly declared that Berklāvs' policy had also been his own. Only repeated pressure, including personal intervention by Khrushchev, carried the day. As a result, Lācis, Chairman of the Council of Ministers, and Jānis Kalnbērziņš, First Secretary of the LaCP, both occupying their positions since 1940, were forced to resign soon after they agreed to dismiss Berklāvs.

While it is impossible for us to ascertain the accuracy of the entire preceding account, both Kalnbērziņš and Lācis were replaced in late 1959. On 25 November, Kalnbērziņš was "released from his post at his own request" during a Plenum of the CC. The speech of his successor, Arvīds Pelše, indicated that the stated reason for his ouster was an inability to educate youth in the proper spirit of internationalism (code word for subservience to things Russian). Perhaps because of his long-standing service, Kalnbērziņš retained membership in the Latvian CC and in its Bureau. Furthermore, he was appointed Chairman of the Presidium of the republic's Supreme Soviet, i.e., titular head of state. His replacement as First Secretary, Pelše, came from a prosperous farmer's family. He had joined the party in 1915 while studying in Petrograd, returned to Latvia only in 1940, and soon became one of the LaCP secretaries (1941–59). He was known as a prominent opponent of "localism and nationalism."

The following day, Lācis was "for reasons of health" released from his position as Chairman of the Council of Ministers. Like Kalnbērziņš, he retained his position in the Latvian CC. As a writer, he continued publishing and participating in cultural events. His successor, prominent agricultural chemist Jānis Peive, was born in Russia and had resided in Latvia only since 1944. He had been Rector of the Latvian Agricultural Academy (1944–50) and President of the republic's Academy of Sciences (1951–59). Although he was Chairman of the USSR Soviet of Nationalities (1958–66), Peive became a member of the Latvian CC and of its Bureau only with his appointment as Chairman of the Council of Ministers, which was to last until 1962 (see Appendix A).

The purge rapidly encompassed the Latvian party and government. While some of the changes may have been planned in advance and cannot be directly ascribed to the purge, others showed an unmistakable connection. In November 1959, the ministries of Justice and of Communal Economy were abolished, but their incumbent heads were appointed to newly created successor bodies.

Wide-scale changes were revealed during the Seventeenth Congress of the party in February 1960. Second Secretary Krūmiņš was again replaced by a Russian. Another CC Secretary, Nikolajs Bisenieks, was discharged. The Commander-in-Chief of the Baltic Military District, Iosif Gusakovskii, was co-opted into the Bureau. Only 3 members of the outgoing Bureau — Pelše, Kalnbērziņš, and Ādolfs Migliniks — remained; and Migliniks resigned a year later, ostensibly for reasons of health. Only 57 of the 91 members of the outgoing CC remained in the new body. The number of Russians increased from 33 to 35, but the body as a whole was also enlarged to 93. The number of CC members openly connected with the security apparatus increased from 2 to 11.

The purge in the Latvian Komsomol can be said to have preceded that of the party as a whole. On 22 September 1959, both the First and Second Secretaries were removed. At the March 1960 Congress, an entirely new leadership was installed, now headed by a Latvian from Russia as First Secretary and a Russian as Second Secretary. The speech of the recently appointed head of the LaCP, Arvīds Pelše, to the Komsomol provided a clear tenor of the pervasive purgative mood. Its attack on nationalism was laced with the words "serious defects," "it is bad," and "it is not tolerable." He found fault with the youth for an insufficient struggle against bourgeois ideals.

> Anti-Soviet rumors and fiction are not being sufficiently unmasked, and no counterattack is being launched against the manifestations of bourgeois nationalism and the chauvinism of the great powers. Young people are being inadequately educated in the spirit of international proletarianism and friendship among the peoples. The friendship of the Latvian people with the other nationalities of our country, and primarily with the great Russian nation, is the object of national pride and one of the great sources of happiness for the Latvian people.[22]

The mass media were accused of a lack of political vigilance, and many serious "mistakes" were found in the work of the State Publishing House. Not long thereafter, almost all the editors of the major newspapers were replaced.

The purge continued through 1960. At the April Plenum, Pēteris Plēsums, Chairman of the Party Commission, was among those discharged. No native Latvians were left as heads of CC

---

[22] ACEN, VIII, p. 119, based on a Radio Riga broadcast of 3–4 March 1960.

departments. In June, Jānis Augškāps, Deputy Director of the Latvian *sovnarkhoz*, was replaced. Although he was pensioned, it was an open secret that he had belonged to the Berklāvs group. His successor was not a native Latvian. Later in the year, the Office Director of the Council of Ministers, the Senior Editor of the State Publishing House, and the Senior Engineer of the State Geological and Mineral Department were all expelled from the party. They had previously been reproached for bourgeois "narrow-mindedness." Likewise, two prominent economists, Pauls Dzērve, Director of the Institute of Economics, and his deputy P. Treijs were forced to resign. Both had been drafting plans for the Latvian *sovnarkhoz* which presumably favored local interests.

The removals extended to municipal and rural self-government bodies. It seems that several thousand party members were expelled within less than two years. In 1961, the party membership represented about 3.5% of the population of Latvia. However, since this included 33,000 members in the armed forces and security apparatus stationed in Latvia, the actual figure was not quite 2% of the population. Latvians may have made up about half of the resident party membership.

Nativization of the LaCP was given a considerable setback by the purge. The leadership of the party would remain dominated by Latvians from Russia. When Pelše was promoted to the all-Union Politburo in 1966, he was replaced by Augusts Voss, another immigrant (in 1945) of the period after the imposition of Soviet power. The indigenous percentage of party membership continued to be lower than in the other two Baltic republics. In 1967, it stood at 45% (including Latvians from Russia), as compared to 52 and 66% in Estonia and Lithuania, respectively.[23]

In 1963, Peive left Latvia again for his native Russia. The new LaSSR Premier (1962–70), Vitālijs Rubenis, was also a Russian Latvian. The pattern of disproportionately low representation of native-born Latvians in leadership positions was paralleled on lower levels. A 1967–68 study for Riga showed that while the local-born population of the city was 51% and made up 39% of the workforce, only 27% of the leadership positions were held by

---

[23] *Estonian Events* and *Baltic Events* [henceforth cited as *EE/BE*], no. 37, p. 8 (1973). The Latvian figure of 45% comes from Jānis Sapiets, "The Baltic Republics," in George Schöpflin (ed.), *The Soviet Union and Eastern Europe* (New York, 1970), p. 224. A similar figure of 46.3% for 1965 if given by Widmer, p. 144. The ethnic composition of the LaCP has never been published, so these are in all likelihood estimates. Another calculation based on 1973 figures for the total LaCP membership concludes that the native composition of the LaCP in that year could not have been higher than 43%: V. Stanley Vardys, "Modernization and Baltic Nationalism," *Problems of Communism*, XXIV/5 (1975), p. 40.

members of this group. Immigrants, on the other hand, making up 25% of the population and 32% of the workforce, held 48% of the leadership positions.[24]

The Reaction in Lithuania and Estonia

The shift in Kremlin policy passed much more uneventfully insofar as the Lithuanian and Estonian Communist leaderships were concerned. In Lithuania, this was in no small measure due to the adroitness of Antanas Sniečkus, a member of the LiCP CC since 1926 and its First Secretary since 1936, in adapting to changes in Moscow. While he had been prompt in his condemnation of Beria in 1953, he seems to have adopted a cautious wait-and-see attitude after the Twentieth Party Congress. In February 1956, the Lithuanian party organ *Tiesa* carried a mere *pro forma* condemnation of the cult of personality. Only on 29 March did the paper elaborate, in a reprint from *Pravda*, that the cult referred to Stalin. The stability of the top party and government personnel appears remarkable by Soviet standards. The only change came in 1956 with the replacement of the Chairman of the Council of Ministers, Mečys Gedvilas, by Motiejus Šumauskas. It appears that the move was prompted more by problems in agriculture than by shifts in the Kremlin. At any rate, Gedvilas, one of Sniečkus' old-time colleagues, was merely demoted to the position of Minister of Education.

Sniečkus faithfully echoed the shift toward a reassertion of centralization. At the time of the expulsion of the "Anti-Party Group" in Moscow, he deemed it wise to warn the LiCP of the dangers of decentralization. In a speech to the Lithuanian Supreme Soviet in June 1957, he observed:

> Separate tendencies toward *localism*, attempts to create a closed economy and attempts to solve economic problems on the basis of limited local tasks, may become evident. Such tendencies must be combatted from the very beginning.[25]

Soon thereafter, he launched a purge of the Lithuanian cultural establishment (see section below on "The Thaw in Culture").

Nevertheless, a quiet "Lithuanization" of party cadres which had begun after the death of Stalin continued. While the CPSU increased about 26% during the years 1956–60, the LiCP grew over 40%.[26] The "Lithuanization" of the party continued through the anti-nationalism campaign of the early 1960s, in spite of a slight

---

[24] Dreifelds 1976, p. 144.
[25] *Tiesa*, 8 June 1957.
[26] Remeikis 1965, p. 116.

increase of Russians in leadership positions. Its CC became only slightly more Russian — 28.4% in 1961, as compared to 22.7% in 1960 and 21.7% in 1958; in 1952, this figure had stood at 33.3%. Its Presidium had only 1 non-Lithuanian; in 1949, there had been 5. The only marked increase of Russians, perhaps for significant show purposes, came in the 1962 Lithuanian delegation to the USSR Supreme Soviet — 23%, up from 11.5% in 1958. Three of the 35-member delegation were not even residents of the republic and had no ostensible connection with it. This ratio seems to have been maintained in subsequent years; the 1966 delegation was 24% Russian.

The party as a whole continued to become more Lithuanian. Its younger members with technical competence began to replace older revolutionaries. While the latter, in view of their pre-war experiences found it more difficult to be nationalists, such problems apparently did not affect the younger group, which was more attuned to the population from which it stemmed. While some friction seems to have developed between them and the old revolutionaries, Sniečkus managed to keep the peace and to prevent the situation from boiling over as it had in Latvia. In 1964, the Lithuanian party (2.5% of the republic's population) was still smaller than the Soviet average. However, its indigenous element stood around 60%. The notable "Lithuanization" of the party can also be seen in the republic's Komsomol. In spite of the anti-nationalism campaign, its membership rose rapidly. By 1964, it stood at 209,000, double that of 1957; 40% of the Komsomol-age youth of the republic belonged. As Lithuania was still pre-dominantly populated by Lithuanians, this pool of prospective party members was likewise predominantly indigenous. In 1965, Lithuanians made up 61.5% of the LiCP; by 1968, the figure had grown to 66.2%.[27]

In Estonia, the possibility of a purge of top native administrators could not even arise, because they had already been purged prac-tically out of existence in 1949–52. Ever since 1951, Estonia had been ruled through people of the type of Pelše and Peive: First ECP Secretary Käbin, who had been in Russia from 1910 to 1941, and Chairman of the Council of Ministers Aleksei Müürisepp, who had been in Russia from 1908 to 1944. The only remaining home-grown figure was August Jakobson, like Lācis a writer, who joined CP only in 1942 and was Chairman of the Estonian Supreme Soviet Presidium from 1950 to 1958. For health reasons, he was replaced by polar biologist Johan Eichfeld, who was in Russia from about 1915 to 1950 and, remarkably, became a party member only in

---

27 *Mažoji lietuviškoji tarybinė enciklopedija*, II, p. 386.

1961, the year he handed the chairmanship over to the ailing Müürisepp. The new Chairman of the Council of Ministers (from 1961 on) was another "Yestonian," Valter Klauson.

Starting from such a baseline, the degree of nativization of top administration could only proceed upward, or stay the same. It did increase somewhat. Some ranking native Communists purged around 1950 recovered some of their rank. Former Chairman of the Council of Ministers Arnold Veimer became its Vice-Chairman and head of the Estonian *sovnarkhoz* in 1957. He was even readmitted to the ECP Bureau in 1961 — a pale reflection of Gomułka's comeback in Poland. Former Vice-Chairman of the Council of Ministers (1943-50) Hendrik Allik returned from forced labor in 1956 and, through smaller jobs, worked his way back to the same post (1965-73). Rehabilitation and nativization were more extensive at lower levels, where incompetent outsiders were often replaced with more competent natives. There was also some re-acculturation of Yestonians. In particular, Ivan Käbin gradually re-Estonianized his first name to Johannes, and improved his poor Estonian considerably (although his language goofs always remained a butt for popular jokes). Many other Yestonians remained Russian in their language and culture.

The ECP largely remained an alien organization in which home-grown Estonians formed about one-third of the total membership. The total Estonian share (including "Yestonian" immigrants from Russia) gradually rose from a low of 41.5% in 1952 to 44.6% in 1956 and 49.1% in 1961. After 1966, it levelled off around 52% — much below the Estonian share in the population (74% in 1959, 68% in 1970) or among the specialists with higher or special secondary education (76% in 1970).[28] The latter figure implies that Estonians were overrepresented in most jobs where skills were needed, but grossly underrepresented in the power structure. The hopes for more national autonomy within a Communist framework made many young Estonians join the party around 1956 — an act they would have considered treasonable only a few years earlier. Such hopes did not last. It would be hard to sort out to what extent the party discouraged Estonian membership, and to what extent Estonians chose not to join. In fact, desistance from joining under colonialist conditions could be interpreted in both ways. Either way, Estonians were underrepresented in the ECP, and remained so.

In the rubber-stamp assemblies, on the other hand, Estonians

---

[28] Pennar 1978, p. 118; *EE/BE*, April 1973, p. 8; ECP Party History Institute, *Nekotorye voprosy organizatsionno-partiinoi roboty* (1971); *Nõukogude Õpetaja*, 22 July 1972, p. 2.

were generously overrepresented. The ESSR Supreme Soviet was 86% Estonian (or Yestonian) in 1959, and 85% so in 1966. In the local soviets (councils), the figures were 88 and 89%, respectively. The 1966 ESSR delegation to the USSR Supreme Soviet was 80% Estonian. In the same year, the 111 members of the more powerful ECP CC included 26 Russians, 45 Yestonians, and only 26 home-grown Estonians.[29]

The Fall of Khrushchev

During the early 1960s, the Soviet reactions of the preceding years continued as a full-fledged campaign affecting many aspects of Baltic national life. The purge in Latvia and the general hardening in all three republics, however, did not affect the de-Stalinization which followed the Twenty-Second Congress of the CPSU in 1961. In its aftermath, 6 Latvian old Bolsheviks, members of the party since 1906–13, published an article "That Is Correct!" expressing their approbation of the decision to remove Stalin from the mausoleum on Red Square.[30] In general, not much needed to be done to eradicate his presence in the Baltic republics. In Latvia, one monument in Cēsis and one publicly displayed bust in Riga were removed, along with more numerous framed portraits; in Lithuania, 42 collective farms had to be renamed.

The fall of Khrushchev in 1964 seems to have come as a surprise to the leading Baltic administrators. On 13 October, during the celebration of the twentieth anniversary of liberation from the Germans, Latvian First Secretary Pelše repeatedly mentioned Khrushchev and his Leninist wisdom. The next day, Khrushchev was toppled. Riga papers only included a short note on 18 October and made no commentary until 30 November. Pelše, however, hastened to render homage to the new leadership through an article "The Strength of the USSR Lies in Loyalty to Lenin's Heritage" which appeared in *Pravda* on 6 November, praising Lenin's supposed supreme desire to lead the party according to the principles of collective leadership. Public reactions in the other two republics were similarly delayed.

As could be expected, the ascendancy of a collective leadership meant a slackening of the policies pursued by its predecessor. During his last years in power, Khrushchev had begun to take a rather strong assimilationist course. The 1961 party program adumbrated an eventual disappearance of republic boundaries and organization of the state along regional economic lines. The concept of merging of the nations made its appearance, and the

---

29 Pennar 1978, p. 119; Uustalu 1970, p. 358.
30 *Padomju jaunatne*, 1 November 1961.

creation of regional *sovnarkhozy* in 1962 seemed to point toward further changes which could even threaten the existence of the "sovereign" republics. The uncertainty of the future of regional *sovnarkhozy*, as well as of other issues in a situation of collective leadership, led to a relaxation of the anti-nationalist campaign and to a distinct diminution in prominence of the "growing together" theme. Such abatement favored the continuing assertion of the national cultures.

Even some modest expansion in efforts to stress the "sovereignty" of the republics could be noted. (The contrary trend toward economic recentralization will be discussed later.) Prominent Baltic figures were included in symbolic Soviet delegations. Chairman of the Presidium of the Lithuanian SSR Justas Paleckis frequently represented the USSR at the Interparliamentary Union. In 1966 he became Chairman of the all-Union Soviet of Nationalities, replacing Peive. The Soviet delegation to the UN General Assembly occasionally included such individuals as Juozas Matulis, President of the Lithuanian Academy of Sciences, and ESSR Foreign Affairs Minister Arnold Green. At times, prominence was given to the republics' "trade negotiations" with other countries, which were in reality little more than discussions of implementation of the provisions of USSR trade treaties with those countries.

THE SUCCESSFUL STRUGGLE FOR CULTURAL AUTONOMY

The Thaw in Culture

The Thaw raised high hopes in cultural circles. Artistic and literary production increased rapidly in quantity and, even more important, in quality. Cultural rebirth was the major development of the late 1950s and early 1960s. Therefore the cultural scene for this period will be described here in more detail than that of the previous period, when cultural achievement was dismal, or the recent (post-1968) one, when it was again taken for granted.[31]

[31] For more details on cultural affairs in 1955–68, see: Ekmanis 1978, pp. 181–235; Šilbajoris; Grinius, pp. 197–213; Jonas Vėlaikis, "Lithuanian Literature Under the Soviets," *Lituanus, XII/3* (Fall 1966), pp. 25–43; Arvo Mägi, *Estonian Literature* (Stockholm, 1968); Ivar Ivask, "Recent Trends in Estonian Poetry," BA, XLII13 (Autumn 1968), pp. 517–520; Ivask (ed.), "A Look at Baltic Letters Today" — a special theme issue with articles by 12 authors, BA, XLVII/3 (Autumn 1973), pp. 623–716; Nirk; Rolfs Ekmanis, "Soviet Attitudes toward Pre-Soviet Latvian Writers," JBS, III/1 (Spring 1972), pp. 44–70; George Kurman, "Estonian Literature," in Parming and Järvesoo, pp. 247–280; Mardi Valgemäe, "Drama

The Thaw removed the obligatory models and simplistic declarations of formulae which had dominated in the arts during the Stalin years. More personal introspection along with some stylistic and structural interpretation based on Western trends appeared. Literature began to include such earlier taboos as stream-of-consciousness, non-chronological narrative forms, and psychological introspection. In general, three tendencies can be seen in literary output. The first was an attempt to formulate a more modern and updated version of the standard socialist-realist form. A second group went even further and tried to update the socialist-realist content. It sought to introduce a considerably wider dimension to the earlier stereotyped characters. Themes such as collectivization, guerrilla warfare, or the impact of industrialization on personal lives were no longer treated as simple elements in a Communist propaganda scheme. The heroes of works in this category became genuine human individuals who were seriously considering the changes facing them and honestly struggling with such change in their attempts to find genuine meaning in the new scheme of things. While the essence of socialist realism was still there, its form had entirely vanished. A third category eschewed any of the questions which were central to socialist realism and which still concerned writers in the first two groups. For writers in the third group, modernism, including all the latest literary techniques, was representative of matters far more complex than those which could be treated within the official ideological structure.[32] While the official cultural establishments were not always pleased with writers in this category, some of their work began to be published.

Several deported Latvian writers returned from Siberia in 1954 (Harijs Heislers) and 1955 (Jānis Medenis, Andrejs Kurcijs). In 1955, most of the Estonian poets who had been publicly denounced for ideological crimes were readmitted into the Writers' Union. The works of pre-war writers who had become unmentionable were reissued. One of the earliest seemed to be Jānis Ezeriņš (1891–1924), whose selected short stories were published in Latvia in 1955. In Lithuania, Vincas Krėvė-Mickevičius, the first Acting Prime Minister of the Soviet occupation regime in 1940, who had died in the United States in 1954, was rehabilitated and his works began to appear in 1956. Six volumes of the writings of Balys Sruoga, who died in 1947 after returning from wartime internment

---

and the Theater Arts," *ibid.*, pp. 281–317; Ilmar Mikiver, "The Great Breakthrough of Youth in Soviet Estonian Literature," Seventh Conference on Baltic Studies (Washington, 1980); Marite Sapiets, "Lithuania's Unofficial Press," *Index on Censorship*, IX/4 (1980), pp. 35–38.

[32] Šilbajoris.

in the Stutthof concentration camp, began to appear in 1957. The prominent pre-war writer Ieva Simonaitytė, who had become virtually silent in spite of the eminently acceptable flavor of her works — social critiques of her native Klaipėda area — resumed publication. Another repressed pre-war writer, the left-wing Kazys Boruta, was reintegrated into Lithuanian cultural life. Several pre-war writers, Antanas Miškinis, Kazys Inčiūra, Petras Juodelis, and Juozas Keliuotis, returned from Siberian exile in the late 1950s. In December 1956, publication in the popular Latvian magazine *Zvaigzne* of the long autobiographical poem *Unfinished Song* by returned deportee Harijs Heislers caused a literary sensation; it was one of the first Soviet works dealing with the theme of the Gulag. In another work, Heislers also minced no words in criticizing Stalinist literature:

> We still remember too well the infamous epoch in our poetry
> when the lyric hero loved only because his betrothed fulfilled the
> plan, when kisses were exchanged only on scaffolds of newly
> erected buildings. . . .[33]

Another returnee, Andrejs Kurcijs, succeeded in publishing a novel on the 1905 revolution which had displeased several authoritarian regimes: upon its publication in 1938, *Gates of Life* had been banned by Ulmanis' censors, and it was not republished under Stalin. It finally was, in 1956 — but in revised form. In Estonia, Rudolf Sirge's novel *The Land and the People* (1956) created a sensation with its realistic description of the 1941 deportations.

De-Stalinization permitted the resurrection of several Latvian writers like Fricis Bārda (1880–1919) and the poetess Aspāzija (1868–1943), whose works were published in 1956. The former practice of publishing classical works with new "proletarian" characters slipped in started to be condemned.

Several writers like the Lithuanian Vincas Mykolaitis-Putinas, who had been prominent in the salon-liberal sector of pre-war society and who had become silent, albeit not formally repressed, now resumed their literary activity. Estonia's Friedebert Tuglas, a non-person since 1951, saw publication of 8 volumes of his selected works in 1957–62. The pervasive thirst for classics was demonstrated by the sellout within a few months in 1956 of a 25,000-copy edition of the poems of Jonas Maironis, a Lithuanian clergyman who had become the bard of the turn-of-the century national renaissance. None of his religious poems, however, were included. The emergence of new Baltic talent, slowly starting in 1956, will be discussed in the next sections.

---

[33] *Literatūra un māksla*, no. 23 (1956), as translated by Ekmanis 1978, p. 198.

A greater variety and substance were tolerated in the plastic arts, and the creative legacy of some artists who had been unmentionable in Stalin's time was restored. The most prominent example was Mikalojus Konstatinas Čiurlionis (1875–1911), whose works had been considered expressions of individualism and symbolism and were removed from public exhibition in the pre-war Kaunas museum which had been built specifically as a home for his work. His *de facto* position as Lithuania's national painter re-emerged with the publication of a collection of reproductions, accompanied by reopening the exhibition of his works. Preparation of the edition of reproductions came after considerable debate among the party's cultural authorities. Its appearance after lengthy wrangles and procrastinations was widely viewed as a milestone in the official acceptance of Lithuania's cultural heritage.

A greater latitude of themes, styles, and outside contacts appeared in the theater. In 1956, theaters in the three republics began to cooperate, and Lithuanian performers began to tour Poland. In music, modern experimentation started.

In Latvia, an effort to revive Latgalian culture was tolerated. The Latgalian dialect had lost its official status as a language in Soviet times. In 1957, two small newspapers with a circulation of 1,000 were started. They were closed the following year. It is not clear whether this was because of a change in policy or whether the effort proved unviable for other reasons. The summer solstice celebration, a major national holiday in Latvia (and also Estonia), was allowed again in 1956, after a long ban.

In 1957, even the Stalin Prize winner Andreijs Upīts joined in condemning a style of which he had been a most successful practitioner. In a volumious book on *Problems of Socialist Realism in Literature*, he ridiculed stories full of "extremely stupid and revulsive half-wits, instead of quite normal bourgeois professors," and of kulak villains "who force rusty nails and pieces of glass down the throats of Soviet cows."[34]

By 1957, *Neierastā Amerika* (*Strange America*), by the Latvian émigré Anšlāvs Eglītis, started being serialized in the popular magazine *Zvaigzne*, but this "import of bourgeois nationalism" was attacked and discontinued after the first installment. However, several plays by the eminent playwright Mārtiņš Ziverts, resident in Sweden, were staged. Five books of another Latvian émigré, Jānis Jaunsudrabiņš, were published in 1957–59, and one of them was even filmed. Republication of Latvian Communist writers purged in the pre-war Soviet Union was slower to come. As persons they were "posthumously rehabilitated" starting from

1956, but the first works were apparently published only slowly, starting in 1958 (selected works by Red Army General Roberts Eidmanis).

Expressions of the need to strengthen the role of the national languages in the Baltic republics appeared. One Estonian commentator felt that Russians in Estonia should be obliged to learn Estonian:

> The party organizations have to deal more seriously with teaching the Estonian language to those comrades who do not speak it, and more resolutely to require it from responsible workers who have lived for many years in the country and whose success in learning the Estonian language is insignificant.[35]

The ideological hardening noted at the end of 1956 slowed the Thaw in cultural life. The reaction was most marked in Lithuania, where a series of dismissals of cultural functionaries can be said to have amounted to a purge in 1957-58. Juozas Bulavas, Rector of the University of Vilnius, was relieved of his post, dismissed from the CC, and excluded from the party for "political mistakes." Somewhat later, his successor, the mathematician Jonas Kubilius, provided a detailed exposé of the problems at the institution:

> Quite recently some instructors at the university committed grave ideological errors; certain nationalist tendencies were intensified. Leninist principles for the selection of cadres were violated. No attention was paid to the multi-national composition of the population of the republic. . . . Some instructors of Lithuanian literature began to deny analysis and evaluation of literature based on a viewpoint of the class struggle. . . . The value of proletarian writers was minimized. . . . Shortcomings . . . were also reflected in the activity of various circles — young writers, folklore, and ethnographic studies.[36]

Bulavas had been a pre-war member of the party in the underground, and his past services may now have secured him employment in the Academy of Sciences. His removal was accompanied by a purge of the University faculty. The dismissal of several prominent scholars of Lithuanian language and literature markedly altered the tenor of study of these subjects at the institution. Other dismissals included the Deputy Rector of the Vilnius Pedagogical Institute and the Minister of Culture. Others engaged in the administration of scholarly work received public reprimands for the defense of religion, "apolitical thinking," and "objectivist research."

[35] "V bratskoi seme sovetskikh narodov," *Kommunist Estonii*, 1957/5, p. 15.
[36] *Tiesa*, 2 October 1960.

The changed climate was also reflected in some other cultural areas. A new Lithuanian opera, based on a recent novel about the 1863 uprising (Vincas Mykolaitis-Putinas, *The Rebels*, 1957), was scheduled to be premiered in 1958. Apart from a 1960 announcement of a revised version, nothing ever came of it. Perhaps the social and national elements in the 1863 revolt simply could not be credibly divorced.

It is difficult to explain this reaction regarding culture in Lithuania. One possible hypothesis is that Sniečkus, sensing moods in the Kremlin, sought to deflect the coming anti-nationalist reaction from the nativization of his political machine, the LiCP, by such an evident crackdown in the cultural sphere.

By 1959, the cultural atmosphere in the Baltic republics had changed almost beyond recognition, compared to what it had been only six years earlier — while yet remaining very much the same. Those who measured the gap still remaining between the Western and Baltic degrees of cultural freedom correctly saw very little change indeed. Those who compared the foul air of 1959 to the suffocation of 1953 saw the immense difference between cultural survival and death. There was new hope, and the coming decade was to see a veritable resurrection of Baltic cultures. The fact that it did not come about easily only added to its significance.

The Re-emergence of Estonian Culture

Around 1960, more than one whole new generation of writers and artists made their appearance on the Estonian scene. The new wave included not only the age cohort whose time had come, but also those whose time was overdue since 1945, and those whose start had been stopped short, after 1940. One might distinguish the following phases: the Thaw (1955–59); the "remarkable fluorescence of new, vital, and aesthetically satisfying verse"[37] and other cultural achievements, in 1960–68; and a period of consolidation which began around 1968.

In poetry, the first major debut was *The Coal Concentrator* (1958) by Jaan Kross, already 38: a collection based on the former law instructor's personal experience in the coal mines.

> Fresh, polemical, erudite, witty, and controversial, this volume, the publication of which had been delayed for years, opened new vistas in subject matter and technique. . . . The fresh breezes loosed upon the literary landscape by Kross . . . drew in their wake those who earlier had meekly submitted, those who had

[37] Kurman 1978, pp. 251–252.

maintained silence, and those who were about to launch their first verses.[38]

Almost every year produced a new landmark. A group of young nature-sensitive poetesses debuting in the late 1950s (Helvi Jürisson, Ellen Niit, Lehte Hainsalu) were dubbed the Spring Maidens, implying an active role in proceeding from Thaw to full-fledged Spring. The delayed war-involved generation produced the intellectual strophes of Ain Kaalep and Kaljo Kangur. Among those silent for almost two decades, August Sang and Betti Alver again started publishing powerful verse. Even half-a-dozen previous party bards freed themselves from declarative, prepackaged rhetoric and produced non-preprogrammed poetry.

In 1962, a poetry "cassette" of five slim debuting collections was an instant hit with youth at home and in exile. Almost unbelievably, it later proved to have introduced three writers who were to loom large in Estonian poetry, prose, and drama for the next two decades: Paul-Eerik Rummo, Mats Traat, and Enn Vetemaa. Rummo's brief introductory poem, "The First Calf," characterized well the new period's mix of humor and quiet determination, as he contradicted the Estonian proverb that a cow's "first calf always will perish." In non-rhyme translation:

> I stand with straddled legs
> and wonder at the world.
> I have a funny tail
> and two big eyes.
> And I don't want
> to be a goner.[39]

Out of the continuing post-Thaw flood of talent, we should at least mention Artur Alliksaar's surrealism (first allowed into print in 1968, two years after his death) and Jaan Kaplinski's resonance with nature, religion, and the fate of Vercingetorix and the American Indians:

> . . . There are no witnesses. The dead
> are good Indians. Marry.
> Get children. Kill. Try to be happy.
> Try to be happy if you can.[40]

In prose, Arvo Valton (whose high-school education was in postwar Siberia) emerged with Mrożek-style allegorical and

[38] *Ibid.*, p. 252.
[39] Translated from Paul-Eerik Rummo, *Ankruhiivaja* (Tallinn, 1962), p. 5.
[40] Jaan Kaplinski, "Meie peame ju väga tasa käima," *Tolmust ja värvidest* (Tallinn, 1967), p. 13; full translation by Rein Taagepera in *Akwesasne Notes*, IX/1 (Spring 1977).

grotesque stories and miniatures. Mati Unt, a teen-ager writing about teen-agers, broke new ground in sex and politics, responding to the protest of one of his own characters:

> Our books have a damnably small vocabulary for that kind of thing: "He stayed for the night"; "She spent the night with him"; "He turned off the nightlamp." Don't you sometimes have the feeling that most Estonian writers are eunuchs?[41]

Problems of personal conscience during the Stalinist years were tackled in Vetemaa's short novels *The Monument* (1965) and *The Musician* (1967).[42] Touches of realism started to penetrate novels on war and postwar topics by old-guard writers such as Paul Kuusberg, Lilli Promet, and Raimond Kaugver, whose *Forty Candles* (written by 1959, published in 1966) provoked official displeasure by having its narrator serve in the German and Finnish armies, lose his last shreds of decency in Stalin's labor camps, and end up a venal, respected, and wealthy Soviet industrial executive. Since it received the Lenin Prize, Juhan Smuul's colorless Antarctic travelogue, *The Icy Book* (1959), probably should be mentioned. While poetry stabilized by 1968, prose was still rapidly developing. Longer works not only took longer to write after the Thaw had given the signal, but they also were hit harder by censorship.

Poetic symbolism might escape the censor's attention, or a single controversial poem could be slipped into a journal, though it might later be omitted from a collection. Such was the case with a poem by Arvi Siig (1967) about a kindergarten teacher, Masha (a Russian name), who was good at heart but ineptly bossed the children (all with Estonian names), whose initials formed the Estonian word for "nation." Also, Estonia's main cultural monthly commemorated the fiftieth anniversary of the October Revolution with a poem by Hando Runnel that started: "And yet I keep thinking about a small country," discussed at length Estonia's world role, and only in the few last lines remembered to add that the country was now "tacking" with the "October wind." Both poets later published a number of books of poetry, but without the above poems.[43] With

---

[41] Mati Unt, *Võlg* (Tallinn, 1964); translation in Kurman 1978, p. 261; full translation by Ritva Poom: "The Debt," *Literary Review*, XXIV/4 (Summer 1981), pp. 461–513.

[42] *The Monument* was published in English in Enn Vetemaa, *Three Small Novels* (Moscow, 1977). For brief analyses of various Soviet Estonian works up to 1968, see also BA, XLII (1968), pp. 310, 472, and 621; XLII (1969), pp. 289–290 and 446–448; and XLIV (1970), pp. 157–158.

[43] Rein Taagepera, "Nationalism, Collaborationism, and New-Leftism," in Parming and Järvesoo, pp. 75–103; full translation of Runnel's poem in *EE/BE*, no. 2, p. 2 (1967).

novels, partial pre-publication was usually not possible, and any cuts by censorship affected the balance of the whole, leading to protracted struggles. As an example, Heino Kiik's aforementioned *Spook Hostel* on collectivization misery received the first prize at the republic-level contest for novel manuscripts in 1967. Typesetting was started on 4 July 1968, but printing was authorized only 18 months later, on 29 December 1969. Meanwhile, a major negative character's Russian name was Estonianized, along with numerous other changes and cuts.[44] Publication occurred in 1970.

In drama, socialist realism was supplemented by the rise of a theater of the absurd which was influenced by similar trends in Western Europe, Poland, and Czechoslovakia. In late 1966 and 1967, three of Sławomir Mrożek's short plays were performed on Estonian television, and a translation of Eugene Ionesco's *Rhinoceros* saw print in 1967. However, already in 1966 the first original absurdist play was published — *The Nameless Island* by Artur Alliksaar. Another play in the same vein, by Ain Kaalep, was performed in 1967, but apparently was never published (except abroad). As with prose, the emancipation was still continuing in 1968. Both in the performing arts and in publishing, Estonia was leading (and possibly influencing and conditioning) Russia, ever since the first postwar Brecht production in the Soviet Union took place in Tallinn (in 1957–58).[45]

Western literary works continued (since the Thaw) to be translated into Estonian in great numbers, and often earlier than into Russian (e.g., Kafka's *Trial*, 1966). Even Fedor Dostoevskii, still shunned in Russia, was more available in Estonian. Moreover, some works by Estonian refugee authors were reprinted in Soviet Estonia, starting with the poetry of Marie Under (1958) and Gustav Suits (1964) and continuing with Karl Ristikivi's novel *The Island of Wonders* (1966). The struggle for recovery of literary heritage was largely completed by republication of Jaan Oks (1967) and Karl-August Hindrey (1968). One major voice continued to be silenced — that of ex-deportee Uku Masing, a theologian and orientalist. In 1965 his *Jungle Songs* were smuggled out and published in Sweden. No visible repression followed.

In the figurative arts, Tallinn rapidly emerged as the third Soviet center for abstract art, along with Moscow and Leningrad. In contrast to Russia, the avant-garde movement in Estonia operated with strong support by the general population and was tolerated by local party officials. From its definitely "unofficial" status in the

---

[44] Private communication to one of the authors by a Soviet subject who prefers to remain anonymous.
[45] Valgemäe, p. 291.

early 1960s, it was inching toward a "semi-official" status. While the Russian avant-garde continued to exhibit in private apartments, in Estonia they moved into the galleries of the Union of Artists and Tartu University as early as 1964. What was banned when called abstract art became acceptable when called "geometric art" or "experimental art." "I don't understand them at all," ECP First Secretary Käbin reportedly said at a 1967 "experimental sculpture" exhibition at the library of the Academy of Sciences. ". . . No, you don't have to remove them. I am no art specialist."[46] Artists like Ülo Sooster (who died in 1970) were reestablishing links with the pre-war experimental tradition, and prepared the ground for a new generation which was to emerge around 1970. In the graphic arts, Vive Tolli gained wide recognition with her semi-abstract style. Applied and decorative arts rapidly rejoined pre-war Scandinavian lines, helped by the widening contacts with Finland.

Music saw a deepened understanding and revival of Estonia's thousand-year-old folk-song tradition, alongside of (and some-times combined with) modern dodecaphonic experimentation. In the latter line, Arvo Pärt's "Perpetuum Mobile" gained early recognition at the Ninth Autumn Festival of Music in Warsaw (1965) while still under attack in Moscow. Veljo Tormis became the leading proponent of folk-song inspiration.[47] The first Soviet jazz festival was held in Tartu around 1964. Film production, however, remained stuck in clichés.[48] Architecture was often innovative on the drawing-board level, but construction was restricted to more conservative approaches, due to bureaucratic attitudes combined with limitations on construction materials.

Every gain in the re-emergence of national culture was achieved in an uphill struggle against reactionary and imperialist forces within the republic and outside. In literature, attacks against innovation occurred throughout 1959; it was branded revisionist, subjectivist, abstract humanist and pacifist, narrowly personal, and nihilistic. A concerted attack on Jaan Kross, Ain Kaalep, and Ellen Niit took place. Free verse was condemned. In 1962 the fighting words were symbolism, impressionism, futurism, expres-sionism, surrealism, and existentialism, which were all declared decadent in an ill-disguised neo-Stalinist attack. The waves of reactionary criticism rose, and ran aground, but they had to be taken seriously, and at times such harassment caused considerable personal harm. Publishing remained under full Soviet state

---

[46] Stephen C. Feinstein, "The Avant-Garde in Soviet Estonia," in Norton Dodge and Alison Hill (eds.), *New Art from the Soviet Union* (Washington, 1977), pp. 31–34; *EE/BE*, no. 3, p. 2, (1968), and no. 4, p. 1 (1968).
[47] Harry Olt, *Modern Estonian Composers* (Tallinn, 1972).
[48] *Eesti nõukogude entsüklopeedia*, II, p. 152.

control. Works could reach the page-proof stage and then be prohibited without explanation. Works of popular authors could sell out, but they would not be reprinted. Meanwhile, stores would be full of second-rate works approved by the party censors, published in new editions regardless of limited demand.

The Re-emergence of Latvian Culture

While the general pattern in Latvia was similar to that in Estonia, the purges of 1959 cast a long shadow over all of the 1960s. The start before 1959 was promising. Although remaining well within the framework of socialist realism, short stories by Jēzups Laganovskis (*When the Winds Rustle*, 1956) represented a landmark by their rather realistic depiction of the sad state of the collectivized Latgalian countryside. Ojārs Vācietis (*The Wind of the Distant Roads*, 1956) emerged as a promising poet.

In 1957–58, new stimulating prose tended to be published in *Karogs*. Republication in the form of a separate book usually required conformist alterations, and often never occurred. In a short story by Dagnija Cielava-Zigmonte (*Golden Dust*), a college student is sleeping around, especially with her father's chauffeur. Being the daughter of a Stalin Prize-winning biologist, she would never consider marrying her lower-class lover. Angry establishment critics paid Cielava the compliment of comparing her story to Françoise Sagan's recent *Un certain sourire*. A novel by Laimonis Purs (*Have I Mused on It?*) extended the description of pleasure-oriented children of the managerial new class. Zigmunds Skujiņš provoked a heated controversy with a story on postwar guerrilla struggle (*One Night's Chronicle*).

As mentioned earlier, establishment attacks became threatening in 1958. Laganovskis, Cielava, and even ex-deportee Heislers were forced to declare repentance. However, in late 1958 a relatively liberal climate returned. A strong demand for aesthetic criteria in literature and the arts was spearheaded by poet Ojārs Vācietis. His first novel (*Through the Eyes of Those Days*, 1958, in *Karogs*; 1959, revised, as a book) depicted the hypocrisy and inhumanity of the collectivization and deportations of 1948–49. The peak of artistic achievement in post-Thaw novels may have been reached with *The Water Lily* (1958) by Visvaldis Eglons-Lāms, where the disappointments of the modern "superfluous man" are compounded by past and present Soviet practices.[49]

The political purge of 1959 changed the cultural atmosphere thoroughly. Starting in November 1959, it felt as if a new *Zhdanovshchina* (cultural purge) were blowing over Latvia. The

[49] For details of the 1957–60 period, see Ekmanis 1978, pp. 235–288.

chill was to continue for many years. As late as 1967, an ex-Stalinist critic considered the stagnation in Latvian literature to be worse, in some aspects, than under Stalin. As one reason, he mentioned

> the distrust that reigned some time ago and hindered development of free thought. Many writers suffered from severe and unmerited accusations. Latvian literary critics did not know how to protect the autonomy of literature during these times when literature was subjugated to rigid canons which turned young immature writers into obedient conjecture literati instead of artists and searchers for new truths.[50]

In 1968, the cultural weekly *Literatūra un māksla* published a complaint that, in comparison with their colleagues in some other Soviet republics, the overseers of Latvian cultural affairs were excessively insensitive to their nation's cultural values.[51] The fact that such a critique could be published in itself suggested some improvement. But the struggle was hard.

The pressures of the early 1960s reinforced the "literature of compromise," although that of protest and exposure did not vanish altogether. A novel about Russian Latvians caught up in the pre-war purges (*My Greetings to Daugava*, by Mārtiņš Krieviņš), originally published in *Karogs* in 1959, was published in book form in 1961, with alterations. Eglons' *Smoke is Rising* (1960) painted a realistically drab picture of day-to-day working-class life, contrasting it with the life-style of the ruling class. It was condemned by LaCP Secretary Augusts Voss, and Eglons did not get into print again until 1968. His fate seemed to reflect that of Latvian culture as a whole.[52]

National classics such as Bārda and Aspāzija, republished during the Thaw, were banned again in the early 1960s, after attacks against an uncleansed literary heritage in the local press and even in *Pravda* (3 January 1960) in Moscow. Only in 1968, a half-dozen literary critics managed to publish articles protesting the gross mistreatment of Bārda's and Aspāzija's work, and opened the way to gradual republication. In Estonia such struggles were fought more quietly, and were essentially won by 1968.

Poetry recovered first. Among the generation born in the 1930s, Ojārs Vācietis continued to publish. Always careful not to overstretch the regime's patience, his elliptic and penetrating *Time of the Cuckoo* (1968) was praised in Latvia and in exile. In clear

---

[50] Edgars Damburs, in *Karogs*, 1967/6, as reported through *Looming*, 1968/11, in *EE/BE*, no. 4, p. 1 (1968).

[51] Rasma Lāce, *Literatūra un māksla*, 30 March 1968; see Ekmanis 1972, p. 61.

[52] The extensive overview by Ekmanis 1978 mentions and describes numerous works from 1956 to 1960, but almost none from 1962 to 1966.

protest against the merciless religion of progress, Vācietis claimed that:

> This century has a metallic voice
> And a steely hand
> And talks too much of: dominating,
> conquering,
> forcing,
> And too little of protecting and preserving.[53]

Vācietis was joined by the impatient and impulsive Imants Ziedonis with *Sand of Land and Dreams* (1961), Vitauts Ļudēns, Māris Čaklais, Jānis Plotnieks, Vizma Belševica, and Imants Auziņš. Among the silenced pre-war poets, Mirdza Bendrupe reappeared. In her *Voice Unceasing* (1967), she told people beyond the seas:

> Between us stand space and time.
> Oceans. Years.
> But we are one breath.
> We're kin.[54]

The nation was repairing broken ties to itself and to the world. Another major pre-war poet, ex-deportee Elza Stērste, also emerged from a long silence. A selection of her pre-war poems, announced in 1960, was finally published, along with some new poems, in 1967.[55] The delayed generation (those born in the 1920s) which so powerfully boosted the early post-Thaw phase in Estonian poetry, was less conspicuous in Latvia.

Prose and drama required a longer recovery period than poetry. However, by 1967, *The Investigator*, a short novel, immediately established Alberts Bels as a major novelist acclaimed by émigré critics and, after brief hesitation, by the Soviet ones. The novel's main character, a 29-year-old sculptor, has a family which mirrors the recent fate of the whole nation: an Old Bolshevik grandfather shot by Stalin, a father bending to all political winds, one brother dead in the German army, and another one wounded in the Soviet army. Many of his classmates were deported around 1947, and one of them survived and returned — a toothless "old man at twenty" — since his father now was declared erroneously condemned.

---

[53] Ojārs Vācietis, "Naktsmājas," *Dzegužlaiks* (Riga, 1968); translation by Vaira Vīķis-Freibergs, "Echoes of the Dainas and the Search for Identity in Contemporary Latvian Poetry," JBS, VI/1 (Spring 1975), pp. 17–29.

[54] Mirdza Bendrupe, in *Nerimas balss* (Riga, 1967); translation by Vīķis-Freibergs, p. 28.

[55] See Astrid Ivask, short review, BA, XLII/3 (Autumn 1968),p. 629; Ekmanis 1978, p. 217.

He clasps me with both hands, and starts crying. "I hate, hate all of those who did the beating — hate them!" "Did they beat you, then?" I asked. I am a naive child, compared to Ivanovs, I do not know many a thing as yet. I thought only the Gestapo was beating people. "Not me," Ivanovs replies. "They beat my father, and it comes to the same!"[56]

The sculptor has decided to be an optimist regarding the future, and avoid getting entangled in the past, without forgetting it. But the past keeps resurfacing in his mind. He half-despises his weathervane father, without suspecting how much he resembles him. It's just that the circumstances are different. The importance of "picking the right birthdate" keeps coming up, just as it does in Vetemaa's *Musician*, also published in 1967, in Estonia. Bels' writings could make one believe "that not all the ideas of socialist realism must be discarded in order to write good literature." Among other prosaists emerging in the late 1960s, one might mention Ija Meldere-Dzērve, who transposed the Daedalus myth into the life of a Soviet manager (*Wax Wings*, 1967), and Andris Jakubāns, whose very short stories form a mosaic of everyday life (*My White Guitar*, 1968).[57]

The most prominent dramatist of the period was Gunārs Priede. Debuting prior to the Thaw in the officially prescribed style, he gradually evolved toward more varied techniques and a wider scope of problems. Nonetheless, even by 1968, Latvian drama remained at what one critic abroad called "one of its lowest ebbs."[58]

In figurative art, a monumental straight-line painting style was developed in the late 1950s, and in the early 1960s influenced all of the official art in the USSR. "Masters of the Land" (1960) by Edgars Iltners became one of the best-known examples of this style, combining Stalinist traditions with moderate modernization: bold-stepping, close-fisted men presumably meant to represent collective farmers. More modern and politically disengaged approaches also came to be accepted gradually, especially in

---

[56] Alberts Bels, *Izmeklētājs* (Riga, 1967); translated from the Estonian translation (Tallinn, 1969), p. 73. See also Juris Silenieks, "Alberts Bels: In Search of Man," JBS, V/1 (Spring 1974), pp. 34–39; Ojārs Krātiņš, "Society and the Self in the Novels of Ilze Skipsna and Alberts Bels," BA, XLVII/3 (Autumn 1973), pp. 675–682, and short review, BA, XLII/3 (Autumn 1968), p. 628.

[57] See Gunārs Irbe, short reviews in BA, XLII/2 (Summer 1968), pp. 477–478, and XLIII/3 (Autumn 1969), p. 635. For other brief analyses of various Soviet Latvian works up to 1968, see also BA, XLII (1968), pp. 162, 316, 478, and 627; XLIII (1969), pp. 269 and 458; and XLIV (1970), p. 164.

[58] Juris Silenieks, short review in BA, XLIII/2 (Summer 1969), p. 458.

graphic arts of the generation born in the 1930s (Gunārs Krollis, Semjons Šegelmans).

The Re-emergence of Lithuanian Culture

Developments in Lithuania paralleled those in Estonia, and even preceded them in prose writing. Furthermore, Lithuanian graphic arts, film, and urban architecture achieved wide recognition by the late 1960s.[59]

As in Estonia and Latvia, poets were among the first to react to the Thaw. Seeking to update the socialist-realist form, some established figures began to shift from Stalinist rigidity to individual themes and a more experimental style. Justinas Marcinkevičius, a talented and unorthodox poet, attempting to present real social problems and their resolutions in the spirit of faith in the official progressive force of history, supplemented clichés in his *Twentieth Spring* (1956) with subtle lyricism and a lively, easy-flowing prosody. *Devil's Bridge* (1957) by Algimantas Baltakis added a new youthful flair but retained a rather traditional declamatory style. The only Lenin Prize of the period, however, went to Eduardas Mieželaitis for his skillful and expressive, though at times somewhat contrived, improvisations in *Man* (1962). This product of his implicit belief that Soviet poetry could become "modernistic" without losing its basic function as a style of propaganda received wide acclaim throughout the Soviet world.

While Marcinkevičius, Baltakis, and Mieželaitis can be clearly placed in the aforementioned first and second general categories of literary reactions to the Thaw (changes in form and in content of socialist realism), some younger poets like Alfonsas Maldonis began to emancipate themselves entirely from socialist realism. In particular, Janina Degutytė, in her first collection (*Days Are Presents*, 1960), related her feelings and moods to nature and landscape. Judita Vaičiūnaitė displayed a fresh childlike outlook toward life in *As Green Wine* (1963). By the end of the decade, some had clearly abandoned any attempts resolving the dichotomy between art and politics. The first edition of Sigitas Geda's *Steps* (1966) is a curious hybrid including a poetic homage to Lenin and Castro:

> The continents fall into Lenin's step,
> The world will fit into his straight finger!

---

[59] A comprehensive overview of 1956–66 Lithuanian literature is given by Vėlaikis. A Soviet view can be found in *Istoriia litovskoi literatury* (Vilnius, 1977) and Algimantas Buchis [Bučys], *Roman i sovremennost: stanovlenie i razvitie litovskogo sovetskogo romana* (Moscow, 1977).

> Fidel is strolling through Cuba's countryside,
> The laced shoes of the bearded one creak![60]

However, the bulk of the booklet is a paean to a continuum with the past, a notion which is hard to politicize:

> The steep eyes of the little wooden gods —
> Are they not my,
> Not your eyes?
>
> How close you are,
> My ancestors![61]

New trends in prose appeared during the early 1960s, although political relaxation was already marked in 1957 by Vytautas Rimkevičius' *The Students*, which even described the huge pro-independence demonstration on All Souls' Eve, 1956.[62] At first, prose works seemed to be more intent on discovering a more modern form of socialist realism. The not-so-successful *Red Roses Bloom* (1959) by Alfonsas Bieliauskas, and some of the early (1958) descriptions of war and guerrilla resistance by Mykolas Sluckis, fit into this category. By the mid-1960s, both writers were seeking to fuse modern forms with a socialist-realist essence. In his novel *Steps to the Sky* (1963), set in the turbulent countryside of postwar collectivization, Sluckis uses the Indriūnas family as a cross-section of Lithuania's peasantry. The story unfolds through the perspective of an idealistic member of the intelligentsia, perhaps an autobiographical double of the author. Although the hero is idealized for his faith in humanity and a socially better future, he discovers that social realities in the village are considerably more complex than the officially sanctioned simplistic schemes would have it. The peasantry's attachment to the land is pervasive and insurmountable. The head of the small-landowner family sacrifices the fates of his loved ones to his perception of what is necessary to maintain land-ownership, and tragedy is inevitable. One of the novel's most surprising facets was its presentation, perhaps for the first time in Soviet Lithuanian literature, of the postwar partisans as human beings, albeit ones motivated by an alien ideology.

Sluckis subsequently pioneered the introduction of stream-of-

---

60 Sigitas Geda, *Pėdos* (Vilnius, 1966), p. 5.

61 *Ibid.*, p. 13.

62 Excerpts from Vytautas Rimkevičius' *Studentai* (Vilnius, 1957), with comments by Thomas Remeikis and Rimvydas Šilbajoris, in *Lituanus*, VI/2 (September 1960), pp. 68–74. For the 1960s, see Velaikis, pp. 30–40; Bronius B. Vaškelis, "The Short Stories of Romualdas Lankauskas," in Arvids Ziedonis et al. (eds.), *Baltic Literature and Linguistics* (Columbus, Ohio, 1973); Ilona Gražytė-Maziliauskienė, "Variations on the Theme of Dehumanization in the Short Stories of Juozas Aputis," BA, XLVII/3 (Autumn 1973), pp. 695–701.

consciousness narration into the Lithuanian novel in *Adam's Apple* (1966) and *My Harbor Is Turbulent* (1968). Both focus critically on problems among the contemporary intelligentsia, delving into the bureaucratic mentality and various facets of urban life.[63] Bieliauskas subsequently applied a stream-of-consciousness technique in *Romance in Kaunas* (1966), which treats the new Soviet bureaucracy, including its seamy side. While apparently bold and daring in its contention that truth — even Soviet truth — is more multi-faceted than may be inferred from official ideology, his novel also presented a "correct" historical viewpoint, suggesting to the reader that present shortcomings are merely a passing phase in the development of Soviet morality.

The most notable Lithuanian work of prose which sought to fuse a socialist-realist essence with the complexities of the real world and to present them in contemporary form was Jonas Avyžius' *The Village at the Crossroads* (1964), which attempted seriously to portray the shortcomings of collective farms and to depict the full moral as well as social chaos introduced into the lives of the peasants by collectivization. It gives an appearance of moral courage through raising tough questions. However, its point, the ultimate resolution of the problems raised, is not unacceptable to official orthodoxy. An individual needs to make a conscious decision to join in the new order of things, as continued resistance will yield only more bloodshed which cannot be justified historically. Perhaps as a very good example of this new type of socialist realism, the novel received considerable all-Union publicity. His subsequent novel, *The Time of the Emptying of Homesteads* (1970), set in the period of German wartime occupation, likewise received official attention and praise. Not long after its appearance, Avyžius was awarded the Lenin Prize.

A similar approach appeared also in the novels of Vytautas Bubnys. His guerrillas are portrayed as human individuals who are idealistic in their own nationalist way, but who also reach the realization that continued opposition will only result in more misery without any historical justification.

Some Lithuanian prose works also clearly passed beyond the realm of socialist realism. Jonas Mikelinskas debuted in 1960 with *The Old Man Under the Clock*, trying to analyze psychological crises and subtle conflicts with a somewhat detached curiosity. With *Wandering Sands* (1960), Romualdas Lankauskas introduced into Lithuanian literature a melancholy, disillusioned, and alienated individual. This was followed in 1963 by two novels,

[63] For a study of the work of Sluckis, see L. A. Terakopian, *Mikolas Slutskis* [Mykolas Sluckis] — *Ocherk tvorchestva* (Moscow, 1976).

In the Middle of a Wide Field, which objectively depicted the horror of a senseless war where Germans as well as Soviets die without knowing why, and *A Bridge into the Sea*, which viewed childhood reminiscences as "our only inviolable possession." The latter was severely criticized, and not published in book form.[64] Two works of Juozas Aputis (*The Flowering Bread of the Bees*, 1963, and *September Birds*, 1967) were only reluctantly published, because of alleged subjectivism and pessimism. Another far-reaching departure from socialist realism in both style and content was Icchokas Meras' *A Tie Lasts a Wink* (1963), in which a flash-back technique is applied to describe the thoughts of a Jewish prisoner playing a fatal chess game with a Nazi guard.

The only notable exception to such trends appears in the work of Juozas Baltušis, whose literary career began during the pre-war years. Although the populist quality of his approach had never fallen afoul of the dictates of socialist realism and his loyalty to the party was never questioned, the quantity of his literary output declined during the Stalin years. His most notable work during the Thaw is the novel *Sold Summers* (two parts, 1957 and 1969), a realistic view of social conditions among the pre-war peasantry, depicted through the consciousness of a poor child. Although the novel can be said to be eminently acceptable to the classical canons of socialist realism, it also gained genuine popularity for its masterful recreation of peasant speech. His subsequent work con-tinued along a similar vein, though he fell somewhat into disfavor among the ideological establishment for a favorable impression of the United States after a trip there (*In the Paths of Fathers and Brothers*, 1967).

The ferment among the Lithuanian intelligentsia during the early 1960s comes through in the work of Justinas Marcinkevičius, *The Pine Tree That Laughed* (1961), and in the circumstances of its appearance.[65] It has been claimed that the book was written upon request by the KGB, which recognized the talent of Marcinkevičius for seeming to be "one of the boys" as far as intelligentsia circles are concerned, but who was actually continually selling himself out to the party ideologues. Several of the protagonists could be readily identified as prominent younger members of the intelligentsia. One of them, currently an émigré, has claimed that entire passages, set in dialogue, are taken verbatim from the record of his interrogation by the KGB which he had signed. The interrogation followed an abortive attempt by some members of the intelligentsia to gather a

[64] Vėlaikis, p. 35; R. Lankauskas, "Tiltas į jūrą," *Pergalė*, 1963/3, p. 22.
[65] Justinas Marcinkevičius, in *Pergalė*, 1961/8, p. 38; also published in book form the same year.

Lithuanian issue of Aleksandr Ginzburg's *Samizdat* publication *Sintaksis* in Moscow. Marcinkevičius' book appeared in the aftermath, became widely discussed, and was quickly sold out. By 1963 it was translated into Russian, Latvian, and Estonian, and achieved some attention throughout the USSR and Eastern Europe. Its format may have inspired the path-breaking short novels of Vetemaa in Estonia and Bels in Latvia, in 1965–67. While a main object of youth interest and subsequent attack in the novel was German existentialism, there were interesting parallels with an earlier official attack against student interest in living Marxism:

> Some students are, with the help of dictionaries, reading the works of Western aesthetes. . . . They are interested in the writings of the Hungarian revisionist G. Lukacs, whose works have reached our republic in German translation [*sic*]. In the meantime, we have not produced any works for our youth in their native language which reveal the nature of such bourgeois aestheticism.[66]

Socialism, Communism, or the party never received a mention in *The Pine Tree* — the attack lines were reactionary rather than Marxist.

History was used in drama to reflect the current Soviet dilemma between art and politics. Perhaps hoping that the issues of the present would attain a timeless immortality when expressed on stage by prominent figures from the past, Marcinkevičius wrote the play *Mindaugas* (1968), a study of the philosophy of history set in a recreation of the harsh rule of the founder of the medieval Lithuanian state. It clearly falls into the second category of literary works of the period, attempting to reconcile contemporary social problems and even personally reprehensible actions with long-term positive benefits. On one level, Mindaugas can be said to have been a murderer and adulterer; on another, he is a national hero. Juozas Grušas, a pre-war Catholic novelist, broke a long silence with a comedy in 1955, and continued with romanticized historical dramas such as *Herkus Mantas* (1957), a dramatization of a thirteenth-century revolt by the Old Prussians against the invading Teutonic Knights. He reached psychological realism with the landmark *Love, Jazz, and the Devil* (1967).

Moving even further away from didactic realism toward the theater of fantasy and the grotesque, Kazys Saja reached a peak in "socialist allegory of the absurd" with *The Maniac* (1966), *The*

---

[66] Kostas Korsakas, Third Congress of Soviet Lithuanian writers (21–23 January 1959), as reported in ACEN VI, 112.

Orator (1966), and *The Prophet Jonah* (1968).[67] In the first, a maniac takes over a train by launching a campaign to unmask a maniac who is planning to take over the train, in a transparent parody of Stalin's takeover of the Revolution.

> Do you know how many people have already been locked up in the other cars? Five in some, seven in some. And how many do *we* have? A mere one-and-a-half. . . .
> — But after all, there is only one maniac!
> — However, we do not know who he is. Everyone looks the same. Even so, we are all quite humane, aren't we?[68]

On the whole, the emergence of a national theatrical tradition as a key element in the country's cultural life proved to be a significant and lasting development of the Thaw. The theater in the provincial center of Panevėžys headed by the veteran director Juozas Miltinis, who had received his training in pre-war France, achieved considerable renown and became a sort of cultural mecca whose performances attracted a wide audience from throughout the country. The official cultural establishment favored such popularity with a modern building to house the company in 1968.

Along with the other Baltic republics, Lithuania became a leading center of the rebirth of graphic arts in the Soviet Union. The tradition of stained glass, banned because of its church connotations, was revived. In architecture, the Žirmūnai residential district in Vilnius was the first in the USSR to apply Finnish and Scandinavian city-planning concepts. The achievement was a double one: to have the concepts approved, and to have the actual construction carried out with Soviet construction materials.

The Lithuanian film industry, which up to that time had hardly produced anything noteworthy, began to explore relevant themes. In 1966, two rather surprising films by Soviet standards, *No One Wanted to Die* by Vytautas Žalakevičius and *Steps to the Sky* by Raimondas Vabalas, treated the extremely sensitive issue of the postwar guerrilla resistance. Although reviews stressed their ideological correctness, both films were not void of artistic merit. It

---

[67] Mardi Valgemäe, "Death of a Sea Gull: The Absurd in Finno-Baltic Drama," *BA*, XLVI/2 (Summer 1972), pp. 374–379; Tomas Venclova, "Echoes of the Theater of the Absurd and of the 'Theater of Cruelty' in Modern Lithuania (K. Saja, J. Glinskis)," in H. Birnbaum and T. Eekman (eds.), *Fiction and Drama in Eastern and Southeastern Europe* (Los Angeles, 1980), pp. 429–441. English translations of Kazys Saja's *The Orator* and *The Maniac* in *Lituanus*, XIII/3 (Fall 1967), pp. 29–71, and XIV/4 (Winter 1968), pp. 73–94, respectively.
[68] Kazys Saja, *Mažosios pjesės* (Vilnius, 1968), p. 152. For brief analyses of various Soviet Lithuanian works up to 1968, see also *BA*, XLII (1968), pp. 479–480 and 629–631; XLIII (1969), pp. 297 and 636; and XLIV (1970), pp. 166–167 and 347.

was also possible to reach interpretations which could be question-able from the ideological point of view. While the latter was somewhat less extolled, perhaps because of a greater subtlety in political differentiation, both won Soviet cinematographic prizes.[69] Another Lithuanian film, *The Last Day of Vacation* by Arūnas Žebriūnas, was awarded the Grand Prix at the 1966 Youth Film Festival at Cannes.

Soviet Socio-Cultural Pressure

A renewed Soviet anti-nationalism campaign of the early 1960s sought to replace the generally perceived feelings of national distinctiveness with an all-Union identification.[70] Accordingly, the effort to stress the communality of the Baltic peoples with the rest of the USSR increased again. Grandiose all-Union development projects in Central Asia or Siberia came again to occupy places of prominence in the mass media. An earlier Virgin Lands campaign had died down, perhaps because of poor reception. Now populari-zations of such projects reappeared. In June 1962, it was reported that 10,000 youths from Lithuania were helping in Kazakhstan with the harvest; large numbers had gone to other places.[71] In March of the same year, Latvian youths participated in road-building projects at Kuibyshev, and Komsomol members from Liepāja worked as construction laborers in Saratov on the Volga. Recruitment articles with titles such as "Siberia is Romantic," "Siberia and I," or "The North Awaits Strong Men" proliferated.

Although its facilities were still quite underdeveloped, internal Soviet tourism started to serve as a vehicle for the mingling of Soviet peoples. The Baltic republics, endowed with attractive beaches, woodlands, and lakes, began to be flooded with seasonal visitors, mainly from the Russian republic. By 1968 it was reported that about a million summer vacationers from the RSFSR had visited Lithuania[72] (which has the least extensive beaches of the three republics).

Glorification of Russia and of things Russian continued as an intrinsic element of the stress on internationalism. As the Latvian party journal *Padomju Latvijas komunists* stressed in August 1960:

One should explain the force that stands behind the friendship of

---

[69] M. Maltsene [Malcienė], *Kino sovetskoi Litvy* (Leningrad, 1980), pp. 67-74, 112-116.
[70] Cf. M. Suslov, *Pravda*, 18 July 1960.
[71] *Komjaunimo tiesa*, 9 January 1962.
[72] *Tiesa*, 10 December 1968.

nations, the extent of the assistance rendered by the brotherly Soviet republics, and principally by the trusted friend of the Latvians — the Russian nation — in reconstructing the Latvian economy and culture.

The campaign also involved a limited return to a Stalinist use of history in stressing an alleged age-old affinity of the Baltic peoples for Russia. Vasilii Savchenko, a Russian historian at the Latvian Academy of Sciences, asserted that "Many times, Russians were assigned by history the role of being other people's saviors." Similar themes of an age-old affinity with the Russian nation appeared in Lithuania. The Chairman of the Presidium of the Supreme Soviet, Justas Paleckis, perhaps mixed metaphors in his *Thoughts about the Elder Brother* (1959) in comparing Russia "to a wise and good mother who unceasingly cares about her children."[73] The historian Kostas Navickas produced a booklet on *The Historical Significance of the Leninist Nationalities Policy to the Lithuanian Nation* (1960), and somewhat later, the dean of official Lithuanian historiography, Juozas Žiugžda, published a survey of Lithuanian ties with its "historical" ally, the Great Russian Nation. Considerable contortion of facts was necessary in view of the long-term medieval rivalry between Moscow and Lithuania, as well as the role of Imperial Russia in the eighteenth-century partitions of Poland-Lithuania and suppression of the nineteenth-century national uprisings. A new aspect of the integration of Baltic history into a tighter all-Union pattern was the glorification of the abortive Soviet Baltic republics of 1918–19 as precursors of the 1940 variety. This had been avoided in Stalin's time, as it might have required mention of some leading Baltic Communists like Jānis Rudzutaks and Roberts Eidmanis (Latvia), Zigmas Angarietis and General Vytautas Putna (Lithuania), and Jaan Anvelt and Hans Pöögelmann (Estonia), who were victims of the Great Purge.

In 1961, Khrushchev in person complained (at the January Plenum of the CPSU CC) about the planned restoration work in Lithuania of castles which even the feudal lords themselves had abandoned, and pointed to ideological mistakes in appraising the traditions of Lithuania's past. He was particularly incensed by initiation of the restoration of Trakai Castle, the capital of the medieval Lithuanian state (20 km southwest of Vilnius), which had been in ruins since early modern times.[74]

Three years later, the writings of the historian Juozas Jurginis

[73] Justas Paleckis, *Mintys apie vyresnįjį brolį* (Vilnius, 1959), p. 8.
[74] *Pravda*, 22 January 1961. Speech of N. S. Khrushchev to Plenum of CPSU CC, 17 January 1961.

were attacked for minimal attention to historic interaction with Russia and for faulty application of Marxist periodization, which had been set up on the basis of the Russian past. However, the full canon of Stalinist historiography was not restored.

A glorification of the military, which intensified during the 1960s, could be seen as another element in the stress on all-Union ties. The Red Army and Navy, organized along centralized principles, could serve as an integrating element among non-Russians. Articles on the heroism of World War II and the friendship between Soviet forces and Baltic Pioneers and students proliferated. In February 1956, the Lithuanian party magazine *Komunistas* reproached writers for "trends toward pacifism and an abstract negation of war." Groups of "young cosmonauts" or "young border guards" were formed under the tutelage of officers to popularize the military among children throughout the Soviet Union.

A shift occurred in emphasis on the roles of the native languages in the republics. This became particularly important, since national feelings among the Balts were to a large extent based on linguistic distinctiveness. Officially, all languages of the USSR were equal. During the Thaw, it became more of a reality. A reaction accompanied the anti-nationalism campaign. One Soviet theorist depicted the goal of Soviet nationality policy as a melting-pot for "the creation of a single nation with a single language."[75]

The linguistic reaction appeared most strident in Latvia after the Berklāvs purge. LaCP Secretary Augusts Voss exuded love, respect, and gratitude toward the "brotherly Russian nation" in an extensive editorial in *Cīņa* (10 June 1960). He admonished Latvians to learn Russian because it was "the language of socialist culture, of the most progressive literature and art, and of twentieth-century technology and progress." Some comrades, however, he observed, "lean toward national seclusion and do not support the progressive influence of the Russian language." All speeches at the joint session of the Latvian Supreme Soviet and CC held on 22 July 1960 were delivered in Russian. Riga streets began to receive Russian names. Literary evenings in the Russian language proliferated, along with notable visits by prominent guests from Moscow at cultural gatherings.

The cry for vigilance against imperialists and bourgeois-nationalist agents and ideologies resounded through public pronouncements on matters of culture. Attempts to restore the old slogans of socialist realism — a projection of the current party line

---

[75] A. A. Isupov, *Natsionalnyi sostav naseleniia SSSR* (Moscow, 1964), p. 9.

in the arts and a glorification of the mythical new Soviet man and of Soviet patriotism — kept appearing in the mass media. There were complaints about modernism and "a reversion to the old decadent formalistic schools and the outdated art of the bourgeoisie."[76] An absence of Soviet themes was frequently bemoaned. Lithuania's graphic arts section at the 1960 Baltic Art Exposition in Moscow was faulted for an insufficient representation of proper historic, revolutionary, and "international" themes. The Lithuanian State Publishing House was publicly reprimanded in 1961 for "uncritical" acceptance of a manuscript on lake research which gave too much prominence to the earlier work of émigré scientists, neglecting Soviet studies.

Expressions of local identification came under attack. In October 1962, *Komunistas* castigated the allegedly inaccurate and narrow-minded use of the term "our literature" in reference to Lithuanian literature; such an expression could supposedly only refer to the literature of the USSR as a whole. Lankauskas' short story, *A Bridge into the Sea*, was denounced for its numerous references to Lithuania as "the green country covered with the bones of forefathers who for centuries had fought for their freedom." In early 1961, Voldemārs Sauleskalns and Voldemārs Melnis were dismissed from the Latvian Writers' Association. Three other writers (including, surprisingly, two Russians) received "strict party censure" for bourgeois nationalism.[77]

Attacks in literature were paralleled in the other arts. Composer Vytautas Klova, who was preparing an opera on the theme of the 1410 Battle of Grünwald (Tannenberg) which had ended the threat of the Teutonic Knights to the medieval Lithuanian state, was faulted for seeking inspiration "behind the thick walls of the castle at Marienburg or the battlefields at Tannenberg," and his colleague Rimvydas Žigaitis was criticized for working on an opera based on Mickiewicz's long romantic poem *Konrad Wallenrod*.[78] The Kaunas State Opera was criticized for staging works by Lehar, Offenbach, Gounod, and Strauss while ignoring current Soviet production.[79]

The writer Mykolas Sluckis was in effect subjected to a public self-criticism session at the 1963 Congress of the Lithuanian Writers' Union. The event — staged, perhaps significantly, in the Vilnius Russian Drama Theater — was attended by First Secretary Antanas Snieckus. According to accounts current among Lithuanian intelligentsia circles, Snieckus was late for his

[76] *Sirp ja Vasar*, 24 February 1961.
[77] *Literatūra un māksla*, 8 April 1961.
[78] *Literatūra ir menas*, 11 February 1961.
[79] *Ibid.*, 4 April 1964.

speech — having been, as he claimed, delayed by some agricultural business. He liked to present the image of a good farmer, and apologized in a rather Khrushchev-like manner: that morning, he is supposed to have claimed, the leadership had been concerned with manure, and now it would proceed to remove the dung from literature.

The exhibition of young artists at the Sixth Congress of the Union of Lithuanian Artists (December 1966) evoked another party blast against works permeated with "alien aesthetic conception," and even against "striving for world standards" if it did not help shape the common national characteristics of Soviet art.[80]

Folk ensembles of song and dance were admonished to perform Soviet songs in place of archaic folk-songs. In early 1960, the popular Latvian ethnographic ensemble *Saulgrieži* was disbanded as an undesirable propagator of nationalist ideology.

The poem "This Year's March" (1963) by Justinas Marcinkevičius unmistakably reflects the mood of uncertainty which had crept into the national cultural scene by the early 1960s:

> Maybe it is not spring, maybe only
> A new variety of winter?
> The earth appears through snow and frost
> As the shore of the sun.[81]

Consolidation of Cultural Autonomy

The absence of Stalinist methods of control, however, weakened the attempts to re-impose orthodoxy in the realm of culture. The yearning of the younger cultural figures for a reunion with the mainstream of Western culture could hardly be dissipated by threats, admonitions, or special seminars attended by party and Komsomol dignitaries designed to explain the party line on national characteristics in art or the role of the party leadership in creative work. Highly heralded trips by young writers for inspiration in the Virgin Lands of Siberian construction projects yielded little results. The anti-nationalism campaign could not undo the cultural revival which had begun with the Thaw.

Celebrations of particularly significant native cultural anniversaries came to be tolerated, provided that some ideological bows were made. The 1964 anniversary celebration of the 250th birthday of the Lithuanian poet Kristijonas Donelaitis tried to portray this eighteenth-century Lutheran parson in East Prussia as a pioneer of socialist realism. A similar approach was taken to Jānis Rainis, the most eminent figure in Latvian poetry, whose birth centenary was

---

[80] *Ibid.*, 24 December 1966.
[81] Justinas Marcinkevičius, *Duoną raikančios rankos* (Vilnius, 1963), p. 77.

celebrated with commemorative evenings at the Opera and other theaters, and by the unveiling of a large monument to him in Riga. Rainis had been a member of the Parliament and Minister of Education of the independent republic.

One reason for the failure of the cultural repression was an inability of the cultural authorities to agree consistently on what was permissible. Estonian modernist composer Arvo Pärt won one of the seven first prizes awarded at the All-Union Final Competition for Young Composers held in November 1962 and involving some 1,200 works, although he had been criticized the previous March by Tikhon Khrennikov, perennial head of the all-Union Society of Composers, for his susceptibility to foreign influences. On the level of popular culture, such a lack of definition could be seen in the 1964 Lithuanian controversy over the twist, a dance then popular in the West. A sign at a Vilnius youth center read: "Dancing the twist on our premises is strictly forbidden." The center's manager observed that "the twist is an unrealistic, unaesthetic, lewd dance of young Americans of a wealthy background. We have to uproot that dance by its roots." A critic argued that the twist was no better or no worse than any other dance, and wondered whether proscription would stop it from being danced.[82]

The failure to reintroduce cultural orthodoxy also stemmed in no small part from the mood of the indigenous populations. Cultural orthodoxy was identified with Russification. The Balts frequently refused to speak Russian in public, even when they knew it. Parents opposed intermarriage with Russians. Baltic tourists refused to pass for "Russians" in the East Bloc countries, and even managed to complain in the press of being introduced abroad as Russians. Under such circumstances, any talk of a common Soviet style or school was immediately identified with attempted impositions of Russian culture. Conversely, the striving for Western styles became viewed as cultural opposition to Russification.

Massive demonstrations of national cultural solidarity were evidenced by the Latvian and Estonian song festivals. These prominent events in the national cultures, dating from the national renaissance in the nineteenth century, emerged as cultural expressions of non-Soviet moods. A large postwar Latvian festival, held at Daugavpils in July 1959, involved 5,000 singers, 2,500 musicians and dancers, and an audience of 70,000. The only principal conductor of pre-war festivals still alive was asked to come to the podium to conduct a song and was extremely warmly received, as were several songs by exile composers included in the program. The

[82] *Meno saviveikla*, 1964/11, p. 23.

next Latvian festival, held in Riga the following summer, was billed as a festival of "friendship of nations." The Red Army garrison chorus and orchestra drew little applause. Lithuanian and Estonian folk-dances were applauded much more than the Russian ones. The popular Latvian song "With battle-cry on your lips," dating from the 1905 Revolution, was inexplicably dropped from the program. In 1965, the only encore was for the song "Jāņu vakars," about the Summer Solstice holiday which had been officially abolished (after being allowed during the Thaw).[83]

Estonian festivals were even more massive, and followed a similar pattern. The 1965 festival involved 26,000 singers and an audience of 120,000 — one-eighth of the nation! The song "My Homeland is My Love," which had become the unofficial anthem of the Estonian people, was repeated at the insistence of a standing audience.[84] Although the tradition of massive song festivals was somewhat younger in Lithuania than in Latvia or Estonia, the intensity of national fervor exhibited at such events was similar. As in Estonia, a particular song, "Lithuania Dear, You Are My Homeland," emerged as the de facto anthem of the Lithuanian people.

The creative intelligentsia soon learned to live with the new ebb and flow. The attacks, criticism, "opposition to one-sided depictions of the recent past in literary works and exaggeration of shortcomings in Soviet life," and warnings continued to flow sporadically from party leaders and artistic hacks. In part, these might have served as ritual incantations to demonstrate alertness on the cultural front. The constant probing continued to test the regime's tolerance for efforts to preserve a national identity and culture. The tolerance of experimentation in the satellite People's Democracy countries provided some relief by making possible the argument that modernism or a contemporary style were not necessarily anti-socialist. The anti-nationalism campaign in the Baltic republics abated after the fall of Khrushchev. As a result, the late 1960s saw a considerable expansion of cultural possibilities.

Conditions for such an expansion of cultural horizons proved most auspicious in Lithuania. The local regime, the machine of Sniečkus — by now dean among republic First Secretaries — felt

---

[83] ACEN, VII, pp. 79-80; IX; pp. 77-78, 109.

[84] The number of singers was 25,800, according to Nõukogude Eesti: entsüklopeediline teatmeteos (Tallinn, 1975), p. 236. Including dance and gymnastics groups, the figure rises to 31,400, according to A. Mesikäpp et al., Laulusajand, 1869-1969 (Tallinn, 1969; no page numbers), which also confirms the standing-up event. The unbelievably large audience actually doubled to a quarter of a million at the next festival in 1969, according to Olt, p. 30 — nearly one-quarter of the nation!

most secure against the political pitfalls of charges of cultural laxity. The quiet process of nativization of the party apparatus had continued unabated. And a certain sympathy among some of the new *apparatchiks* for cultural modernization and Westernism cannot be excluded.

Compared to Russia, greater cultural latitude prevailed in the Baltic republics. In part, it was due to lack of scrutiny by the world press. In Moscow, Western correspondents had become careful observers and commentators on any unusual or unexpected developments, a circumstance which maximized caution among the cultural bureaucracy, for fear of political consequences. The lack of knowledge of the Baltic languages, both by the Moscow bureaucrats and the Western newsmen, and the infrequent visits by the latter to the Baltic republics, insulated these cultures from scrutiny and thus lessened their politicization. While Camus was published in Estonia and subsequently in Lithuania without comment, this could hardly have been the case in Moscow.

In sum, the decade after the Thaw was a period of clear re-emergence of national, Western-oriented, and modernistic aspects of culture. While the organizational form saw little change toward autonomy, the effective increase in cultural autonomy was considerable as far as the content was concerned. Broadly speaking, under Stalin only a few specified topics were allowed, and everything not explicitly authorized was forbidden. By 1968, quite a few topics remained on the forbidden list; but everything not explicitly forbidden was allowed, or at least negotiable. For the national cultures, it meant the difference between suffocation and ability to develop within limits. The limits were set by a balance of forces and wills between Moscow's desire to control the republics' cultural life and each republic's desire and willingness to struggle for cultural autonomy. In the Baltic republics, the struggle for cultural autonomy was quite successful from the vantage point of 1968, compared to 1953.

EXPANSION OF CONTACTS ABROAD

An important psychological factor introduced by the Thaw was a reopening of foreign contacts. The Baltic populations had been virtually cut off from the West since 1945, and vice versa. During the mid-1950s, Soviet publications aimed at foreign audiences began to feature the Baltic republics. Specially selected foreign groups began to visit Riga and Tallinn. Riga was opened to foreign tourists in 1957, Vilnius and Tallinn in 1959. Apart from special exemptions, the bulk of the three republics, however, remained closed to foreign travel.

The appearance of foreign visitors was accompanied by the establishment in all three republics of Societies for Friendship and Cultural Ties with Foreign Countries, to arrange for exchanges of ·artists, tourists, and publications. These societies were complemented by republic branches of the all-Union Societies for Friendship with specific countries, such as the USSR-France Society. They were responsible for enriching the cultural offerings in the three republics by inviting foreign performers. While most were from Eastern Europe, some Americans like the pianist Van Cliburn and the baritone Leonard Warren performed in Latvia. In June 1964, on its second visit to the USSR, the *Comédie française* gave a performance of *Andromaque* in Riga. Educational programs involving foreigners were also arranged. In 1962, a one-week seminar for teachers of French in all three republics was held in Riga, with instructors from France.

As a contiguous neighbor and one with a friendly socialist government, Poland assumed a special role in Lithuania's cultural life as a window to the outside. The shared Catholic milieu and, to a lesser extent, a common historic past, enhanced Poland's position as a bridge to the West. Polish publications, albeit constrained by censorship, were considerably less fettered than the local output, and as a rule they were available. While Joyce, Kafka, and Proust were as yet culturally unmentionable entities locally, an intimation of their work could be gleaned by way of Poland. Two special Polish publications in 1957 on Lithuanian art and literature, issued in conjunction with an exchange of folk-art festivals between the two countries, praised the works of the pre-war period and almost disregarded more contemporary Lithuanian production. *Tiesa*, on 18 June 1957, carried a complaint by an "official" writer over such "unfair treatment of Soviet Lithuanian literature."

By the end of the 1960s, some Polish publications were no longer available in Lithuania. A general history of Lithuania published in Poland in 1967, for instance, contained too many objectionable items from the Soviet point of view. Subscribers in Lithuania could not receive their copies, and these had to filter into the republic by way of Moscow or other parts of the USSR.

Although a good portion of Lithuania's Polish minority had been repatriated, in the 1940s, enough remained to effect a continuous flow of personal visits. The better-stocked Polish market for clothes and consumer items thus began to supply a limited Lithuanian market, particularly for more contemporary Western-style clothing. Prayerbooks and Bibles, even though written in a foreign language, were other important items of import. By 1968, Polish TV, available to two-thirds of Lithuania, had become particularly popular because of its greater variety and freshness of programming.

Finland, although not an East Bloc country, assumed an analogous role for Estonia, especially since 1965 when the Helsinki-Tallinn boat connection, broken since 1940, was reestablished. However, travel here consisted much more of short Finnish visits for a drinking spree in Tallinn. The closeness of the Estonian and Finnish languages facilitated contact, but Finnish publications were not as readily tolerated by Soviet authorities as those from Poland. Finnish TV became available in northern Estonia. In 1964, Finland's President Kekkonen visited Tallinn — the first visit to the postwar Baltic republics by a Western head of state.[85]

The opening of the Baltic republics to foreign contacts also enabled some of their residents to catch a glimpse of the outside world. Initially, only highly selected individuals were allowed to travel abroad, starting with the Soviet-appointed Archbishops Gustavs Tūrs of Latvia and Jaan Kiivit of Estonia, who visited Great Britain in 1955 and the United States in 1956. In 1958, Latvian First Secretary Kalnbērziņš and Chairman of the Latvian Council of Ministers Vilis Lācis visited the Brussels World's Fair. Baltic sports teams began to appear in international competitions. In 1958, the Latvian basketball team captured the European championship.

Even a trickle of legal emigration appeared. In 1956, ten elderly women from Latvia were allowed to join their children abroad. The stringent limits on legal exit were dramatized by the Estonian sailor Viktor Jaanimets, who, on 10 October 1959, defected from the Soviet ship *Baltika*, then moored in New York, on the occasion of Khrushchev's visit.

In spite of such occasional defections, the number of Baltic performing groups allowed to tour foreign countries, and of individuals allowed to visit relatives abroad, continued to increase throughout the 1960s. In 1962, the Estonian Academic Male Choir was allowed to perform in Helsinki, for the first time, possibly in reaction to a similar performance by the refugee New York choir. Some of the performers began to acquire international recognition. The Lithuanian String Quartet placed second in a Brussels competition in 1965.

The opening of the three capital cities of the Baltic republics to foreign travel affected the regime's policies on relations with the sizable bodies of emigrants in the West, particularly those who had left in 1944–45. The emphasis changed from the postwar invitations to return to the fatherland to promotion and regulation of

[85] *Teataja*, 7 March 1964.

rather one-sided cultural contacts, with some intelligence work included. The earlier committees for repatriation mutated during the late 1950s into local "Groups of Initiators" within the USSR Committee for the Return to the Homeland and for Cultural Relations with Countrymen Abroad. Special newspapers were aimed at an émigré audience, such as the Lithuanian *Tèvynès balsas* (*Voice of the Homeland*). They were mailed free of charge from East Berlin, and were unavailable within the Baltic republics. They could afford to treat issues not mentioned by the local press, such as religion and some aspects of pre-war history. By 1964 the repatriation issue was dropped completely.

The new cultural contacts were accompanied by attacks aimed at refugee political organizations and activities which had earlier been largely ignored. The Soviets appeared to be especially touchy regarding refugee efforts which resulted in U.S. Congressional resolutions on Baltic self-determination. In an effort to discredit refugee activists, several individuals prominent in pre-war society were harnessed to make anti-émigré statements in *Izvestiia* (e.g., Vilhelms Munters, the pre-war Latvian Minister of Foreign Affairs, 8 April 1962). While such declarations had little effect on refugee activity, they did reveal considerable information on refugee organizations to readers in the Baltic republics.

After the reopening of contact, many expatriates began to send parcels to relatives and friends in the home countries. Resale, especially of clothes, in the consumer-goods-starved Soviet milieu made some individuals quite wealthy by Soviet standards. The regime reacted by press attacks against those who had "lost the dignity of Soviet people and stretch a begging hand for some foreign rags,"[86] and by court actions against unearned income. In one instance, a hospital employee had built a small house for himself from the proceeds of only ten parcels sent by his sister in Canada. The local Executive Committee decided to confiscate it as having been built from funds not earned through "socially useful work," but a local judge reversed the decision, to the dismay of *Tiesa* (20 August 1965). While the attacks on speculation continued, the Soviet Treasury also profited directly from the parcels: duties, usually prepaid by the senders in hard currency, were set at extremely high levels.

Discussions of cultural interaction with the refugees were expanded during the late 1960s. In April 1966, a special conference of Soviet Lithuanian youth representatives met in Vilnius, and two years later the Committee on Foreign Affairs of the Lithuanian Supreme Soviet called a special conference on the matter. A

---

[86] *Tiesa*, 15 April 1960.

Lithuanian Minister of Foreign Affairs was appointed after a vacancy of several years. The propaganda newspapers mailed from East Berlin to refugees in the West were replaced by weeklies published in and available in the republics as well. The works of several prominent émigré figures became available, at least in part, to residents of the home countries. One Estonian and two Lithuanian anthologies published in 1967 included some émigré writers, even though they had uttered quite a few pro-independence statements. The émigré theme was featured at the Vilnius Opera in 1967 with the première of the opera *Lost Birds*.

The level of personal interaction increased markedly. War-time refugees and their children began to visit the home countries. In 1967, approximately 500 such visitors went to Lithuania; six girls from Great Britain vacationed in a Pioneer Camp, and a Lithuanian-American basketball team played a series of games with local Lithuanian teams. Extended visits to relatives, while not numerous, had become fairly common.

SOCIO-ECONOMIC TRENDS

The major features of the Baltic socio-economic scene between 1953 and 1968 were industrialization and, in Latvia and Estonia, the accompanying immigration of Russians and other non-Baltic Soviet peoples. In agriculture, centrally enforced attempts to grow maize eventually gave way to a return to the dairy-centered approach of the independence period. Urbanization increased, birth rates decreased, divorce rates soared, and Protestant religious practices plummeted.

Industrialization and Regional Economic Councils

After the intense and erratic reconstruction during the preceding decade, Soviet economic policy and practice in the Baltic republics stabilized in 1955–68. A set pattern of economic activity emerged by the mid-1960s and was to continue in the 1970s. Economic cost calculations agreed with imperial socio-political goals in the Baltic region: this area was cheaper and easier to develop than the eastern part of the USSR, due to its relatively good rail and road network and, above all, its skilled and well-trained labor force. Natural resources were limited to oil shale, fertilizers, construction materials, and fairly good soil. Although some oil was discovered during the 1960s in western Latvia and Lithuania, the amounts were small. Ten tons a day spouted from two drill-holes in Lithuania in late 1968, but not much has been heard about this oil since that time.[87]

In industry, the emphasis was on labor-intensive products requiring few raw materials. Skilled Baltic labor tended to be complemented by an influx of unskilled Russian labor. Only Lithuania maintained a considerable internal labor pool. The last cooperative enterprises were squeezed out of urban industrial production. In Estonia, their share declined from 12.6% in 1950 to 5.5% in 1960 and 4.9% in 1965. The rest belonged directly to the state.

The product mix largely continued and diversified the tradition of the independence period (radio-technical, food and footwear industries) or even of Tsarist times (electro-technical, machinery, transportation and textile goods). With only 2.8% of the total Soviet population, the Baltic republics by the late 1960s produced 3.6% of the Soviet gross national output.[88] This production included more than half of the Soviet oil shale (Estonia), electric railway coaches (Latvia), telephones and automatic telephone stations (Latvia), electric welding equipment (Lithuania), various types of scientific and computing hardware, and motors for refrigerators and washing machines. The Baltic republics also produced 10 to 50% of Soviet lightbulbs, radios, motorbikes (Latvia), refrigeration equipment, and fish. For the sake of proper perspective, we should not forget that they produced little or no coal, iron, cars, or cotton.

In money terms, Baltic visible exports tended to exceed visible imports by 10%.[89] Such disparity might be interpreted as economic exploitation or an involuntary "foreign aid" to the less developed Soviet republics, but it may also have simply reflected an overpricing of industrial consumer goods by the Soviet non-market price system. Baltic wage and retail sales levels exceeded the USSR average, but so did their national incomes — so the question of possible exploitation by Russia cannot be easily settled on that level. The question of what the Baltic national income could have been in the absence of Soviet occupation remains open. The Baltic nations certainly were paying for the upkeep of the Soviet troops and police on their soil who, depending on one's point of view, were either protecting or oppressing the Baltic nations.

Within the USSR, the Baltic republics increasingly surpassed the other republics in per-capita national income. In 1958, Latvia and

---

[87] Benedict V. Mačiuika, "The Role of the Baltic Republics in the Economy of the USSR," JBS, III/1 (Spring 1972), pp. 18-25. For more details on the economy in 1955-68, see King, pp. 207-295; Zundė 1965, pp. 141-169; Järvesoo 1978, pp. 131-190; Remeikis 1977, pp. 116-120.

[88] Calculated from data in Remeikis 1977, p. 117. His figure of "almost 10%" (p. 118) must be a misprint.

[89] Mačiuika, "The Role," p. 21.

Estonia were 29 and 19%, respectively, above the Soviet average, while Lithuania trailed it by 8%. By 1968, Lithuania exceeded the average by 15%, Latvia by 42%, and Estonia by 44%. Compared, in particular, to the Russian republic, Latvia and Estonia were always higher, and Lithuania surpassed it in 1966. However, they all trailed the Moscow and Leningrad regions of Russia. Higher tax collections, and purchases by Russian tourists and soldiers, also worked to lower the actual Baltic income. On the other hand, the strong Baltic "underground" economy had the opposite effect. While USSR per-capita income increased 67% from 1958 to 1968, Estonia's and Latvia's went up by about 90%, and Lithuania's by 108%.[90]

The rise in living standards was more modest, since the production increase largely went into industrial investment. Compared to the early postwar period, private consumption increased, but in many aspects it remained below the level reached during the independence period. It has been calculated that, compared to pre-war industrial workers' families, urban Latvian families in 1961 consumed 30 to 50% less meat, eggs, and dairy products.[91] Regarding consumer durable goods, the pre-war consumption level was reached again in the 1960s. Given the rapid advances in the West, this meant that the gap between Baltic and West European living standards had increased since the pre-war period — and by the 1960s, war destruction could no longer be taken as even a semiplausible alibi. Introduction of the Soviet system had advanced the local time by one hour, but set back its growth in welfare by two decades.

It is not even clear whether income distribution had become more equal (as it did in Western Europe). Typical industrial wages in 1961 were around 90 new rubles per month. Many office clerks and female workers received the minimum wage of 45 rubles, but the director of a Latvian textile trust received 450 rubles, plus a hefty bonus and income in kind. Measures like socialized medicine worked to reduce this gap in formal wages, but small income taxes and large indirect taxes worked to re-widen the gap. Nonetheless, median earnings increased by about 90% from 1960 to 1974, while price inflation was less than 1%.[92]

The quality of life improved considerably from what it had been in postwar times, yet still left much to be desired. As in the

[90] H.-J. Wagener, "Regional Output Levels in the Soviet Union," *Radio Liberty Research Paper*, no. 41, 1970.
[91] King, p. 266.
[92] King, p. 273; Järvesoo 1978, p. 144. The new ruble introduced in 1961 was worth 10 pre-1961 rubles.

remainder of the USSR, the service sector had been particularly backward in the Stalin years. During the late 1950s, visible efforts were made to improve the situation, although progress reported was at times pathetically limited. Between 1959 and 1961, some 500 new shops and restaurants were opened in Latvia.[93] Between 1959 and 1964, 10 laundries, 53 public baths, 5 dry-cleaning shops, 5 auto-service stations, and 2 tailor shops were reported opened in Lithuania.[94] The positive effect of a greater number of better-stocked sales outlets in the Baltic republics was considerably offset by the influx of numerous shoppers from other parts of the USSR. A newly opened radio repair shop in a small Lithuanian town began to attract a swarm of customers, some from as far away as the Kaliningrad Oblast, after its reputation for good service had circulated.[95] Service problems continued to persist. According to First Secretary of the Lithuanian Komsomol Vaclovas Monkūnas, in 1966 some 5,456 stores in Lithuania had an outdated "material technical structure," service was frequently rude, and prices were arbitrary. Meat stores were insufficient in number and poorly stocked. Stores in outlying areas had particularly meager offerings, and long lines were frequent when items in short supply appeared.[96]

Industry shared in the series of all-Union reforms and reorganizations and mirrored the all-Union errors and inefficiencies. The most significant reorganization was the aforementioned establishment of the *sovnarkhozy* (regional economic councils) in mid-1957. Each republic now became a unit of economic administration. The *sovnarkhozy* gave considerably more autonomy to the republic administrators and reduced interference by central Soviet ministries. A number of industrial Union-republic ministries were transformed into branches of the republic *sovnarkhoz*, for the most part headed by their former ministers. Estonia and Latvia now had 10 such administrations, and Lithuania 11. About 420 Estonian enterprises responsible for about 80% of the republic's industrial production were now subordinated to the republic *sovnarkhoz*. The Latvian *sovnarkhoz* was responsible for 486 enterprises, and that of Lithuania for 443 (approximately 83% of all industry). This was in marked contrast to 1956, when central Moscow ministries had been in charge of 90% of Latvia's industrial output.

In the long run, the *sovnarkhoz* system proved especially beneficial to Lithuania, which unlike its two northern neighbors had not

[93] *Cīņa*, 28 September 1961.
[94] *Tiesa*, 26 February 1965.
[95] *Valstiečių laikraštis*, 8 January 1965.
[96] Komjaunimo tiesa, 29 November 1966; *Tiesa*, 5 November 1966.

been subjected to a rapid centrally directed industrialization during the postwar years. The later start of its industrialization allowed for a greater impact of the Khrushchev era on the manner in which it was carried out. The *sovnarkhoz* system gave local planners a far greater input than had been the case earlier. This allowed the dispersal of industrial projects within the republic in such a way as to maximize local natural and labor resources. The Khrushchev years also saw a modest shift in emphasis on consumer-oriented production. Such an ability by local authorities to disperse new plants, as well as the increased possibilities in opting for labor-intensive industries, somewhat differentiated the industrial profile of Lithuania from those of Latvia and Estonia. Important social consequences stemmed from the fact that there was little need in Lithuania for an immigration of labor from other parts of the USSR, as had occurred in Latvia and Estonia.

Formal recentralization began in 1962 throughout the Soviet Union. Baltic power production, construction, and fisheries were subordinated to supra-republic regional *sovnarkhozy*. The Northeast Power Industry System, for instance, included the three Baltic republics as well as the Leningrad and Kaliningrad Oblasts of the RSFSR. However, much was still left under local control. In 1964, the 160 republic *sovnarkhoz* enterprises in Estonia still represented 70% of the republic's industrial output. This output doubled from 1958 to 1965. In spite of their seeming success in greatly increasing production, the *sovnarkhozy* of the Baltic republics were abolished in 1965, along with those in the rest of the USSR.

The following reorganization has become known as the Kosygin Reform. Launched in September 1965, the move aimed to introduce a criterion for appraisal of an enterprise according to results obtained through execution of production and profit plans. The USSR State Planning Committee was transformed from an all-Union to a Union-republic institution. The republics' planning committees were enjoined to prepare projects for all branches of the economy except defense, but in close coordination with the all-Union Committee. The majority of each republic's industry was placed under Union-republic jurisdiction. In Lithuania, about 60% of all industry fell into this category; 12% was left under local supervision and 28% was under purely central Moscow supervision.

Friction between local units and a variety of central organs soon became apparent. The Lithuanian construction materials industry, for instance, came under the jurisdiction of at least eight all-Union ministries and agencies. As one critic observed, the all-Union agencies tried to regulate everything from above, to the last detail.[97] Such a situation made local planning efforts futile, especially when central agencies could and did frequently alter plans without full cognizance of or regard for local conditions. Complaints also were heard over attempts by all-Union agencies to impose supplementary production quotas on short notice, thus upsetting the internal work schedules of enterprises.

A lack of coordination between central and local agencies at times led to major problems. In 1965, Juozas Maniušis, head of the Department of Industrial Affairs in the Lithuanian CC, complained to the all-Union Supreme Soviet that since 1961 the USSR State Planning Committee had been cutting down allotments of Lithuanian capital investment for the construction materials industry, in spite of the fact that construction projects within Lithuania were increasing. Hence an acute shortage of construction materials had developed. His request for an increased allotment, reiterated by the Deputy Chairman of the Lithuanian Council of Ministers, was not granted. In 1965, Lithuania's investment allocations in the construction materials industry remained at 1960 levels, while construction had doubled.

Construction of several massive enterprises was undertaken during the *sovnarkhoz* period. The giant thermodynamic station at Elektrėnai, which began operations in 1962 and was fully completed in 1968, made Lithuania an exporter of electrical energy. Other significant Lithuanian projects launched during this period included a chemical plant at Kėdainiai and a liquid-fertilizer plant at Jonava, using natural gas from the Ukraine as inputs.

The growth of Baltic industrial production slowed down somewhat during the 1960s (see Table 16). The main reason for the slowdown was increasing industrial maturity. Obsolescent plants and a lack of mechanization remained a problem. A furniture factory in Lithuania supposedly required four times the labor inputs of one in Finland and took twice the time of a plant in East Germany to build a wooden wardrobe.[98] The high turnover in the workforce was another major concern. During the years 1965-67, about a quarter of the Lithuanian workforce changed jobs annually. Idling, sluggishness, and absenteeism aggravated inadequate or sporadic deliveries of raw materials. Frequently rushing to complete plant quotas toward the end of the month, workers paid little attention to quality. Around 1961, every fourth "Latvija" radio, every third telephone, and every fifth automatic telephone exchange manufactured at the Riga Electronics (VEF) plant proved defective, and 38% of the items manufactured at the Rigas Aditajs

[97] *Liaudies ūkis*, 1967/4-5, p. 127.
[98] *Komjaunimo tiesa*, 27 May 1966.

knitted goods factory were judged to be of inferior quality.[99]

On the whole, industry was developed in the Baltic republics at a more rapid pace than throughout the rest of the USSR. In 1970, Lithuania's industrial production was 6.2 times higher than in 1955. The comparable figure for the USSR as a whole was 3.7, while for Estonia it was 4.2 and for Latvia 4.7 (see Table 7). These were times when any form of industrialization throughout the world tended to be considered "progressive" by Western public opinion, regardless of human or ecological cost; "industrialization" began to lose its luster in the West only in the late 1960s. For a while, Soviet Baltic commentators continued admiring rather than abhorring the fact that the oil-shale ash heaps formed higher peaks than Estonia's highest natural hill.

Agriculture

The relative improvement was most marked for farmers as state interference was reduced, obligatory delivery system was abolished, and prices paid were raised to non-confiscatory levels. Dismantling of the state MTS in 1958 was a major step.

Agriculture, which had languished in the "spook hostel" during the postwar period, presented a particularly sorry picture even in the late 1950s.[100] Total agricultural output had dropped to about 75% of the pre-war level (see Table 8), and possibly much lower. The Latvian party journal *Padomju Latvijas komunists* complained in its July 1958 issue that the total yield, while considerably increased lately, was still insufficient to satisfy completely even the domestic needs of the collective farms alone. The area of land under cultivation had dropped considerably since 1939. The Latvian 1960 figure of 1.9 million ha. was about half that of 1939. Yields were down to half the pre-war level (see Table 8); thus grain production must have been much less than half the pre-war level. A general lack of fertilizer was partly responsible for lower yields. In Lithuania, the single pre-war fertilizer plant had been shut down and farmers were totally dependent on sporadic imports from other parts of the USSR.

The collective sector continued to be reduced in favor of the state sector. Both inefficient and overly efficient collective farms were frequently converted into state farms (*sovkhozes*), whereas the reverse process was not allowed. In Latvia, the number of sovkhozes increased from 93 to 113 between March and October 1958. In Lithuania, collective farms decreased between 1958 and 1961 from 2,185 to 1,867. The process continued through the

99 *Padomju Latvijas Komunists*, 1961/1.
100 Arnold Purre, *Soviet Farming Failure Hits Estonia* (Stockholm, 1964).

1960s, though at a much slower pace. The agriculturally useful area of Estonian kolkhozes decreased from 1,766,000 ha. in 1955 to 790,000 in 1970, while that of the sovkhozes increased from 118,000 to 576,000 ha.[101]

As far as the regime was concerned, sovkhozes represented a higher form of socialist ownership. From the point of view of the peasants, given the state-imposed restrictions on the kolkhozes, conversion to a sovkhoz assured at least minimal and regular remuneration, even though the farms might be operating at a loss. Only 32 to 113 sovkhozes in Latvia showed a profit in 1958.[102] Moreover, membership in a state farm assured some minimal social security. Pension plans for Soviet collective farmers were not introduced until 1965. (A non-mandatory plan based on deductions from income drew few applicants in Lithuania in 1961.)

Initially, the wages of collective farmers under the new system tended to remain low. In 1958, the average *annual* wage for a Lithuanian collective farmer stood at 68.4 new rubles and 452 kilograms of cereal grain. At 1963 prices, which were about the same as those of 1958, a kilogram of sausage cost 2.80 rubles; a man's sweater, 20.2 rubles; and a motorcycle, 980 rubles. Many collective farmers earned less than half of the wages paid to workers at state farms. Because of the enormous expenses for fodder and capital investments, a considerable number of Lithuanian collective farms could only afford to pay their members 10–15% of their annual incomes.[103]

For this reason, a major portion of the livelihood of collective farmers depended on private plots. In Lithuania, the private sector in 1959, comprising 5.8% of the cultivated land, produced 65.4% of the most important livestock products, 72.4% of the total potato crop, and 80% of the total fruit yield.[104] (See also Latvian data in Table 15.) High taxes and compulsory deliveries from private plots were abolished in 1958–59. At the same time, the cessation of payments of kolkhoz wages in grain adversely affected raising livestock on private plots. This, however, proved a temporary problem until new means of securing fodder were found. The rumors, current in 1958, which attended these changes led to a drastic drop in the price of cows from 400–500 new rubles to 250–300. Many collective farmers managed to purchase cows at relatively low prices.

By 1965, a marked improvement in agriculture could be noted.

---

[101] Järvesoo 1978, p. 141.
[102] *Sovetskaia Latviia*, 11 April 1959.
[103] *Komunistas*, 1962/3, pp. 36–41. All values are in the new 1961 rubles, worth 10 earlier rubles.
[104] Zundė 1965, p. 155.

Capital and resource allocations to agriculture had increased. Yields reached and surpassed pre-war levels. In 1965, Estonian grain production reached the 1939 level, even though the area under cultivation was 45% smaller. The high yields could in part be attributed to the increased use of tractors and mineral fertilizers. The use of fertilizers doubled during the 1950s, and did so again during the 1960s.

The earnings of collective farmers increased dramatically. In 1965, the Estonian average daily wage for collective farmers stood at 3.7 rubles; the all-Union figure was 2.5 rubles. By 1964, all Estonian kolkhozes were on a system of guaranteed wages; this was envisaged for the USSR as a whole only for 1966. Various measures during the middle of the decade concerning the private sector increased incomes further. In late 1964, the special tax on private livestock was abolished and permission was granted to sell concentrated fodder to private individuals. Loans for the purchase of private livestock became available in Lithuania in 1965, and the number of privately-owned cattle increased 9.5%, and of pigs 14.6%, over the 1964 level.[105] The average 1965 collective farmer's income exceeded that of 1952 by 360%. During the following two years, the average remuneration on Lithuanian collective farms increased 90% and that on state farms 30%.[106] The comparable increases in Estonia between 1960 and 1974 were 278% for kolkhozes and 177% for sovkhozes. When sovkhoz "self-management" (with no government subsidies) was developed in the Soviet Union in 1967, all Estonian sovkhozes were immediately placed on this system. Latvia and Lithuania readily followed suit in 1970. Throughout the rest of the USSR, only 49% of sovkhozes could get by without subsidies as late as 1973. During the late 1960s, mean rural incomes in the Baltic republics, in marked contrast to other regions of the USSR, were approaching the mean urban incomes.

Urbanization and Immigration

Of the three Baltic republics, Estonia and Latvia tended to exhibit quite similar social characteristics, while Lithuania tended to follow the same path of development, though with some lag. This applies in particular to the urbanization figures shown in Table 10. The percentage of the labor force employed in agriculture was decreasing. In 1968 it stood at 22% in Estonia and 24% in Latvia and Lithuania, compared to 27% throughout the USSR. In this regard, Lithuania had already caught up with Latvia.

[105] *Tiesa*, 29 January and 13 May 1966.
[106] *Liaudies ūkis*, 1968/12, p. 35.

Urbanization proceeded at a fairly constant rate in 1955–68 (see Table 10). The absolute size of the rural population decreased steadily from 1940 on. This trend was briefly interrupted only during the late 1950s and early 1960s, when thousands of deported farmers returned. While the Baltic service sector also grew, agricultural labor shifted mainly to industry. In Latvia and Estonia, industrial employment surpassed employment in agriculture around 1960. The three capital cities increased their shares of the republic populations (see Table 11). However, Tallinn's share in Estonia's industrial employment declined to 43% in 1967, since other cities also grew. Changes were most dramatic in Lithuania. Its three major cities, Vilnius, Kaunas, and Klaipėda, grew 82% between 1950 and 1965.

The flight to the cities had a significant effect on the countryside. During the period 1960–65, 100,000 Lithuanian farmers left to work in industry. Some kolkhozes, depleted of manpower, were left with 35–45 ha. of arable land per collective farmer, in contrast to the average of 6 ha. Some farms were left with no males in the 15–30 age group. In the district of Jurbarkas, 58 of the 165 kolkhozes had no working-age males under 65 left.[107] Because of poor living conditions, over half of the newly graduated agricultural specialists failed to stay on the farms for more than two years.[108] Inadequate living conditions in the countryside resulted in part from the policy of discouraging private rural construction. Collective farmers preferred to hold on to their old homesteads, many of them in dilapidated condition, rather than engage in construction of new centralized settlements.

The rapid urban growth aggravated the housing shortage which had appeared after the war (see Table 10). Moreover, a 1962 all-Union decree, motivated as much by cost as by ideology, prohibited the construction of individual dwellings in the republics' capital cities and allowed republic authorities to apply this prohibition to other cities as well. In June of that year, Estonia limited house ownership to one dwelling per family. Bachelor-owned apartments in Vilnius were proscribed.[109] In spite of shortages of construction materials, a large building campaign was undertaken. While 7.5 million square meters of living space had been added in Lithuania during 1946–64, another 5.2 million sq. m was built in 1965–68 — i.e., about 3 sq. m per urban inhabitant. Some Baltic urban projects, such as the Vilnius residential complexes of Žirmūnai and Lazdynai, stood out because of their

---

attempts to vary the usual drab regularity of Soviet prefabricated housing.

Marriage patterns underwent a marked change as the countries urbanized and modern technology penetrated the countryside. Even while the marriage rate decreased, the divorce rate increased dramatically (see Table 12).

Birth rates in Estonia and Latvia continued to be below the Soviet average, and reached their lowest values in 1967 (14.2 and 13.5 per thousand, respectively), after which a slight increase occurred (see Table 13). In 1966–70, Lithuania's birth rate, though decreasing, temporarily surpassed the Soviet average, which had been decreasing even faster. This demographic difference, coupled with Soviet industrialization policy, produced a continuing heavy immigration to Latvia and Estonia, but not to Lithuania (see Table 14).

Lithuania's rural labor pool was still large and could fill the labor needs of its relatively few cities. The influx of Russians was small compared to the natural increase of Lithuanians. In the absence of deportations, the percentage of Lithuanians in the country's population was even slightly increasing (see Table 1). The Russians could dominate Lithuania politically, but they were not in the process of swamping it. In contrast, the influx of Russians into Latvia and Estonia constituted a threat to national survival.

Since Latvia and Estonia were already predominantly urbanized, the remaining rural labor reserve was comparatively small, and the low birth rates compounded the problem. Relentless Soviet industrialization plans ignored the shortage of indigenous manpower, or possibly even used this opportunity on purpose to bring in Russians. Latvia was rapidly approaching the point where non-Latvian immigrants would exceed the Latvians in numbers. Estonia was following the same path, though at a slower rate.

The new immigration was different from that of the late 1940s, which had often been involuntary (functionaries assigned and forced labor dispatched to the Baltic area) and had been accompanied by forced emigration of natives. In 1954–59, immigration had remained low (except for Latvia in 1956) and included many returning Baltic deportees. In the early 1960s, the net immigration rate speeded up appreciably, amounting at times to almost 1% of the existing population per year (see Table 14). Actually, many more came, but many also left every year. This flux made social, cultural, and linguistic integration difficult, the more so since the Russian immigrants often expected the Balts to integrate with them. This was the situation that some of the Latvian Communist leaders had sought to alleviate in 1958. The purge of these leaders made it even more difficult to control the influx. A high immigration rate prevailed throughout the decade. By 1970, Latvians formed only 57% of Latvia's population, and Estonians were down to 68% of Estonia's (see Table 1).

The new immigration was voluntary, and largely consisted of individuals attracted by Baltic job vacancies and the more plentiful supply of consumer goods. However, sometimes jobs in the Baltic area seemed to be better advertised in Leningrad and Moscow than on the spot, raising the issue of possible purposeful Russification. Many of the major labor-intensive industries were once again in the 1960s placed under the control of all-Union ministries and agencies which found it simpler to recruit in central Russia. By the late 1960s, immigration was a major irritant to Latvian and Estonian national feelings, the more so since the immigrants often received the scarce housing for which local people had waited for years. At times the Russian newcomers would simply invade newly finished apartments, and no local functionary would dare to evict them and risk being accused of nationalism. "Friendship of peoples" meant accepting Russian colonization.

By 1965, the total number of Russians in the Baltic republics was over 1,000,000. For that date, the Nazi *Generalplan Ost* had envisaged only 520,000 German settlers.[110]

Education

The Khrushchev years saw considerable experimentation within the Soviet educational system. For the most part, developments in the Baltic republics followed the all-Union pattern of curtailing direct admission to higher education from secondary schools, and combining secondary education with on-the-job training. The USSR school-reform laws promulgated in December 1958 were followed by republic counterparts early the following year. They envisaged a gradual transition between 1959 and 1963 to a new system in which pupils would attend classes five days every week and go to factories or kolkhozes to work on the sixth (for the most part Thursdays). Their school week was to consist of 31 hours in class, 6 hours in production, and 2-4 hours in extracurricular activities. Furthermore, the new laws allowed parents to decide what languages their children would be taught. It meant that Russian became a "voluntary" subject in Baltic schools where it was not the language of instruction, and that the Baltic languages became voluntary in Russian-language schools. The realities of Soviet life, however, put pressure on the Balts to become bilingual,

---

[110] For the Nazi *Generalplan Ost*, see the beginning of section in Chapter II on German occupation.

while no such pressure was imposed on Russian residents in the Baltic republics.

The adoption of the new system resulted in numerous criticisms. Latvian CC Secretary Pelše as well as Deputy Chairman of the Council of Ministers Berklāvs raised objections at the Supreme Soviet session adopting the law. In March 1959, Latvia actually expanded compulsory Latvian studies in the Russian schools, and they were made voluntary only after the purge of autonomists.[111]

Problems of implementation appeared with the opening of the new school year. Shortages of adequate textbooks were universal, and resistance from parents and teachers had to be surmounted. The new system led to an immediate drop in the number of applicants to institutions of higher education. For the first time ever, in 1959 there were fewer applicants than places at the Tallinn Polytechnic Institute.

After 1960, complaints appeared over the inability of young people who were sent to kolkhozes as laborers to continue their studies. By the 1961–62 school year, 30% of all Lithuanian pupils in the ninth to eleventh grades combined classes with productive labor.[112] The quality of their production was poor, and many enterprises to which they had been assigned experienced difficulties in putting them to work. Many students did nothing, and 40% of those assigned to kolkhozes were acquainted with tractors and machinery only through illustrations.[113]

In 1964, the optimal length of primary and secondary education became an issue, as it was becoming evident that the work-training programs had failed and would be abolished. Lithuanian Minister of Education Mečys Gedvilas argued in *Izvestiia* on 22 March 1964 for an 11-year system in the national republics (instead of 10 years as in Russia), because of the need to learn a native language as well as Russian. Initially, such arguments did not prevail, and the system was decreased to 10 years in all three Baltic republics for the academic year 1964–65. However, in late 1965, after the fall of Khrushchev, the 11-year curriculum was approved for Baltic schools whose language of instruction was not Russian. At the same time, the moribund work-study program was abolished.

The reinstitution of the 11-year system, as opposed to the 10-year system prevalent throughout the rest of the USSR, was viewed as a victory for those opposing forced Russification and concerned with the maintenance of the national languages as media for professional communication. However, at least in Latvia, nearly all of

---

111 *Pravda*, 24 December 1958; Widmer, pp. 542–545.
112 *Tarybinis mokytojas*, 7 January 1962.
113 *Tarybinė mokykla*, 1963/10, p. 3.

the extra time was allocated to the study of Russian.[114]

The anti-nationalism campaign was accompanied by a renewed stress on the teaching of Russian, with limited success. In 1962, nearly 5,000 students in Riga were made to repeat their whole school year because of insufficient progress in the Russian language.[115] Numerous bilingual schools were introduced in Latvia; in 1967, 240 out of a total of 1,500 schools were bilingual.[116] Some were set up in areas with virtually no Russian population, and therefore became viewed as blatant instruments of Russification. Very few bilingual schools were established in Lithuania and Estonia.

A more orderly pace appeared in higher education. The postponement of obligatory military service for students in institutions of higher learning had been abolished in 1961, but was reinstated in 1966. Talk of a unified Baltic educational system — wherein Estonia would train machine operators and electricians; Latvia, nuclear physicists and technicians; and Lithuania, specialists for the textile and leather industries — remained stillborn suggestions. Difficulties in higher education caused by war-time loss of trained personnel and postwar Stalinist stagnation were to a large extent surmounted by the late 1960s.

The wide-scale evaluations of the education-work curriculum during the early 1960s unveiled numerous shortcomings which had existed since the war. While it had been claimed that by 1949 compulsory seven-year schooling had been enacted in Lithuania, it appeared that in 1961 the drop-out rate in some rural areas reached 45%. Many kolkhozes employed children, preventing their enrollment in school. Teacher shortages proved endemic, since the teaching profession was not considered an attractive career for males. In the 1966-67 academic year, 76.6% of the teachers in Lithuania were women. In rural areas, the shortage of school buildings was chronic. During the academic year 1961-62, more than 4,000 children in Lithuania had to attend school in two or even three shifts.[117] From the middle of the decade, some kolkhozes began to build their own schools, a common practice in the pre-war Soviet Union. Scarcities of textbooks, even of second-hand copies, were alleviated by 1967-68.

---

[114] Dreifelds 1976, p. 140.
[115] *Skolotāju avīze*, January 1962.
[116] Jānis Sapiets, p. 223; Augusts Voss, *Izvestiia*, 5 January 1967.
[117] Vytautas Vaitiekūnas, "Sovietized Education in Occupied Lithuania," in Vardys (ed.), *Lithuania Under the Soviets*, pp. 171-196.

Religion

The Thaw also affected religious life. Atheistic propaganda was toned down in 1954–56.[118] In Lithuania, two new bishops were consecrated in 1955. About 130 priests returned from deportation (one-third of those deported), along with two bishops, though the latter were not allowed to resume their positions. Some discussion of modern religion and its compatibility with socialism was even allowed in the press.

A new Union-wide campaign against religion was launched in 1957. In the Baltic republics, the attack soon merged with the drive against nationalism. A concerted effort ensued to replace the religious customs and holidays which maintained wide currency among the population. A "Spring Holiday" was celebrated a week before Easter, and a "Winter Festival" on the Sunday preceding Ash Wednesday was billed as a Soviet Mardi Gras. A particular effort began in Latvia in 1960 to root out the traditional Summer Solstice feast of St. John, 23–24 June, which had resumed during the Thaw. Its renewed prohibition apparently even led to a slow-down strike in 1960 at the Riga Electronics (VEF) and Railroad Car Plants.[119] The authorities finally yielded in 1968. Name-giving and Adulthood Day ceremonies appeared as efforts to replace baptism and confirmation. A realization that church ceremonies were more attractive and dignified came early, but efforts to spruce up civil ceremonies were slow. The most successful ceremony was the civil marriage, to which some solemnity and aesthetic aura were successfully added. In Lithuania, the former Kaunas City Hall, a restored graceful building in the old town of the city, became a particularly attractive Wedding Palace.

Church closings accompanied the campaign against religion. In May 1959, the towering Gothic Riga Cathedral was taken away from the Latvian Evangelical Church. The edifice, including its massive organ, was restored and opened as a concert hall in June 1962. The eighteenth-century neo-classical cathedral of Vilnius likewise had already been taken over in 1953, and was converted to a picture gallery and concert hall. Other churches were also transformed into concert halls. Such was the fate in 1964 of the Church of St. Simon (dating from 1283) in Valmiera, Latvia. The following year, the seventeenth-century Reformed Church in Riga was closed, because its congregation could not raise the 55,000 rubles needed for repairs, and was turned into a library. The Orthodox Cathedral in Riga was closed in 1961 and emerged four years later

---

[118] Vardys 1978, pp. 80–88; Salo, pp. 191–222.
[119] ACEN, IX, 76.

as a new Museum of Science and Planetarium. The Church of St. Casimir in Vilnius became a Museum of the History of Religion and Atheism in 1962. One case of church closing stands out for its peculiar circumstances: a permit to erect a Roman Catholic church in Klaipėda was issued during the Thaw, but the completed edifice was confiscated around 1960, and the pastor of the parish was subsequently sentenced for alleged speculation. The Lutheran Aleksander Church in Narva, destroyed during the war and restored by congregation members in 1958–60, was also confiscated and turned into a clubhouse.[120]

The campaign against religion included slander and police action against some clergymen. Archbishop Julijonas Steponavičius of Vilnius was exiled to Žagarė (25 km east of Akmenė) in January 1961, apparently because he expelled two police infiltrators from the seminary in Kaunas and refused Soviet demands to issue orders contrary to canon law. Two other Lithuanian bishops, Teofilis Matulionis and his successor Vincentas Sladkevičius, had been banished from their diocese in 1958. In 1961–65, only one bishop was not exiled.[121]

A slackening in the anti-religious campaign set in during the mid-1960s, especially regarding Roman Catholics, whose church is formally a part of a highly structured international organization. Delegations of Lithuanian clergymen (none of them bishops) were allowed to visit Rome. In November 1964, Monsignor Vaivods, who had been permitted to attend the Vatican II Council, was consecrated Bishop of Latvia. A year later, Bishop Juozapas Matulaitis-Labukas of Lithuania was also consecrated in Rome.

However, while the Kremlin was willing to go along with the Vatican's *Ostpolitik* on the official level, a crackdown on organized religious practices reappeared toward the end of the decade. State interference in the posting of clergymen and prohibition of religious activities such as the catechization of children had formed the basis of the conflict between Archbishop Steponavičius and the regime for a long time. They were enacted into law in May 1966, when the Presidium of the Supreme Soviet of the Lithuanian SSR explained in detail the application of Article 143 of the republic's Penal Code, which concerned the separation of church and state. An artificially low limit on seminarians accepted for study in the sole functioning Catholic seminary, and various restraints on religious practice, in all likelihood triggered

---

[120] Klaipėda: Vardys 1978, p. 84; Narva: former congregation member A. Alliksaar's account in the bulletin of Estonian St. Peter's Church, Toronto, December 1967.

[121] For the rather complex details, see Vardys 1978, pp. 83–86.

the reactions by the faithful during the late 1960s which blossomed into dissent during the subsequent decade (see section on dissent in Chapter V).

Soviet policy toward religion was characterized by two seemingly contradictory trends. On the one hand, there was the constant struggle against the "survival of superstition from the past." On the other, the churches and their dignitaries could be used as instruments of Soviet foreign policy within a context of the struggle for peace and coexistence. Jaan Kiivit, the Lutheran Archbishop of Soviet Estonia, and Archbishop Gustavs Tūrs of the Soviet Latvian Evangelical Church, were even earlier travelers abroad, visiting Great Britain in 1955 and the United States in 1956. Two years later, Tūrs was a member of the delegation to a Stockholm Peace Conference which included, among others, Secretary of the Latvian CC Arvīds Pelše. Kiivit went on the air in 1958 to condemn the American intervention in Lebanon — the first time that a clergyman was permitted to speak on the Estonian radio since 1940. He travelled widely in the 1960s, attending Lutheran councils and lobbying with the World Council of Churches to unseat refugee Archbishop Johan Kõpp. In 1967 Kiivit resigned for health reasons, after close questioning in Moscow about his doings on the foreign visits.[122]

It is difficult to judge the effectiveness of the anti-religious campaign. Statistical data regarding believers are not only hard to ascertain, but the concept itself is hard to define precisely. While some decline in religious practice could be expected under any circumstances of modernization and industrialization, such losses could well have been considerably offset, especially in Lithuania, by an identification of religious practice with national distinctiveness. In 1958, Archbishop Kiivit claimed that 80–85% of Estonians were active members of the Lutheran Church, but his successor Alfred Tooming claimed only 300,000 by 1969.[123] An East German "progressive" Catholic journal estimated in 1969 that 75% of the population of Lithuania confessed to the Catholic faith.[124] The Lithuanian and Polish populations of the republic, its two traditionally Catholic groups, made up 88% of the total.

Whatever internal convictions were, it was clear that external religious practices declined sharply during the 1960s. In Estonia, christenings went down from 56% of all children in 1957 to 12% in 1968. Church weddings dropped from 30 to 3% of all weddings, and funerals from 64 to 46%. The secularization trend visible ever

---

[122] Uustalu 1970, p. 364; Salo, p. 204.
[123] ACEN, V, p. 69; Salo, p. 204.
[124] Vardys 1978, pp. 213ff.

since 1920 may actually have been slowed down by the Stalinist onslaught, and was now catching up. Introduction of more dignified civil ceremonies also had an effect. Lutheran confirmations in Estonia reached a peak of 9,200 in 1957, the year Komsomol coming-of-age camp rituals were started. By 1959, both competitors netted about 6,200, with some youths possibly taking part in both rituals. By 1964, confirmations stabilized around 500 and Komsomol camps around 6,000. The pattern may have been similar in Latvia. In Lithuania, the percentage of children christened dropped from 80% in 1958 to 46% in 1972. The corresponding figures for marriages were 60 and 25%, and for church funerals 79 and 51%.[125]

HOW THE BALTIC STATES LOOKED IN 1968

For the Baltic nations, the outlook was markedly different in early and late 1968. Soviet invasion of Czechoslovakia in August made the difference. It marked the end of the post-Stalin optimism, and also of a hesitantly sprouting Baltic mood of cooperation with Soviet rule.

The late 1950s had proved to be a period of considerable improvements in individual security and well-being as well as in national culture, despite major setbacks such as the Latvian purge. By any standard other than the Stalinist past, the regime was still very oppressive, but the change that had already taken place encouraged optimism regarding changes still to come. The early and middle 1960s saw a decelerating pace of reforms, but a feeling of making headway lasted, despite Latvian and Estonian unease about the resurging influx of Russians.

Readiness to cooperate within the Soviet framework increased, and confrontational tactics were avoided, for various reasons. The Soviet debit in foisting Stalinism on the Baltic nations was gradually being cancelled out by credit for overcoming it. Russia evolved, and so did the Baltic image of Russia. The renascent Baltic culture was increasingly appreciated by Russian cultural circles. This recognition, combined with grudging Baltic respect for Soviet stability, for the first time added a fleeting element of goodwill to the complex mix of Baltic feelings toward the regime, a mix which previously had mostly ranged from passive total negation to abject slavish eagerness in some cases. It seemed that problems could eventually be talked out with Moscow on a rational level based on respect for mutual interests. The general tenor may well have been

125 Salo, pp. 202–204, Vardys 1978, p. 214.

expressed by Rudolf Rimmel, an Estonian born in Kazakhstan in 1937, through the opening verses of his poem "Looking Forward":

> mildew will wither forever wither
> and winds will carry away its musty stench
> eternal idols having become decrepit
> will scatter like seeds of daisies
> the air will be full as if with pollen
> unable to germinate unable to germinate
> shouts of joy will ring unable to germinate
>
> the hijacked ship will be cleared of pirates
> the rescued will discover a new New World
> sailors will not revolt against columbuses
> small fish will turn into dolphins
> so will the sharks so will the sharks because
>   it has to be so[126]

It was not a cry of triumph over the sharks, but an expectation of their evolving into dolphins and a willingness to accept mutation without rancor. The term for "unable to germinate" (*idanemisvõimetu*) could also be understood as "unable to orientalize." The poem was published in the August 1968 issue of the Soviet Estonian cultural monthly *Looming*. By the end of the month, the shark forecast was out of date.

Toward the end of 1968, the expectation of a general cultural purge appeared. It was not to come, but the fleeting goodwill had been lost. Some, especially in Lithuania where the earlier process had been the most successful, began to wonder what benefit, if any, the nativization of the Communist party had brought or could bring. Many adopted a resigned, cynical stance of pursuing material goods, which were still scarce, though considerably less so than earlier. Others became passive or active dissidents. Dissent, hardly evident in the mid-sixties, was born. It was a peaceful confrontation, but a confrontation nevertheless. August 1968 can be said to have been a psychological watershed, marking the end of a cooperative evolution of Moscow's rule in the Baltic republics.

---

[126] Rudolf Rimmel, "Ettepoole," *Looming*, 1968/8, p. 1211.

CHAPTER V

CENTRALIZATION AND WESTERNIZATION: 1968–1980

The period from 1968 to 1980 might be termed the years of contradictions for the Baltic countries. On the one hand, centralization of the economy and politics under Moscow control continued and set in more deeply; immigration also continued to strengthen the Russian hold on the Baltics. On the other hand, the development of a Western-oriented Baltic culture and life-style also continued; in particular, despite continuing strict controls, direct contacts with the West expanded considerably. Dissent arose in the midst of increasing Soviet conformism. Russification of education contradicted cultural autonomy. If a major theme can be said to have characterized this period, it could not yet be distinguished from the short perspective of the early 1980s.

POLITICS AND IDEOLOGY

Immobilisme *in Administration*

In 1968, a variety of political developments seemed possible in the Soviet Baltic republics. On the one hand, a genuine political process could have evolved to complement the provincial administrations which, despite their trappings of autonomy, deferred all political decision-making to Moscow. On the other hand, the invasion of Czechoslovakia raised the possibility of a Stalinist crackdown on Baltic autonomy, as limited as it already was. Neither of these potentialities materialized during the 1970s. We can hardly speak of government or politics in the republics, as such functions were reserved for Moscow; we can merely follow the rather uneventful changes of personnel within the Soviet Baltic bureaucracy. Beyond their names, people tended to know little of Moscow's lieutenants in their countries, and politics was not a frequent topic for social discussion.[1]

Nativization of the ruling apparatus could have been expected in Estonia and Latvia during the 1970s. The Russianized cadres with native surnames, imported during the 1940s, had been subjected to gradual re-nativization as well as to mortality. At the same time, the indigenous pool of available talent was expanding in both numbers and seniority. Maintenance of an immigrant lieutenancy did not seem to be a basic element in Moscow's policy; in Lithuania, native cadres have held most of the top posts since 1940. Nonetheless, no change occurred in Latvia or Estonia. The chief cause was perhaps the increasing gerontocratic *immobilisme* in Moscow. This seemed particularly evident in 1978, when Estonia's First Secretary Käbin retired. He was replaced by a totally lackluster Yestonian technocrat, Karl Vaino, whose main qualification seemed to be an Estonian surname. During thirty years in the country, he had scarcely been able to learn his ancestral language.

The formal external relations of the Baltic republics seemed to expand somewhat around 1970. Like the other western republics of the USSR, they joined the East European International Radio and Television Organization on a par with Poland and Finland. Some trade treaties were concluded on relatively minor matters with East Germany, Hungary, Czechoslovakia, and Finland. However, this could not be considered even a formal extension of sovereignty, as the Leningrad Oblast also concluded comparable "border trade agreements" with Finland.

The death in office in 1974 of Lithuanian First Secretary Antanas Sniečkus was the first such occurrence among republic First Secretaries in the history of the USSR. By that time, Sniečkus, who had been LiCP First Secretary since underground days in 1936, was second in seniority among national CP First Secretaries, being surpassed in tenure only by Mao Zedong. The Lithuanian party had become its First Secretary's personal machine probably to a greater extent than that of any other Soviet republic. Sniečkus secured such relative control through unhesitant allegiance to Moscow and through his ability to foresee shifts in Kremlin policy. Although the Kremlin tended to have more trouble with Lithuania

---

[1] For details of politics and ideology, see Pennar 1978, pp. 105–127; Taagepera 1978, pp. 75–103; Yaroslav Bilinsky, "The Background of Contemporary Politics in the Baltic Republics and the Ukraine: Comparisons and Contrasts," in Ziedonis, Taagepera, and Valgemäe (eds.), *Problems of Mininations: Baltic Perspectives* (San Jose, Calif., 1973), pp. 89–122; Rein Taagepera, "Dissimilarities Between the Northwestern Soviet Republics," *ibid.*, pp. 69–88; Bruno Kalniņš, "How Latvia Is Ruled," JBS, VIII/1 (Spring 1977), pp. 70–78; Remeikis 1970, pp. 121–156; also *EE/BE*.

than with the other two Baltic republics, somehow Sniečkus seems to have metamorphozed the unruliness of his fief into proof of the toughness of his job, rather than of his inability to handle it.

If one is to believe the interpretation of an alleged personal friend of Sniečkus who sent an unofficial obituary to an émigré publication, the successful Lithuanization of the party over which he presided during the 1950s and 1960s was in part due to a change in outlook by the First Secretary. According to this thesis, Sniečkus, who had been a fanatic Communist, ruthlessly executing orders from Moscow in Stalin's time, had later mellowed into an astutely pragmatic politician not blind to the intense nationalism among his charges. Utilizing a combination of such a pragmatic outlook with the inevitable expansion of prerogatives sought by the head of any bureaucracy and with the influential support in the Kremlin which he had built up during his long tenure in office, he managed to secure some tangible benefits for his bailiwick which might not normally have been forthcoming in the Soviet order of things.[2] In spite of his seniority, it appears that Sniečkus was posthumously snubbed. His funeral was a low-key affair, and no major Politburo figure attended. (The absence of Mikhail Suslov, a long-time personal friend, who had headed the CPSU Special Bureau for Lithuania in 1944-46, was perhaps particularly notable.)

His successor, Petras Griškevičius, was a party member since 1945, and gradually rose through positions in press censorship (1950-55), the Vilnius Party Secretariat (1956-64), and the CC (1964-71) to become First Secretary of the Vilnius City Committee (1971-74). The earlier situation of indigenous staffing of the republic's top posts continued. By 1970, native Lithuanians made up 67% of the party (see Table 6). One of the few immigrant top functionaries was Juozas Maniušis, Chairman of the Council of Ministers from 1967 to 1981 (see Appendix A for other administrators).

The Latvian administration remained in the hands of Russian Latvians with a significant admixture of Russians and other non-Latvians. In 1971, only 3 of the 13-member Bureau of the LaCP CC had been born in Latvia. In 1975, 12 out of 42 members of the Council of Ministers had completely non-Latvian names.[3] The LaCP was headed by Augusts Voss, who had grown up in Siberia

---

[2] T. Ženklys [pseud.], "Su A. Sniečkaus mirtimi pasibaigusi Lietuvos gyvenimo epocha," *Akiračiai* (Chicago), March 1974; republished as T. Zhenklis, "Proshchaias s Antanasom Snechkusom; chego my zhdem ot emigratsii, vstupitel'naia zametka A. Shtromasa," *Kontinent*, XIV (1977), pp. 229-250.

[3] See lists in *EE/BE*, no. 27, p. 2 (1971), and no. 50/51, pp. 3-4 (1975).

before being dispatched for party work in Latvia in 1945. He rose to the position of a CC Secretary in 1960, and succeeded Pelše as First Secretary when the latter was transferred to the all-Union CC Politburo. Pelše is the only person of Baltic origin to have become a full member of the Soviet Politburo in postwar years. He had left Latvia in his teens, joined the Bolsheviks in Petrograd in 1915, and returned to Latvia in 1940. After his move to Moscow, he demonstratively downplayed any Latvian ties. While most non-Russian Politburo members have themselves voted into the Supreme Soviet from their respective republics, Pelše chose throughout most of the 1970s to represent Volgograd in Russia rather than Riga. The ceremonial Chairmanship of the USSR Soviet of Nationalities has been held since 1974 by Vitālijs Rubenis, who was previously Soviet Latvia's titular head of state.

In 1970, Jurijs Rubenis, another Latvian from Russia, was appointed Chairman of the Council of Ministers. His official biography actually listed him as Russian, not Latvian, by nationality.[4] Only in 1974 was an indigenous Latvian, Pēteris Strautmanis (member of the party since 1944) given the ceremonial post of Chairman of the Presidium of the Supreme Soviet. By 1980, Latvians seemingly represented considerably less than half of the LaCP membership. No direct Soviet data on this embarrassing issue seem to be available (cf. Table 6).

Estonia continued to have fewer native top administrators than Lithuania, but many more than Latvia. In 1970, Estonians formed 52% of the membership of the ECP. An appreciable number of the Estonian members had grown up in Russia. However, after thirty years in Estonia, many of them were being re-Estonianized linguistically as well as culturally — a process which seems to have proceeded more extensively than in Latvia.

Top posts in Estonia still seemed to be awarded to those who remained the most Russianized. Johannes Käbin, First Secretary since 1950, was in 1978 kicked upstairs to become Chairman of the Presidium of the Supreme Soviet, the top ceremonial post previously held by Aleksei Müürisepp and Artur Vader until their deaths. Käbin had spent the years from 1910 to 1941 in Russia, from which he had returned as Ivan Kebin. Initially he had been vocally anti-nationalist, but gradually he re-Estonianized his name and relearned his mother tongue. Estonians came to consider him as a tolerable middleman, under extant conditions, between them and Moscow. Käbin's successor Karl Vaino (born in Tomsk, Siberia) initially came to Estonia in 1947, apparently carrying the

---

[4] *Deputaty Verkhovnogo Soveta Latviiskoi SSR Vosmoi Soziv* (Riga, 1972), p. 122.

Russian name Kirill Voinov. He rose through a variety of party positions to become one of the CC Secretaries in 1960. His selection for the top position surprised many Estonians. His extremely limited ability and willingness to speak Estonian insulted national feelings. The deepening consumer goods shortage was blamed on his overeagerness in shipping food products to Russia. In 1979, there was at least one attempt on his life: on his way to his country cottage, he was shot at by Imre Arakas, member of an underground armed group, who was given a 12-year sentence — which he was serving, as of 1981, in Vilnius.[5]

Valter Klauson continued as Chairman of the Council of Ministers. By 1978, however, it was rumored that he was in poor health. The two ranking home-grown administrators of the mid-1970s did not last: First Vice-Chairman of the Council of Ministers Edgar Tõnurist was demoted not long after Vaino's promotion in 1978; and Vaino Väljas, one of the CC Secretaries since 1971, was removed in March 1980, later to become Soviet Ambassador to Venezuela. After that date, the top administrators included only two home-grown Estonians, both with low party seniority: Arnold Rüütel, who replaced Tõnurist; and Rein Ristlaan, who replaced Väljas. Of all cabinet ministers, however, about 80% were born in Estonia.

Civic Culture and Consumerism

Administrative *immobilisme* and the absence of legal politics could not impede change in civic culture. Generational change was fading the memories of the Stalinist terror as well as of independence. Consumerism arose to challenge both official ideology and dissent. Any study of it has to remain based on anecdotal accounts. Little social research has been carried out, and even less published.

By 1980, the Baltic population below age 40 had no experience of the independence period and little experience with Stalinism. Such a self-evident statement implies a series of consequences. A generation whose knowledge of the pre-Soviet period was hazy had matured. Soviet schools distorted facts. Corrective home education was limited by people's fears of challenging a police-backed version of history as well as by a prevalent modern tendency to leave education to the schools. For increasing numbers of Balts, the independence period was receding into a past beyond that crucial personal watershed between the contemporary and the historical: one's own date of birth. As one of the authors had occasion to observe personally, some could speak of the formation date of the Soviet Baltic republics in 1940 as ''the anniversary of the republic''

5 *USSR News Brief* (Munich), 31 May 1981, pp. 4-5.

with an indifferent matter-of-factness devoid of any pro-Soviet fervor, and yet so incongruous to those who applied the same term to the creation of the independent republics in 1918. In this sense, time was definitely on the Soviet side. However, the new generation also lacked the obeisance which had been beaten into their elders by Stalinist terror. And even the older generation was opening up. People were less afraid than before to talk, to ask questions, and, in some cases, to dissent openly. In this sense, time was working against Soviet efforts to maintain a tight police state.

Police-state methods certainly were not abandoned. Yet the penalties for real or imagined transgressions were obviously more lenient than the prison terms so easily meted out in Stalin's time. Foreign correspondence seemed to be registered and opened routinely (with contents sometimes intermixed), and phone calls abroad were sometimes interrupted at sensitive points, indicating continuous monitoring. Many people believed their rooms were bugged, and counteracted by lifting the phone, playing the radio or television loud, letting the kitchen faucet run, speaking habitually in a low voice, or going to the park when talking about anything that might displease the authorities. Uncertainty over microphones and police reports as well as over unexplained professional setbacks became powerful weapons in the hands of a quasi-monolithic bureaucracy. Individuals could be put on the defensive by hours of puzzled self-questioning over which of their inevitable minor transgressions could have been the cause of a non-promotion or a friendly police chat. Even open dissent could be repressed by indirect means (such as firing from a job, house searches, interrogations, beatings of family members by "hooligans" whom the police would not catch, and general harassment) before open resort to imprisonment. The change in the totalitarian methodology was partly due to the rise of consumerism.

Consumerism developed with the rise of income — a Union-wide phenomenon — in which the Baltic republics were ahead of the Russian republic. After a period of general scarcity, the material good things of life now came within one's reach, if one concentrated on getting them and did not rub the system the wrong way. A car, a summer cottage with a sauna bath, fancy food (often merely of the U.S. supermarket variety), elegant tableware and furniture, a trip abroad, and even an encyclopedia set made scarce through oversubscription by other, similar consumerists — these were attractive items for personal enjoyment and for keeping up a prestige struggle with one's closest peers. The accompanying collaboration with the regime began to be rationalized not only in terms of yielding to the inevitable but also in terms of transcending the whole issue: Communist ideology was declared so despicably emptied of any content that it was beneath one's dignity even to bother taking an open stand against it. One voiced one's complete opposition by going through all the required motions with an ironical meticulousness, thus presumably making the Communist liturgy even more void of content.

The regime's reaction to consumerism was mixed. Emphasis on material goods for private (or even group) consumption went against the official interpretation of Marxism. The regime lost idealistic supporters who succumbed to creature comforts, but it also lost idealistic opponents in even larger numbers. Consumerism faced political dissent with a weapon in some ways more powerful than terror or bureaucratic harassment: a mix of ridicule and boredom. While peaceful dissent looked criminal to the regime and morally imperative to the dissenters, to the consumerists it looked merely foolish. Consumerism was thus weakening the ideological underpinnings both of the regime and of dissent. It was not clear by 1980 which one would be more affected.

For those less cynical or egoistic, coping with repression led to a somewhat schizophrenic pattern of behavior, the combination of public collaboration with private dissent. The contrast became most marked among those doing professional writing: managers, scholars, writers, and educators. While praising the regime in their written output, such people frequently condemned it privately. The repression of loyal dissent blocked constructive criticism. Total public support was obtained at the cost of cumulative private frustration and disaffection. As daily tasks continued to be performed, such split behavior served immediate Soviet objectives. Long-range effects remain to be seen.

During the late 1970s, two new developments seemingly made it more difficult for the Baltic populations to maintain the stances of cynical consumerism or schizophrenic collaboration: an economic slowdown, and Russification. The rise in the standard of living slowed and probably even reversed itself. Food availability worsened markedly; inflation could not be indefinitely masked by new, supposedly improved brands. Specific crises had their effect. The disruption of the natural gas flow from Iran in 1979, coupled with Soviet military moves during the Chinese border war with Vietnam, coincided with unexpected power cut-offs in the Baltic republics.[6] For several decades, the Soviet regime had managed to deliver a rising standard of living to individuals willing to accept political restrictions as part of the bargain. By 1980, such times

6 Personal communications by Soviet citizens. Much in the section on consumerism is based on personal communications and on direct or indirect observation.

seemed to be approaching an end. Economic failures could lead to questions about the regime's legitimacy. The Great Russian chauvinism, revived by the regime in its search for legitimacy at the Russian core of the state, affected all minority nationalities of the USSR, the Balts among them.

The Russification Campaign of the Late 1970s

The slackening in the anti-nationalism campaign which followed the replacement of Khrushchev and the assumption of power by a collective leadership showed signs of ending by the late 1960s. By the beginning of the following decade, a renewed pressure could be distinctly felt. The concept of a "Soviet people" continued as a clear ideological tenet, present here and now. This may have been perceived in the Baltic republics as a threat to the national cultures and thus contributed a stimulus to their development as well as to dissent. The tightening of ideological controls and an intensification of "internationalist" propaganda was unmistakable. In Lithuania, the brunt of the visible attack seems initially to have fallen on the popular ethnographic societies which had emerged as points around which national cultural feelings tended to crystallize. Ethnography study groups and organizations were directed to shift their attention to the "ethnography" of the Soviet period: revolutionary lore and war-time experiences of the Soviet military.

The renewed effort to Russianize the non-Russian population of the USSR seems to have gained in intensity during the second half of the 1970s. Ever since 1960, the Russian people had lost ground demographically within the USSR. Although, according to the 1979 census, they still maintained a narrow absolute majority, already by the mid-1960s over 50% of the Soviet newborn were non-Russian. In 1970, only 47% of the children under ten were Russian. Major growth in the non-Russian population occurred in Central Asia, but Moscow's response was Union-wide.[7]

The brunt of the attack came in the realm of language. Union-wide conferences were called to consider methods of extending the use of Russian in public affairs and education. Secret instructions dispatched to the republics mandated implementation of that which was only under discussion.[8] Nursery schools were ordered to

[7] Rein Taagepera, "National Differences Within Soviet Demographic Trends," *Soviet Studies*, XX/4 (April 1969), pp. 478–489; Lubomir Hajda, "Nationality and Age in Soviet Population Change," *Soviet Studies*, XXXII (1980), pp. 475–499; Michael Rywkin, "The Political Implications of Demographic and Industrial Developments in Soviet Central Asia," *Nationality Papers*, VII/1 (Spring 1979), pp. 25–52.
[8] An unpublished decree of the USSR Council of Ministers, on 13 October 1978,

use Russian for half the day, and Russian was to be taught systematically, starting with the first grade. In the high schools, at least two subjects were to be taught in Russian in their entirety. Such ordered use of Russian extended to parts of the university curriculum as well as to more informal activities such as amateur theatrical groups. Radio and television programs in Russian were expanded. Estonia's Pedagogical Institute expanded the training of Russian teachers for Estonian-language schools, while preparing absolutely no teachers of Estonian for the republic's Russian-language schools. Estonian First Secretary Karl Vaino conceded that one should love one's own language, and speak it every day, but he also maintained that Russian was the *lingua franca* even within the Estonian republic, and that it was the key to world culture. During the 1980 song festival, for the first time, all speeches at official receptions were in Russian only, although Estonian was used in some of the public speeches.[9]

The most blatant expression of this new Russification came from Latvian Minister of Education Mirdza Kārkliņš, who boasted of the moral superiority of Russian over other languages in *Sovetskaia Latviia* of 6 January 1979: "Russian safeguards the effectiveness of patriotic and internationalist education, promoting the development of high moral and ideological-political qualities among pupils." She confirmed in detail the planned expansion of instruction in Russian, and reproached Latvians for not "adequately appreciating the value of speaking Russian among themselves." Deepened and thorough mastery of the Russian language is possible only, she claimed, when informal conversation in the language is not restricted to discussions with Russian teachers; all teachers must speak Russian, "thus creating a Russian-speaking environment." The pressure of overt Russification seemed to be approaching that of the Tsarist government during the 1890s.

---

was followed by a major conference in Tashkent, 22-24 May 1979. Its detailed and largely unpublished "recommendations" reached the West and were published in "The Tashkent Conference and Its Draft Recommendations on the Teaching of Russian," *Radio Liberty Research Bulletin*, no. 232 (August 1979), pp. 4-24. The October 1978 decree was apparently delivered to republic educational officials by special couriers, to be read and memorized in a special room, without making written notes; the decree copy was then returned to the courier. (Private communication to one of the authors.) In their turn, the republic CP CC Bureaus issued detailed confidential decrees. That of the Estonian Bureau (Minutes no. 105, par. 1, dated 19 December 1978) was obtained and published in *Eesti Päevaleht* (Sweden), 15 November 1980.

[9] Personal communications; *Perspektyvos* (a Lithuanian *samizdat* journal), no. 11, as reported in ELTA, October 1979, p. 11; *Nõukogude Kool*, no. 3 (March 1980), p. 14; *Rahva Hääl*, 14 June 1980; *Helsingin Sanomat*, 13 July 1980, p. 3.

The well-developed Lithuanian underground press responded to the pressures with protests and calls to boycott classes taught in Russian. In Estonia, the first reaction was shock and despair, yet combined with a determination not to yield a single cultural or educational position without argument or delay. The 1979 census brought surprising results regarding the self-declared competence in the Russian language of the Estonians. From 1970 to 1979, this self-declared knowledge of Russian as a second language increased in all Soviet republics except Estonia. Latvians went from 45.2 to 56.7%, and Lithuanians from 35.9 to 52.5%. In view of continuing Soviet schooling, and of the mortality of the pre-Soviet older generation, such a trend was to be expected. However, only 29.0% of Estonians declared themselves proficient in Russian in 1970, and in 1979 the figure actually dropped to an unbelievable 24.2%. The only explanation could be that the Russification campaign had brought about a backlash.[10]

The open attack on national education may have elicited an active stand from many who had previously accepted the status quo. Pleas for support in the West were smuggled out by those who had previously never taken such risks. Consumerists, who had rationalized the harmlessness of slow Russification through immigration, could hardly pretend any longer that the national culture was not in danger. If the reaction to the Tsarist Russification drive of the 1890s could be taken as a guide, means would be developed to resist denationalization. The end result could be a heightened national consciousness and increased resentment of a regime which had turned more blatantly Russian-chauvinist.

DEMOGRAPHIC AND SOCIAL TRENDS

Interaction between birth rates and immigration continued in 1968–80 to be of far-reaching importance for Baltic social, political, and cultural processes. Urbanization continued, but service industries replaced production as the main growth sector. Many new aspects common to all technologically overdeveloped countries emerged, but the basically established Soviet and Baltic patterns were maintained.

---

[10] Data from *Naselenie SSR: Po dannym Vsesoiuznoi perepisi naseleniia 1979 goda* (Moscow, 1980). One of the present authors has direct information on specific cases where persons fluent in Russian denied such knowledge in a Soviet census report, and where census-takers casually suggested that overly extensive reporting of fluency in Russian might result in cuts in book publication in the language of the republic.

Demography

The gap between the labor demands set by imperialist economic goals and the labor-supply capacity of the Baltic population continued to be filled by immigration of Russians and Russianized members of other Soviet nations. Compared to the 1960s, the influx in the late 1970s decreased in Latvia and Estonia. In Lithuania it expanded, but was still less than in the other two countries. The differences could be explained in terms of the birth rates in the Baltic countries and in Russia.[11]

In Latvia and Estonia, the crude birth rate per thousand population reached a low of 14 in the mid-1960s, and stayed in the 14-to-16 range thereafter (see Table 13). The rate seemed to be nearly the same for Estonians and Latvians (who had a high percentage of old people) and for immigrants (who were younger, but included many footloose transients without children). Due to the aging of the native population, the yearly death rate climbed from 11 per thousand population in 1970 to more than 12 in 1980, and was much higher for the local nationals (around 15) than for the immigrants (probably around 8). Because of this lower death rate, the number of foreigners would have increased faster than the number of Latvians and Estonians even if there had not been any further immigration in the 1970s. Immigration compounded the threat of demographic denationalization of the two republics. It reached alarming proportions in 1970: about 11,000 into Estonia, compared to a natural increase of about 2,500 Estonians and 4,000 non-Estonians. In Latvia, immigration peaked in 1973–74, with a net inflow of 15,000 per year, compared to a natural increase of about 2,000 Latvians and 4,000 non-Latvians. However, net immigration decreased appreciably thereafter (see Table 14). The decrease was clearly due to the drop in the Russian birth rate two decades earlier. The supply pool of immigrant labor was rapidly being reduced.[12]

[11] For details on demography, see Taagepera, "Baltic Population Changes" and "The Population Crisis and the Baltics," JBS, XII/3 (Fall 1981), pp. 234–244; Gundar J. King and Juris Dreifelds, "Demographic Changes in Latvia," in Ziedonis et al. (eds.), *Problems of Mininations*, pp. 131–136; Tönu Parming, "Population Changes and Processes," in Parming and Järvesoo, pp. 21–74, and "Population Processes and the Nationality Issue in the Soviet Baltic," *Soviet Studies*, XXXII/2 (July 1980), pp. 398–414; *EE/BE*; *National Economy* yearbooks of the Baltic SSRs; Arnold Purre, "Ethnischer Bestand und Struktur der Bevölkerung Sowjetestlands im Jahr 1970," AB, XI (1971), pp. 41–60; Andrivs Namsons, "Nationale Zusammensetzung und Struktur der Bevölkerung Lettlands nach den Volkszählungen von 1935, 1959 und 1970," *ibid.*, pp. 61–86; Benedict Mačiuika, "Auswertung der Volkszählungsergebnisse von 1970 in Sowjetlitauen," *ibid.*, pp. 87–116.

[12] Detailed data and calculation of estimates in this paragraph are given in Taagepera, "Baltic Population Changes."

Even during its peak period, the net immigration actually represented the combined effect of massive influx largely cancelled out by almost as massive an outflow. In 1963 there were 72 departures for every 100 new arrivals in the Baltic cities; in 1968–69, Estonia received 35,300 immigrants but saw an outflow of 19,700 people.[13] By 1980 the ratio could stand at more than 90 departures for every 100 arrivals, with both flows largely consisting of footloose young Russians hunting for the "long ruble" (easy money) throughout the Soviet Union. The net emigration of Estonians seemed to be negligible, with a small outflow cancelled by a similarly small return flow of previous Estonian settlers in Russia. Emigration of Latvians was also quite limited. The considerably transient nature of the Russian-speaking colonies in Latvia and Estonia helped to reduce their vested interest and social power, but it also impeded cultural integration. They were guests who largely chose to ignore the republic language and culture, and expected their hosts to adjust themselves. Such behavior caused resentment well expressed in an Estonian ditty which was sung widely in private, and often openly in the streets during festivities such as New Year's Eve:

> *Välja, välja vabariigi seest,*
> *kes söövad eesti leiba ja ei räägi eesti keelt!*
>
> [Out, get out from this republic's reach,
> All eaters of Estonia's bread who do not use its speech.]

Lithuania's birth rate was relatively high and, from 1965 to 1970, it even surpassed the rapidly decreasing Soviet Russian birth rate by an appreciable margin (18 per thousand against 15). However, by 1980 Lithuania's birth rate also had dropped to 15. Net immigration actually was slightly larger in the 1970s (7,000 per year) than it was in the 1960s (an average of 4,300 per year). Even so, it remained small compared to Latvia's, and raised little concern for national survival. The mechanization of agriculture, a higher birth rate, and the successful decentralization of industrial development during the 1960s assured that Lithuania's labor increase predominantly came from Lithuanian cradles.

In 1959, Estonia's population had been 75% Estonian. By 1970 there was an alarmingly rapid decrease to 68%. The third postwar census in 1979 showed a further decrease, but a noticeably smaller one, to 65% (see Table 1). Similar trends brought the Latvians even closer to the prospect of being reduced to a minority in their own country. Already down to 62% of Latvia's population in 1959, Latvians represented 57% in 1970 and 54% in 1979. The

---

[13] V. I. Perevedentsev, in *Soviet Geography* (April 1969); Uno Mereste and Maimu Saarepera, *Rahvastiku enesetunnetus* (Tallinn, 1978), pp. 257–258.

psychologically important 50% level was close, but further attrition was slowing down. The Lithuanians continued to preserve a strong majority position in their country. They actually increased their share in Lithuania's population from 79% in 1959 to 80% in 1970 and 1979, partly through a slow assimilation of the Polish minority.

Republic-wide trends in national composition were accentuated in the capital cities (see Table 11). In Tallinn, the Estonian share dropped from 60.2% in 1959 to 55.7% in 1970, and to 51.3% in 1979. In Riga, Latvians, down from 44.7% in 1959 to 40.9% in 1970, were outnumbered by Russians (42.7% in 1970), and the remaining population tended to know Russian better than Latvian. In Vilnius, which historically had been a multi-national city, the Lithuanian share (33.6% in 1959) continued to rise, reaching 42.8% in 1970 and 47.3% in 1980.[14]

The image of the poorly educated and uncultured Russian construction worker seemed to loom large in the Baltic popular image of the immigrants. However, statistics showed the Russians and Ukrainians in the Baltic republics to have more schooling than the Balts had. They dominated not only among bricklayers and miners, but also in civil aviation, fishing fleets, and railroad engineering. Reflecting the general lack of social interaction, inter-marriage between Balts and immigrants remained quite low in the 1960s. It may have risen in the 1970s, with most of the offspring apparently opting for Baltic nationality.[15] Around 1970, there was some propaganda for the immigrants to master the local language, and cases of some who had done so were described in newspapers. Results were limited. Especially in Latvia, even a single Russian within a *kollektiv* would often insist that the official business be transacted in Russian.

Urbanization continued, at a gradually decreasing rate (see Table 10). In Estonia, the most urbanized of all Union republics, the percentage of people living in cities and towns rose to 70% in 1980. Latvia's figure was almost as high. Lithuania's degree of

[14] *Itogi Vsesoiuznoi perepisi naseleniia 1970 goda*, vol. IV (Moscow, 1973), pp. 275, 283, and 320; *Õhtuleht* (Tallinn), 27 February 1980; *Mokslas ir gyvenimas*, 1981/3, p. 27.

[15] Of a total of 15,552 Estonians who married in 1968, only 5% (729) married Russians, according to *Nar. khoz. ESSR 1969*, p. 26. Of the children from Russian-Baltic mixed marriages who reached adulthood in 1960-68, 62% opted for the republic nationality in Tallinn, 57% in Riga, and 52% in Vilnius, according to L. N. Terenteva, *Sovetskaia etnografiia*, no. 3 (May-June 1969), pp. 20-30, translated in *Bulletin of Baltic Studies*, no. 4 (December 1970), pp. 5-11. In Baltic mixed marriages with non-Russians, about 80% opted for republic nationality. The percentages are likely to be higher in the countryside, but lower for those settled outside the republic.

urbanization in 1970 was still below the Soviet average, but it almost caught up by 1980 (62%, compared to 63% for the USSR). The high degree of urbanization in Latvia and Estonia reflected the tendency of immigrants to settle in the cities. The urbanization of ethnic Latvians and Estonians was more limited. The Russian-penetrated cities continued to contrast with the overwhelmingly Baltic countryside, except in some eastern districts.

Agriculture's share in employment and national product continued its slow decline. However, industrial employment also peaked in Estonia (with 35.2% of total employment in 1970, and 34.4% in 1976), Latvia (down from 34.3% to 33.1%), and probably, by 1980, in Lithuania as well.[16] As in all technologically mature countries, service became the major sector of growing employment.

Latvia's economy and culture continued to be dominated by a single large city — Riga (835,000 inhabitants in 1979). Lithuania maintained a two-center system, although Vilnius (481,000) was slowly gaining an edge over Kaunas (370,000). Estonia could be said to have a one-and-a-half-center system, with Tallinn (430,000) sharing some cultural leadership with Tartu (102,000 inhabitants in 1979).[17] An increasing proportion of the total population was living in the capital cities (see Table 11).

Western-Like Trends in Life-Style

In many ways the Baltic life-style underwent changes similar to those in the West, with a time lag that tended to decrease as communications improved. Sometimes there was clear imitation of Western fads, while at other times similar technological changes may have brought similar results even independent of foreign examples. Analogous developments in Russia tended to lag behind the Baltic, and may at times have been affected by the Baltic examples.

Youth culture visibly imitated the West, and some establishment members were accepting it. "If a hippie plays a violin naked above the waist and with a cross around his neck . . . this does not mean that the music is bound to be bad," composer Uno Naissoo wrote. "Let us remember that in fact we have always sanctioned (tacitly or even officially) everything that has acquired international

---

16 *Nar. khoz. ESSR 1977*, p. 171, and *Nar. khoz. LaSSR 1977*, p. 212. In Lithuania, the combined share of industry and construction advanced very slowly from 37.6% in 1971 to 38.0% in 1975: *Ekonomika ir kultūra 1975*, p. 187.

17 Tõnu Parming, "Roots of Nationality Differences," in Edward Allworth (ed.), *Nationality Group Survival in Multi-Ethnic States* (New York, 1977), pp. 24–57.

circulation; only we have been late by up to ten years."[18] Long hair was shocking some Baltic parents and teachers throughout the early 1970s; they accused television of promoting "hairiness" which affected even the star team of the Estonian Student Corps, an apparently unique Estonian enterprise for summer work by high school students. Some schools had daily dress controls, insisting on school uniforms, removing rings, and rejecting long-haired boys and girls with tight pullovers. But at school dances, leather jackets, Beatle outfits, weirdly-dressed bands, and rock instead of polkas tended to prevail. In July 1971 a "Union-wide Congress of Hippies" reportedly brought 100 guests to a Vilnius restaurant. Unable to expel the "Texas pants" (blue jeans), and unwilling to give up on having a school uniform, Estonian schools finally made the jeans compulsory.

Telemania expanded as in the West, despite a rather different program mix (except for Tallinn, where Finnish TV could be seen). TV broadcasting began in 1954, and started to reduce movie attendance by 1961. Color broadcasting was introduced in 1972. A Latvian study found people spending 7 of their weekly total of 20 leisure hours on TV, and poetess Lija Brīdaka felt the nation had become "comfortably ensconced on the couch in an intellectual stupor."[19] Since most programs were in Russian (74% in Estonia, 1975-76), for sheer reason of cost, the stupor also had a Russianizing component.

The Baltic republics were ahead of the rest of the Soviet Union in acquisition of private cars. Although the "car explosion" was modest compared to American excesses, it began to overstrain the limited road, parking, and servicing facilities. By 1970, Lithuania had 30,000 private cars and 160,000 motorcycles. Estonia's car sales quintupled from 1971 to 1972. Rush hours in Riga made planners start thinking about a subway. Waiting lists were still long, and some people in Latvia were ready to pay embezzlers 18,000 rubles cash for fake lottery tickets enabling one to get a 9,200-ruble "Volga" without waiting.[20] In Estonia's Kingissepa district (Saaremaa island), the right to buy a car without waiting was made a major prize in a socialist competition. Service remained so limited that a new 8-pump gas station (with no repair facilities) in Tallinn was first-page news, with photo, in the republic's main daily.[21] An almost unbelievable degree of gasoline pilfering took place, with 30% of all gasoline assigned to kolkhozes and state

[18] *Sirp ja Vasar*, 29 October 1971; *EE/BE*, no. 29, p. 5 (1971).
[19] *Literatūra un māksla*, 23 November 1974; *EE/BE*, nos. 48–49, p. 17 (1975).
[20] *Cīņa*, 1 July 1975.
[21] *Rahva Hääl*, 29 September 1972.

enterprises ending up in private hands through illegal speculation.[22]

Traffic accidents killed 667 people in Lithuania in 1970, 637 in Latvia in 1971, and 271 in Estonia in 1972. These seemed to be peak levels before the population adjusted to car expansion. Of Lithuania's 4,678 car accidents in 1970, drunk driving caused 989. Truck drivers caused 57% of Latvia's accidents, and tractor drivers 34%. While 22,302 people received driving licenses in Estonia, 4,812 lost them for drunk driving in 1973. Fines were heavy. ESSR Agriculture Minister Harald Männik was demoted to sovkhoz director in 1970 because of a drunken U-turn in which he himself was the only injured party. He was reinstated in 1975.[23]

As in the rest of the Soviet Union, highway construction failed to keep pace with the increase in vehicles. The situation may have been marginally better in the Baltic republics. The four-lane highway linking Vilnius to Kaunas, a stretch of some 100 kilometers completed in 1970, was perhaps the longest such interurban expressway in the USSR.

Consumer goods variety and quality improved, although continuing short supply was suggested by bulging savings accounts (one-third of yearly retail turnover around 1972, and close to half by 1977). Stereo hi-fis, vacuum cleaners, refrigerators, and tape cassettes reached a sizable fraction of the population. In 1970, "Estonia-Stereo" was the first Soviet stereophonic radio set. Meat began to be sold in vacuum-sealed plastic bags, and aluminum foil appeared. Even a Soviet invention of mailing-strength carton boxes was announced.[24] Washing-machine sales in Estonia and Latvia peaked in 1968, indicating market saturation at least for the models available (and the place to put them, in cramped apartments). The partial switch from the traditional Soviet sellers' market to a buyers' market brought along "socialist commercial advertising," in papers and on TV. Created in 1967 as a self-managing enterprise (see section below on "Recentralization and Self-Management"), "Eesti Reklaamfilm" netted 3 out of 4 prizes at a 1971 Union-wide advertising film seminar, received in 1975 at least 120,000 rubles from regular customers, and was accused in the press of creating new artificial needs by persuading people that consumer goods can bring prestige and family happiness. In 1972, *Rahva Hääl* (23 February) for the first time ever ran an ad for credit buying: a 300-ruble TV set for 85 rubles down and the rest in

---

[22] *Ibid.*, 9 July 1969.

[23] Traffic accident statistics compiled from Soviet press, in *EE/BE*, nos. 33, p. 3, and 35, p. 4 (1972); nos. 37, p. 4, 40, p. 3, and 41, p. 4 (1973); and nos. 44, pp. 9 and 11, and 47, p. 12 (1974). For Männik: no. 24, p. 8 (1971), based on private communications; and *Rahva Hääl*, 25 December 1970.

[24] *Rahva Hääl*, 12 May 1971.

monthly installments over two years. TV trade-in offers started in June 1972. By 1975, Latvia's *Padomju jaunatne* (6 June) was advertising a two-day moped, tent, and boat motor sale with no money down. It was a far cry from the Soviet Baltic market of the 1950s or even 1960s.

In 1972, the Soviet Union gingerly entered the bank-check age, and the following year personal checks were instituted for large purchases, with sums rounded off to the next hundred rubles. However, most Baltic customers still seemed to pay for their cars and apartments with thousands of rubles of cash nervously tucked into coat pockets.

The first comic book in Soviet Estonia (and possibly the Soviet Union) was published in 1973 — 128 pages of "Donald Duck, Mickey, and others" — but no others followed. Two books on sex and family were published in massive quantities to take care of the backlog (1970: 50,000 copies; 1974: 80,000) for an Estonian-speaking population of one million, with about 8,000 marriages and 3,000 divorces per year. Estonia's first funeral home was established in 1975. Monthly TV press conferences by party and government leaders started in 1971, but did not seem to last long.

While officially there was no inflation, the only combined price index published (that for the kolkhoz markets in four Latvian cities) showed a yearly price increase of 1% in 1965–70, 4% in 1970–75, and 13% in 1975–77. Price indices for individual goods on the Estonian kolkhoz markets tended on the average to increase by 2% per year in 1965–70, and by 4% in 1970–77.[25]

Other Social Trends

In many other aspects, life continued to follow established Baltic or Soviet patterns. Food remained a major concern for the population, in terms of both cost and availability. In 1968, Estonians were spending 62% of their personal income on food, with another 21% spent on clothing. The imbalance partly reflected the low-cost apartments (if one could get one), medical expenses, and transportation. But food expenses also reflected recurring shortages of staple foods in state stores, and the high prices at the kolkhoz and the black market. Depending on domestic harvests and Soviet foreign-trade vagaries, there would be periods without meat, coffee, spice, onions, and even potatoes. The Vietnam-China border war in 1979, and the United States' partial grain embargo in 1980, triggered panic buying during which the daily

---

[25] Calculations based on data in *Nar. khoz. LaSSR 1977*, p. 292, and *Nar. khoz. ESSR 1977*, p. 233.

sales of flour and grits in Tallinn increased sixfold.[26]

Official estimates of Baltic diet indicated higher protein content than in other Soviet regions and even in most other East European countries. Around 1970, egg consumption was rapidly increasing, and meat was on a par with Hungary. Milk and dairy-products consumption (over 400 kg per capita) stood far above the East European countries. On the other hand, grain products were low in the Baltic diet, and only Poles were eating more potatoes. Potato consumption was decreasing rapidly (from 194 kg per capita in 1965 to 140 in 1975, in Estonia), but it was replaced by fats rather than vegetables. Rapid modernization resulted in people doing little physical work and yet eating the dream foods of their peasant grandparents. Rural Latvians were estimated to be 20 kg overweight, on the average; in Estonia, fats formed 69% of the caloric intake; and Lithuanian protein consumption decreased. The recurring meat shortages were aggravated by Russian tourists and vacationers raiding the stores in major cities and even in small resort towns, sending food packages back to Moscow and leaving the local residents unhappy.[27]

Servicing in the late 1960s compounded the shortages, since it, too, was often set up to suit the convenience of the store rather than the customer. To buy food, one often had to stand in three or four separate waiting lines, and then take the streetcar to separate bakery and vegetable stores, only to find some of them closed for lunch.[28] By 1980, the majority of shops seemed to have shifted to self-service, and overspecialization was attenuated.

After 1975, however, shortages of the goods themselves became increasingly frequent and acute, especially in Latvia. By 1979 people from Riga were encountered in Tallinn, trying to purchase butter. In Tallinn itself, ham was practically absent from stores in the late 1970s, and according to some local residents, by May 1980 little meat of any kind was available, apart from pork feet.

Housing shortage remained a major social problem. By 1978, urban per-capita living space in Estonia finally caught up with the pre-Soviet level of 1940, after 30 years of peace and worldwide technological progress. The pre-war level remained unsurpassed in Latvia, and probably in Lithuania (see Table 10). Cramped quarters sharpened marital and generational friction. Living space was not redistributed because of such purely personal reasons as divorce, and some remarried professional people avoided the

---

[26] *Rahva Hääl*, 12 January 1980.
[27] Food consumption data from *EE/BE*, nos. 23, p. 4 (1970); 29, p. 8 (1971); 35, p. 3 (1972); and 44, pp. 7–8 and 47, p. 10 (1974). "Sausage tourists": nos. 29, p. 2 (1971); and 32, p. 3 (1972).
[28] *Eesti Kommunist*, May 1968, p. 36; *EE/BE*, no. 9, pp. 2–3 (1968).

resulting nightmare by sleeping in their offices. Distribution was unequal, and many people just above the legal minimum of 3 square meters were not even eligible for improved quarters around 1970. New construction tended to be sloppy. Parents would move into a brand-new apartment before children, to fill drafty cracks, adjust doors and windows, and make sure the porch would not fall down. Architect Mart Port wondered whether city planners used apartment dwellers as guinea pigs in some socio-biological experiment:

> Will they exist without stores and barber-shops? They will. How about trash-collection points a thousand feet away? They will carry it. Hoisting baby carriages up a narrow stairway to the fifth floor? They'll do it. No laundering facilities? They'll manage. But lower the room temperature by 10°C? They'll start complaining. So let us make a note: a boiler room is a must — that's the survival threshold. [29]

Some notable improvement in the urban environment took place during the decade. Housing continued to grow, as new neighborhoods sprawled outward from the major cities, especially the capitals. Some construction of public buildings and restoration changed the older centers. Tallinn especially profited from its selection as the site for the yachting competition of the 1980 Olympics. In addition to a new yachting center on the outskirts of the city, linked to it by a 5-km four-lane expressway, Tallinn was also endowed with a new 800-bedroom hotel and other conveniences. Its picturesque center received a facelift. Throughout the decade, Riga and Vilnius also received considerable restoration work. The 400th anniversary celebration of Vilnius University in 1979 occasioned a renewal of its centrally located old campus, and a new campus was opened in the suburbs. Earlier in the decade, Vilnius had also constructed a new Sports Arena (1971) and a new Opera House (1974), both of which were considered noteworthy by Soviet standards.

Due to space shortage, nearly 18% of Latvia's schools were operating in two shifts in 1970. About 14% of Lithuanian and 10% of Latvian and Estonian students attended night shifts in 1975. This involved only about 1% of all students in grades 1 to 8. However, in grades 9 to 11, the night shift was attended by 48% of all students in Lithuania, and by 41% in Latvia and Estonia. Hotels were crowded, too. Tartu, with 100,000 inhabitants in 1977, had only two hotels, with a total of 319 beds and a remarkably high average occupancy: 1.31 persons per bed per night. Estonia's

[29] *Sirp ja Vasar*, 13 June 1969.

average was 0.97 persons per hotel bed, and Latvia's 0.95.[30]

Family structure showed some loss of masculine domination, but no let-up on the disproportionate share of housework done by women. Women also did most of the time-consuming everyday shopping, often during work hours. Life for single women was sometimes not any easier in places like the Ogre textile firm in Latvia, which had dormitories for 4,000 girls without a single cafeteria, experienced a 20% labor turnover in half a year, and was used by mothers as a threat to lazy schoolgirls. After a major increase in the 1960s, the divorce rate grew only slowly in the 1970s (see Table 12). Abortion continued to be the most prevalent birth-control method, reaching the proportions of an epidemic "in all social layers." Throughout the three Baltic republics, the number of abortions tended to equal or surpass those of live births. In 1973, Latvia registered 60,000 abortions and 34,000 births. When asked their reasons for avoiding even a single child, most women stressed inadequate housing. Venereal disease became an acknowledged issue, favored by more relaxed sexual mores, continuing prostitution, and hidden brothels. As for rape, Latvian Minister of Internal Affairs A. Kavalieris cavalierly dismissed 60% of the cases as provoked by the victim's "lustful behavior."[31]

Shoplifting tended to increase as more stores switched to self-service. For those caught in Riga's "Children's World," the average hoard was under 7 rubles. On the more organized side, 34 people were indicted in 1972 for selling Riga Trade Institute's exam copies for 200 rubles apiece. As in the West, crime rates were increasing (by 8.5% per year in Lithuania, from 1968 to 1970), police complained of growing passivity of citizens in the face of criminal acts (partly in order to avoid tedious witness duty), and juvenile delinquency seemed to spread to the middle class.[32] People depended heavily on "under-the-counter" dealings, to make ends meet. "We are living on our *income*, not on our salaries," was a frequent explanation given to innocent visitors from the West.

Alcoholism became a source of worry both to Soviet managers concerned with labor efficiency and to Baltic patriots concerned with national survival. Around 1970, Estonia consumed 50% more

---

[30] Schools: *Skolotāju avīze*, 25 March 1970; *Nar. khoz. LaSSR 1977*, p. 305, and *Nar. khoz. ESSR 1977*, pp. 261–263; *Ekonomika ir kultūra* [LiSSR] *1975*, p. 260. Hotels: calculated from *Nar. khoz. LaSSR 1977*, p. 297, and *Nar. khoz. ESSR 1977*, pp. 246–247.

[31] Ogre: *Padomju jaunatne*, 28 May 1975; abortion epidemic: *Nõukogude Õpetaja*, April 1972, and Dreifelds 1976, p. 147; venereal disease: *Veseliba*, no. 2, 1974; rape: *Literatūra un māksla*, 14 July 1973.

[32] For crime reports, see *EE/BE*, nos. 3, p. 3 (1968); 24, p. 2 (1971); 34, p. 4 (1972); 37, p. 2 (1973); 45, p. 9 (1974); and 48, p. 16 (1975).

absolute alcohol per capita than did the RSFSR or the United States; Lithuania and Latvia were close behind. The level was on a par with beer-drinking West Germany, and much below wine-drinking France, but the Balts consumed mostly hard liquor (and cheap wine substitutes). In Estonia, the yearly per-capita consumption had risen from 3 liters of absolute alcohol in the 1930s to 6 liters in 1965. From 1965 to 1970, it increased by 52% (while wages went up by 35%, and per-capita retail sales by 51%), and was coming close to the previous historical record of 10 liters established around 1800 during the hopeless days of serfdom. Lithuania's hard-liquor consumption doubled from 1959 to 1968 (from 4.5 to 8.9 liters of alcohol per-capita), in line with the general Soviet trend.

Drinking at work was widespread. Even during a 1972 Union-wide anti-alcoholism campaign, a major Tallinn plant ("Ilmarine") was proud to announce that it had broken up "group drinking," conceding only partial success on individual drinking. Penalties involved not only losing a bonus, but also one's position in the apartment waiting list. Truck and tractor drivers were the worst offenders, but they were also among the most indispensable workers. It was privately conjectured in Lithuania that were the laws on drinking and driving strictly enforced, the republic's truck fleet would become paralyzed. The leadership was accordingly not interested in full enforcement. Over 7% of Estonia's tractor drivers lost their permits in 1968 for drunken driving, and the pattern was similar in 1972.[33]

Most collective farmers in a Latvian study continued to feel that drinking during work hours was "not necessarily bad." Vodka had become standard payment for kolkhoz tractorists willing to plow up a farmer's private plot, and many other such services. Alcohol was implicated in three-quarters of all drownings and crimes, half of all auto accidents and fire deaths, and many divorces. The death toll due to alcohol was estimated to be 1,500 in Latvia in 1972. It accounted for one-third of male deaths in the 20-to-50 age bracket. Official responses ranged from producing more beer (to displace liquor) to increasing the penalty for selling moonshine to three (Latvia) or five (Estonia) years in prison.

Special services continued to be supplied to the upper class of the classless society. There were special stores for Communist Party members. Pharmacies were keeping special reserves for these privileged elements. For the others, there were instances of a prescription's being filled after an eleven-month delay. Republic CP CC

---

[33] "How Estonia Drinks," *ibid.*, no. 29, pp. 6–7 (1971), and various other reports; A. Garonas, "Gerti ar negerti?" *Švyturys*, 1964/9, pp. 25–26.

buildings had other, better stores off-bounds even to the party rank-and-file, and distribution of foreign lingerie highlighted top-level party meetings even in the late 1970s. The development of a sense of hereditary elitism was illustrated by the angry establishment reaction to a short story in which a manager's son rejects middle-class values, cops out, and becomes a truck driver. Although he was described in the story as a skilled and conscientious worker, he was termed a superficial anarchist in the anonymously authoritative critique which, interestingly, did not object to the description of workers living in hovels without hope of raising a family.[34]

Militarism in propaganda and education may have increased around 1970, combined with aggressive peace propaganda. Since 1968 all factories and high schools have been required to have permanent military workshops to get the boys "interested in warfare" and to develop "soldierly habits." Estonian Lenin-Prize-winning author Juhan Smuul proclaimed that "nowhere else is human character unveiled so well, nowhere do superficial virtues . . . crumble so quickly as in war." This mood was echoed in teachers' and children's magazines. Obligatory military training started in the 9th grade, including practice with combat weapons. High school competitions featured shooting and grenade-throwing from motorcycles, with gas masks on.[35] The great majority of Baltic youths spent their two or three years of obligatory Soviet army, navy, border guard, or KGB service outside the Baltic area. In contrast to the Tsarist and early Bolshevik period, the developed Baltic area supplied very few officers to the Soviet army; those above the rank of colonel seemed to include less than half a dozen native-born Balts. Distrust may have been mutual.

Large numbers of Soviet troops continued to be stationed in the Baltic republics. Soviet-inspired proposals for a denuclearized northern Europe did not include the eastern shore of the Baltic. An "earthquake" in northern Estonia (Fall 1976) looked more like a nuclear accident at the Paldiski naval base 40 km west of Tallinn. *The Guardian* (U.K.) reported Soviet nuclear submarines stationed in Liepāja (9 April 1978). Forced to serve as nuclear missile bases against western Europe, the Baltic countries became potential nuclear targets themselves.

[34] E. Tennov, "Margiti kadumine," *Looming* (October 1974), pp. 1592–1651; *Rahva Hääl*, 6 December 1974, pp. 2–3; *EE/BE*, no. 48, pp. 14–15 (1975).
[35] Warfare interest: *Eesti Kommunist* (May 1970), p. 73; Smuul: *Rahva Hääl*, 10 October 1970; grenades: *Skolotāju avīze*, 18 November 1970.

ECONOMY AND ECOLOGY

The Baltic economic scene was characterized by a deepening labor shortage, and by two somewhat contradictory trends: a continuing shift of control from the republic to Moscow, but also an increasing self-management on individual plant and farm level. The labor shortage contributed to a reduction in industrial growth rate, and helped to boost the labor-saving aspects of self-management, which in turn consolidated the role of the Baltic republics (especially Estonia and Latvia) as a sort of socio-economic laboratory or testing grounds for potential Union-wide reforms. Agriculture improved considerably. Economic over-development started to create ecological problems. All these questions will be discussed in greater detail. [36]

Recentralization and Self-Management

The *sovnarkhoz* economic councils of 1958-64 marked the peak of economic autonomy for the Soviet Baltic republics. The new leaders who replaced Khrushchev in 1964 clearly preferred administration on the basis of production branches rather than territorial units. Abolition of the *sovnarkhoz* was one of their very first steps. The need for territorial coordination was recognized in principle, but in practice the power of central ministries expanded considerably in the mid-1960s, and continued to expand later at a slower rate. Traditionally some Soviet ministries existed only in Moscow, with no counterparts in the republics, while some others were republic responsibility, with no central ministry in Moscow. A third category consisted of "Union-republic" ministries, where ministries of the same name existed both in Moscow and in the republics, interacting tightly. This latter category was expanded at the expense of purely republic-level ministries. In this way, recentralization could take place without any republic ministry being conspicuously abolished. Yet the Union-republic format in practice shifted major decision-making from republic capitals to Moscow. The asymmetrical relationship was well illustrated by an Estonian delegate's complaint voiced at the 1969 Supreme Soviet session: if the combined operations result in a surplus, the Union ministry gets it; but if the year ends with a deficit, the Republic

[36] For details on economy, see *EE/BE*; Benedict Mačiuika, "The Role," pp. 18-25; George J. Viksnins, "Current Issues of Soviet Latvia's Economic Growth," JBS, VII/4 (Winter 1976), pp. 343-351; I. S. Koropeckyj, "National Income of the Baltic Republics in 1970," *ibid.*, VII/4 (Spring 1976), pp. 61-73; Järvesoo 1978; Endel Jakob Kolde, "Structural Integration of Baltic Economies into the Soviet System," JBS, IX/2 (Summer 1978), pp. 164-176; and the various annual editions of the *National Economy* of the Lithuanian, Latvian, and Estonian SSRs.

ministry has to absorb it. The scope of the purely Union ministries (with no republic-level counterparts) also expanded. In Latvia, only 3% of industrial production had been under Union control in 1960. By 1971 the Union ministries controlled 34%, and Union-republic ministries accounted for 56%, leaving only 10% (mostly light and food industries) under Latvian control.[37]

Baltic reactions to excesses of centralization ranged from academic demonstrations of its inefficiency to complaints at Supreme Soviet sessions about central ministries' shortcomings, and attempts to widen the centrally mandated plant self-management program to include some republic ministries. Estonian economist Vello Tarmisto argued that centralization may function well in less-developed areas, where economic structure is simple, but hurts in well-developed industrial areas such as Latvia and Estonia. Prior to 1964, all of Estonia's industry was directed from 6 local centers, but by 1969 about 40 local and Union-wide command centers were involved. Union ministries often had a single plant in Estonia, with its day-to-day management carried out from Moscow, at a distance of 1,000 km. Estonia's metallurgy and machine construction were subject to 15 different planning and command agencies, most of them outside Estonia. Industry often was expanded into cities where communal facilities were already overstrained, Tarmisto wrote, because the central planners were not obliged to consult with city agencies responsible for the well-being of the population. Others proposed that the efficiency measurements practiced at single-plant level be expanded to ministerial level, in order to determine whether territorial or production-branch management would be more efficient in any given case. A similar argument was made in 1978 by the Lithuanian economist Algirdas Maniušis, who underscored the importance of republic organs of administration in the establishment of genuinely efficient industrial units. He noted that management at the republic level was less fettered by rigid administrative boundaries, which could facilitate the creation of enterprises overlapping several existing industrial branches as well as draw on the results of diverse research and planning institutes.[38]

At the Supreme Soviet session of 1970, Artur Vader (who soon thereafter became Chairman of the Presidium of the Supreme

---

[37] *Nar. khoz. LaSSR 1971*, p. 79; *EE/BE*, no. 35, p. 3 (1972).

[38] Vello Tarmisto, "Territorial Concentration and Decentralization of Industry in the Soviet Baltic Republics," *Eesti NSV Teaduste Akadeemia Toimetised — Ühiskonnateadused*, XVIII/3 (1969), pp. 208–211; M. Kuniavskii, "Territorialnye problemy upravleniia," *Kommunist (Litvy)*, no. 11 (1979), p. 86; review of A. Maniushis [Maniušis], *Sovershenstvovanie upravleniia narodnym khoziaistvom soiuznoi respubliki* (Vilnius, 1978).

Soviet of the ESSR) scored the Union Building Materials Ministry for its costly, shoddy, and insufficient deliveries, and all Union ministries for giving premiums to plants located in Estonia and failing to fulfill their plan regarding locally needed products. Such detailed complaints by Baltic Supreme Soviet delegates continued in the 1970s, but without raising the general issue of decentralization.

During the late 1960s, a "new planning and incentive system" of self-management was gradually introduced in Soviet enter- prises. It involved relative administrative autonomy, financial self-dependence (and hence need for profitability), and tieing the workers' incomes to the enterprise's profits. This partial return to Western economic criteria was eagerly accepted and rapidly implemented in the Baltic republics. In Estonia, plants using the new system represented 49% of total industrial production in 1967 and 96% by the end of 1970. In Lithuania, the figure was 90% by the end of 1969. Progress was slower in industries which were dominated by Union ministries, where the mentality that "production determines consumption" persisted and administrative methods were preferred to economic levers. Material stimulation of labor efficiency slowed down when payments into stimulation funds increased, but increased payments to the workers out of those funds were not allowed. Adjustments were gradual.

Stymied in their quest for decentralization from above, some Baltic technocrats tried to make use of the plant self-management approach for consolidation of republic authority from below. In 1973, ESSR Food Industry Minister Jaan Tepandi argued that his ministry should be given self-management rights throughout the republic, reducing food industry decision-making by both local and all-Union enterprises. He thought this approach was suitable for many ministries in the smaller republics. The degree of implementation of such proposals was limited. The ESSR Transportation Ministry's Highway Agency apparently could not shift to self-management under that name, but could do so once it was reorganized as a "Highway Construction and Maintenance Trust" in 1970. Even minor production and personnel decisions continued to be made in Moscow. Knowledgeable Balts combined frequent business trips with making personally sure that their file in Moscow was "in the right pile."

Agricultural Efficiency

Agricultural efficiency of the Baltic republics continued to surpass the Soviet average by wide margins (86% in Estonia, 1968), and farmers' living standard continued to improve.[39] State farm employees profited from enterprise self-management, and relaxation of various restrictions turned some kolkhozes into genuine collective farms which at times became relatively wealthy. By 1972, collective farmers' average income (including income from private plots) had surpassed that of urban workers in Estonia and Latvia, and the traditional labor flow from the countryside to the cities started to be cancelled out by an opposite flow. Kolkhoz chairmen continued to be effectively appointed by the party-state apparatus, but in some cases the kolkhoz council came to be genuinely elected.

The number of farms continued to be slowly reduced through mergers. Both very poor and very rich kolkhozes ran the risk of being turned into sovkhozes, after an irreversible *pro forma* vote by the collective farmers. The poor ones would receive improved management, while the state could extract a fatter slice of profits from wealthy farms under the sovkhoz format, even though total profits might suffer. Kolkhoz-sovkhoz mergers almost always resulted in sovkhozes, but at least one reverse instance also occurred.

Auxiliary industry on collective farms was a major factor in their new wealth. Although a 1938 edict prohibited any kolkhoz industry, many kolkhozes started to process their products in the mid-1960s. By the time farm industry was declared legal in 1967, it already produced 54% of all Estonia's starch and 27% of its sawed timber. By 1970 many Baltic collective farms derived most of their profits from mills, canneries, wine factories, and mineral-water bottling. They made furniture, bakery products, barbed wire, special nails, and various wooden and metal consumer goods. Inter-farm industry developed, such as a large cannery built by 24 kolkhozes in Latvia's Liepāja district. Some kolkhozes (and sovkhozes) built their own stores in the cities. The kolkhozes were supposed to use only their own labor and agricultural raw materials, but in practice, successful farms often bought raw materials from other farms and brought in city labor. The 1972 plan for Latvia foresaw 64,000 minks, but farms produced 36,000 more for the private market. State pleas for "party-mindedness" only partially convinced kolkhozes to deliver cheap milk and grain rather than make more profitable maltose and starch. A firm line was drawn by state control when four Estonian kolkhozes started

---

[39] For details on agriculture, see (in addition to sources in note 36) Elmar Järvesoo, "Progress Despite Collectivization," in Ziedonis et al. (eds.), *Problems of Mininations*, pp. 137–149, and "Private Enterprise in Soviet Estonian Agriculture," JBS, V/3 (Fall 1974), pp. 169–187; Jonas Glemža, "Die Landwirtschaft Sowjetlitauens, 1960–1973," AB, XV (1975), pp. 211–279.

to act as marketing agents for individual producers of wooden buttons throughout several districts. Farm industry made headway in many parts of the Soviet Union, but the Baltic farms seemed to be among the most active. In 1972, auxiliary industry formed 14% of Estonia's total agricultural production.[40]

The Kirov fishing kolkhoz near Tallinn seems to have become a species by itself. It gradually acquired nearly a hundred trawlers, boats, and processing ships, but most of its income came from fur animals, trout, canning, furniture, garden products, and souvenirs. Mergers made it stretch 120 km along the coastline. Already by 1971, the monthly income was 650 rubles per member (compared to an ESSR average of 240 and USSR average of 140 rubles). Membership stood at 3,400, with a long waiting list. This piece of the Adriatic on the Baltic coast seemed to be accepted by authorities because it was a convenient showcase of collective-farm well-being. VIPs visiting Tallinn, from Romania's President Ceauşescu to the Shah of Iran, could be taken to admire Kirov's health and consumer services building, its restaurant, clubhouse, and sports stadium, as could tourist groups from abroad.

Despite occasional collective wealth, a large part of collective farm income continued to come from the tiny private plots — 44% in Latvia in 1970, and 43% in Lithuania five years later. In 1975, the private sector was still producing 39% of Lithuania's total agricultural output, and 17% of Estonia's *marketed* agricultural produce, on a basis of 5 to 7% of total arable land and an obviously much larger share of labor input.[41] However, the state and collective sectors were expanding; the Latvian figures in Table 15 are typical.

Soviet feelings toward private agriculture were negative in principle. Attempts were frequently introduced to make it inconvenient. Some of these clearly backfired. As livestock feed came to be priced higher than bread, many private pigs, not surprisingly, started to be fed bread and even macaroni. On the practical level, however, the Soviets realized the importance of private farming in feeding the cities. As thousands of farmers were being relocated from the traditional scattered farmhouses into newly created kolkhoz villages, it was determined by a Latvian survey that many had given up their cows and most planned to stop all private farming as inconvenient. While official social

---

[40] For documentation on farm auxiliary industry, see "Can Farmers Can?" *EE/BE*, no. 20, pp. 3–4 (1970); and also nos. 14, p. 8 (1969); 19, p. 2, and 23, p. 5 (1970); 24, p. 6, and 29, p. 8 (1971); 33, p. 4 (1972); 37, p. 2 (1973); and 42, p. 3 (1974).

[41] *Ibid.*, no. 47, p. 13 (1974); *Ekonomika ir kultūra* [LiSSR] *1975*, pp. 104 and 113; *Nar. khoz. ESSR 1977*, pp. 90 and 97.

commentators were pleased over the apparent diminution of the instinct for private ownership, they also noted that a collective farmer who gives up his cow "not only stops producing milk but also will demand milk from the local store."[42] When Baltic efficiency seemed to bring a completely deprivatized agriculture possibly within their reach, the Soviets hesitated. Official support for the vanishing private cow reappeared. The Tartu Experimental Automotive Plant even constructed a special bus for collecting milk from private cow owners.

Although rural incomes, counting in the significant proceeds from private plots, tended to exceed those of urban industrial workers, the rural environment continued to present a less attractive life-style than the cities. In 1973, about half of Lithuania's rural population lived in some 200,000 scattered individual homesteads (down from 265,000 in 1967). Some 100,000 of these were still nineteenth-century log constructions badly in need of repair. Their rate of diminution was low, about 10,000 annually. Apart from a few showplace settlements, their replacements were not uniformly attractive, either. Of the 130,000 residential units in Lithuania's 3,870 rural settlements (38% of the total rural housing), only 17% had running water and 6% a working sewage-disposal system. Only one-fifth of the settlement streets were paved, and most had no trees or greenery.

The aging of the rural population also continued. By 1970, two-thirds of Lithuania's pensioners lived in the countryside, numbering 357,000 or 23% of the rural population. The strain on the underdeveloped social-care and social-welfare systems was great. The average rural pensioner found it difficult to live on his pension, which in 1972 averaged 23 rubles. In 1968, it had been calculated that a monthly expense of 45 rubles was necessary to maintain a minimum standard of living. This led many to continue working for their collective farms after retirement, to continue backbreaking labor on their private plots for supplemental income, or to join their children in already overcrowded urban housing. Such solutions did not alleviate hardship and could serve as examples for younger people of the eventual hardships of remaining in the countryside. The prevalent attitude of looking down on rural workers continued to be widespread.

While Baltic agricultural efficiency continued to be much higher than the Soviet average, it also remained much below the Scandinavian. The average 1970 milk production per cow was 2,110 kg throughout the USSR, 2,950 in Latvia, but 3,950 in Denmark. Disparities led to an interesting cooperation between

---

42 *Literatūra un māksla*, 27 January 1973.

Estonia and the neighboring underdeveloped Russian Pskov Oblast, which delivered Estonia's flax quota while Estonia took care of the Pskov potato deliveries to the state and helped in land drainage. Baltic experimentation with an extensive type of farming offered a possible development model for the less advanced regions of the USSR.[43]

Laboratory Role and Labor Shortage

According to the French Communist journal *Démocracie Nouvelle*, in 1965 Estonia, because of its highly developed material, social, and humanistic culture, was explicitly assigned a role as a socio-economic laboratory for the Soviet Union, which made it in the journal's opinion a representative miniature, a "reduced model" of the future economy of the Soviet Union.[44] This laboratory role, which can be said to have been shared by Latvia, probably receded by the late 1970s. Around 1970, however, its importance in determining the direction of Soviet planning seems to have been appreciable. It was not so much a question of having the largest milk tank in the Soviet Union, or building the world's most powerful crane (although these achievements also were announced by the Soviet Estonian press), or even realizing by 1970 that trucks are more economical than railroads for small freight — Estonia's main role was in the adoption of computerized methods in economic management.

Estonian scientists were assigned "a leading role" in developing republic-wide automatized management systems.[45] They were to write the standards regarding the structure, data banks, and transmission. The Cybernetics Institute in Tallinn, founded in 1960, had been the first Soviet institute devoted entirely to cybernetics. In 1969 an econometric model of Estonia's economy was constructed, computerized scheduling of trucks started, and two years later republic-wide automatized planning and managing of construction were introduced — all Soviet "firsts." Increasingly, all-Union ministries were turning to Estonia and the other Baltic states for first implementation of systems to be later applied Union-wide. Computerization of agricultural management was another focus of Baltic pioneering. The limited supply of advanced computers was compensated for by ingenuity.

Baltic industrial product mix remained basically the same as

[43] M. L. Bronshtein, "Estonskii eksperiment," *Pravda*, 18 June 1972. For preceding description of rural life, see Benedict Mačiuika, "Contemporary Social Problems in the Collectivized Lithuanian Countryside," *Lituanus*, XXII/3 (1976), pp. 9, 14-16.

[44] *Démocracie Nouvelle*, March 1965, p. 91.

[45] *Rahva Hääl*, 15 March 1973.

before. Overall, the structure of Baltic industry differed from the average of the USSR in the preponderance of light and food-processing industries. In 1970, 32.7% of Lithuania's industrial workforce was engaged in machine construction, 24.8% in light industry, and 13.0% in food processing. Per capita, Lithuania in 1970 was fifth in the USSR in the production of electrical energy, third in mineral fertilizer, second in wool fabrics, first in meat, and third in fish. In 1977, Estonia stood first in the USSR in per-capita production of electrical energy, mineral fertilizer, paper, cotton fabrics, fish, and butter. Latvia continued to produce about 30% of all Soviet electric railroad cars, 50% of all motorcycles and mopeds, and 20% of radio sets.

The share of consumer goods varied. In Estonia, consumer goods industries expanded, and surpassed heavy industry in 1973. In Latvia, on the contrary, the share of heavy industry expanded from 50% of the total in 1965 to 57% in 1977. In Lithuania, it expanded from 58% in 1970 to 60% in 1975.[46]

Quality still remained a problem. A 1973 check in Latvia found 106 out of 185 production units producing substandard goods. Merger of small production units met resistance, and bureaucratic squabbles sometimes became grotesque. For more than a year, no door hinges could be bought in Estonia, Deputy Minister of Trade Aleksander-Voldemar Rebane complained in 1970, because the Price Committee refused to assign a price for hinges without screws, and no suitable screws could be found.[47]

Despite such impediments, industrial production in the late 1960s continued a hefty rise (see Table 16). The growth was slightly above the Soviet average in Estonia and Latvia, and much higher in Lithuania. As Baltic industry matured, growth slowed down in the 1970s, falling below the Soviet average (which itself was decreasing) in Latvia and Estonia, and barely maintaining this average in Lithuania.

The increase in produced national income followed a similar pattern (see Table 16). In 1965–70, it was very close to the Soviet average for Latvia and Estonia, and higher for Lithuania. In 1970–75, it was very close to the Soviet average in all three Baltic republics.

Around 1970, Soviet sources were claiming that Baltic per-capita national incomes were among the highest in Europe, with Estonia slightly ahead of Denmark, Latvia, and West Germany. However, Baltic visitors to the West felt their people had markedly lower

[46] Järvesoo 1978, p. 143; *Nar. khoz. LaSSR 1977*, p. 68; *Ekonomika ir kultūra* [LiSSR] *1975*, p. 57.
[47] *Rahva Hääl*, 23 September 1970.

purchasing power and living standards. But Baltic per-capita national incomes were certainly about 50% above the Soviet average, and larger than those of any other Union republic.

Integration of the Baltic economies into the all-Soviet framework was extensive. Nonetheless, a somewhat surprising degree of self-sufficiency was maintained. In 1971, Estonia exported 31% of its "material production" (88% of it into other parts of the USSR), which is low compared to other world countries of comparable small population size.[48] Import pattern was similar, with imports and exports in approximate equilibrium. It seemed that restrictions on trade with non-Soviet countries were partly compensated by Soviet trade, but partly also by producing locally what could have been found more cheaply on the world market. Soviet trade through the Baltic ports expanded, with Klaipėda and Ventspils exporting coal and oil. Riga shipped iron, timber, and industrial products, with regular connections to Le Havre, France. Tallinn's ship lines to West Africa specialized in sugar imports. Throughout the 1970s, rumors circulated that Moscow pondered making Tallinn the main Soviet Baltic maritime center, doubling its population to nearly a million. Local planning in all three republics stressed the need to develop smaller towns around which rural labor reserves still existed.

Labor shortage, indeed, became a major problem for the Soviet Union in the 1970s. In the Baltic states it was becoming a visible brake on the plans of industrial expansion. By 1969, Lithuanian economists began to speak of labor shortage (which already prevailed in Latvia and Estonia), and suggested a slowdown, since Lithuania's industrial production was on the point of reaching the Soviet average. In Latvia, the number of industrial workers did not increase in 1970-72, and in Estonia the increase was much less than 1% per year. On the highest level in Moscow the labor shortage was acknowledged, and emphasis was placed on raising labor efficiency. Baltic republic agencies, keenly aware of the shortage in their own republics, generally tried to achieve the planned production growth through efficiency increases only. However, the basically territorial issue of labor economy was hard to solve through the mechanisms inherent in centralized management. Thus Latvia's Deputy Director of Planning Elerts Āboliņš protested against the five-year plans for industries under Union-wide control which, instead of freeing labor for other needs,

[48] Laine Tulp, "Meie vabariik Nõukogude Liidu majandussüsteemis," *Eesti Kommunist*, XXVIII/2 (February 1972), pp. 11-18, and "The Estonian SSR and Socialist Integration," in *Estonia: Geographical Studies* (Tallinn, 1972), pp. 151-159; Rein Taagepera and J. P. Hayes, "How Trade/GNP Ratio Decreases with Country Size," *Social Science Research*, VI/1 (March 1977), pp. 108-132.

expected "an increase in the number of workers by an unrealistic 13,000."[49]

Baltic labor efficiency was markedly above the Soviet average, but below Western standards. The candy factory "Kalev" in Tallinn exported some of its product and used the resulting foreign currency bonus to buy an assembly line from Italy around 1969. Designed for 11 Italian workers, the line was set up to operate with 18 Estonians. A series of 24-hour analyses of all machine and instrument construction factories in Latvia, 1967 to 1971, found 25 to 32% of basic production equipment idle, mainly for lack of workers. Auxiliary tasks consumed an increasing share of labor — 42% in 1971.[50]

The very shortage of manpower which mandated higher efficiency made its achievement more difficult, since workers fired for continual tardiness, absence, and drinking on the job could easily find jobs elsewhere. The yearly turnover in apparently typical plants and farms was around 15 to 20%, saddling the economy with additional time losses and retraining costs, on top of a heavy bureaucratic overload. In the words of Senior Engineer Heino Tominga: "Building organizations unfortunately have so much empty senseless paperwork that it is hard to take it seriously. We make fun of these documents, but we must nonetheless have them in by the deadline." He further said that labor shortage forced the management "to treat the construction workers with more tender loving care than they merited."[51] In Tartu, the competition between construction enterprises led to wage increases, but such regulation through market mechanisms was stopped in 1972; strict wage ceilings were imposed, and scarce labor was distributed by administrative means.

Labor shortage ranged from police to milkmaids. Seasonality of agricultural work emerged as another labor drain, with 70,000 farm workers underemployed in Latvia alone. Farm auxiliary industry gave only limited help, since its peak periods tended to coincide with those of field work. Commuting to winter work in nearby cities was under discussion both in Latvia and Estonia, but the non-market wage structure imposed by bureaucratic fiat did not seem to offer incentives. A major way to avoid wage ceilings was to work on two full-time jobs simultaneously, and 40,000 people were officially acknowledged to do that in Latvia in 1973.[52]

In 1969, pension rules for retired persons were relaxed in

49 *Padomju Latvijas komunists*, May 1973, p. 12.
50 *Cīņa*, 23 July 1972.
51 *Sirp ja Vasar*, 15 September 1972.
52 *EE/BE*, nos. 25, p. 4 (1971); 32, p. 3 (1972); 37, p. 3 (1973); and 42, p. 2 (1974).

Estonia, where 17% of the population was over 60, compared to the Soviet average of 11%. In some fields, pensioners could now receive full retirement benefits on top of a salary of up to 300 rubles per month, if they continued to work (which 55% did). An official "people's industry enterprise" named *Kodu* ("Home") also was created to distribute materials and collect products from a sort of cottage industry where pensioners, invalids, housewives, and seasonal workers produced various consumer items. In addition to such efforts to collectivize private production, restrictions on non-cooperative work were relaxed. Private tailoring and photo work were already legal under the previous 1949 rules. Legal private enterprise was now extended to barbering, watch and TV repairs, and toy and furniture manufacture. Printing, brewing, and transportation remained expressly forbidden. Private enterprise had to be registered. In Latvia, construction and carpentry income up to 730 rubles was tax-free in 1973.[53]

As spontaneous labor inflow from Russia levelled off in the late 1960s, enterprises took to active recruitment through advertisements in the Baltic Russian-language press, and directly in Russian cities. The accompanying promises of housing especially irked the Balts, who were themselves short of living space. In Estonia, a special Labor Reserves Committee was created in 1968. Its centralized employment bureau ran ads in the Estonian and Russian-language press for unskilled and construction laborers, typists, electricians, salespeople, nurses, and farm tractor drivers. There was visible inconsistency between the Baltic economic goals set by Moscow and official statements that manpower recruitment from outside the republic was "not in agreement with our Party's policy."[54] While 22,000 vacant job positions in Estonia were allegedly caused by decreased labor influx from the outside, an increasing population growth rate around 1970 could be explained only by increased immigration. The labor demands of the economic plan had been excessive from the viewpoint of Baltic national interests ever since 1945, but now they also surpassed the availability of the Russian labor supply. In the course of the late 1970s, the planned overexpansion was reduced, and a better balance with the still decreasing labor supply seemed to come about.

Energy and Ecology

The policy of overdevelopment brought increasing ecological

---

[53] *Ibid.*, nos. 10, p. 4 (1968); 14, p. 4 (1969); 18, p. 1, and 23, p. 5 (1970); 25, p. 2 (1971); and 43, p. 9 (1974).
[54] Agu Köörna, in *Eesti Kommunist*, June 1971, pp. 3–10.

problems, especially in connection with boosted energy needs.[55] Baltic energy supply remained limited. Oil was discovered in Lithuania's Klaipėda district in 1968, but in quantities insufficient for exploitation. Instead, a large oil refinery was built in Mažeikiai to refine crude oil piped in from Bashkiria and the Ob region. Begun in 1972, it was scheduled to be completed in the early 1980s. The refinery had originally been planned for Jurbarkas. However, a protest by 21 members of the intelligentsia over its danger to the Nemunas River delta led to the inland site at Mažeikiai, near the Latvian border. In Latvia, a large hydroelectric power station was constructed at Plaviņas, on the Daugava River, 120 km from Riga. More industrialized than the other two Baltic republics, Latvia received 42% of its 1970 energy from Lithuania and Estonia.

Estonia's oil-shale mining exceeded by far its internal energy needs, but due to energy export Estonia's own needs were barely covered. The degree of electrification of Estonia's industry in 1970 was only 64% of the Soviet average. It produced 10 billion kilowatt-hours, but consumed only 3.5 billion. The oil-shale use pattern changed over time. Gas made from oil shale had been supplied to Leningrad in the 1950s. In 1968 the flow direction was reversed, as Tallinn started to receive cheaper natural gas from the Urals, and oil-shale gasification remained static. Shale-based electricity continued to expand. The "Baltic Thermoelectric Station" was completed in 1965, and the "Estonian Thermoelectric Station" reached its full capacity of 1.6 million kilowatts in 1973. While growth worshippers waxed enthusiastic about Estonia's having the world's two largest shale-based power plants, scientists increasingly questioned the wisdom of digging up 30 million tons of oil shale yearly, and then just burning most of it. Shale oil was seen as a valuable chemical raw material. An ammonia fertilizer plant was opened in 1969, but few other chemical applications followed. For most chemical uses, it was cheaper to import oil than to extract it from shale. At the least, Estonian oil shale activity brought to Tallinn a nine-day UNESCO-sponsored International Oil Shale Symposium in 1968, bolstering the self-confidence of the long-secluded Estonian technologists and engineering students.

By 1975, all major Baltic cities were connected to natural gas

---

[55] For details on energy and ecology, see Henry Ratnieks, "Baltic Oil Prospects and Problems," JBS, VII/4 (Winter 1976), pp. 312–319, "Baltic Oil Shale," *ibid.*, IX/2 (Summer 1978), pp. 155–163, and "Energy Crisis and the Baltics," *ibid.*, XII/3 (Fall 1981), pp. 245–259; Mare Taagepera, "Pollution of the Environment and the Baltics," *ibid.*, pp. 260–274; Augustine Idzelis, "Response of Soviet Lithuania to Environmental Problems in the Coastal Zone," *ibid.*, X/4 (Winter 1979), pp. 299–308.

pipelines. In the face of this cheap and convenient energy supply, oil-shale mining seemed to level off. But by 1980 the energy outlook had changed. With its oil and gas projections reduced, Moscow seemed to want to increase oil-shale mining to levels that could deplete the Estonian reserves in much less than the previously envisaged 200 years. From the empire's viewpoint, it was a quick energy fix. From Estonia's viewpoint, it was colonial over-exploitation of the country's only energy and industrial raw material reserves.

Considerable reliance on nuclear energy was apparently foreseen in the future. In the late 1970s, construction began by Lake Drūkšiai in northeastern Lithuania on the first fourth of a planned massive generation complex. A new city named after the late First Party Secretary Sniečkus was also begun in the vicinity, to house construction workers and, eventually, operations personnel.

Baltic concern about ecology first emerged in the mid-1950s with a Latvian debate about clean rivers.[56] In Estonia, a debate took place in *Eesti Loodus* (March 1965) about pesticides. In 1968 Rachel Carson's *Silent Spring* was translated. Both Latvia (around 1966) and Estonia claimed to be the only republic in the USSR (and possibly the world) to ban completely the use of DDT, hexachlorane, and other long-lasting and highly toxic organic chlorine and phosphorus preparations. River pollution was the next concern. In 1969, the effluents of a chemical factory in Panevėžys killed all the fish in the Nevėžis River; the Venta, the Šešupė, the Minija, and other Lithuanian rivers were also reported polluted. The fresh-water fish catch in Estonia had been reduced to one-eighth of what it had been ten years earlier, and several popular beaches were becoming unhealthy.

> This is the last song about this river.
> No new ones will be made
> and the old ones will soon be forgotten.
>
> Nothing but a dead, dirty flow
> circling around mounds of ashes.
> This river no more has a soul.
>
> The factory, this bright-eyed titan,
> has buried the sun and the moon
> with hot flakes of soot,
> while it pours its excrements
> into the river.[57]

[56] Juris Dreifelds, "Implementation of Pollution Control Policy in Latvia: A Case Study of the Sloka Pulp and Paper Mill," *Co-Existence* (Glasgow), XVII (October 1980), pp. 178–192.
[57] Kersti Merilaas, *Kuukressid* (Tallinn, 1969), pp. 141–142.

These excerpts of Estonian verses by Kersti Merilaas were a far cry from the Soviet First of May slogans which in 1970 still made no mention of the need to abate pollution; just "Improve product quality in every way, and reduce production costs!" (Slogan 24). Sewage-disposal problems occurred even in minor cities such as Viljandi, and water-supply problems arose. By 1980, Tallinn was receiving water from all over Estonia, from Lake Peipsi in the east to the Pärnu River in the southwest. In 1972, an ESSR Water Code was promulgated to regulate water usage and prohibit construction of new plants without pollution-control devices. The paper industry was a main polluter, but talks with the visiting USSR Minister for the industry seemed to remain talks. The republic's code was not binding on the Union-wide ministry. Soviet industry in Estonia recirculated only 22% of its water, compared to 81% in Lithuania, and to a Soviet average of 53%.

Protection of the environment gradually became accepted by Moscow as necessary in principle. However, continued emphasis on Union-wide management by production branch made it very difficult to preserve the inevitably territorial ecological balance. Pollution in Lithuania's fragile coastal zone increased despite republic-level efforts. The Klaipėda Cellulose and Paper Combine continued to discharge 35,000 tons of waste per year into shallow waters. Construction of waste treatment facilities began only in 1974, and was not yet finished in 1978. Despite moderate fines, 63 ships released waste oil into the Klaipėda harbor in 1974. Protests at the USSR Supreme Soviet (e.g., by Vilnius CP Secretary Vytautas Sakalauskas, in 1977) brought only partial response from Union-wide ministries, and LiSSR Deputy Prime Minister Aleksandras Drobnys started to advocate "the adoption of terri- torial principles in the planning of surface-water protection measures."[58] However, the Lithuanian Party and government appeared to be powerless vis-à-vis the all-Union ministries. A number of international conferences and projects on pollution took place in the Baltic states, mostly with Soviet and Finnish, but also with some American participation (December 1974, in Jūrmala).[59]

CULTURE AND THE EXPANSION OF WESTERN CONTACTS

One of the most striking socio-cultural developments in the Baltic

---

[58] *Liaudies ūkis*, no. 5, 1979; see Idzelis 1979, pp. 304–308.
[59] *Veseliba*, no. 2, 1975.

republics after 1968 was the expansion of contacts with the West. The submerged Western traditions had resurfaced during the rebirth of national cultures under the Thaw, and direct contacts with the contemporary West had begun to develop during that period. Their expansion after 1968 was so gradual that only a comparison with the reports and comments of the mid-1960s reveals the extent of cumulative change by 1980.[60]

The Expansion of Travel

By the 1970s, the trickle of travel which had begun in the late 1950s had become an appreciable flow, though hardly a torrent. In 1967, 2,500 individuals from Estonia toured outside of the USSR, most of them probably in Eastern Europe. In 1970, about 1,700 Estonians visited Finland alone. While still very limited in comparison with West European countries, these figures were probably considerably higher by 1980.

Increasing numbers visited relatives abroad, sometimes for several months. More scholars spent up to a year abroad, sometimes accompanied by their spouses, though with children usually left behind. Soviet Baltic attendance at international scholarly conferences increased markedly. In 1979, several Soviet Baltic scholars attended the biennial Conference on Baltic Studies in Scandinavia, for the first time ever. Artistic performances abroad by Soviet Baltic individuals and ensembles continued to increase in frequency.

Nevertheless, impediments to foreign travel continued. Many people repeatedly applied for permission to travel abroad, without success, even though relatives abroad were willing to cover all expenses. Scholars and scientists with papers accepted for presentation at international conferences were at times denied exit visas at the last minute, with no explanation. Permission and denial of foreign travel had become one of the means for social control by the authorities.

Permanent emigration was also somewhat expanded. During the 1970s, the bulk of emigrants from the Baltic area were Jews or Volga Germans who had settled in the Baltic republics during the Thaw.

The flow of Western visitors continued, at probably ten times the rate of Balts going to the West. During the early 1970s, several Scandinavian lines supplemented the Helsinki-Tallinn boat line which had been started in 1965, attracting vodka week-enders from

---

[60] For details of travel and interactions, see *EE/BE*; V. Stanley Vardys, "The Role of the Baltic Republics in Soviet Society," in Roman Szporluk (ed.), *The Influence of East Europe and the Soviet West of the USSR* (New York, 1977), pp. 147-179.

Finland. Several hundred Finnish construction workers came to Tallinn between 1969 and 1972 to build the modern high-rise Viru Hotel, and a number of them married Estonians. However, such projects did not continue after that time.

Émigrés continued to make up a large percentage of Western visitors. In 1968 at least 600 Estonian émigrés revisited their homeland, and over 900 Latvians did so in 1972. By 1980, the number for all three countries together was very likely several thousand. Some of the relatives stayed for several months. A few students from abroad began to attend courses at Vilnius University and in Tallinn. A special annual Lithuanian summer program at Vilnius University, designed for the children of émigrés, was started in the early 1970s, and similar programs were later started in Latvia and Estonia.

Cultural Interactions

Increasing numbers of Baltic performing artists were allowed to make themselves known abroad. The most eminent was probably the Estonian conductor Neeme Järvi, who performed extensively in the West. He was favorably received at the Metropolitan Opera in New York in 1978. The following year, he and his Jewish wife emigrated permanently, and instantly became unmentionable in the Soviet Estonian press. The Lithuanian tenor Virgilijus Noreika gave some performances abroad.

In many cases, attempts by Baltic performers to participate in Western musical life met obstruction from the authorities. The Estonian composer Arvo Pärt, whose music had become known outside the USSR since the mid-1960s, had several premières of his works in Finland and Great Britain. However, his own travel abroad was severely restricted, motivating him to ask for a permanent emigration permit. It was granted in 1979; Soviet bureaucracy seemed to prefer a total loss of talent to sharing it with the West. The Lithuanian bass Vaclovas Daunoras, who won a Gold Medal at the Toulouse competition in 1971, apparently also experienced difficulties in performing outside the USSR until 1979.

In spite of such pettiness, Soviet Baltic artists and their art continued to reach the West far more widely than earlier, and began to create a modernist Baltic image which was distinct from the general Soviet one. Writers also travelled more widely than ever before, and ties with émigré communities were expanded.

Western impact on the Baltic cultures, occurring through reciprocal visits, radio, and Finnish (and somewhat less so, Polish) TV, translation of Western books, production of Western plays and musicals, and screening of Western films, expanded steadily throughout the 1970s. The effect was striking, not only in comparison with the previous decade, but also in comparison with the rest of the USSR.

Serious Western drama seems to have been more in evidence on Baltic stages than in those of other Soviet republics. Eugene Ionesco's *Rhinoceros*, which had already been published in Estonia in 1967, and Samuel Beckett's *Krapp's Last Tape* were notably staged in Tallinn. Riga saw a production of Tennessee Williams' *Night of the Iguana* in 1973. Arthur Miller's *Death of a Salesman* opened in Panevėžys during the late 1960s, and his *The Price* appeared in Vilnius somewhat later. Friedrich Duerrenmatt's *The Visit* and *The Physicists* and Tennessee Williams' *Orpheus Descending*, *The Glass Menagerie*, and *A Streetcar Named Desire* all received Lithuanian performances during the 1970s.

The 1968 Vilnius production of Sławomir Mrożek's *Tango* was removed from the repertoire shortly after the invasion of Czechoslovakia. Its author, resident in France, had taken public exception to Poland's participation in the affair, and as a result became unmentionable in his home country. The story was widespread in Vilnius that the Cultural Attaché of the Polish Embassy in Moscow had lodged a protest over this sole remaining production of a Mrożek play in the bloc. The Lithuanian production of *The Price* also disappeared, because of Miller's public expressions of opinion unwelcome to the Soviet authorities.

Popular Western theatrical entertainment also made inroads. The Estonian production of *West Side Story* in 1965 seems to have been the first in the USSR of an American musical. By 1968, the "Estonia" Theater had also staged *Kiss Me Kate* and *My Fair Lady*. In 1974, a sexually explicit Estonian musical based on *Love Story* was performed. In 1969, a Latvian musical based on Mark Twain's *The Prince and the Pauper* was produced in Liepāja, and *Oklahoma*! appeared on the same stage four years later. *My Fair Lady* also was given a Lithuanian production in Kaunas, and *Man of La Mancha* was staged in Vilnius. While such Baltic productions can hardly be considered unique, their number appears greater than anywhere else in the USSR, especially when the size of the potential audience is taken into account.

Interaction with émigrés sometimes proved fruitful in explaining Western phenomena to Soviet Balts who, in turn, were able to "translate" them into concepts understandable to Soviet Russians. Émigrés continued to supply contacts with Western scholars and artists, and channelled Western consumer goods and fashions to the Baltic countries. In the absence of Stalinist methods of persuasion, Russian cultural attraction clearly was losing out to Western appeal.

Interaction with Eastern Europe and the Soviet Union continued, of course, but it became more balanced in several ways. In addition to Western works, the Balts translated Mrożek from Polish and Havel from Czech. They also discovered the Soviet East beyond Russia, from medieval Central Asian classics to contemporary Georgian and Armenian ways to cope with Russian hegemony. The Balts may have had some Westernizing influence on Russia itself during the 1960s through their earlier establishment of Western ties.

Baltic impact on the smaller Soviet nationalities within the Russian republic has been little noticed, but it may prove to have been of more than local importance, especially in the case of Estonia. Developed Estonian culture within the Soviet Union was an obvious role-model for other Soviet nations of around one million people, and Estonians were aware of it. In 1968 the "Vanemuine" theater in Tartu organized a seminar for theater producers of the autonomous republics and oblasts within the RSFSR. Estonia became the natural leader in Finno-Ugric language studies in the USSR, and attracted graduate students from all five Finnic autonomous republics. In 1970, a week-long Mari Cultural Festival was held in Estonia, to introduce Estonians to this emerging fellow-Finnic culture in the Volga Bend, and vice versa.

The Development of National Cultures

The powerful cultural rebound of the early 1960s was followed in 1968–80 by a period of more mature and less spectacular development. Conditions continued to be the most difficult in Latvia, where the battle for cultural autonomy was still undecided.[61] In June 1968, Czechoslovakia's National Assembly Chairman Josef Smrkovsky visited Latvia and spoke on the "need to democratize socialism." In August, students in Riga grilled and shouted down the regime spokesmen who tried to justify the Soviet invasion of Czechoslovakia. In December, LaCP secretary Jurijs Rubenis launched a counterattack. Seven leading literary figures were accused of writing "from unacceptable positions": Priede, Bels, Belševica, Čaklais, Vācietis, Auziņš, and Purs. In Summer 1969, the editors of the cultural weekly *Literatūra un māksla* were replaced, but the new team also was soon criticized for publishing ideologically erroneous works. (Estonia's cultural weekly *Sirp ja Vasar* also lost its editors in early 1969, after they were accused of "ugly attacks" against Stalinist attackers of modernism.)

---

[61] For details of cultural developments, see Ekmanis 1978; Kurman 1978, pp. 247–280; Valgemäe, pp. 281–317.

However, later criticism (e.g., at the January 1976 LaCP Congress) tended to become more impersonal.

Attacks went beyond words. A play by Laimonis Purs, *To Behold the Sea*, became a box-office hit, and was lauded in the press, until it was suddenly ordered removed from the repertory, in September 1968, because of "politically equivocal dialogues." The censors banned Gunārs Priede's *Mushrooms Are Fragrant* even before it could open. Vizma Belševica became the most denounced writer of the period, because of her double-level symbolism "liable to create utter ideological chaos among politically inexperienced readers" (*Cīņa*, 7 June 1969). Starting with her fourth poetry collection (*Annual Rings*, 1969), the witch-hunt continued for years. Many were bound to be displeased with verses like

> O servile nation! In sweet joy you tremble
> Because the master whips your brothers
> Instead of you. Waiting, you bare your teeth
> To fall upon a brother's bloodied nape,
> For in the master's hand a medal glitters
> To be bestowed on you . . .[62]

The setting of the poem was medieval, with one marked anachronism. For three years (1971–74), not a single poem by Belševica was published, but later she was gradually allowed to return. Another member of the Writers' Union, French translator Maija Silmale, was arrested in 1971 and made to testify in a political-dissidence case. Never tried herself, she was nonetheless confined to the prison psychiatric ward in Riga until shortly before her death.

Despite such harassment, Latvian culture made headway. In literature, new young talent appeared. Established poets sometimes shifted to prose (Imants Ziedonis, *My Kurzeme*, 1970–74, and *Epiphanies*, 1971 and 1974; Belševica, *Misfortune at Home*, 1979). Poems were published that would have sounded bold even by the reputedly more relaxed standards in Lithuania and Estonia:

> Like pestilence, the regiments of Sheremetev
> Brought you double bondage
> Because His Excellency Peter the First
> Felt like hewing a wider window to Europe.

This 1968 observation was generalized in 1970 by another poet:

> No one shall transform our land

---

[62] Vizma Belševica, "The Notations of Henricus de Lettis in the Margin of the Livonian Chronicle"; translation by Baiba Kaugara, *Lituanus*, XVI/1 (Spring 1970), pp. 15–21, followed by comments by Gunārs Saliņš, pp. 22–32.

> neither with Bibles
> nor various theories, courts, idols, hells.
> Alas, many have come to remake us,
> to give us their faith, their gods,
> to take our harbors — ice-free!
> to occupy our shores — amber shores![63]

Latvian prose was finally allowed to catch up with that of its neighbors, in terms of stylistic experimentation. Poignancies of everyday life, alienation (*The Pedestrian*, 1974, by Jānis Mauliņš), war and postwar events (*Joker and a Puppet*, 1971, by Visvaldis Lāms), and sexual activity (*Nakedness*, 1970, by Zigmunds Skujiņš) became acceptable topics. Drama remained a weak point, partly because of the aforementioned harassment.[64]

In Estonia, prose and drama caught up with the earlier expansion of poetry. Here, too, a number of established poets shifted into a new genre. Historical novels by Jaan Kross set out to "reconquer the national past" by demonstrating the Estonian ties of reputedly Baltic German cultural figures such as the sixteenth-century chronicler Balthasar Russow or the fifteenth-century painter Michel Sittow. Mats Traat described more recent tribulations in novels like *Dance Around the Steam Engine* (1971), where every potential central figure dies, mostly in wars, as soon as the author tries to focus on him. Aimée Beekman presented vividly realistic pictures of contemporary life, Arvo Valton supplemented increasingly abstract short stories with a major novel on Mongol-Chinese intellectual interactions, Vaino Vahing emerged with psychological short stories, and Aino Pervik shocked many with her merciless description of sterile consumerism, sleeping-around, and pseudo-intellectuality.

In poetry, the major new debut was that of actor-TV performer Juhan Viiding (whose early collections were signed Jüri Üdi), whose playful tone and ironic bite at times hides deep despair. Writing in a somewhat similar tragi-comic vein, Hando Runnel was repeatedly attacked in the official press for "improprieties" and "statements tending to nationalism," such as the following description of the postwar guerrillas:

> Many men were found, deported,
> Many men to arms resorted.

[63] Imants Auziņš, *Skumjais Optimisms* (Riga, 1968), p. 35; Māris Čaklais, *Karogs* (May 1970), p. 59; both as translated in Ekmanis 1978, pp. 344 and 347. Only one European power has been chronically short of ice-free ports.
[64] *The Blue One*, a play representative of Gunārs Priede's production in the 1970s, is available in English translation by Andre Šedriks, in Alfreds Strautmanis, ed., *Confrontations with Tyranny* (Prospect Heights, Ill., 1979), pp. 225–262.

Bunkers in the woods were built.
Many mouths were filled with silt.[65]

Absurdist theater reached a major peak with Mati Unt's *Phaethon* (1968) and Paul-Eerik Rummo's *Cinderella Game* (1969; performed at La Mama in New York in 1971), and continued with a series of plays by Enn Vetemaa.[66] Political pressures in Estonia were similar to those in Latvia, but in general they remained milder.

Lithuania had reached post-Thaw stability already by 1968, in virtually all literary fields, and further change was less eventful. The highly complex and intellectually sophisticated poetry of Tomas Venclova (*A Sign of Speech*, 1972) provided a clear example of the incompatibility of art and politics. The allusion to Lithuania in "Tell Fortinbras" is unmistakable:

> So may they rest. White islands,
> Rock salt replenish their blood,
> Snowstorms rise from the shores of Connaught,
> The forests wrapped in steam, the shaggy orchards,
> And Denmark, Denmark is no more.[67]

Kazys Saja emerged as Lithuania's most prominent exponent of the didactic function of drama, focusing on such diverse questions as public morality, alcoholism, and the conservation of natural resources. His *A Hunt for Mammoths* (1968) employs grotesque hyperbole and psychological paradox to lampoon a variety of bureaucratic and social shortcomings. *The Holy Lake* (1970) treats the negative effects of the overdrainage of swamps. Perhaps his most successful effort, one which has seen considerable translation into other Soviet and East European languages along with several productions within the bloc, is *Nine-Calamity Village* (1976), an American-style musical based on folk themes.[68] *The House of Terror* (1968) by Juozas Glinskis is a philosophic investigation on the life of the early nineteenth-century folk bard Antanas Strazdas. Elements of the grotesque are effectively employed, along with stylistic and linguistic contrast and juxtaposition, to approach

[65] Hando Runnel, *Lauluraamat ehk mõõganeelaja ehk kurbade kaitseks* (Tallinn, 1972); for full translation of the poem quoted, see Taagepera, "A Portrait," p. 85. For documentation on official attacks, see *EE/BE*, no. 37, p. 4 (1973).

[66] *The Cinderella Game* has been translated into English by Andres Männik and Mardi Valgemäe, in Strautmanis 1979, pp. 273-322.

[67] Tomas Venclova, *Kalbos ženklas* (Vilnius, 1972), p. 29; English translation by Algirdas Landsbergis in *Lituanus*, XXIII/4 (Winter 1977), p. 27.

[68] Translated under the title of *Village of Nine Woes* by Eglė Juodvalkis, in Alfreds Straumanis (ed.), *The Golden Steed* (Prospect Heights, Ill., 1979), pp. 277-325.

social, ethical, and in a veiled form, political issues. The production enjoyed unprecedented success. *Barbora Radvilaitė* [Barbara Radziwiłłowna] by Juozas Grušas (1972), an extremely poetic treatment of the tragic fate of the beautiful sixteenth-century queen, has perhaps become the longest-playing production on the modern Lithuanian stage. The original production was still in the active repertoire in 1980.

A significant chill, however, crept into the Lithuanian cultural scene in 1972, a follow-up on the local level of slightly earlier all-Union developments. In Vilnius, the new atmosphere was heralded by a review in *Tiesa*, "The Poetization of Chaos," of the latest poetry by Sigitas Geda, *26 Chants of Autumn and Summer* (1972). While the attack on Geda for his "subjective, super-individualistic manner of depiction" remained somewhat restrained, its weighty message of official dissatisfaction resounded clearly throughout cultural circles. The party organ did not usually concern itself with reviews of poetry. The same year, the editors of the official cultural weekly *Literatūra ir menas* and of the trendy youth magazine *Nemunas* were removed; the tenor of both magazines was noticeably changed. The year can also be said to have marked an end, for a time at least, to the theater's ability to discuss contemporary issues through allusions in historical drama. The innovative director of the Kaunas State Theater, Jonas Jurašas, was removed from his post and became a stone-cutter, after his public protest against political tampering with his productions (see next section, on dissent).

Besides the modern West, Baltic cultures also received inspiration from their folkloric past, and often the two influences were blended. Remarkable ethnographic films of Finno-Ugric peoples were made by Lennart Meri. The oral folk-song tradition, with motifs and styles going back centuries or even a millenium, still survived through the mouths of aging bards, in the middle of the century. However, people in general were more familiar with written texts and "Europeanized" tunes than with the original musical style. The spread of tape recorders and the worldwide interest in folk-song coincided with the advent of a self-assured Baltic generation no longer ashamed of the simplicity of the folk-tunes. The archaic singing style became quite popular with some groups in Estonia, while some others produced jazzed-up versions. A modernistic folk-song-based oratory by Veljo Tormis, *The Cursing of Iron* (1975), was officially criticized as pacifist. Folklore influenced many Baltic writers, from Latvian poets like Imants Auziņš and Jānis Peters to Lithuanian playwrights like Saja.

DISSENT

Dissent — a disagreement with or opposition to the system — could be said to be, almost by definition, endemic within the Baltic republics.[69] The realization that persisting dreams of independence, or at least of genuine autonomy, required fundamental change in political conditions throughout the USSR, fostered ongoing attempts to secure or maintain whatever piecemeal benefits to national self-identification were possible under extant circumstances. A whole spectrum of individuals, encompassing a major portion of the Baltic populations, could be characterized as falling within this group. Its general goal was shared, among others, by passive nationalists seeking to preserve and maximize the national forms of the Soviet system; members of the intelligentsia striving to enrich the national cultures, thus making them more attractive and immune to denationalization; and even some national Communists. They all seemed to strive for a change for the better within the system. In a broad sense, Soviet reality made a dissident out of any non-Russian Soviet citizen fully aware of his identity, because the compatibility of the survival of his ethnic group with the aims of the regime was questionable.[70]

However, dissent was normally used to describe a more narrow type of overt activity. It included dramatic action like mass demonstrations or rioting, though such were infrequent and sporadic. Usually, the term connoted more restrained activity by those who felt a need to protest publicly or to counteract any of the basically negative influences permeating Soviet society. Dissidents generally sought to protest within Soviet law. By so doing, they evoked repression indicative of the pervasive hypocrisy of the system, one of its basic negative features.

At times, dissent which could be labelled "apolitical" achieved its purpose. The 1966 appeal by 21 members of the Lithuanian intelligentsia over the planned construction of a refinery at

---

[69] For current English-language reports on dissent and its repression, see various Amnesty International publications on the Soviet Union; *UBA Information Service* (United Baltic Appeal, New York), news release series; ELTA Information Service monthly newsletter (Supreme Committee for the Liberation of Lithuania, New York, from 1956 on); *Latvian Information Bulletin* (Latvian Legation, Washington, D. C.); *EE/BE*; *Lituanus*. Overviews and translations of underground publications: Vardys 1978; *Documents from Estonia on the Violations of Human Rights* (Stockholm, 1977); full texts (in German) of *The Chronicle of the Lithuanian Catholic Church*, from no. 7 on, in *Acta Baltica* (from 1975 on); Peter Reddaway (ed.), *Uncensored Russia: The Human Rights Movement in the Soviet Union* (London, 1972); Andres Küng, *A Dream of Freedom* (Cardiff, Wales, 1980).

[70] Alexander Shtromas, *Political Change and Social Development: The Case of the Soviet Union* (Frankfurt, 1981), p. 80.

Jurbarkas led to its relocation at Mažeikiai. Within a Soviet context, however, such issues which could appear to be apolitically inspired were limited.

At the other end of the spectrum, some survivors of the postwar guerrillas still maintained an armed existence in the Baltic woods. August Sabe, 70, drowned rather than surrender on 5 October 1978.[71] He had been a forest brother in southern Estonia since 1944. Other such cases have been reported, but opposition to Soviet rule since 1954 has tended to use non-armed means.

Spontaneous Manifestations of Dissent

Numerous minor indications of the latent opposition smoldering beneath the surface constantly reappeared on the Baltic scene in the late 1960s and 1970s. The simplest forms were usually the most numerous, consisting of demonstrative refusals in everyday situations to speak Russian when addressed in that language. Another form consisted of small symbolic gestures such as placing flowers at places whose significance the regime was seeking to minimize. An Estonian hero of the 1919 War of Independence, Julius Kuperjanov, had no living relatives, yet flowers appeared by his grave on a regular basis. The pre-war Latvian independence monument in downtown Riga which had not been destroyed by the authorities was a similar magnet. Unobtrusive introduction into souvenir items of the colors of the pre-war national flags was also being noted. Surreptitious hoistings of these flags at prominent public places were more dramatic occasional occurrences. It was reported that the slogan "Sakharov — our conscience" was painted on trains as well as in the Riga Railroad Station during the Spring of 1976.

A somewhat more demonstratively active form consisted of cheering at spectator sports events for non-Soviet competitors, particularly when such contestants had somehow acquired resistance symbolism. Czech teams were particular Baltic favorites during the period after 1968. Sports events also triggered more massive demonstrations. At times, these did not even have to be live performances. On 20 April 1972, for instance, several hundred students from the Tallinn Polytechnic Institute celebrated a televised Czech hockey victory over the Soviets by shouting "We won" on the streets. In Vilnius, a soccer match against a Russian team from Smolensk, on 10 October 1977, provided the occasion for a demonstration against the new Soviet Constitution. A crowd of sports fans took to the streets shouting "Down with the Constitution of the occupying power!" Four months after the event,

---

[71] *Sõnumid* (Stockholm), no. 71 (March 1979), pp. 3–5.

the Soviet press confirmed the events by castigating the émigré press for having exaggerated them, and "interviewed" some of the "rowdy" participants to demonstrate that simple hooliganism had triggered the outburst.[72]

Pop concerts sometimes led to similar events. In the Estonian university town of Tartu on 3 December 1976, local officials decided to prohibit a program, supposedly because of its political nuances. The crowd of students, estimated by some at around a thousand, streamed through the town shouting anti-Soviet slogans from the evening until around 2:30 the next morning. A similar incident took place in the aftermath of a concert held in the Latvian port city of Liepāja on 11 August 1977. Around 11 p.m., when an Estonian rock group was not allowed to perform at an open-ir theater, the audience of young people proceeded to vent their anger at the authorities by wrecking the place. Afterwards, about a thousand of them roamed through the streets shouting "Freedom!"[73]

Full-scale riots occurred in Lithuania on at least three postwar occasions. The first instance, in 1956, coincided with the dramatic events in Hungary and Poland. In July 1960, public disturbances broke out in Kaunas after a boxing match between Lithuanian and Uzbek teams. Moscow chief ideologue Mikhail Suslov was reputedly in Kaunas that day, the eve of the anniversary of Lithuania's incorporation into the USSR. Few details are available.

The most serious massive manifestation occurred in Lithuania during the late Spring of 1972. On 14 May, a 19-year-old student named Romas Kalanta poured gasoline over himself at noon in a Kaunas park, struck a match, and subsequently died in a hospital. Rioting, involving several thousand youths, began on the day of his funeral. Youths roamed the streets shouting "Freedom for Lithuania!" and fought the authorities, who had to be reinforced by paratroopers and KGB units. Some 500 arrests were made. Within a few days, three other self-immolations took place in other places in Lithuania. Some claims have been made that the Kalanta suicide had been planned as a joint Baltic protest, but that the Latvian and Estonian participants were prevented from carrying out their actions.[74]

---

[72] Rein Taagepera, "Estonia: Uppity Satellite," *The Nation*, 7 May 1973; *Literatūra ir menas*, 11 February 1978, p. 12.

[73] "Student Demonstrations in Tartu, Estonia," *Radio Liberty Research Paper*, no. 107 (May 1977); "Reports of Youth Demonstration after Pop Concert in Latvia," *ibid.*, no. 243 (October 1977).

[74] The events in Lithuania received widespread press coverage. Among others, see *New York Times*, 22, 26, and 28 May and 8 June 1972; *The Economist*, 27 May 1972; and *Le Monde*, 23 May 1972. The reference to an abortive joint Baltic demonstration appears in the Lithuanian *samizdat* publication *Aušra*, no. 1 (1975).

The meat shortage in Latvia led to an economically motivated protest apparently expressed through a workers' strike on an officially imposed "fish day" in May 1976. Four Riga dock workers reportedly were sentenced to two to three years in labor camps.[75]

October 1980 saw unprecedentedly large student demonstrations in Estonia, and up to 200 workers went on strike, possibly for the first time since the "Red Krull" workers did so in December 1940. Youth protest started on 22 September when a pop concert following a soccer game was abruptly interrupted by officials. Several thousand young people marched toward Tallinn's city center, and 200 were briefly arrested and expelled from school. Repression triggered new and more organized marches on 1 and 3 October, with 2,000 high school students converging on the government buildings from four separate assembly points. Some were severely beaten by the police, and several hundred were briefly arrested. Demonstrations spread to the Tallinn Polytechnic Institute, to the Pärnu Merchant Navy School, and to Tartu University, and recurred in Tallinn on 10 October. Demands ranged from better cafeteria food to "Russians, get out!" A particular target was Elsa Gretškina, Soviet Estonia's newly appointed semi-Russian Minister of Education. *Rahva Hääl*, 14 October 1980, announced court proceedings against the "initiators and propagators" of "recent gross breaches of public order by groups of youths." Meanwhile, workers went on strike on 1 October at the Tartu Experimental Repair Factory, asking for reduced work norms and the payment of long-withheld premiums. They may have been encouraged by the success of Polish workers. The next day a special commission rushed in from Moscow and acceded to strikers' demands.[76]

Persistent manifestations of dissent are reflected in non-state-approved writings called, in Russian, *samizdat*. The varied documents, magazines, memoirs, appeals, open letters, and accounts, although generally produced by the intelligentsia, collectively represented the tip of an iceberg of gradually mounting internal pressure for change affecting all levels of society. On the all-Union scene, the early 1966 trial of the writers Siniavskii and Daniel is usually considered the beginning of the *samizdat* age. Most of

---

[75] *The Times* (London) and *New York Times*, both 1 November 1976.

[76] Alex Milits, in *Välis-Eesti* (Sweden), 10 November 1980, p. 2; *New York Times*, 5 and 18 October 1980; *Daily Telegraph*, 6 October 1980; *The Economist*, 11 October 1980, p. 57; *Los Angeles Times*, 23 October 1980, p. 1–2; *Time*, 3 November 1980, p. 57. Exaggerated figures have been reported. Dissidents who later emigrated put the number of strikers at "200 workers at most" (personal communication).

those who as a result of the Khrushchev years had anticipated continued within-the-system amelioration and removal of negative Stalinist social shackles, now realized the futility of their expectations. As official channels for real criticism remained practically closed for the foreseeable future, the most eager advocates for change began to act unofficially.

Lithuania

As has been noted, the Khrushchev Thaw proved somewhat longer-lasting in Lithuania than it had in Moscow. CP First Secretary Sniečkus had managed to avert unseemly problems such as those posed by national Communism in Latvia. Although carefully controlled, there was a genuinely greater latitude on the cultural scene which was enriched by the not entirely faded pre-war heritage. A growing cultural diversity, including achievements of unquestioned value, nourished a hope for the preservation of a distinct Lithuanian culture. The feeling of futility arrived more slowly than it had in Moscow. From 1968, however, Lithuanian *samizdat*, first appearing in a trickle, began to reflect mounting dissident activity. The trickle later reached massive proportions. Around 1980, Lithuania produced perhaps more *samizdat* per capita than any other area of the USSR.

Unlike Moscow, where dissent was a phenomenon among the secular intelligentsia, the first manifestations of *samizdat* activity in Lithuania showed a clear religious orientation encompassing a broader segment of society. Roman Catholicism provided a core for the national opposition, and the issue of religious discrimination attracted widespread attention. In Lithuania, as in neighboring Poland, religious strength had come to be equated with national identity. Soviet reality, however, curiously metamorphosed the generally conservative political traditions of Roman Catholicism into the championing of political ideals traditionally associated with a secular orientation. Although religiously oriented *samizdat* may not reflect the entire spectrum of opposition, they were by far the most extensive in terms of publications.

The first phase of overt Lithuanian religious dissent, dating from 1968, consisted of petitions to the authorities as well as to the Church hierarchy. Some two dozen documents of this nature have become known. A counterattack by the regime through prosecuting several priests for teaching religion to children only served to inflame the issue. In December 1971, a mass petition was organized. The document asked the Soviet government

to grant us freedom of conscience that is guaranteed by the
Constitution, but which has so far not been secured in practice.

We do not want beautiful words in the press or over the radio; we ask for serious governmental efforts to make us, Catholics, feel that we have equal rights as Soviet citizens.[77]

In spite of KGB obstructions to gathering signatures, 17,054 were appended to sheets of paper each carrying a full text of the petition. The collection, addressed to Brezhnev, was sent to him through UN Secretary Kurt Waldheim. Two other mass petitions followed in 1973. One, with 14,604 signatures, went to the Ministry of Education of the Lithuanian SSR; the other, with 16,800 names, went to the republic's Commissioner for Religious Affairs. The government's reply consisted of an intensification of propaganda alleging freedom of religious practice, plus coercion of the Church hierarchy to condemn such "divisive" practices by religious activists. Mass appeals of this nature seemed to cease after 1973. In 1979, however, a new one appeared regarding the church in Klaipėda, containing some 150,000 signatures (4% of the republic's population).

The chief *samizdat* publication of religiously oriented dissent in Lithuania is *The Chronicle of the Lithuanian Catholic Church*. Its first issue was dated 19 March 1972, and the journal has appeared continuously since that time. Evidently modelled on the Moscow *Chronicle of Current Events*, this publication initially sought to register events connected with the repression of religious practice in Lithuania. Each issue of some 40–70 single-spaced typewritten folded-sheet pages provides a glimpse, at times in rather minute detail, into various facets of everyday life in the republic. While the first six numbers were largely documentary, later issues included opinion pieces as well. The initial exclusive focus on specific violations of religious rights expanded into treatment of other matters of general national interest, especially the influence of ideological demands on Lithuanian culture. This expanded approach introduced a clear change in tone. The earlier issues sought a level factual approach. An inventory of social ills introduced by the system — the physical destruction of the population, denationalization, and moral decay (including alcoholism, juvenile delinquency, venereal disease, and a rise in the divorce rate) — inexorably led to the expression of judgments of the system as a whole, which had initially been avoided. In 1976, the *Chronicle*, in view of the diversification of Lithuanian *samizdat*, reverted to its initial exclusive focus on religious questions. By 1980, nearly 40 issues had reached the West.

In late 1973, a major KGB offensive labelled Case 395 seems to

[77] Full text in Vardys 1978, pp. 261–262.

have been launched against the *Chronicle* as well as other religious activism in Lithuania. Within a year, several prominent activists were arrested. Five were tried in December 1974 on charges of having produced and distributed "libelous fabrications directed against the Soviet system." The youngest of the group, 27-year-old Virgilijus Jaugelis, was also its most outspoken member:

> Here we stand before the Supreme Court. It is here that the most law-abiding and just people should be in charge. But what do we see? Corruption, lies, and brute force . . .[78]

The trial, as reported in a subsequent issue of the unvanquished *Chronicle*, bore out his evaluation. The judges disregarded evidence in favor of the defendants, two of whom publicly repented, acted as prosecution witnesses, and were rewarded with suspended sentences. Jaugelis received two years.

Another *Chronicle*-related trial, that of Nijole Sadūnaitė, followed in June 1975. Although the proceedings were held in closed chambers, the *Chronicle* managed to present her defense speech. In it, she compared the publication to a mirror

> . . . which reflects all the criminal acts of atheists against those who believe. No evil act likes to look at its own horrible image, it hates its own reflection. That is why you hate everyone who tears off the veil of falsehood and hypocrisy behind which you are hiding. But the mirror does not lose its worth for all that.[79]

She was sentenced to three years in a labor camp, to be followed by three years in exile inside the USSR but outside Lithuania.

Case 395 also involved two prominent Moscow dissidents. In December 1974, Andrei Tverdokhlebov was interrogated, and Sergei Kovalev, a biologist and founding member of the Moscow chapter of Amnesty International, was arrested. His trial followed nearly a year later in Vilnius. He was given seven years in a labor camp and three in exile from his region of residence.

In 1976-79, several additional religiously oriented *samizdat* journals joined the *Chronicle* (and the non-religious *samizdat*, discussed below). They varied from a nationalistic and somewhat intolerant *Dievas ir tėvynė* (*God and Fatherland*) to one with a primarily pastoral function, *Rūpintojelis* (*Sorrowing Christ*). General consensus seems to hold that the issue "Bažnyčia ir *LKB Kronika*: mintys, svarstymai ir pageidavimai" ["The Church and *The Chronicle of the Lithuanian Catholic Church*: Thoughts, Reflections, and Desiderata"] (1977), and attempt to present an

---

[78] *Lietuvos Katalikų Bažnyčios Kronika 13* (Chicago, 1975), II, p. 304.
[79] *Ibid.*, *17*, III, p. 64.

alternative loyal Catholic position, was KGB-inspired. Apart from its content, this "*samizdat*" publication was alone in being able to enjoy double-spaced typing, at least in those copies earmarked for foreign consumption.

Around 1980, religiously oriented dissent in Lithuania seemed to be moving somewhat in the direction of greater confrontation with the regime. This could be reflective of the boost in morale which the 1978 election of Pope John Paul II gave to religious activism. In the Fall of that year, a five-member Committee for the Defense of the Rights of Catholics was announced at a Moscow news conference. Together with the attention that some recent issues of the *Chronicle* devoted to the rights of Roman Catholics in Moldavia, this seemed to indicate an expansion of concern by Lithuanian Catholic dissenters beyond purely Lithuanian questions.

Religious dissent was the most long-standing and widespread manifestation of organized opposition in Lithuania. The country's strong religious heritage, and its interrelation with nationalism, rendered such dissent potentially the most powerful. However, it did not appear alone on the scene.

On the level of individual action, several prominent figures on the Lithuanian cultural scene became dissidents through public protests against some negative facets of Soviet reality. As mentioned earlier, in August 1972 Jonas Jurašas, Senior Director of the Kaunas State Theater addressed a letter to several cultural agencies in the republic, denouncing the compromises that he, as an artist, was forced to make by the arbitrary limitations placed on his activity by cultural officials. He was removed from his post and, over two years later, allowed to emigrate.

In May 1975, the poet Tomas Venclova, son of a pre-war leftist writer who in 1940 had become the People's Commissar for Education, declared in a letter to the CC of the LiCP:

> The Communist ideology is alien to me and, in my opinion, is largely false. Its absolute reign has brought much misfortune to our land. . . . I take a serious view of Communist ideology, and therefore I refuse to repeat its formulas in a mechanical or hypocritical manner.[80]

He was subsequently allowed to accept an invitation to a visiting professorship at the University of California, during which time he was stripped of his Soviet citizenship.

The case of Mindaugas Tomonis should also be included in the category of individual action. In November 1975 he was found dead along a railway track, supposedly a suicide, though many felt that he had been driven to the act, if not killed outright beforehand, by the KGB. As head of the laboratory in the Institute for Monument Restoration, Tomonis refused to inspect a crumbling monument to the Red Army at Kryžkalnis (40 km north of Jurbarkas) and stated his critical opinion of the significance of the memorial in writing. He was placed under psychiatric care, but continued public manifestations of dissent by entering his opinion in the visitors' book of the Vilnius Museum of the History of Religion and Atheism, and by sending the Lithuanian Soviet administration memoranda on the Helsinki Agreement. Tomonis had been known as an unofficial poet who had published abroad; after his death, his poetry circulated in *samizdat* form.

Several standing groups emerged, formed for specific non-religious purposes, though some of their individual members were also religious activists. The most significant of these was the committee established by five individuals in November 1976 for the purpose of monitoring Soviet compliance with the Helsinki Accords. In effect, it fulfilled the function of a citizens'-initiative civil rights committee. Its name and concerns paralleled similar committees in several other parts of the USSR with which it maintained ties. Its method of operation was through *samizdat* publication of statements on alleged human rights violations brought to its attention. As human rights were of a wider than national concern, the documents of the Lithuanian committee were not limited to purely Lithuanian questions. Document no. 7 (26 May 1977), for instance, dealt with the case of Erik Udam, an Estonian electrical engineer and former wrestling champion who had been approached by the KGB to form a Soviet-controlled "dissident" committee with ties to American diplomats in Moscow. The Lithuanian Helsinki Committee's ties with its Moscow counterpart made its memoranda more accessible to the outside world.

Although the original membership of the Lithuanian Helsinki Committee was affected by death, arrest, and emigration, new members continued the group. Of the five founders, Reverend Karolis Garuckas died a natural death in April 1979. Tomas Venclova, as already mentioned, came to reside in the United States. Viktoras Petkus was arrested in the Summer of 1977, and a year later received an especially harsh sentence of ten years' imprisonment, to be followed by five years of internal exile. The two others, Ona Lukauškaitė-Poškienė and Eitan Finkelstein, were interrogated by the KGB; Finkelstein was accused of "collecting and transmitting to foreign intelligence centers and anti-Soviet propaganda organs slanderous fabrications and information defaming the Soviet social and state system."[81]

Samizdat intimated the existence of several other Lithuanian groups. A National People's Front — consisting, among others, of a Lithuanian Free Democratic Youth Alliance and a Lithuanian Catholic Alliance — claimed in 1975 to have been in existence since 1955 and to have organized an illegal country-wide conference in June 1974. The program of struggle supposedly discussed at that time, and submitted to the entire freedom movement, was predicated on a rather gloomy world-view and appeared rather general and unrealistic. A subsequent strongly worded declaration in May 1976 warrants doubt as to its authenticity. At best, the authors may have consisted of a small unrepresentative group. This was probably also the case with a "Lithuanian Communist Movement for Secession from the USSR," for which there are two *samizdat* references.

A second Lithuanian *samizdat* periodical began to appear in 1975. Its name, *Aušra (Dawn)*, and numeration attempted to establish a symbolic continuity with the first Lithuanian newspaper, published in East Prussia between 1883 and 1886 and smuggled into the Russian Empire. *Aušra* was not a chronicle of specific events or issues, but a magazine with an avowed emphasis on spiritual values and cultural progress as indispensable elements for preservation of a Lithuanian national character. The implicit feeling in its advocacy of nonviolent resistance was that the Lithuanian nation will survive if it manages to maintain a cultural superiority over its oppressors. *Aušra* focused attention on a series of questions involving human rights as well as social, economic, and cultural issues. It devoted considerable attention to various facets of Russification as well as to questions of the distortion or insufficient coverage of the nation's history. By 1980, 21 issues had appeared.

At least six other Lithuanian *samizdat* periodicals have appeared since 1975. Some indicate the circulation of source materials unavailable to Soviet citizens under normal conditions; others refer to ties and cooperation with dissident elements outside Lithuania. The most recent magazine of the 1970s was *Alma Mater*, which began its appearance in 1979, the year of Vilnius University's 400th-anniversary celebration. It was a thick quarterly of some 300 typed pages with a distinctive cover. In the late 1970s, several books also made their appearance in Lithuanian *samizdat*. One volume

---

[81] As reported in *Draugas* (Chicago), 9 September 1977. See also Yaroslav Bilinsky and Tönu Parming, "Helsinki Watch Committees in the Soviet Republics: Implications for Soviet Nationality Policy," *Nationality Papers*, IX/1 (Spring 1981), pp. 1–26.

consisted of the memoirs of Petras Klimas, a pre-war statesman and diplomat; another, those of the second President of the interwar republic, Aleksandras Stulginskis. *Tarybų Sąjungos Komunistų Partijos Programa ir Gyvenimas* (*The CPSU Program and Life*), by Gintautas Tautvytis (pseud.), analyzed political and socio-economic realities in the republic. *Sofijokratija ir geodoroviniai jos principai* [*Sophiocracy and Its Geomoral Principles*] (1977) is a theological-philosophical work by a dissident activist, Algirdas Statkevičius, who was subsequently repressed. A 300-page manuscript entitled *Spiritual Genocide in Lithuania* was confiscated in November 1979 during a search of the apartment of another prominent dissident, Vytautas Skuodis.[82]

Latvia

The first intimations of Latvian opposition date from the early 1960s. In 1960, three individuals were tried for allegedly plotting an armed uprising. One of them, Vilnis Krūkliņš, received a ten-year sentence; he was released in 1970. In 1961, poet Knuts Skujenieks was sentenced to seven years of forced labor for patriotic activities. In 1962, eight Latvians were sentenced to from eight to fifteen years for planning to form an organization, to be named the Baltic Federation, to oppose Russification and economic exploitation of the Baltic republics. Viktors Kalniņš, who served a ten-year sentence, continued dissident activities after his release and was allowed to emigrate in 1977.[83]

In early 1968, Jānis Jahimovičs, Chairman of a collective farm near Daugavpils, sent a letter to Mikhail Suslov and the CPSU CC protesting the persecution of Iurii Galanskov, Aleksandr Ginzburg, and others:

> Only one remedy can liquidate *samizdat* — the development of
> democratic rights, not their violation; observance of the
> Constitution, not its violation; the realization in practice of the
> Declaration of Human Rights.[84]

Jahimovičs was expelled from the party and subsequently removed from his post, but continued signing protests over human rights violations. He considered himself a national Communist, a stance clearly reflected in a moving letter written in March 1969, just

---

[82] Richard J. Krickus, "The Case of Vytautas Skuodis, U.S. Citizen," *Commonweal*, CVIII/17 (25 September 1981), p. 525.

[83] Interviews with Viktors Kalniņš have been published in several Canadian newspapers, including *St. Catharines (Ont.) Standard*, 8 May 1978, and *The Daily Mercury* (Guelph, Ont.), 14 May 1979.

[84] Text in *Sunday Telegraph*, 3 March 1968, and *New York Times*, 8 March 1968. For dissent in Latvia, see Ekmanis 1978, pp. 305-308.

before his arrest. While the people are sovereign, he claimed, "they are made up of living persons, of real lives. When human rights are violated, especially in the name of socialism and Marxism, there cannot be two positions."[85] Jahimovičs was declared to be mentally ill and forced to receive treatment continuing until 1971.

1969 proved to be a dramatic year for individual Latvian dissent. On 13 April, a young Jewish student, Ilia Rips, set himself on fire by the Riga Independence Memorial, publicly protesting the Soviet occupation of Czechoslovakia. He survived and was allowed to emigrate to Israel in 1972. In 1970-71, at least a dozen Latvian Jewish activists were sentenced. A journalist, Ivars Žukovskis, received a five-year sentence for criticizing the intervention in Czechoslovakia. After finishing his sentence, Žukovskis was re-arrested and imprisoned for six months for carrying a petition addressed to the UN Commission on Human Rights. Later, he was again arrested, receiving a two-year sentence on an apparently fabricated charge of shoplifting. In November 1969, three young people, Gunārs Bērziņš, Laimonis Markants, and Valerijs Luks, distributed 8,000 leaflets commenting on various aspects of Soviet foreign policy. They were sentenced to up to three years for anti-Soviet propaganda as well as for alleged illegal possession of weapons. One of the signers of the 1918 Latvian Declaration of Independence, Social Democrat Fricis Menders, was also tried in November for "anti-Soviet agitation and propaganda": he supposedly gave some notes and memoirs to a visiting émigré couple. Banished from Riga, he was allowed to return a year later and soon thereafter died at the age of 86.[86] In December 1970, Lidija Doronina-Lasmanis and several others received shorter sentences, and in 1971, as we have noted, it was the turn of translator Maija Silmale.

The most notable document of Latvian dissent, dated July-August 1971, was the long "Letter of the Seventeen Communists" addressed to party leaders in Romania, Yugoslavia, France, Austria, and Spain.[87] Although its origin in Latvia and authorship by Communists in particular has come to be questioned, the "Letter" received considerable attention in the West. Its anonymous authors claimed to be veterans of 25 to 35 years who had joined the party when it operated underground in the pre-war

[85] *New York Times*, 13 April 1969.
[86] See Bruno Kalniņš, "The Social Democratic Movement in Latvia," in *Revolution and Politics in Russia: Essays in Memory of B. I. Nicolaevsky* (Bloomington, Ind., 1972), pp. 134-156.
[87] English text in George Saunders (ed.), *Samizdat: Voices of the Soviet Opposition* (New York, 1974), pp. 427-40, and in *Congressional Record*, 21 February 1972, pp. E1426-E1430; German text in AB, XI (1971), pp. 117-130.

republic. They detailed numerous violations of Marxist-Leninist nationality policy and called upon the fraternal parties to help correct "certain actions and events that cause great harm to the Communist movement, to Marxism-Leninism, and to our own as well as other small nations." They said that Latvians (including Russian Latvians) formed only 42% of the LaCP CC staff, 47% of District Secretaries, and 17% of the basic Party Group Secretaries; in Riga, LaCP membership was 18% Latvian and there were no Latvians among the City Committee section leaders. They listed by name and function 25 native Communists purged in 1959. The authors said they all fought on the Soviet side during the war, and had actively participated in building socialism in Latvia. They had long thought that Russification was an unintentional temporary phenomenon, but had reluctantly come to believe that the Soviet Communist Party had "deliberately adopted a policy of Great Russian chauvinism."[88]

The Baptist Khristianin Publishing House near Cēsis provided the most prominent manifestation of religious dissent in Latvia. Its publications, however, appeared only in Russian, and individuals connected with the effort seem to have come together from all over the USSR. Another facet of religious dissent in Latvia was the tortuous process of emigration by Baptist Pastor Jānis Šmits and his relatives, the Bruvers family, which stretched over three years (from 1973 to 1976), and involved hunger strikes, harassment, and even sentencing one member of the family to a six-month term in a labor camp.[89] A 1975 Roman Catholic petition in Daugavpils signed by 5,043 faithful, over threatened demolition of their church, can also be considered Latvian religious dissent.

The activities of three political dissent groups in Latvia also became known. A letter dated 27 July 1975, addressed to Latvian émigrés, provided the first indication of the existence of the Latvian Independence Movement. It contrasted the positive developments of the independence period with the overwhelming problems of the present — among them oppression, Russification, moral degradation, family instability, and alcoholism — which placed the survival of the nation in question. Émigrés were asked to remind the world of this reality. The second group, Latvia's Democratic Youth Committee, likewise sent a letter to Latvians abroad, on 5 October 1975, surveying the steps which had to be

---

[88] Factual information in the "letter" was not contradicted in Soviet Latvian press comment ("Atbilde apmelotajiem," *Cīņa*, 24 February 1972) after the "letter" was published in the West. Western press reports included *The Economist*, 26 February 1972; *New York Times*, 27 February 1972; and *Le Monde*, 8 March 1972.

[89] See, e.g., "Latvian Minister Tells of Plight of Clergy in the Soviet Union," *Christian Science Monitor*, 17 August 1976.

taken in order to reestablish independent Baltic states. It carried the signature of the group's Chairman, Jānis Briedis, as well as a seal of the organization. Later that year, the clandestine Pali Publishing House in Riga printed a New Year's greeting card from the Committee. The third group, Latvia's Christian Democratic Organization, became known from a late 1975 letter to émigré leaders written after a clandestine observance of Latvian Independence Day, 18 November. In addition to voicing political concerns, it indicated a need by Latvians to lead Christian lives as a prime condition for regaining independence, and expressed a special concern for the plight of the Baptists in Latvia.

The three groups coordinated their efforts in 1976. The first two were responsible for a handbill in March. In June, they sent a letter to the government of the Latvian SSR signed by their Chairmen. Written on the anniversary of the entry of the Red Army in 1940, the document protested the subsequent Sovietization and Russification. All three organizations sent a joint letter to Australian Prime Minister Fraser thanking him for his new government's decision to abrogate the earlier Australian recognition of the incorporation of the Baltic states into the USSR. Each of the three groups sent greetings to the United States on its bicentennial.[90]

A fourth Latvian group of this type, the Organization for Latvia's Independence, became known from a small pamphlet (Spring 1977) calling for a referendum on the republic's secession from the USSR. The four-page pamphlet was said to be the third statement of the organization, an abridgment from a larger work, and to have an edition of 25,000. The group claimed to be composed of 210 representatives, each from a particular constituency. The tract provided some practical suggestions for showing discontent: these included whistling whenever ideological statements are being expressed, boycotting elections, and using the tritest phrases of official jargon as often as possible. Whenever anyone is arrested, the population could show solidarity by turning on all lights and appliances for ten minutes during the peak period of usage; the resulting blackouts would be noticed by the authorities. A list of positive goals for a liberal independent state was also appended.[91]

Less copious than Lithuania's, Latvian *samizdat* did exhibit a pessimistic concern for the future of the nation. As in the other two

---

[90] Aina Zariņš, "Dissent in the Baltic Republics: A Survey of Grievances and Hopes," *Radio Liberty Research Paper*, no. 496 (December 1976), pp. 18–20.
[91] The untitled four-page pamphlet was republished in 1978 in Bonn by the émigré publisher Gaismas Akcija.

republics, the emphasis was on implementation of human rights. Latvian dissidents managed to smuggle to the West a unique three-minute film of a Soviet labor camp near Riga: columns of prisoners, armed guards, watchdogs, trucks with barred cages, and watch-towers. The documentary was seen on television in 1975-76 in Great Britain, the United States, Canada, West Germany, and France.

The case of Žanis Skudra is particularly notable. In 1979 he was tried and sentenced to twelve years for allegedly transmitting photographed information about military objectives to the West. This was done with the help of Jānis Niedre, a Swedish citizen of Latvian birth, who was arrested during a visit to Latvia and sentenced to ten years, but was released after six months and returned to Sweden. The material, published in two volumes by the Latvian National Fund in Stockholm, consists among other things of photographs of churches, farmsteads, rural scenes, and architectural monuments. The pictures were accompanied by a diary. Together, they present a panorama of the changes in the Latvian countryside under Soviet rule and become an indictment, in illustrated travelogue form, of the neglect and destruction of Latvia's national heritage.[92]

The existence of an underground branch of the Latvian Social Democrat Party (complementing its exile branch in Sweden) became known when its leader, electrical engineer Juris Bumeisters, was arrested in 1980; he was sentenced in June 1981 to 15 years.

Estonia

Organized Estonian dissent became known mainly through a series of *samizdat* essays and memoranda which began to reach the West during the late 1960s. Nearly all such items were characterized by reflective concerns over the survival of the Estonian nation, coupled with appeals for moral regeneration and the fostering of spiritual values.

The earliest notable piece was a July 1968 essay entitled "To Hope or to Act," written by "Numerous Members of Estonia's Technical Intelligentsia" as a reply to Andrei Sakharov's *Thoughts on Progress, Peaceful Coexistence, and Intellectual Freedom.*[93] Its anonymous authors took issue with Sakharov's implicit belief in

---

[92] J. Dzintars, *Okupētas Latvijas dienas grāmata, 1944-1972* (Stockholm, 1976 and 1980; 2 volumes); see also Jānis Sapiets, "Out of Latvia," *Index on Censorship*, X/2 (1981), p. 58.

[93] *Münchener Merkur*, no. 306 (1968); *Frankfurter Allgemeine Zeitung*, 18 December 1968.

the basic goodness and common sense of mankind, as well as with his faith in the ability of science and technology to solve contemporary problems. They felt that Sakharov ignored the spiritual facets of human nature, and they argued the need for new moral values. Materialist ideology, they claimed, had destroyed Christian values without providing any adequate alternative. On a more practical plane, they called for a specific program of action which they felt Sakharov failed to enunciate: renunciation of the aggressive foreign policy of the Soviet Union, establishment of a democratic form of government, and the right of nations to exercise self-determination.

About a year later, a group of officers of the Soviet Baltic fleet were tried in Tallinn on charges of having founded a society, "The Union for Struggle for Political Rights," whose membership extended beyond Tallinn to Leningrad and Kaliningrad, among other places. Some Estonians were involved. It was reported that searches connected with the affair uncovered a printing press. On 11 December 1969, four Estonians were arrested in Tartu for membership in a secret organization as well as alleged possession of weapons.

In 1972, evidence reached the west of the existence of two Estonian resistance groups: the Estonian National Front (ENF) and the Estonian Democratic Movement (EDM). The ENF supposedly published a political program in the fifth issue of the *samizdat* periodical *Eesti demokraat*, published since 1971. The publication did not reach the West. As summarized in the Moscow *Chronicle of Current Events* (no. 25), the program sought to work out principles for the political and social systems of an independent Estonia and to strive for a referendum on self-determination. In October 1972, both groups addressed a joint memorandum to the UN General Assembly and a letter to Secretary-General Kurt Waldheim.[94] The letter outlined the *raison d'être* for both groups, and detailed the course of Russification in Estonia. The memorandum demanded restoration of an independent Estonia and its admission to the UN, as well as formation of a democratic government in the country through free elections administered by the world body. The Soviets responded to the publication of these documents by house searches and arrests in December 1974, as reported in a new appeal to Waldheim by the two groups (23 December 1974):

In spite of these gloomy events, we consider that our primary goal

---

[94] The road to the West was long. Texts were first published in *Baltic Events*, no. 46 (October 1974), and later in *Documents from Estonia*, pp. 19–26.

has been achieved. . . . The monopoly of the Soviet Estonian puppet regime to represent the Estonian people has ended. No one can state any more that the Estonian nation as a whole agrees with the 35 years of occupation and perspective of assimilation.[95]

The same themes appeared in a letter written on 25 December 1974 by a group of "Estonian Patriots" addressed to several principal instruments of the Western mass media such as the BBC and the *New York Times*. In June 1975, "Representatives of Estonian and Latvian Democrats" addressed all governments participating in the Helsinki Conference on Security and Cooperation in Europe. In September, the ENF and the EDM joined four other Baltic organizations in an appeal to Baltic émigrés as well as to leaders of freedom-loving nations and organizations throughout the world. All of these activities may have been interrelated.

Five members of the EDM were tried in Tallinn in October 1975. The proceedings underscored a connection between the group and the human rights movement in other parts of the USSR. One of the defendants pleaded guilty and received a suspended sentence in return for testimony against the other four, all engineers. The defendant Kalju Mätik argued that the EDM had not sought to overthrow the Soviet regime: "The constitution guarantees the right of the constituent republics to secede from the Soviet Union. We demanded a referendum. This is not the same as to overthrow the regime." His colleague Mati Kiirend found it difficult to believe that anyone could be tried for activities which were sanctioned by the Soviet constitution. Sergei Soldatov, whose dissident activity had already surfaced during the trial of the Baltic fleet officers, characterized EDM activity as having been motivated by moral and ethical principles in its struggle for human rights. Artjom Juskevitš protested against being imprisoned in a dirty and dark cellar, a treatment which had made him believe Solzhenitsyn's *Gulag Archipelago*. The 4 unrepentant defendants received sentences of five to six years in strict-regime labor camps. But they were not silenced. In February 1976, they joined 15 other political prisoners in the Potma camp in Mordovia in an appeal to all who cherish "the principles of democracy, freedom, and human rights," asking them to demand that the USSR adhere to the provisions of the Helsinki Agreement which it had signed.[96]

---

[95] The 1974-75 texts in *EE/BE*, nos. 48, pp. 2-6, and 52, pp. 2-10 (1975), and *Documents from Estonia*, pp. 10-18 and 27-31; the June 1975 text also in *Lituanus*, XXI/3 (Fall 1975), pp. 63-73.

[96] Texts of court proceedings and of Potma appeal in *Newsletter from Behind the Iron Curtain*, nos. 490/491 (April-September 1976) and no. 492 (December 1976), and also in *Documents from Estonia*, pp. 32-61.

Kiirend and Juskevitš were released in 1979, and Soldatov and Mätik in 1980. Given the choice between permanent rural residence and emigration, Soldatov chose Western Europe, in 1981.

A long statement dated April 1976 was addressed by an "Association of Concerned Estonians" to ESTO '76, an American-Estonian festival of culture. It expressed concern over the moral erosion which had accompanied 32 years of Soviet rule. Christian ideals and faith in the future had been replaced in Estonia by widespread skepticism, materialism, pragmatism, and egoism. A moral renaissance of the Estonian people was seen as a *sine qua non* for the re-achievement of independence. In October 1976, "Representatives of Estonian Democrats" sent another plea to Amnesty International and to UN and United States human-rights bodies.

In May 1977, an anonymous letter by 18 naturalists was addressed to colleagues in northwestern Europe. It protested against ecological damage by Soviet oil-shale and phosphorite mining in Estonia, which was described as a short-sighted colonialist practice of turning large stretches of land into a moon landscape.

One later manifestation of organized Estonian dissent exhibited some unusual facets for such activity in the USSR, though it too shared the reflective concern over the future of the nation which seemed to be the leitmotif of Estonian *samizdat*. In late 1978, a "White Key Brotherhood" and a cultural organization calling itself Maarjamaa circulated six issues of a mimeographed periodical called *Poolpäevaleht* (which could mean either "The Saturday Paper" or "The Semi-Daily") in the university town of Tartu. The first issue outlined the goals of the magazine, principally the uncensored publication of literary and cultural writings of the membership. One editorial in the journal viewed Christianity as the "carrier of the idea of Germanism" and, as such, poison. The Estonian people were in need of spiritual independence from Europeanization. In May 1979, several members and contributors were expelled from the University.

In addition to identified individuals connected with some of the groups, several other names were significant in Estonian dissent. Mart Niklus was first arrested in 1958 for sending abroad photos of shoddy construction and of a radio-jamming station, and a year thereafter was sentenced to ten years in a labor camp for "agitation and the spread of anti-Soviet propaganda." He was again taken into custody for a couple of months in 1976 when he went to the prosecutor's office to demand the return of tape recordings and texts seized during a search of his apartment. In 1970, 4 young workers were sentenced to two to five years for political organizing and alleged possession of firearms. In 1971, Vladimir Eichvald was committed to a psychiatric ward for, among other things, protesting the expulsion of Alexander Solzhenitsyn from the USSR Writers' Union. Olev Meremaa, a mathematician with the Tallinn Construction Institution, kept applying unsuccessfully for permission to attend international conferences which had accepted his papers. On 1 May 1974, he publicly carried a placard in Tallinn with the inscriptions "Put human rights into practice" and "Sakharov-Solzhenitsyn." He was physically attacked by four party activists, arrested, and held for nearly four days before being released, and he lost his position. In January 1975, theater employee Sven Kreek was arrested for distributing poems and a socialist reform manifesto. Subjected to forced mental treatment, he soon died. Soviet authorities claimed suicide, but they buried Kreek secretly in an unknown place.

A new major phase in Baltic dissent was introduced on 28 October 1980, when 40 Soviet Estonian writers, artists, and scholars signed an open letter to *Pravda* (which did not publish it). Among the signers — 13 of whom were listed in the *Estonian Soviet Encyclopedia* — were writers Lehte Hainsalu, Jaan Kaplinski, Heino Kiik, Paul-Eerik Rummo, Mati Unt, Arvo Valton, and Juhan Viiding, and sociologist Marju Lauristin, the daughter of the first (1940–41) Chairman of the ESSR Council of People's Commissars. Their unprecedented step was triggered by the "violence associated with the events in Tallinn" during the aforementioned high school student demonstrations, which they termed "an unexaggerated reflection of the dissatisfaction of numerous older Estonians." They mentioned food shortages, but more specifically called for a candid discussion of Russian-Estonian relations:

> The rapid relative decline of the Estonian segment of the population
> Circumscription of the use of the Estonian language in business, everyday matters, and science
> The growing scarcity of Estonian-language journals and books
> The hyperbolic and inept propaganda campaign pushing the teaching of Russian
> Immoderate and overtaxing development of industry
> Unilateral demand for bilingualism among Estonians, without a similar effort being made among aliens
> The appointment of persons with inadequate knowledge of Estonian culture[97]

---

[97] Full text in *Radio Liberty Research Paper*, no. 477 (15 December 1980). Interviewed by Sweden's State Radio on 4 May 1981, ESSR Minister Gustav Tõnspoeg acknowledged the letter's existence, but declined to discuss its details (*Vaba*

While half a dozen less well-connected dissidents were arrested in late 1980, the regime's response to the memo of the 40 intellectuals seems to have been limited to a search of Jaan Kaplinski's apartment on 6 November. Their writings continued to be published.

Cooperation Among Baltic Dissidents

In the late 1970s, some hints of cooperation among dissidents appeared in the three republics. There has been no indication that the 1962 Baltic Federation extended beyond Latvia. The Estonian Democratic Movement defendents in 1975 were accused of contacts with Moscow, Latvia, and especially Lithuania. There was the June 1975 Estonian-Latvian appeal. A Baltic dissident gathering in August 1976 is mentioned in the Lithuanian *samdizat* periodical *Perspektyvos* (no. 9, 1979). A decision was made to appeal to the West with a memorandum outlining the reality of conditions in the Baltic republics and pointing out Western indifference to the situation; Estonian human-rights activist Mart Niklus was arrested during the drafting of the memorandum. Some of the participants in the Riga gathering also sought to establish an Estonian-Latvian-Lithuanian National Movement Committee and to appeal to the democratic states of the world in its name. According to the account in *Perspektyvos*, one of its organizers, Viktoras Petkus, was arrested before the final stage of establishment of the Committee, and its activity ceased. A Committee decision of 20 August 1977 was reported in the Lithuanian *samdizat* publication *Aušra* (no. 8). Three days later, 23 August 1977, Petkus was arrested.

On 23 August 1979, a statement protesting the Molotov-Ribbentrop Pact of 1939 and demanding publication by the USSR of its full text, including the secret protocols on the division of Eastern Europe, appeared in Moscow.[98] Although most had Lithuanian names, 4 Latvians and 4 Estonians were among the 45 signers. Estonian signers Mart Niklus and Erik Udam had been mentioned in Lithuanian *samizdat* since 1977. The statement requested that the Pact be specifically declared null and void by the USSR as well as by the two German states, which were further requested "to assist the Soviet Government to nullify the consequences of that Pact: namely, to withdraw foreign troops from the Baltic states." Unconfirmed reports claim that 35,000 signatures were gathered in Lithuania in support of this statement, which

---

Eestlane, 30 June 1981). See also Rein Taagepera, "Peril of Uprising Keeps Moscow Cautious," *Los Angeles Times*, 20 May 1981, p. II-15.
[98] *New York Times*, 25 August 1979, p. 5. Full text in *UBA Information Service*, news release nos. 330/331 (11 November 1979), supplement.

stands out for its skillfulness in avoiding terms that could be interpreted as "anti-Soviet" and by its specific nullification request placed on West Germany's doorstep.

Police harassment of signers began immediately. Among others, Antanas Terleckas was arrested in October 1979, and Mart Niklus in March 1980. Also arrested was Tartu University chemistry lecturer Jüri Kukk, after a January 1980 condemnation of the Soviet invasion of Afghanistan, signed by 21 persons from all three Baltic countries.[99] On 8 January 1981, Kukk was sentenced to two years in prison, and died under questionable circumstances on 27 March, while Niklus received a harsh sentence of ten years in prison plus five years of internal exile.[100] Terleckas was sentenced to three years in prison plus five years of internal exile.

These varied manifestations of dissent indicated gradually mounting Baltic pressures for a more pluralistic society which would grant legitimacy to indigenous nationalism, including the religious heritage in Lithuania. The continued existence and circulation of Baltic *samizdat* seemed to underscore an increasing defensiveness on the part of the regime, whose power, as a result of long erosion by institutionalized hypocrisy, was paralleled by an astounding moral weakness.

[99] David K. Willis, "Fresh Burst of Baltic Nationalism Hits Kremlin," *Christian Science Monitor*, 29 January 1980; further articles on 16 January and 6 February 1980.

[100] *Rahva Hääl*, 13 January 1981; Murray Seeger, "In Estonia, an Uncelebrated Martyr," *Los Angeles Times*, 20 May 1981, p. II-15; Rein Taagepera, "The Death of Jüri Kukk: A Case Study in Erratic Repression," *Social Sciences Research Report* R97, (University of California, Irvine, July 1981); Jānis Sapiets, "New Waves of Dissent," *Index on Censorship*, X/3 (June 1981), pp. 51-53.

CHAPTER VI

THE OUTLOOK FOR THE 1980s

After the years of deepening despair from the mid-1940s to the mid-1950s, and the years of rising hopes from the mid-1950s to the late 1960s, the 1970s were years of contradictions for the Baltic nations. Internal autonomy did not increase, but neither was there marked erosion of the modest gains of the early 1960s. Centralization of economic decision-making was counterbalanced by more plant-level autonomy. Economic development continued, new products whetted consumers' appetites, but food shortages reappeared. Russian immigration reached alarming new peaks, but then started to subside rapidly. Western influences penetrated Baltic culture and life-style more than ever since 1940, but a new campaign for the Russification of culture started in the late 1970s. Travel contacts with the West became commonplace, but heavy and petty restrictions remained. The structure of Moscow's rule in the Baltics did not change appreciably, but the very lack of reforms represented a change. In terms of passive submissiveness, the Soviet rule gained further acceptance by simply lasting for another dozen years and sinking deeper into the collective memory. Yet dissent became vocal. It was repressed harshly, but less brutally than before.

In 1940, the Soviet Union annexed three nations with ancient roots, but with very recent national identities in a modern sense. It was possible to wonder whether they would survive under new conditions, or whether political annexation would soon be followed by socio-cultural absorption. The fact that their linguistic and cultural roots were quite different from the dominant Russian veneer in Soviet society argued against easy absorption. However, their modern national framework in 1940 was recent and fragile. Sustained national-language literature, press, and theater were less than a century old. Higher education in the national languages had come with the emergence of the nation-states in 1918, as had administration above the commune level. Nearly every adult in the three national groups was a child or grandchild of peasants. The possibility existed that the sense of national identity could be shaken, that gifted individuals could be lured to Moscow or elsewhere in the empire, and that the collective sense of identity would shift from the local to the empire level. In many ways, Lithuanian, Latvian, and Estonian identities might have appeared to rest on shallower ground than those of the Basques, the Welsh, or the Bretons — who, in spite of their linguistic distinctiveness, also looked like vanishing peoples in 1940.

Predictions of imminent demise were still there 40 years later; so were the nations involved. It has been said that, according to the laws of aerodynamics, the bumblebee should not be able to fly. But it does so anyway, too ignorant to know any better. Perhaps according to the social laws of modernization, devised for the most part by members of large national groups, such entities as the Baltic or the Ibero-Celtic mini-nations should have been collapsing, but they did not know it, and kept going. Culturally more suppressed than the Balts during 1940–75, the Basques seemed to achieve, in 1979, a meaningful political autonomy which was still beyond the reach of the Balts. Autonomy for Wales was an issue more alive in 1980 than 40 years earlier, and there were new stirrings in Bretagne.

Cultural assimilation in the Soviet Union may have been overestimated by many earlier observers. Correctly noting the utterly limited political and economic autonomy of the republics within the Soviet Union, such observers underestimated the boost to national identity supplied by the mere existence of national republics, not to mention the very real cultural autonomy extant in many of them. The Baltic nations made full use of restricted opportunities. In so doing, they have, compared to 1940, extended appreciably their historical depth as modern nations.

By 1980, the Baltic nations could look back to 60 years rather than 20 years of native-language universities and republic-level administration. In the 40-year perspective, the use of Russian in those fields had advanced; but in the 80-year perspective, the overall picture still was one of a massive shift from Russian to the national languages. The very territorial units called Estonia, Latvia, and Lithuania, as applied to the corresponding ethnolinguistic areas, were in 1940 only 20 years old. They, too, had now tripled in age: 20 years of real sovereignty had been augmented by 40 years of shadow sovereignty in the form of secession rights in the Soviet Constitution, and of non-recognition of Soviet annexation by the United States and other Western powers.

The increase in socio-cultural depth may be the most important consideration. Large numbers of young Balts in 1980 saw college-educated grandparents as nothing unusual. Forty years earlier, this was highly unusual. Instead of vehement doubt-tinged declarations that one's co-nationals were as capable as members of any large

Western nation, the Balts of 1980 took such parity as self-evident. The centennial celebrations of national press and theater came and receded into the past. Factually and mentally, the Baltic nations were now living in their second century of modern cultural nationhood. They could expect to be there for their bicentennial. The bumblebee continues to fly.

Within this long-range general prognosis, the most likely scenario for the 1980s was one of gradual evolution. Radical changes, of course, could never be considered impossible — they were merely unforeseeable. Current trends seemed to indicate that urbanization of the Baltic society would slowly continue, with an ever-larger fraction of people going into service professions rather than industry. The depopulation of the countryside would likewise continue, but at a reduced rate. As the population ages, the death rate would increase. The Lithuanian birth rate would still fall slightly, and the natural increase would slow down markedly. The already minimal growth of the ethnically Latvian and Estonian population might come to a complete halt as deaths among the relatively large older-age groups would surpass the new births generated by the smaller fertile-age cohorts. However, as the large older cohorts died, a constant fertility level could result in a slightly increased crude birth rate by 1990. The outcome would be zero population growth rather than major population decrease.

Net immigration could fall to near-zero by 1985. By 1990, a net outflow of non-Balts from all three republics could take place. The next census (be it 1989 or 1990) might find only a minor decrease, if any, in the percentage of ethnic Balts in the population of the Baltic republics.[1]

The knowledge of Russian as a second language would increase, due to schooling and TV exposure. But the small percentage of Balts declaring Russian as their main language could decrease, as some denationalized Balts who returned from Russia in 1945–65 would die or be reassimilated. As the Russian settlement in the Baltics stabilized, intermarriages could be expected to increase, with most of the offspring likely to acquire a Baltic identity, except in the heavily Russian cities of eastern Latvia and Estonia. In Lithuania and Estonia, appreciable integration of immigrants into the national language and culture could become visible by 1990.

The national cultures would continue to develop, integrating national tradition with worldwide trends, increasing amounts of Western culture, and limited Russian influence. Emergence of worldwide literary and artistic figures would be limited not only by

[1] For detailed population projections, see Taagepera, "Baltic Population Changes."

the small population pool, but also by Soviet bureaucracy super-imposed on Baltic provincialism, both of which encourage high-quality imitation but discourage true innovation. A continuing major cultural problem would be the impossibility of emigration with "honorable discharge," whereby a promising Baltic artist or intellectual could establish long-term residence in world locations where worldwide reputations could best be established, without being denounced back home as a political or cultural renegade. It was likely that promising talent would be kept permanently home, never to bloom fully, or permanently abroad, if it ever managed to leave.

Open peaceful dissent was likely to continue. The trend of the 1970s toward longer pre-arrest harassment and relatively short sentences might continue, due to the built-in mechanisms of a maturing political system. If so, then the level of popular frustration would increase — because repression, although less brutal, would become more visible. It was, however, unlikely that a flash point, with widespread unrest, would be reached prior to 1990, unless it were triggered by events outside the Baltic area.

The *immobilisme* in Baltic Soviet administration was likely to continue, with little native input (except in Lithuania), and little in the way of a republic-level political process. While leadership change in Moscow was highly probable during the 1980s, it was not likely to affect the Baltic lieutenants, if one could judge on the basis of precedents: both Käbin and Sniečkus managed to last through the 1953–56 and 1964 leadership changes in Moscow, as did the Latvian administrators.

In economic matters, one might be tempted to extrapolate from the fairly stable trends of 1960–80 in the same way we have done for socio-demographic characteristics. We would thus project further economic growth, though at a gradually decreasing rate. Consumer industry might become more dominant. Major current projects such as the Mažeikiai refinery would become operational. Major new projects (such as overexpansion of the Tallinn harbor) would not yet be completed by 1990. Decision-implementation lag-times would bar any sharp economic changes. However, the increasing worldwide energy squeeze makes passive extrapolation from past economic performance questionable. The Soviet Union would be no exception to worldwide trends, and any major disruptions of the Soviet energy structure would be fully felt by Baltic consumers and producers, not to mention the Baltic energy industry (such as refineries, hydroelectric projects, and oil-shale mining). Any possible political repercussions of an energy and raw material shortage, if generated elsewhere in the Soviet Union, would also be felt in the Baltic republics.

Baltic ability for political initiative would be limited by size, and by absence of political autonomy. Reform initiative had been blocked previously by Soviet practices, and was likely to remain so. Revolutionary initiative beyond a few days of mass protest (as in Kaunas in 1972) was not likely, either. Hungary, Czechoslovakia, and Poland not only had larger cities, but also preserved a semi-autonomous political structure which came to play a crucial role during the revolutionary processes of 1956, 1968, and 1980. The only way the Balts could alter the scene markedly during the 1980s would be in the reverse direction, were the national will of one of the Baltic nations suddenly to collapse under the combined load of Russification, immigration, repression, and consumerism. There were no signs to that effect — and, indeed, no relevant precedents in world history.

Unforeseeable major changes in the Baltic scene that could be triggered by external forces were, of course, innumerable, ranging from catastrophes like nuclear war to Amalrik's visions of 1984.[2] A Great Russian military takeover in Moscow would be unlikely but not impossible, and could lead to an abolition of the formal union republics and their concomitant cultural autonomy. A large fraction of Russian technocrats asked for just that, on grounds of economic efficiency, during pre-1977 discussion of the new Soviet Constitution. On the other hand, the coming change of leadership in Moscow could also bring about some liberalization.

In the longer perspective, Baltic developments were still wide open. In the 1980s, Baltic political initiative was likely to be severely limited, but socio-cultural initiative was possible. The Lithuanians, Latvians, and Estonians were likely to make the utmost use of these limited opportunities.

In the words of a poem by Vizma Belševica:

> Winds rage. Winds howl. Riga is silent.
> The nude stone women are silent.
> The heraldic beasts are silent.
> The steeples are silent. Rooster
> Weathervanes are silent.
>
> Winds rave. Winds roar. Riga is silent.
> Like a key that is silent
> When the pulse beat of the sweaty hand
> That took it throbs around the iron.
> Struck down, the conqueror shall always fall,
> And on the cobblestones his blood
> Will guard its silence.

---

[2] Andrei Amalrik, *Will the Soviet Union Survive Until 1984?* (New York, 1970).

Winds whip. Winds beat. Riga is silent.
Indifference? Obtuseness? Cowardice?
Ask not. You won't be answered.
The transitory must shout.
Must plead. Must prove.
The eternal can dwell in silence.[3]

[3] Vizma Belševica, *Gadu gredzeni* (Riga, 1969), p. 55.

APPENDIX A

MAJOR BALTIC ADMINISTRATORS AND GOVERNMENT LEADERS, 1938-1980

	ESTONIA	LATVIA	LITHUANIA
		1938 — Early June 1940	
President	Konstantin Päts 1938 — 21 July 1940	Kārlis Ulmanis 1936 — 21 July 1940	Antanas Smetona 1926 — 15 June 1940
Prime Minister	Kaarel Eenpalu 1938 — October 1939	Kārlis Ulmanis 1934 — 19 June 1940	Jonas Černius March — November 1939
	Jüri Uluots October 1939 — 21 June 1940		Antanas Merkys November 1939 — 15 June 1940
		Late June 1940 — Early August 1940	
Soviet Emissary	**Andrei Zhdanov 17 June — 6 August 1940	**Andrei Vyshinskii 17 June — 5 August 1940	**Vladimir Dekanozov 15 June — 3 August 1940
Prime Minister	Johannes Vares 21 June — 25 August 1940	Augusts Kirhenšteins 20 June — 25 August 1940	Justas Paleckis 17 June — 1 July 1940

	ESTONIA	LATVIA	LITHUANIA
		August 1940 — Summer 1941	
CP First Secretary	Karl Säre 12 September 1940 — Fall 1941	Jānis Kalnbērziņš June 1940–1959	Antanas Sniečkus 1936–1974
Chairman of the Council of People's Commissars	Johannes Lauristin 25 August 1940 — 28 August 1941	Vilis Lācis 25 August 1940–1959	Mečys Gedvilas August 1940–1956
Chairman of the Presidium of the Supreme Soviet	Johannes Vares 25 August 1940 — 29 November 1946	Augusts Kirhenšteins 25 August 1940–1952	Justas Paleckis 25 August 1940–1967
CP Second Secretary	Nikolai Karotamm 1940–1944	Žanis Spure August — December 1940	Icikas Meskupas-Adomas 1940–1942
		Summer 1941–1944/45	
German General Commissioner	**Karl Litzmann December 1941 — September 1944	**Otto Drechsler September 1941 — May 1945?	**Adrian von Renteln September 1941 — January 1945?
First Director/General Counselor	*Hjalmar Mäe 15 September 1941 — September 1944	*Oskars Dankers 21 August 1941 — 27 September 1944	Petras Kubiliūnas 22 August 1941–1944

	Lithuania	Latvia	Estonia
Head of Provisional Government	Kazys Škirpa Juozas Ambrazevičius 23 June — 3 August 1941	Roberts Osis 7-8 May 1945	Jüri Uluots 18-22 September 1944
Head of CPSU CC Special Bureau for the Republic	**Mikhail Suslov 11 November 1944 — Spring 1946 **V. V. Shcherbakov Spring 1946-1947?	*1944–1980* **Nikolai Shatalin? 1944-1945? **V. F. Riazanov? 1945-1947? **S. G. Zelenev? 1945-1947?	**Nikolai Shatalin 11 November 1944-1945? **Georgii Perov 1945?-1947 **Konstantin Boitsov 1947-1948?
CP First Secretary	Antanas Sniečkus 1936-1974 Petras Griškevičius 1974-	Jānis Kalnbērziņš 1940 — November 1959 *Arvīds Pelše 1959-1966 *Augusts Voss 1966-	Nikolai Karotamm 22 September 1944 — March 1950 *Johannes (Ivan) Käbin 1950-1978 *Karl Vaino 1978-
Chairman of the Council of Ministers	Mečys Gedvilas 1940-1956	Vilis Lācis 1940 — November 1959	Arnold Veimer 1944 — April 1951

	ESTONIA	LATVIA	LITHUANIA
Chairman of the Presidium of the Supreme Soviet (i.e., ceremonial head of state)	*Aleksei Müürisepp 1951–1961	*Jānis Peive 1959–1962	Motiejus Šumauskas 1956–1967
	*Valter Klauson 1961–	*Vitālijs Rubenis 1962–1970	*Juozas Maniušis 1967 — January 1981
		*Jurijs Rubenis 1970–	Ringaudas Songaila 16 January 1981–
	Johannes Vares August 1940 — 29 November 1946	Augusts Kirhenšteins 25 August 1940–1952	Justas Paleckis 25 August 1940–1967
	*Eduard Päll 1946–1950	Kārlis Ozoliņš 1952–1959	Motiejus Šumauskas 1967–1975
	August Jakobson 1950–1958	Jānis Kalnbērziņš 1959–1970	Antanas Barkauskas 1975–
	*Johan Eichfeld 1958–1961	*Vitālijs Rubenis 1970–1974	
	*Aleksei Müürisepp 1961–1970	Pēteris Strautmanis 1974–	
	*Artur Vader 1970–1978		
	*Johannes Käbin 1978–		

CP Second Secretary

**Sergei Sazonov November 1944–1950?	**Ivan Lebedev 1944 — January 1949	Vladas Niunka May — December 1944
**Vassilii Kosov 1950? — August 1953	**Fedor Titov January 1949–1952?	**A. N. Isachenko 1945–1946
*Leonid Lentsman August 1953–1964	**V. N. Ershakov 1952? — June 1953	**Aleksandr Trofimov 1946–1952
*Artur Vader 1964–1970	Vilis Krūmiņš June 1953 — January 1956	**V. Aronov 1952 — June 1953
**Konstantin Lebedev 1971–1982	**Filipp Kashnikov January 1956 — January 1958?	Motiejus Šumauskas June 1953–1955
	*Arvīds Pelše? January — April 1958?	**Boris Sharkov 1956–1961
	Vilis Krūmiņš April 1958? — February 1960	**Boris Popov 1961–1967
	**Mikhail Gribkov February 1960–1963	**Valerii Kharazov 1967–1978
	**Nikolai Belukha 1963–1978	**Nikolai Dybenko 1978–
	**Igor Strelkov 1978–1980	
	**Valentin Dmitriev 1980–	

* Persons who were not residents of the pre-war Baltic states, or who received German citizenship in 1939 — early 1941.

** Persons with no ethnic or pre-war ties to the Baltic area.

TABLES

TABLE 1

POPULATION AND ETHNICITY OF THE BALTIC REPUBLICS, 1939–1980

Year (1 January)	Total Population (in Millions)			Percentage Belonging to the Republic Nationality		
	Estonia	Latvia	Lithuania	Estonia	Latvia	Lithuania
1939, pre-war borders	1.134[a]	2.00[b]	2.575[c]	88.2%[a]	75.5%[b]	80.6%[c]
1939, postwar borders	1.052[d]	1.93[d]	3.1[d]	92	77	76(?)
1945	0.854[e]	1.4[f]	2.4[f]	94(?)	83(?)	80(?)

Source: Data from Rein Taagepera, "Baltic Population Changes, 1950–1980," JBS, XII/1 (Spring 1981), pp. 35–57, except as indicated below.

a. *Eesti entsüklopeedia,* supplementary volume (Tartu, 1940), pp. 232–234.

b. Jānis Rutkis (ed.), *Latvia: Country and People* (Stockholm, 1967), pp. 293 and 302.

c. V. Stanley Vardys (ed.), *Lithuania Under the Soviets, 1940–1965* (New York, 1965), p. 22.

d. Rein Taagepera, "Population Crisis and the Baltics," JBS, XII/3 (Fall 1981), pp. 234–244.

e. Estimate in *Eesti NSV ajalugu* (Tallinn, 1971), III, p. 601.

f. Estimate based on considerations shown in Table 2.

TABLE 1—continued

Year (1 January)	Total Population (in Millions)			Percentage Belonging to the Republic Nationality		
	Estonia	Latvia	Lithuania	Estonia	Latvia	Lithuania
1950	1.097	1.944	2.57	76(?)	63(?)	75(?)
1955	1.157	2.010	2.61	74(?)	62(?)	75(?)
1960	1.209	2.113	2.756	74.1	61.7	79.4
1965	1.285	2.254	2.954	70.9	58.8	79.8
1970	1.356	2.364	3.128	68.2	56.8	80.1
1975	1.427	2.465	3.295	65.7	54.5	79.9
1980	1.474	2.529	3.420	64.5	53.5	80.1

TABLE 2

POPULATION CHANGES, 1939–1945[a]
EDUCATED GUESSES (in thousands)

	Estonia	Latvia	Lithuania[b]
Population in mid-October 1939	1,130	2,000	2,950[b]
Emigration and territorial changes, November 1939 — May 1941[c]	−20	−70	+50
Soviet deportations and executions, 1940–41[d]	−15	−35	−35
Soviet army mobilization, 1941 and 1944–45[e]	−35	−20	−60
Evacuation to USSR, 1941[f]	−30	−40	−20

a. The figures presented are often very approximate "guesstimates," and should not be requoted without inclusion of this warning. Presenting these guesstimates in this book serves two purposes: to give the reader *some* idea of the type and order of magnitude of the changes, and to induce scholarly readers (East and West) to come up with better-documented figures.

b. After loss of Klaipėda (150,000) and gain of Vilnius (500,000).

c. Emigration mostly to Germany (October-November 1939 and January-March 1941). Additional territory near Vilnius (August 1940): about 100,000.

d. Including executions by local henchmen.

e. Including the Baltic units existing in early 1941; excluding the Destruction Battalions. Excluding those who surrendered to the Germans and were released, or returned home otherwise, by 1942.

f. Voluntary evacuees (including Jews fleeing the Nazi terror, and the Destruction Battalions), and involuntary ones not fitting the deportation or mobilization categories (e.g., railway workers).

TABLE 2—*continued*

	Estonia	Latvia	Lithuania
Nazi executions and deportations, 1941–45[d,g]	–10	–90	–200
German army mobilization, 1941–45[h]	–70	–150	–50
German labor mobilization, 1941–44[i]	–15	–35	–75
Evacuation and flight to the West, 1942–45[j]	–60	–100	–50
Return from Germany and German army, 1944–45	+60	+80	+50
Soviet executions and deportations, 1944–45[k]	–30	–70	–50
Return from USSR and Soviet army, 1944–45[k]	+20	+20	+50
Territorial changes, 1945[l]	–70	–50	+25
Emigration to Poland, 1945	0	0	–150
Birth deficit	–15	–30	–35
Population in late 1945 (estimate)[m]	850	1,400	2,400
Percentage of loss since 1939	25%	30%	15%

g. Includes about 250,000 Jews (Lithuania, 180,000; Latvia, 70,000; Estonia, 1,000).

h. Includes those stationed in their homelands, and in military Labor Battalions.

i. Includes only those sent to Germany (and other parts of Central Europe).

j. Voluntary and semi-voluntary. Excludes deportees and mobilized labor and military.

k. Highly speculative figures. Soviet demobilization largely came only later.

l. Klaipėda regained; about 25,000 people remaining. Abrene, Petseri, and trans-Narva areas transferred to RSFSR in January 1945.

m. Includes non-registered local population (guerrillas, etc.); excludes imported forced labor and POWs.

TABLE 3

WAR AND OCCUPATION DEATHS, 1940–1945[a]
EDUCATED GUESSES (in thousands)

	Estonia	Latvia	Lithuania
Soviet executions, 1940–41	2	1.5	1.1
Soviet deportee deaths, 1940–43	15	20	20
Soviet evacuee deaths, 1941–43	10	10	5
Soviet army and labor battalion deaths	25	5	20
Nazi executions, 1941–45	5	65	140
German deportee deaths, 1942–45	5	10	50
German and Finnish army deaths	15	40	10
Deaths among civilians moving West	5	10	5
Bombing and other war deaths	5	10	15
Soviet executions, deportee deaths, and guerrilla war losses, 1944–45	5	10	15
Totals	90	180	280
Percentage of the 1939 population	8%	9%	9%

a. Very approximate "guesstimates" — not to be quoted without this qualification. See Table 2, note a.

TABLE 4

LITHUANIAN GUERRILLAS, 1944–1952: ARMED FORCES INVOLVED
(in thousands)

	Guerrillas	Repression Troops
Mid-1944	10[a]	
Spring 1945	30	
Spring 1946	30 to 40	
January 1947		50
February 1947		110
Mid-1947	25	50
1948	30	100
Early 1950	5[b]	20[c]
Early 1951		20[c]
Early 1952	0.7[b]	

Sources: Thomas Remeikis, "The Armed Struggle Against the Sovietization of Lithuania After 1944," *Lituanus,* VIII/1–2 (1962), pp. 29–40, except as indicated below:

a. Zenonas Ivinskis, "Lithuania During the War," in Vardys (ed.), *Lithuania Under the Soviets,* p. 84.

b. Stasys Žymantas, "Twenty Years of Resistance," *Lituanus,* VI/2 (September 1960), pp. 40–45.

c. Inferred from Burlitski, in *Fourth Interim Report of the Select Committee on Communist Aggression* (U.S. Congress, 1954).

TABLE 4—*continued*

	Guerrillas	Repression Troops
Battle losses suffered:		
Soviet estimates	20[d]	20[e]
Guerrilla estimates	25 to 50[bf]	80
Civilians killed by	4[f] to 13[g]	24[b]
Civilians deported by	0	320

[d]. George Weller, *Chicago Daily News*, 17 August 1961.

[e]. Vardys (ed.), *Lithuania Under the Soviets*, pp. 85–108.

[f]. K. V. Tauras, *Guerrilla Warfare on the Amber Coast* (1962), p. 52.

[g]. Usual Soviet estimate, according to Benedict Mačiuika, personal communication.

TABLE 5

POPULATION CHANGES, 1945–1955[a]
(in thousands)

	Estonia	Latvia	Lithuania
Population, end 1945: total	850	1,400	2,400
republic nationality	800	1,200	1,900
Deportations and arrests, 1946–53	−80	−100	−260
Guerrilla war deaths[b]	−15	−25	−50
Birth excess over natural deaths: republic nationality	+50	+60	+300
others	+20	+40	+50
Immigration: republic nationality	+100	+100	+40
Russians and others	+230	+535	+160
Population, early 1955: total	1,157	2,010	2,613
republic nationality	865	1,250	1,980

a. Includes some very approximate "guesstimates" — not to be quoted without this qualification. See Table 2, note a.

b. Includes guerrilla and native repression troop losses, and executions by both sides.

TABLE 5—continued

	Estonia	Latvia	Lithuania
Losses in home-grown population:			
1945–55[c]	–90	–125	–310
1939–45[d]	–280	–600	–700[e]
Total, 1939–55	–370	–720	–1,000[e]
1939–55 change as percentage of 1939 population	–33%	–36%	–32%[e]
Immigration as percentage of 1939 population	29%	31%	6%[e]

[c]. Home-grown population losses = (1955 pop.) – (1945 pop.) – (immigration) – (birth excess over natural deaths)

[d]. From Table 2.

[e]. Based on 1939 population of the Republic of Lithuania and the Vilnius region.

TABLE 6

COMMUNIST PARTY SIZE AND ETHNICITY, 1930–1980
(Size in thousands of members and candidates)

Year (1 January)	Estonian CP[a]		Latvian CP[b]		Lithuanian CP[c]	
	Size	%Est.	Size	%Latv.	Size	%Lith.
1930	0.3[d]		1.0[e]		.65[f]	
1934	0.387[d]		1.15[e]		1.10[f]	
1936	—		—		1.942[f]	
1937	—		—		1.499[f]	
1938	0.11[g]		—		—	
1939	—		0.4[e]		—	

a. Source, unless otherwise indicated: Aleksander Panksejev, "EKP tegevusest partei ridade kasvu reguleerimisel, aastad 1944-1965," Töid EKP ajaloo alalt, vol. II (1966), pp. 149–204.

b. Source, unless otherwise indicated: I. M. Muzykantik (ed.), Kommunistitsheskaia partiia Latvii v tsifrakh, 1904–1971 (Riga, 1972), pp. 6-174.

c. Source, unless otherwise indicated: Thomas Remeikis, "Berücksichtigung . . . ," AB, X (1970), pp. 132–138.

d. G. Naan (ed.) Nõukogude Eesti: entsüklopeediline teatmeteos (Tallinn, 1975), pp. 85, 86, 92; the 1934 figure is for August.

e. Seppo Myllyniemi, Die baltische Krise, 1938–1941 (Stuttgart, 1979), p. 84.

f. Leonas Sabaliūnas, Lithuania in Crisis (1972), p. 54.

g. "On 21 June 1940, there were in Estonia 133 ECP members, 3 of them in prison." About 22 had joined since Spring 1938. Olaf Kuuli, Revolutsioon Eestis, 1940 (Tallinn, 1980), pp. 47–50.

TABLE 6—continued

Year	Estonian CP[a]		Latvian CP[b]		Lithuanian CP[c]	
(1 January)	Size	%Est.	Size	% Latv.	Size	% Lith.
1 June 1940	0.133[g]	88%[g]	0.967		1.741[i]	
1941	2.036		2.798		3.138	53.3%
21 June 1941	3.75[j]	65[k]	3.13		4.62	
1945	2.41[l]		5.0		3.54[l]	31.8
1946	7.14	48.1[m]	10.99		8.06	
1947	12.97		21.04		16.2	
1948	16.4		28.7		22.2	
1949	16.9		31.2	53%[h]	24.5	
1950	17.6		34.2		27.8	
1951	18.9		37.3		29.9	
1952	21.2	41.5[m]	40.3		34.7	

h. Gundar King, *Economic Policies in Occupied Latvia* (1965), pp. 180–183.

i. Thomas Remeikis, "The Administration of Power," in Vardys (ed.), *Lithuania Under the Soviets*, p. 118.

j. Johannes Jakobson et al., *Ülevaade EKP ajaloost* (1972), III, p. 94.

k. Rein Taagepera, unpublished calculations.

l. Without Red Army units.

m. Jaan Pennar, "Soviet Nationality Policy and the Estonian Communist Elite," in Tõnu Parming and Elmar Järvesoo (eds.), *A Case Study of a Soviet Republic* (1978), p. 118.

TABLE 6—continued

Year (1 January)	Estonian CP[a]		Latvian CP[b]		Lithuanian CP[c]	
	Size	%Est.	Size	% Latv.	Size	% Lith.
September 1952	—		42.0[c]		37.1	
1953	22.3		42.2		36.2	38.0
1954	21.2		42.7		34.5	
1955	21.5	43.6	45.1		35.5	
1956	22.5	44.6	48.5		38.1	
1957	25.7	44.8	53.9		42.2	
1958	27.7	45.6	57.3		44.8	
1959	30.5	47.5	61.4	35[h]	49.1	55.7
1960	33.4	48.6	65.9	32[h]	54.3	
1961	37.8	49.1	72.5		60.6	
1962	42.5	49.4	78.2		66.2	
1963	45.7	50.5	82.0		71.1	
1964	49.8	51.1	88.2		77.5	

n. Thomas Remeikis, "Modernization and National Identity in the Baltic Republics," in Ihor Kamenetsky (ed.), *Nationalism and Human Rights* (1977), p. 128.

TABLE 6—continued

Year	Estonian CP[a]		Latvian CP[b]		Lithuanian CP[c]	
(1 January)	Size	%Est.	Size	%Latv.	Size	%Lith.
1965	54.8	51.9	95.7	39(?)[p]	86.4	61.5
1970	70.2[m]	52.3[m]	122.4		116.6	67.1[n]
1975	81.5[d]		140.0[o]		140.2[q]	68.5[q]
1980	95.4[o]		158.0[o]		165.8[o]	

[o.] *Ezhegodnik Bolshoi Sovetskoi Entsiklopedii* (1976 and 1980).

[p.] The Latvian share of the LaCP would be 46.3%, if all ethnically Latvian CPSU members resided in the LaSSR (Remeikis 1970, p. 137). However, 16% of Estonian and 14% of Lithuanian CP members resided outside their own republic. Applying a 15% correction to the LaCP figure yields an estimate of 39%.

[q.] *Lietuvos Komunistų Partija skaičiais, 1918–1975: statistikes duomenų rinkinys* (Vilnius, 1976), p. 123.

TABLE 7

INDUSTRIAL EMPLOYMENT AND INDEX OF PRODUCTION, 1940-1980

Year	Employment (in thousands of workers)			Production (last 5 mos. of 1940 = 1.00)			Production (full year 1940 = 1.00)[e]		
	Est.[a]	Lat.[b]	Lith.[c]	Est.[b]	Lat.[b]	Lith.[c]	Est.	Lat.	Lith.
1940	73	114[f]	57	(2.4)	(2.4)	(2.4)	1.00	1.00	1.00
1945	52	71[h]	42[g]	0.73	0.47[j]	0.40[g]	0.30	0.20	0.17
1950	99	171[f]	97	3.42	3.03	1.91	1.42	1.26	0.79
1955	127	218[d]	153	6.7	5.85[d]	4.9[g]	2.8	2.4	2.1
1960	161	280	212	11.5	11.0	10.3	4.8	4.6	4.3

a. *25 aastat Nõukogude Eestit* (1965), pp. 23, 28.

b. *Narodnoe khoziaistvo LaSSR*, 1977, pp. 65 and 76; *Nar. khoz. ESSR*, 1975, p. 224; and calculations based on *ibid.*, 1978, pp. 66 and 72.

c. *Ekonomika ir kultūra* [LiSSR], 1975, pp. 56 and 78.

d. King 1965, pp. 69, 107, 124.

e. 5/12 of the 5-month values. Soviet data in the previous column seem to take as baseline the 1940 production of *Soviet* Baltic republics, which only existed for 5 months of 1940. The proper 12-month comparison base is restored in the last column of the table.

f. *Padomju Latvijas tautas saimniecība* (Riga, 1968), p. 72.

g. Pranas Zundė, in Vardys (ed.), *Lithuania Under the Soviets*, pp. 158, 164.

TABLE 7—continued

Year	Employment (in thousands of workers)			Production (last 5 mos. of 1940 = 1.00)			Production (full year 1940 = 1.00)[e]		
	Est.[a]	Lat.[b]	Lith.[c]	Est.[b]	Lat.[b]	Lith.[c]	Est.	Lat.	Lith.
1965	207[b]	350	313	18.4	17.4	17.9	7.7	7.2	7.5
1970	226[b]	400	414	27.8	27.3	31.2	11.6	11.4	13.0
1975	234[b]	410	458	39.1	37.1	46.4	16.3	15.5	19.3
1980	240[i]	—	—	48.3[i]	45[i]	58[i]	20.1[i]	19[i]	24[i]

h. Based on the 1950 figure and the 1950/1945 ratio of 2.48, as given in A. Šumiņš, *Apcerējums par Padomju Latvijas ekonomisko attīstību, 1940–1958* (Riga, 1960), p. 46.

i. Calculations based on *Nar. khoz. ESSR*, 1980, pp. 79, 80, 86.

j. Šumiņš, p. 45.

TABLE 8

AGRICULTURAL PRODUCTION AND EFFICIENCY, 1940–1978

Year	Production Index (1940 = 1.00)			Cereal Yield (in metric tons per hectare)		
	Estonia	Latvia	Lithuania	Estonia	Latvia	Lithuania
1940	1.00	1.00	1.00	1.15	1.21	0.94[g]
1945	0.6	0.5[i]	—	0.89[a]	0.87[i]	0.88[g]
1950	0.88[a]	0.77	0.85	1.15[a]	0.91[d]	0.79
1955	0.8[b]	0.62[h]	0.70	0.65[a]	0.75[e]	0.5[f]
1960	1.20	1.06	1.30	1.33	1.01[d]	0.93
1965	1.32	1.15	1.51	2.20	1.52	1.62
1970	1.49	1.35	1.89	2.13	2.31	2.45
1975	1.69	1.35	2.08	2.67	1.93	2.00
1978	1.69[c]	1.38[c]	2.21[c]	2.00[c]	1.51[c]	2.50[c]

Sources: Unless otherwise indicated, obtained or calculated from *Nar. khoz. ESSR,* 1977, pp. 20, 95, and 105, and 1978, pp. 105 and 116; *Nar. khoz. LaSSR,* 1977, pp. 115 and 126; and *Ekonomika ir kultūra* [LiSSR] 1975, pp. 100 and 121, and 1977, p. 98.

a. *25 aastat,* pp. 23 and 51.

b. Estimate based on *Nar. khoz. ESSR,* 1977, p. 95.

c. Based on *Nar. khoz. SSSR,* 1978, pp. 197 and 221.

d. *Bolshaia Sovetskaia entsiklopediia* (1975), vol. 19, articles on LaSSR and LiSSR.

e. Andrivs Namsons, "Die Sowjetisierung . . ." (1962), p. 75.

f. Pranas Zundė, "Die Kollektivierung . . ." (1962), p. 105.

g. Benedict Mačiuika, private communication.

h. *Padomju Latvijas tautas saimniecība,* p. 175.

i. Calculations and estimates based on Šuminš, pp. 18 and 143.

TABLE 9

RURAL ADMINISTRATIVE UNITS, 1939–1980

	Estonia	Latvia	Lithuania
1939–41[a] districts	11 maakond	19 apriņķi	23 apskritys
townships	233 vald	516 pagasti	261 valčius
1942–44 Kreisgebiete[b]	6	5	4
1945–49[c]	11 to 13 maakond	19–25 apriņķi	26–37 apskritys
	233 vald	510 pagasti	320 valčius
	637 külanõukogu	1,306–1,362 ciemu padomes	3,032–2,774 apylinkes
Date of introduction of Soviet units[c]	26 September 1950	1 January 1950[d]	20 June 1950
1950 raions/village councils	39/626	58/1,229–1,358	87/2772
Spring 1952–April 1953, oblasts	3	3	4[e]

Sources: Main source for 1939–60: Gottlieb Ney, "Administrative Gliederung . . . ," AB, II (1962), pp. 9–34. For 1960–77: *Nar. khoz. ESSR*, 1977, p. 10; *Nar. khoz. LaSSR*, 1968, p. 22, and 1977, p. 22; *Ekonomika ir kultūra* [LiSSR], 1975, p. 9; and 25 *aastat*, p. 19.

a. Because of territorial changes, the numbers are approximate. Prior to the 1939 consolidation, Estonia had 365 *vald*.

b. Superimposed on previous units. Myllyniemi, *Die Neuordnung . . .* (1973), p. 88.

c. *Eesti NSV ajalugu*, III, p. 594; *Lietuvos TSR istorija*, IV, pp. 146 and 151–152; Rutkis, pp. 165–167; Ney, "Administrative Gliederung . . . ," p. 16.

d. Rutkis, p. 167; George Carson (ed.), *Latvia: An Area Study* (1956), p. 4; Ney's date of 31 December 1948 seems questionable.

TABLE 9—*continued*

	Estonia	Latvia	Lithuania
Raions/village councils			
1960	24/319	32/643	44/1,160
1965	15/239	21/564	44/623[f]
1970	15/235	26/539	44/650
Late 1970s	15/194	26/481	44/600

e. In Lithuania, oblasts were introduced as early as 20 June 1950.

f. P. Adlys and A. Stanaitis, *Soviet Lithuania: Population* (Vilnius, 1979), p. 11.

TABLE 10

URBANIZATION AND LIVING SPACE, 1940–1980

Beginning of Year	Percentage of Population Living in Cities and Towns				Per-Capita Urban Living Space (in square meters)		
	Estonia	Latvia	Lithuania	USSR	Estonia	Latvia	Lithuania
1940	33.6%	35.2%[b]	24.0%	32.5%	15.5	17.8	—
1945	31.3	—	16.0	—	12.0[d]	—	—
1950	47.1	45.3	28.3	38.9	9.3[e]	12[h]	8.6[c]
1955	54.8	52	34.6	44.4	8.8[c,e]	—	—
1960	57.1	54[a]	39.3	48.8	11.4	12.2[c]	9.4[c]
1965	62.1	59[a]	43.9	52.6	12.4[e]	12.6[c]	10.3[c]
1970	65.0	62.5	50.2	56.3	13.6[c]	13.4[c]	11.3[c]

Sources: Urbanization data from Taagepera, "Baltic Population Changes." Living space data from Nar. khoz. ESSR, 1977, pp. 237 and 12; Nar. khoz. LaSSR, 1968, p. 399, and 1977, pp. 250 and 6; Ekonomika ir kultūra [LiSSR], 1975, p. 247, and 1977, p. 217.

a. Interpolations or extrapolations.

b. 1939 figure.

c. Figure for end of the year.

d. Calculated, using data in Eesti NSV ajalugu, III, pp. 596 and 601.

e. Calculated, using data in Nõukogude Eesti saavutusi . . . (Tallinn, 1960), p. 85, and 25 aastat, p. 105.

TABLE 10—*continued*

Beginning of Year	Percentage of Population Living in Cities and Towns				Per-Capita Urban Living Space *(in square meters)*		
	Estonia	Latvia	Lithuania	USSR	Estonia	Latvia	Lithuania
1975	67.7	65.5	56.2	60.0	14.8[c]	14.3[c]	12.3
1980	70.1[a]	69.0[a]	62[a]	62.8	16.6[f]	15.3[g]	13.2[g]

[f]. *Rahva Hääl*, 20 November 1980.

[g]. 1979 figure, based on *Nar. khoz. SSSR*, 1978, pp. 398 and 17.

[h]. Figure for 1952, based on 11.7 million sq. m total urban living space.

TABLE 11

SIZE, RELATIVE WEIGHT, AND ETHNICITY OF CAPITAL CITIES, 1940–1979

Beginning of Year	Population of Capital City (in thousands)[a]			Capital Population as Percentage of Republic Population[j]			Republic Nationality as Percentage of Capital Population[l]		
	Tallinn	Riga	Vilnius	Estonia	Latvia	Lithuania	Tallinn	Riga	Vilnius
1940	176[b]	348[e]	209[g]	16%	17%	7%	85.6%[k]	63.0%[n]	20%[o]
1945	134	—	110[g]	16	—	4	—	—	—
1950	212	497[f]	176[h]	19.3	25.6	6.9	—	—	—

a. *Eesti nõukogude entsüklopeedia* [*ENE*], vol. VII (1975), p. 450; *Nar. khoz. LaSSR*, 1977, p. 8; *Ekonomika ir kultūra* [LiSSR], 1975, p. 12, unless otherwise shown.

b. 1941 figure from *Nar. khoz. ESSR*, 1977, p. 13. The value of 136,000 for 1940 given in *ENE* applies to restricted city territory, and reflects the recent departure of the Germans.

c. 1959 figure.

d. *USSR in Figures, 1979*, pp. 13–14.

e. 1939 figure, possibly after departure of the Germans. Rutkis, p. 182, gives 385,000 for 1935, of whom 38,500 were Germans.

f. 1951 figure.

g. *Socialistinės visuomenes susiformavimas ir raida Tarybu Lietuvoje, 1940–1980* (Vilnius, 1980), p. 56.

h. Adlys and Stanaitis, p. 25.

TABLE 11—continued

Beginning of Year	Population of Capital City (in thousands)[a]			Capital Population as Percentage of Republic Population[j]			Republic Nationality as Percentage of Capital Population[l]		
	Tallinn	Riga	Vilnius	Estonia	Latvia	Lithuania	Tallinn	Riga	Vilnius
1955	261	567[p]	223[h,r]	22.6	28.2	8.4	—	—	—
1960	288	580[c]	236[c]	23.8	28.0	8.7	60.2[c]	44.7[c]	33.6[c]
1965	329	678[i]	296[h]	25.6	29.7	10.0	—	—	—
1970	363·	732	372	26.8	31.0	11.9	55.7	40.9	42.8
1975	399	796	433	27.9	32.1	13.2	—	—	—
1979	436	843[d]	492[d]	29.6	33.3	14.4	51.3[m]	—	47.3[q]

i. 1966 figure.

j. From city population and the republic population in Table 1.

k. Raimo Pullat, *Linnad kodanlikus Eestis* (Tallinn, 1978), p. 137.

l. Unless otherwise indicated, *Itogi Vsesoiuznoi perepisi naseleniia 1970 goda*, vol. IV (Moscow, 1973), pp. 275, 283, and 320.

m. *Õhtuleht* (Tallinn), 27 February 1980.

n. 1935 census. Carson, p. 168; Rutkis, p. 182.

o. Educated guess, based on considerations in Sabaliūnas, pp. 277–278.

p. Rutkis, p. 182.

q. Algirdas Motulas, *Vilniaus dabartis ir nytdiena* (Vilnius, 1980), p. 32.

r. 1956 figure.

TABLE 12

MARRIAGE AND DIVORCE RATES, 1940–1978
(Per year and per 1000 population)

Year	Marriages				Divorces			
	Estonia	Latvia	Lithuania	USSR	Estonia	Latvia	Lithuania	USSR
1940	9.6	10.8	9.7	6.3	1.1	1.1	0.0	1.1
1945	—	—	—	—	—	—	—	—
1950	9.5	9.9	9.1	11.6	0.6	0.8	0.2	0.4
1955	10.3	10.6	9.7	11.5	1.2	1.1	0.4	0.6
1960	10.0	11.0	10.1	12.1	2.1	2.4	0.9	1.3
1965	8.2	8.8	8.4	8.7	2.3	2.8	0.9	1.6
1970	9.1	10.1	9.5	9.7	3.2	4.6	2.2	2.6
1975	8.7	9.9	9.0	10.7	3.4	4.7	2.7	3.1
1978	8.5	10.1	9.1	10.7	3.8	5.0	3.0	3.5

Sources: Nar. khoz. ESSR, 1969, p. 23, 1977, p. 13, and 1978, p. 21; Nar. khoz. LaSSR, 1977, p. 19, and 1979, p. 9; Nar. khoz. SSSR, 1978, p. 28; Ekonomika i kultūra LaSSR, 1966, p. 20; Ekonomika ir kultūra [LiSSR], 1975, p. 17, and 1978, p. 17.

TABLE 13

BIRTH AND DEATH RATES, 1940–1980
(Per year and per 1000 population)

| Year | Birth Rate | | | | Death Rate | | | |
	Estonia	Latvia	Lithuania	USSR	Estonia	Latvia	Lithuania	USSR
1940	16.1	19.3	23.0	31.2	17.0	15.7	13.0	18.0
1945	15.9[a]	—	—	—	19.4[a]	—	—	—
1950	18.4	17.0	23.6	26.7	14.4	12.4	12.0	9.7
1955	17.9	16.4	21.1	25.7	11.7	10.6	9.2	8.2
1960	16.6	16.7	22.5	24.9	10.5	10.0	7.8	7.1
1965	14.6	13.8	18.1	18.4	10.5	10.0	7.9	7.3
1970	15.8	14.5	17.6	17.4	11.1	11.2	8.9	8.2
1975	14.9	14.1	15.7	18.1	11.6	12.1	9.5	9.3
1980[b]	15.0	14.0	15.1	18.3	12.3	12.7	10.5	10.3

Source: Condensed from year-to-year data in Taagepera, "Baltic Population Changes."

a. For 1943.

b. Nar. khoz. ESSR, 1980, p. 28.

TABLE 14

POPULATION INCREASE, 1950–1979
(in thousands)

Average for	Estonia		Latvia		Lithuania	
	Natural	*Immigration*	*Natural*	*Immigration*	*Natural*	*Immigration*
1950–54	5.6	6.6	9.3	3.9	28.3	–20.6
1955–59	6.8	3.6	12.7	7.9	34.5	– 6.0
1960–64	6.8	8.3	12.5	15.6	36.8	2.8
1965–69	5.3	9.0	7.8	14.2	29.1	5.8
1970–74	6.3	8.0	7.4	12.8	25.4	7.9
1975–79	4.4	4.9	3.7	9.1	18.8	6.2

Source: Calculated from year-to-year tabulation in Taagepera, "Baltic Population Changes." The 1975–79 figures involve estimates for 1979.

TABLE 15

THE SHARE OF PRIVATE PLOTS IN LATVIA'S AGRICULTURAL PRODUCTION, 1950–1977

	1950	1960	1965	1970	1975	1977
Total cultivated land	—	5%[a]	—	4.6%[b]	—	5.0%[d]
Total agricultural production	—	—	—	32.5[c]	—	29[d]
Grain	—	—	2%	1	2%	2
Potatoes	64%	63	60	60	61	54
Vegetables	84	66	64	58	48	32
Meat	73	49	47	35	28	24
Milk	60	49	43	39	34	31
Eggs	93	71	51	34	28	23

Sources: Main source for 1950–60: Andres Küng, Vad händer i Baltikum? (Stockholm, 1973), p. 125, based on Nar. khoz. LaSSR, 1971. For 1965–77: Nar. khoz. LaSSR, 1977, pp. 117 and 119.

a. Rutkis, p. 357.

b. Küng 1973, p. 125.

c. For 1972, from A. Cīce, in Padomju Latvijas komunists, November 1975, p. 69.

d. For 1978, Cīņa, 23 November 1979.

Analogous data available on Estonia and Lithuania are limited, but the general pattern seems to be the same. See Elmar Järvesoo, "Private Enterprise in Soviet Estonian Agriculture," JBS, V/3 (Fall 1974), pp. 169–187.

TABLE 16

AVERAGE YEARLY GROWTH RATES OF PRODUCED INCOME AND INDUSTRIAL PRODUCTION, 1950–1980

	Produced National Income				Industrial Production			
	Est.	Lat.	Lith.	USSR	Est.	Lat.	Lith.	USSR
1950–55	—	10.0%	—	11.2%	14.4%	14.1%[e]	20.9%	13.1%
1955–60	—	—	—	9.1	11.4	13.5[e]	15.9	10.4
1960–65	7.4%	7.2	8.7%	6.5	9.9	9.6	11.7	8.6
1965–70	7.6	7.7	9.4	7.7	8.6	9.4	11.7	8.4
1970–75	5.5	5.8	5.7	5.7	7.1	6.4	8.3	7.4
1975–80	4.2[a]	3.8[d]	—	4.4[b]	4.4[a]	3.6[b]	5.1[b]	4.7[b]
1980–85[c]	2.8[a]	—	—	—	2.9	3.1	4.1	4.9

Sources: Produced national income (*proizvedennyi natsionyi dokhod*) and total industrial production calculated from *Nar. khoz. ESSR,* 1977, pp. 24–28 and 55; *Nar. khoz. LaSSR,* 1977, p. 26; *Ekonomika ir kultūra* [LiSSR], 1975, pp. 23–27; *Mažoji lietuviškoji tarybinė enciklopedija,* II, p. 899; *USSR in Figures,* 1979, pp. 28–37 and 106; Harry G. Shaffer, "Soviet Economic Performance in Historical Perspective," in Samuel Hendel (ed.), *The Soviet Crucible* (North Scituate, Mass., 1980), pp. 293–304.

a. *Rahva Hääl,* 20 November 1980 and 26 February 1982.
b. For 1975–79.
c. Average goals of the 1981–85 five-year plan, *Rahva Hääl,* 2 December 1980.
d. For 1975–78.
e. Calculated from Table 7.

BIBLIOGRAPHY

This is not intended to be a comprehensive listing of all relevant work. Rather, it includes those sources which we have found particularly useful in our work, and a fairly extensive sampling of what is available in English and German.

Abbreviations:
AB — *Acta Baltica*
BA — *Books Abroad*
JBS — *Journal of Baltic Studies*

Documents and Statistical Collections

The Chronicle of the Catholic Church in Lithuania: Underground Journal of Human Rights Violations. Vol. I, nos. 1-9 (1972-1974). Chicago, 1981. Subsequent issues not yet published in book form are available in English translation through the Lithuanian Roman Catholic Priests' League of America, Brooklyn, N.Y. The original title is better rendered as "The Chronicle of the Lithuanian Catholic Church."

Documents from Estonia on the Violations of Human Rights. Stockholm, 1977.

Ekonomika i kultura Litovskoi SSR. Vilnius, annual since 1957. (Russian edition of *Lietuvos TSR ekonomika ir kultūra.*)

Fourth Interim Report of the Select Committee on Communist Aggression. 83rd Congress, 2nd Session. Washington, 1954.

Itogi Vsesoiuznoi perepisi naseleniia 1970 goda, vol. IV. Moscow, 1973.

Kancevičius, Vytautas (ed.). *Lithuania in 1939-1940: The Historic Turn to Socialism.* Vilnius, 1976.

Kollektivizatsiia krestianskikh khoziaistv Litovskoi SSR: sbornik dokumentov i materialov. Vilnius, 1977.

Latviia za gody sovetskoi vlasti: statisticheskii sbornik. Riga, 1967.

Lietuvos Katalikų Bažnyčios kronika. 5 volumes, containing issues 1-39. Chicago, 1974-1979. (See *The Chronicle of the Catholic Church in Lithuania.*)

Lietuvos Komunistų Partija skaičiais, 1918–1975: statistikos duomenų rinkinys. Vilnius, 1976.

Lietuvos TSR ekonomika ir kultūra. Vilnius, annual since 1957. (Lithuanian edition of *Ekonomika i kultura Litovskoi SSR.*)

Lithuania in Figures. Vilnius, 1966.

Narodnoe khoziaistvo Estonskoi SSR. Tallinn, annual since 1957. (Bilingual, Estonian and Russian; separate issues for some years.)

Narodnoe khoziaistvo Latviiskoi SSR. Riga, annual since 1957. (Bilingual, Latvian and Russian; separate issues for some years.)

Naselenie SSSR po dannym vsesoiuznoi perepiski naseleniia 1979 goda. Moscow, 1980.

Nõukogude Eesti saavutusi 20 aasta jooksul: statistiline kogumik. Tallinn, 1960.

Paul, I. (ed.). *Eesti rahvas Nõukogude Liidu Suures Isamaasõjas, 1941–1945: Dokumente ja materjale.* Tallinn, 1975.

Present-day Lithuania in Figures. Vilnius, 1971.

Sontag, Raymond James, and James Stuart Beddie (eds.). *Nazi-Soviet Relations, 1939–1941.* Washington, 1948.

Tarybų Lietuvos dvidešimtmetis: statistinių duomenų rinkinys. Vilnius, 1960.

Tarybų valdžios atkūrimas Lietuvoje, 1940–41 metais: dokumentų rinkinys. Vilnius, 1965.

Third Interim Report of the Select Committee on Communist Aggression. 83rd Congress, 2nd Session. Washington, 1954. Reprinted as *The Baltic States: A Study of Their Origin and National Development; Their Seizure and Incorporation into the USSR.* International Military Law and History Reprint Series, vol. IV. Buffalo, N.Y., 1972.

Tõnurist, Edgar (ed.). *Eesti NSV põllumajanduse kollektiviseerimine: Dokumentide ja materjalide kogumik.* Tallinn, 1978.

25 aastat Nõukogude Eestit: statistiline kogumik. Tallinn, 1965.

25 let sovetskoi Litvy: statisticheskii sbornik. Vilnius, 1965.

1940. aasta sotsialistlik revolutsioon Eestis: Dokumente ja materjale. Tallinn, 1960.

Journals and Newspapers

Cīņa	Organ of the Latvian CP (daily)
Eesti Kommunist/Kommunist Estonii	Journal of the Estonian CP (monthly)
Karogs	Latvian cultural journal (monthly)
Komjaunimo tiesa	Organ of the Lithuanian Komsomol (daily)
Komunistas/Kommunist (Litvy)	Journal of the Lithuanian CP (monthly)
Literatūra ir menas	Lithuanian cultural paper (weekly)
Literatūra un māksla	Latvian cultural paper (weekly)
Looming	Estonian cultural journal (monthly)
Padomju jaunatne	Organ of the Latvian Komsomol (daily)
Padomju Latvijas komunists/Kommunist sovetskoi Latvii	Journal of the Latvian CP (monthly)
Pergalė	Lithuanian cultural journal (monthly)
Rahva Hääl	Organ of the Estonian CP (daily)
Sirp ja Vasar	Estonian cultural paper (weekly)
Sovetskaia Estoniia	Estonian Russian-language paper (daily)
Sovetskaia Latviia	Latvian Russian-language paper (daily)
Sovetskaia Litva	Lithuanian Russian-language paper (daily)
Tiesa	Organ of the Lithuanian CP (daily)

The press of the Baltic republics has been surveyed in Assembly of Captive European Nations, *A Survey of Developments in Nine Captive Countries*. 17 volumes. New York, 1956–1965. Three separate volumes of the survey on Lithuania are also available: Vytautas Vaitiekūnas, *A Survey of Developments in Captive Lithuania*. 3 volumes. New York, 1962–1966.

Estonian Events (1967–1972) and *Baltic Events* (1973–1975), published by Rein Taagepera (University of California, Irvine) and Juris Dreifelds (Brock University, St. Catherines, Ontario, Canada).

Books and Scholarly Articles

Aiszilnieks, Arnolds P. "Sovietization of Consumers' Cooperation in the Baltic States," JBS, V/1 (Spring 1974), pp. 40–50.

Allworth, Edward (ed.). *Nationality Group Survival in Multi-Ethnic States: Shifting Support Patterns in the Soviet Baltic Region.* New York, 1977.

Angelus, Oskar. "Die Russifizierung Estlands," AB, VII (1967), pp. 85–130.

————. "Die Jugend in Sowjetestland," AB, XVIII (1978), pp. 156–193.

Arad, Yitzhak. "The 'Final Solution' in Lithuania in the Light of German Documentation," *Yad Vashem Studies*, XI (Jerusalem, 1976), pp. 234–272.

Balodis, Agnis. *Sovjets och Nazitysklands uppgörelse om de Baltiska staterna.* Stockholm, 1978.

Bilinsky, Yaroslav. "The Soviet Education Laws of 1958–1959 and Soviet Nationality Policy," *Soviet Studies*, XIV (1962), pp. 138–157.

————, and Tönu Parming. "Helsinki Watch Committees in the Soviet Republics: Implications for Soviet Nationality Policy," *Nationality Papers*, IX/1 (Spring 1981), pp. 1–26.

Bilmanis, Alfred. *Latvia Under German Occupation.* Washington, 1943.

————. *Baltic Essays.* Washington, 1945.

————. *A History of Latvia.* Princeton, N.J., 1951.

Bokalders, Jānis. "Urbanisation und Rückgang des Lebensstandards der Landbevölkerung Sowjetlettlands," AB, IV (1964), pp. 92–127.

Borba za sovetskuiu Pribaltiku v Velikoi Otechestvennoi Voine, 1941–1945. 3 volumes. Riga, 1966.

Bourdeaux, Michael. *Land of Crosses.* Devon, UK., 1979.

Brazaitis, Juozas. "Pirmoji sovietinė okupacija (1940–1941)," *Lietuvių enciklopedija*, XV, pp. 356–370. Boston, 1968.

————. "Vokiečių okupacija (1940–1944)," *Lietuvių enciklopedija*, XV, pp. 371–380. Boston, 1968.

Buchis [Bučys], Algimantas. *Roman i sovremennost: stanovlenie i razvitie litovskogo sovetskogo romana.* Moscow, 1977.

Bulavas, Juozas. *Vokiškųjų fašistų okupacinis Lietuvos valdymas.* Vilnius, 1969.

Carson, George B. (ed.). *Latvia: An Area Study.* Human Relations Area Files, no. 41. New Haven, 1956.

Chambon, Henry de. *La tragédie des nations baltiques*. Paris, 1946.

Czollek, R. *Faschismus und okkupation*. Berlin, 1974.

Dallin, Alexander. *German Rule in Russia, 1941-1945: A Study in Occupation Policies*, esp. Chapter 10, "Ostland: Lohse and the Baltic States," pp. 182-187. London, 1957.

Daumantas, J. [Juozas Lukša]. *Partizanai už geležinės uždangos*. Chicago, 1950.

Dovydėnas, Liudas. *Mes valdysim pasaulį*. 2 volumes. Woodhaven, N.Y., 1970. English edition: *We Will Conquer the World*. New York, 1971.

Dreifelds, Juris. "Characteristics and Trends of Two Demographic Variables in the Latvian SSR," *Bulletin of Baltic Studies*, VIII (1971), pp. 10-17.

―――. "Latvian National Demands and Group Consciousness since 1959," in George W. Simmonds (ed.), *Nationalism in the USSR and Eastern Europe in the Era of Brezhnev and Kosygin*, pp. 136-156. Detroit, 1976.

―――. "Belorussia and the Baltics," in I. S. Koropeckyj and Gertrude Schroeder (eds.), *Economics of Soviet Regions*, pp. 323-385. New York, 1981.

Drizul [Drīzulis], A. A. *Borba latyshkogo naroda v gody velikoi otechestvennoi voiny, 1941-1945 gg*. Riga, 1970.

Eesti nõukogude entsüklopeedia. 8 volumes. Tallinn, 1968-1976.

Eesti NSV ajalugu, vol. III. Tallinn, 1971. (Estonian edition of *Istoriia Estonskoi SSR*.)

Eesti riik ja rahvas teises maailmasõjas, vols. I-X. Stockholm, 1954-1962. A polemical continuation under the same title, not authorized by the publishers of the original, was published in the same format in Soviet Estonia: vols. XI-XV. Tallinn, 1964-1972.

Efremenko, A. P. *Agrarnye preobrazovaniia i nachalo sotsialisticheskogo stroitelstva v litovskoi derevne v 1940-1941 godakh*. Vilnius, 1972.

Ekmanis, Rolfs. "Sowjetlettische Schriftsteller in der Sowjetunion und ihre literarische Tätigkeit seit 1940," AB, VII (1967), pp. 171-262.

―――. "Die kulturellen Probleme in Lettland Ende der sechziger Jahre," AB, IX (1969), pp. 229-314.

———. "Soviet Attitudes toward Pre-Soviet Latvian Writers," JBS, III/1 (Spring 1972), pp. 44–70.

———. *Latvian Literature Under the Soviets, 1940–1975.* Belmont, Mass., 1978.

Forgus, Silvia P. "Manifestations of Nationalism in the Baltic Republics," *Nationalities Papers*, VII/2 (Fall 1979), pp. 197–211.

Ginsburgs, George. "Nationality and State Succession in Soviet Theory and Practice — The Experience of the Baltic Republics," in A. Sprudzs and A. Rusis (eds.), *Res Baltica*, pp. 160–190. Leyden, 1968.

———. "Soviet Views on the Law of State Succession with Regard to Treaties and Acquired Rights — The Case of the Baltic Republics," in A. Sprudzs and A. Rusis (eds.), *Res Baltica*, pp. 191–229. Leyden, 1968.

Gitlerovskaia okkupatsiia v Litve: sbornik statei. Vilnius, 1966.

Glemža, Jonas. "Die Landwirtschaft Sowjetlitauens, 1960–1973," AB, XV (1975), pp. 211–279.

Gregorauskas, M. *Tarybų Lietuvos žemės ūkis, 1940–1960.* Vilnius, 1960.

Grinius, Jonas. "Literature and the Arts in Captive Lithuania," in V. S. Vardys (ed.), *Lithuania Under the Soviets, 1940–1965.* New York, 1965.

Gureckas, Algimantas P. "The National Resistance During the German Occupation of Lithuania," *Lituanus*, VIII/1–2 (1962), pp. 23–28.

Hanchett, Walter S. "The Communists and the Latvian Countryside, 1919–1949," in A. Sprudzs and A. Rusis (eds.), *Res Baltica*. pp. 88–116. Leyden, 1968.

Harrison, Ernest J. *Lithuania's Fight for Freedom.* New York, 1952.

Heine, Eerik. "Metsavennad," in R. Maasing et al. (eds.), *Eesti saatusaastad, 1945–1960*, vol. II, pp. 66–75. Stockholm, 1963–1972.

Hoover, Karl K. "The Baltic Resettlement of 1939 and Nationalist Socialist Racial Policy," JBS, VIII/1 (Spring 1977), pp. 79–89.

Horm, Arvo. "Balternas flykt till Sverige," *Symposium om Balterna i Sverige.* Stockholm, 1971.

Idzelis, Augustinas. "Locational Aspects of the Chemical Industry in Lithuania," *Lituanus*, XIX/4 (1973), pp. 51–61.

———. "Response of Soviet Lithuania to Environmental Problems in the Coastal Zone," JBS, X/4 (Winter 1979), pp. 299–308.

Istoriia Estonskoi SSR, vol. III. Tallinn, 1974. (Russian edition of *Eesti NSV ajalugu*.)

Istoriia Latviiskoi SSR, vol. III. Riga, 1957.

Istoriia Latviiskoi SSR, sokrashchennyi kurs. Riga, 1971.

Istoriia litovskoi literatury. Vilnius, 1977.

Istoriia Litovskoi SSR. Vilnius, 1978.

Ivask, Ivar. "Recent Trends in Estonian Poetry," BA, XLII/3 (Autumn 1968), pp. 517-520.

———(ed.). *A Look at Baltic Letters Today*, a special topical issue of BA, XLVII/3 (Autumn 1973).

Ivinskis, Zenonas. "Lithuania During the War: Resistance Against the Soviet and Nazi Occupants," in V. S. Vardys (ed.), *Lithuania Under the Soviets, 1940-1965*, pp. 61-84. New York, 1965.

Jakobson, Johannes; Johannes Kalits; and Aleksander Panksejev. *Ülevaade Eestimaa Kommunistliku Partei ajaloost*, vol. III. Tallinn, 1972. (Estonian version of *Ocherki istorii Kommunicheskoi Partii Estonii*.)

Järvesoo, Elmar. "Die Wirtschaft Estlands und deren strukturelle Veränderungen," AB, IX (1969), pp. 9-45.

———. "Private Enterprise in Soviet Estonian Agriculture," JBS, V/3 (Fall 1974), pp. 169-187.

———. "The Postwar Economic Transformations," in T. Parming and E. Järvesoo (eds.), *A Case Study of a Soviet Republic: The Estonian SSR*, pp. 131-190. Boulder, Colo., 1978.

Jensen, Erik Vagn. *Ukendte naboer — Sovjetrepublikkerne Estland/Letland/Litauen*. Copenhagen, 1977.

Juda, Lawrence. "United States' Nonrecognition of the Soviet Union's Annexation of the Baltic States: Politics and Law," JBS, VI/4 (Winter 1975), pp. 272-290.

Jurašienė, Aušra-Marija. "The Problem of Creative Artistic Expression in Contemporary Lithuania," *Lituanus*, XXII/3 (1976), pp. 28-48.

Jüriado, Andres. "Nationalism and Socialism in Soviet Estonian Drama," *Lituanus*, XIX/2 (1973), pp. 28-42.

Kaelas, Aleksander. *Das Sowjetisch besetzte Estland*. Stockholm, 1958.

Kalniņš, Bruno. *De Baltiska staternas frihetskamp*. Stockholm, 1950.

————. "How Latvia Is Ruled: The Structure of the Political Apparatus," JBS, VIII/1 (Spring 1977), pp. 70–78.

Kaslas, Bronis J. *The USSR-German Aggression Against Lithuania*. New York, 1973.

————. *The Baltic Nations: The Quest for Regional Integration and Political Liberty*. Pittston, Pa., 1976.

Kaufmann, Max. "The War Years in Latvia Revisited," in Mendel Bobe et al. (eds.), *Jews in Latvia*, pp. 351–368. Tel Aviv, 1971.

Kazlas, Juozas. "Social Distance among Ethnic Groups," in Edward Allworth (ed.), *Nationality Group Survival in Multi-Ethnic States: Shifting Support Patterns in the Soviet Baltic Region*, pp. 228–277. New York, 1977.

Kiik, Heino. *Tondiöömaja* (*Spook Hostel*). Tallinn, 1970.

King, Gundar J. *Economic Policies in Occupied Latvia*. Tacoma, Wash., 1965.

Kivimaa, Ervin. "Eesti NSV põllumajanduse kollektiviseerimine aastail 1947–1950," in Edgar Tõnurist (ed.), *Sotsialistliku põllumajanduse areng Nõukogude Eestis*, pp. 69–93. Tallinn, 1976.

Klesment, Johannes. "Die Rechtsordnung in Sowjetestland," AB, II (1962), pp. 9–34.

Kolde, Endel Jakob. "Estonian External Trade Under the Soviet Regime," JBS, VI/4 (Winter 1975), pp. 291–299.

————. "Structural Integration of the Baltic Economies into the Soviet System," JBS, IX/2 (Summer 1978), pp. 164–176.

Koropeckyj, I. S. "National Income of the Baltic Republics in 1970," JBS, VII/4 (Spring 1976), pp. 61–73.

Krakhmalinikova, Z. A. *Romany i romanisty*. Tallinn, 1977.

Küng, Andres. *Vad händer i Baltikum*? Stockholm, 1973.

————. *A Dream of Freedom: Four Decades of National Survival Versus Russian Imperialism in Estonia, Latvia and Lithuania, 1940–1980*. Cardiff, Wales, 1980.

Kurman, George. "Literary Censorship in General and in Soviet Estonia," JBS, VIII/1 (Spring 1977), pp. 3–15.

————. "Estonian Literature," in T. Parming and E. Järvesoo (eds.), *A Case Study of a Soviet Republic: The Estonian SSR*, pp. 247–280. Boulder, Colo., 1978.

Kütt, Aleksander. "Die Wirtschaft Sowjetestlands," AB, II (1962), pp. 107-128.

Kuusik, Mall. "Die sowjetestnische Literatur heute," AB, XIV (1974), pp. 184-196.

Labsvīrs, Jānis. "A Case Study in the Sovietization of the Baltic States: Collectivization of Latvian Agriculture, 1944-1956." Ph.D. diss., University of Indiana, Bloomington, 1959.

Landsbergis, Algirdas. "The Organic and the Synthetic: A Dialectical Dance," in George W. Simmonds (ed.), Nationalism in the USSR and Eastern Europe in the Era of Brezhnev and Kosygin, pp. 181-187. Detroit, 1975.

―――. "Orvell i Kafka eshche zhivy v Litve," Kontinent, V (1975), pp. 207-219.

Latvijas PSR maza enciklopēdija. 4 volumes. Riga, 1967-1972.

Latvju enciklopēdija. 3 volumes. Stockholm, 1950-1955.

Lehiste, Ilse. "Where Hobgoblins Spend the Night," JBS, IV/4 (Winter 1973), pp. 321-326.

Lemberg, Adelaida. "Estonskie dissidenty — za nezavisimost," Kontinent, IX (1976), pp. 157-164.

Lentsman, Leonid (chief ed.). Eesti rahvas Suures Isamaasõjas, vol. II. Tallinn, 1977.

Levin, Dov. "Participation of the Lithuanian Jews in the Second World War," JBS, VI/4 (Winter 1975), pp. 300-310.

―――. "Der bewaffnete Widerstand baltischen Juden gegen der Nazi-Regime, 1941-1945," AB, XV (1975), pp. 166-174.

―――. "The Jews and the Elections Campaigns in Lithuania, 1940-1941," Soviet Jewish Affairs, XII (February 1980), pp. 39-51.

Lietuviškoji tarybinė enciklopedija. Vols. I-VIII published to date. Vilnius, 1972-1982.

Lietuvių archyvas: Bolševizmo metai. 4 volumes. Kaunas, 1942-1943. An abridged one-volume edition: J. Prunskis (ed.). Brooklyn, N.Y., 1952.

Lietuvių enciklopedija. 36 volumes. Boston, 1953-1969. An abridged English-language edition: Encyclopedia Lituanica. 5 volumes. Boston, 1970-1975.

Lietuvos Komunistų Partijos istorijos apybraiža, vol. II. Vilnius, 1978.

Lietuvos TSR istorija, vol. IV. Vilnius, 1975.

Loeber, Dietrich. "The Administration of Culture in Soviet Latvia: Direction of Literature and the Arts in the Mirror of Written Law," in A. Sprudzs and A. Rusis (eds.), *Res Baltica*, pp. 133-145. Leyden, 1968.

Maasing, Richard; Hans Kauri; Arnold Purre; et al. (eds.). *Eesti saatusaastad, 1945-1960*. 6 volumes. Stockholm, 1963-1972.

Mačiuika, Benedict V. *Lithuania in the Last Thirty Years*. Human Relations Area Files, no. 18. New Haven, 1955.

―――. "The Baltic States Under Soviet Russia: A Case Study in Sovietization." Ph.D. diss., University of Chicago, 1963.

―――. "Die Russifizierung Litauens seit 1959: Versuch einer quantitativen Analyse," AB, VII (1967), pp. 289-302.

―――. "Auswertung der Volkszählungsergebnisse von 1970 in Sowjetlitauen," AB, XI (1971), pp. 87-116.

―――. "The Role of the Baltic Republics in the Economy of the USSR," JBS, III/1 (Spring 1972), pp. 18-25.

―――. "Acculturation and Socialization in the Soviet Baltic Republics," *Lituanus*, XVIII/4 (1972), pp. 26-43.

―――. "Contemporary Social Problems in the Collectivized Lithuanian Countryside," *Lituanus*, XXII/3 (1976), pp. 5-27.

Mägi, Arvo. *Estonian Literature*. Stockholm, 1968.

Maltsene [Malcienė], M. *Kino sovetskoi Litvy*. Leningrad, 1980.

Mažeika, Povilas. "Die neuere Entwicklung der Industrie Litauens," AB, IX (1969), pp. 177-225.

Mažoji lietuviškoji tarybinė enciklopedija. 4 volumes. Vilnius, 1966-1975.

Meissner, Boris. *Die Sowjetunion, die Baltischen Staaten und das Völkerrecht*. Köln, 1956.

Mereste, Uno, and Maimu Saarepera. *Rahvastiku enesetunnetus*. Tallinn, 1978.

Meškauskas, K. *Tarybų Lietuvos industrializavimas*. Vilnius, 1960.

―――, et al. *Lietuvos dabartis ir ateitis*. Vilnius, 1973.

Myllyniemi, Seppo. *Die Neuordnung der baltischen Länder, 1941-1944*. Helsinki, 1973.

————. *Die baltische Krise, 1938–1941*. Stuttgart, 1979.

Namsons, Andrivs, "Die Sowjetisierung des Schul- und Bildungswesens in Lettland von 1940 bis 1960," AB, I (1960–61), pp. 148–167.

————. "Die Umgestaltung der Landwirtschaft in Sowjetlettland," AB, II (1962), pp. 57–92.

————. "Stadtentwicklung und Siedlungsformen in Lettland," AB, VII (1967), pp. 131–169.

————. "Neue Errungenschaften in der Industrie Lettlands," AB, IX (1969), pp. 81–134.

————. "Die Entwicklung der Landwirtschaft in Sowjetlettland," AB, IX (1969), pp. 135–176.

————. "Nationale Zusammensetzung und Struktur der Bevölkerung Lettlands nach den Volkszählungen von 1935, 1959 und 1970," AB, XI (1971), pp. 61–68.

————. "Die bürgerliche Bewegung in Sowjetrussland und in den baltischen Ländern," AB, XIV (1974), pp. 138–183.

Ney, Gottlieb. "Administrative Gliederung und Verwaltungsorgane der sowjetisierten baltischen Staaten," AB, II (1962), pp. 9–34.

————. "Sozialistische Industrialisierung und ihre Auswirkungen im sowjetisierten Baltikum," AB, II (1962), pp. 129–145.

Nirk, Endel. *Estonian Literature*. Tallinn, 1970.

Ocherki istorii estonskoi sovetskoi literatury. Moscow, 1971.

Ocherki istorii Kommunisticheskoi Partii Estonii, vols. II-III. Tallinn, 1963–1970. (Estonian version: see J. Jakobson et al.)

Ocherki istorii Kommunisticheskoi Partii Latvii, vol. II. Riga, 1966.

Ocherki razvitiia gosudarstvennosti sovetskikh pribaltiiskikh respublik (1940–1965 gg.). Tallinn, 1965.

Olt, Harry. *Modern Estonian Composers*. Tallinn, 1972.

Oras, Ants. *Baltic Eclipse*. London, 1948.

Paletskis, Iustas [Paleckis, J.]. *V dvukh mirakh*. Moscow, 1974.

Panksejev, Aleksander. "EKP tegevusest partei ridade kasvu reguleerimisel (aastad 1944–1965)," in *Töid EKP ajaloo alalt*, vol. II, pp. 149–204. Tallinn, 1966.

Parming, Tönu. "Negotiating in the Kremlin: The Estonian Experience," *Lituanus*, XIV/2 (1968), pp. 45-96.

———. "Population Changes in Estonia, 1935-1970," *Population Studies*, XXVI/1 (March 1972), pp. 53-78.

———. "Nationalism in Soviet Estonia since 1964," in George W. Simmonds (ed.), *Nationalism in the USSR and Eastern Europe in the Era of Brezhnev and Kosygin*, pp. 116-135. Detroit, 1975.

———. "The Jewish Community and Inter-Ethnic Relations in Estonia, 1918-1940," JBS, X/3 (Fall 1979), pp. 257-259.

———. "Population Processes and the Nationality Issue in the Soviet Baltic," *Soviet Studies*, XXXII/2 (July 1980), pp. 398-414.

———, and Elmar Järvesoo (eds.). *A Case Study of a Soviet Republic: The Estonian SSR*. Boulder, Colo., 1978.

Penikis, Janis J. "Latvian Nationalism: Preface to a Dissenting View," in George W. Simmonds (ed.), *Nationalism in the USSR and Eastern Europe in the Era of Brezhnev and Kosygin*, pp. 157-161. Detroit, 1975.

Pennar, Jaan. "Nationalism in the Soviet Baltics," in Erich Goldhagen (ed.), *Ethnic Minorities in the Soviet Union*. New York, 1968.

———. "Soviet Nationality Policy and the Estonian Communist Elite," in T. Parming and E. Järvesoo (eds.), *A Case Study of a Soviet Republic: The Estonian SSR*. Boulder, Colo., 1978.

———. "Reflections on Union Republics in the New Soviet Constitution," *Lituanus*, XXV/1 (1979), pp. 5-16.

Procuta, Ginutis. "The Transformation of Higher Education in Lithuania During the First Decade of Soviet Rule," *Lituanus*, XIII/1 (1967), pp. 71-92.

Pullat, Raimo (ed.). *Problemy sotsialnoi struktury respublik sovetskoi pribaltiki*. Tallinn, 1978.

Purre, Arnold. *Soviet Farming Failure Hits Estonia*. Stockholm, 1964.

———. "Teine punane okupatsioon Eestis: Aastad 1944-1950," in R. Maasing et al. (eds.), *Eesti saatusaastad, 1945-1960*, pp. 7-65. Stockholm, 1964.

———. "A New Deal in Soviet Industrial Administration," *Lituanus*, XI/4 (1965), pp. 67-70.

———. "Territoriale Einteilung und Verwaltung der Estnischen SSR im Rahmen der allgemeinen Staatsordnung der UdSSR," AB, VII (1967), pp. 9-37.

————. "Estlands Industrie unter sowjetischer Herrschaft," AB, IX (1969), pp. 47–69.

————. "Ethnischer Bestand und Struktur der Bevölkerung Sowjetestlands im Jahr 1970," AB, XI (1971), pp. 41–60.

Rakūnas, A. *Klasių kova Lietuvoje, 1940–1959 m.* Vilnius, 1976.

Raštikis, Stasys. "The Relations of the Provisional Government of Lithuania with the German Authorities," *Lituanus*, VIII/1–2 (1962), pp. 16–22.

Ratnieks, Henry. "Baltic Oil Prospects and Problems," JBS, VII/4 (Winter 1976), pp. 312–319.

————. "Baltic Oil Shale," JBS, IX/2 (Summer 1978), pp. 155–163.

————. "Energy Crisis and the Baltics," JBS, XII/3 (Fall 1981), pp. 245–259.

Rauch, Georg von. *The Baltic States: The Years of Independence, 1917–1940.* London, Berkeley and Los Angeles, 1974.

Raun, Linda. *The Estonians.* Human Relations Area Files, no. 4. New Haven, 1955.

Rei, August. *The Drama of the Baltic Peoples.* Stockholm, 1961. (The second edition (1970) has an appendix by Evald Uustalu, "Events After 1940.")

Remeikis, Thomas. "The Armed Struggle Against the Sovietization of Lithuania After 1944," *Lituanus*, VIII/1–2 (1962), pp. 29–40.

————. "The Communist Party of Lithuania." Ph.D. diss., University of Illinois, Urbana, 1963.

————. "The Administration of Power: The Communist Party and the Soviet Government," in V. S. Vardys (ed.), *Lithuania Under the Soviets, 1940–1965*, pp. 111–140. New York, 1965.

————. "A Latvian in the Politbureau: A Political Portrait of Arvīds Pelše," *Lituanus*, XII/1 (1966), pp. 81–84.

————. "The Impact of Industrialization on the Ethnic Demography of the Baltic Countries," *Lituanus*, XIII/1 (1967), pp. 29–41.

————. "Natur und Prozess der Verstädterung in Litauen," AB, VII (1967), pp. 263–288.

————. "Berücksichtigung der nationalen und verwaltungsmässigen Interessen der Unionsrepublik im Rahmen des zentralistischen

Sowjetsystems, dargestellt am Beispiel Litauens," AB, X (1970), pp. 121-156.

————. "The Decision of the Lithuanian Government to Accept the Soviet Ultimatum of June 14, 1940," *Lituanus*, XXI/4 (1975), pp. 19-44.

————. "Political Developments during the Brezhnev Era," in George W. Simmonds (ed.), *Nationalism in the USSR and Eastern Europe in the Era of Brezhnev and Kosygin*, pp. 164-180. Detroit, 1975.

————. "Modernization and National Identity in the Baltic Republics: Uneven and Multi-Directional Change in the Components of Modernization," in Ihor Kamenetsky (ed.), *Nationalism and Human Rights: Processes of Modernization in the USSR*. Littleton, Colo., 1977.

————. *Opposition to Soviet Rule in Lithuania, 1945-1980*. Chicago, 1980.

Rianzhin, V.A. *Krizis burzhuaznoi konstitutsionnoi zakonnosti i vosstanovlenie sovetskoi gosudarstvennosti v Estonii*. Leningrad, 1971.

Rozītis, Elmārs. "Die evangelisch-lutherische Kirche in Sowjetlettland," AB, I (1960-61), pp. 93-109.

Royal Institute of International Affairs. *The Baltic States*. London, 1938.

Rutkis, Jānis (ed.). *Latvia: Country and People*. Stockholm, 1967.

Sabaliūnas, Leonas. *Lithuania in Crisis, 1939-1940*. Bloomington, Ind., 1972.

Salo, Vello. "The Struggle Between the State and the Churches," in T. Parming and E. Järvesoo (eds.), *A Case Study of a Soviet Republic: The Estonian SSR*, pp. 198-204. Boulder, Colo., 1978.

Sapiets, Jānis. "The Baltic Republics," in George Schöpflin (ed.), *The Soviet Union and Eastern Europe*, pp. 217-224. New York, 1970.

Sapiets, Marite. "Religion and Nationalism in Lithuania," *Religion in Communist Lands*, VII/2 (1979), pp. 76-96.

————. "Lithuania's Unofficial Press," *Index on Censorship*, IX/4 (1980), pp. 35-38.

Savasis, J. *The War Against God in Lithuania*. New York, 1966.

Senn, Alfred Erich. "The Sovietization of the Baltic States," *Annals of the American Academy of Political and Social Sciences*, CCCXVII (1958), pp. 123-129.

————. *The Emergence of Modern Lithuania*. New York, 1959.

Sharmaitis [Šarmaitis], R. "Kommunisticheskoi Partii Litvy — 50 let," *Kommunist* (Litvy), 1968, no. 9, pp. 57-73.

Shtromas, Aleksandras. "The Official Soviet Ideology and the Lithuanian People," to be published.

Šilbajoris, Rimvydas P. "Socialist Realism and the Politics of Literature in Occupied Lithuania," to be published.

Šilde, Ādolfs. *Resistance Movement in Latvia*. Stockholm, 1972.

Simmonds, George W. (ed.). *Nationalism in the USSR and Eastern Europe in the Era of Brezhnev and Kosygin*. Detroit, 1975.

Slavenas, Julius P. "Nazi Ideology and Policy in the Baltic States," *Lituanus*, VI/2 (1960), pp. 47-52.

Smith, Graham E. "The Impact of Modernization on the Latvian Soviet Republic," *Co-Existence*, XVI/1 (April 1979), pp. 45-64.

Sotsialisticheskie revoliutsii 1940 g. v Litve, Latvii, i Estonii. Moscow, 1978.

Spekke, Arnolds. *History of Latvia*. Stockholm, 1957.

Sprudzs, Adolf, and Armins Rusis (eds.). *Res Baltica*. Leyden, 1968.

Stakle, Jānis. "Die Eisenbahnen und das Transportwesen Lettlands in der Zeit von 1940-1970," AB, XV (1975), pp. 175-210.

Šumiņš, A. *Apcerējums par Padomju Latvijas ekonomisko attīstību (1940-1958)*. Riga, 1960.

Survel, Jaak [Evald Uustalu]. *Estonia Today*. London, 1947.

Swettenham, John A. *The Tragedy of the Baltic States*. London, 1952.

Taagepera, Mare. "Pollution of the Environment and the Baltics," JBS, XII/3 (Fall 1981), pp. 260-274.

Taagepera, Rein. "Nationalism in the Estonian Communist Party," *Bulletin* (Institute for the Study of the USSR), XVII/1 (1970), pp. 3-15.

———. "Inequality Indices for Baltic Farm Size Distribution, 1929-1940," JBS, III/1 (Spring 1972), pp. 26-34.

———. "The Problem of Political Collaboration in Soviet Estonian Literature," JBS, VI/1 (Spring 1975), pp. 30-40.

———. "Estonia and the Estonians," in Z. Katz (ed.), *Handbook of Major Soviet Nationalities*, pp. 75-95. New York, 1975.

———. "La demanda de libertad de las naciones bálticas," *Revista de Occidente*, no. 146 (May 1975), pp. 160-174.

——. "The Impact of the New Left on Estonia," *East European Quarterly*, X (1976), pp. 43–51.

——. "Nationalism, Collaborationism, and New-Leftism," in T. Parming and E. Järvesoo (eds.), *A Case Study of a Soviet Republic: The Estonian SSR*, pp. 75–103. Boulder, Colo., 1978.

——. "Soviet Documentation on the Estonian Pro-Independence Guerrilla Movement, 1945–1952," JBS, X/2 (Summer 1979), pp. 91–106.

——. "Soviet Collectivization of Estonian Agriculture: The Taxation Phase," JBS, X/3 (Fall 1979), pp. 263–282.

——. "Soviet Collectivization of Estonian Agriculture: The Deportation Phase," *Soviet Studies*, XXXII/3 (July 1980), pp. 379–397.

——. "A Portrait of the 'Historical Gap' in Estonian Literature," *Lituanus*, XXVI/3 (Fall 1980), pp. 73–86.

——. "Baltic Population Changes, 1950–1980," JBS, XII/1 (Spring 1981), pp. 35–57.

——. "The Population Crisis and the Baltics," JBS, XII/3 (Fall 1981), pp. 234–244.

Tarulis, Albert. *Soviet Policy toward the Baltic States, 1918–1940*. South Bend, Ind., 1959.

Tarybų Lietuva didžiajame tėvynės kare. Vilnius, 1975.

Tarybų Lietuvos valstietija: istorijos apybraiža. Vilnius, 1979.

Tauras, K. V. *Guerilla Warfare on the Amber Coast*. New York, 1962.

Trapans, Andris. "The Role of the Latvian Communist Party in 1940," in *Materials of the Second Conference on Baltic Studies in Scandinavia*. Stockholm, 1971.

Uustalu, Evald. *The History of the Estonian People*. London, 1952.

—— (ed.). *Aspects of Estonian Culture*. London, 1961.

——. "Events After 1940," appendix to August Rei, *The Drama of the Baltic Peoples*, 2nd ed. Stockholm, 1970.

——. "The National Committee of the Estonian Republic," JBS, VII/3 (Fall 1976), pp. 209–219.

Valgemäe, Mardi. "Drama and the Theater Arts," in T. Parming and E. Järvesoo (eds.), *A Case Study of a Soviet Republic: The Estonian SSR*, pp. 281–317. Boulder, Colo., 1978.

Valters, Nikolaus. "Soziale Veränderungen in den baltischen Sowjetrepubliken," AB, IV (1964), pp. 9-35.

Vardys, V. Stanley. "Recent Soviet Policy toward Lithuanian Nationalism," *Journal of Central European Affairs*, XXIII (1963), pp. 313-332.

————. "The Partisan Movement in Postwar Lithuania," *Slavic Review*, XXII (1963), pp. 499-522.

————. "Soviet Colonialism in the Baltic States: A Note on the Nature of Modern Colonialism," *Lituanus*, X/2 (1964), pp. 5-23.

————. "Soviet Colonialism in the Baltic States, 1940-1965," *Baltic Review*, no. 29 (1965), pp. 11-26.

———— (ed.). *Lithuania Under the Soviets: Portrait of a Nation, 1940-1965*. New York, 1965.

————. "How the Baltic Republics Fare in the Soviet Union," *Foreign Affairs*, XLIV/3 (April 1966), pp. 512-517.

————. "The Baltic Peoples," *Problems of Communism*, XVI/5 (September-October 1967), pp. 55-64.

————. "Soviet Nationality Policy as an Instrument of Political Socialization: the Baltic Case," in A. Sprudzs and A. Rusis (eds.), *Res Baltica*, pp. 117-132. Leyden, 1968.

————. "Modernization and Baltic Nationalism," *Problems of Communism*, XXIV/5 (September-October 1975), pp. 32-48.

————. "The Role of the Baltic Republics in Soviet Society," in Roman Szporluk (ed.), *The Influence of East Europe and the Soviet West on the USSR*, pp. 147-179. New York, 1977.

————. *The Catholic Church, Dissent, and Nationality in Lithuania*. Boulder, Colo., 1978.

————, and Romuald J. Misiunas (eds.). *The Baltic States in Peace and War, 1917-1945*. London, 1978.

Vaškelis, Bronius B. "The Assertion of Ethnic Identity in Myth and Folklore in Soviet Lithuanian Literature," *Lituanus*, XIX/2 (1973), pp. 16-27.

Vėlaikis, Jonas. "Lithuanian Literature Under the Soviets," *Lituanus*, XII/3 (Fall 1966), pp. 25-43.

Venclova, Tomas. "Translations of World Literature and Political Censorship in Contemporary Lithuania," *Lituanus*, XXV/2 (Summer 1979), pp. 5-26.

Vīkis-Freibergs, Vaira. "Echoes of the Dainas and the Search for Identity in Contemporary Latvian Poetry," JBS, VI (Spring 1975), pp. 17–29.

Viksnins, George J. "Current Issues of Soviet Latvia's Economic Growth," JBS, VII/4 (Winter 1976), pp. 343–351.

———. "Evaluating Economic Growth in Latvia," JBS, XII/2 (Summer 1981), pp. 173–188.

Widmer, Michael J. "Nationalism and Communism in Latvia: The Latvian Communist Party Under Soviet Rule." Ph.D. diss., Harvard University, 1969.

Žagars, Ē. *Socialist Transformation in Latvia, 1940–1941*. Riga, 1978.

Zhenklis [Ženklys], T. "Proshchaias s Antanasom Snechkusom; chego my zhdem ot emigratsii, vstupitel'naia zametka A. Shtromasa," *Kontinent*, XIV (1977), pp. 229–250.

Ziedonis, Arvids; Rein Taagepera; and Mardi Valgemäe (eds.). *Problems of Mininations: Baltic Perspectives*. San Jose, Calif., 1973.

Zīle, Zigurds. "Soviet Federalism in Criminal Law: A Case Study," in A. Sprudzs and A. Rusis (eds.), *Res Baltica*, pp. 152–159. Leyden, 1968.

Zundė, Pranas. "Die Kollektivierung der Landwirtschaft Sowjetlitauens," AB, II (1962), pp. 93–106.

———. *Die Landwirtschaft Sowjetlitauens*. Marburg/Lahn, 1962.

———. "Lithuania's Economy: Introduction of the Soviet Pattern," in V. S. Vardys (ed.), *Lithuania Under the Soviets, 1940–1965*, pp. 141–169. New York, 1965.

Žymantas, Stasys. "Twenty Years of Resistance," *Lituanus*, VI/2 (September 1960), pp. 40–45.

INDEX

Āboliņš, Elerts (b. 1928), 225
Abortions, 214
Abrene district, Latvia, 71
Administration: changes effected during Thaw, 127–130; *immobilisme* in, 195–199, 263; postwar, 69, 74–81; rural units of, 288–289; sovietization of, 24. *See also* Economy, administration of
Adomas-Meskupas, Icikas. *See* Meskupas
Agriculture: changes in during Thaw, 133–134, 141, 182–184; efficiency of, 182, 219–223; postwar, 91–104; pre-war, 10; production, 103–104, 183–184, 222–223, 287; sovietization of, 33–35. *See also* Collective farms; MKPP; MTS; Private plots; State Farms
Agrogorod proposal, 133
Akmenė district, Lithuania, 35
Alcohol abuse, 102, 214–215, 226, 251
Allik, Hendrik (b. 1901), 80, 143
Alliksaar, Artur (1923–1966), 151, 153
Alma Mater, 248
Alver, Betti (b. 1906), 151
Amalrik, Andrei Aleksandrovich (1938–1980), 264
Ambrazevičius, Juozas (1903–1974), 45
Amnesty International, 245
Andresen, Nigol (b. 1899), 119
Angarietis, Zigmas (1882–1940), 166
Angelus, Oskar (b. 1892), 65
Anniversaries. *See* History, significance of

Anti-Party Group, 134, 141
Anti-semitism, 60. *See also* Jewish population
Anvelt, Jaan (1884–1937), 166
Aputis, Juozas (b. 1936), 162
Arakas, Imre (b. 1945), 199
Aronov, V., 271
Art. *See* Cultural life
Aspāzija [Elza Rozenberga-Pliekšāne] (1868–1943), 147, 156
Association of Concerned Estonians, 256
Atlantic Charter, 63
Audrini village, Latvia, 67
Augškāps, Jānis, 140
Augspils, Latvia, 35
Aukštieji Panėriai, Lithuania, 59
Aušra, 248, 258
Auster, Lydia (b. 1912), 118
Automobile ownership, 209
Auziņš, Imants (b. 1937), 157, 234, 238
Avyžius, Jonas (b. 1922), 161

Baltakis, Algimantas (b. 1930), 159
Baltic Entente, 13, 18
Baltic Federation, 249, 258
Baltic Military District, 136, 139
Baltic Review, 19
Baltic states, period of independence: contingency planning (1939–1940), 17; economy, 10–17 *passim*; foreign relations of, 13, 16–17; formation of, 8–9; peace treaties with Soviet Russia, 9; political structures of, 10–12; Soviet ultimatums to (1939), 18–19
Baltic Thermoelectric Station, Estonia, 228

317